HITLER'S CRUSADE

To my husband and best friend
Geoff Waddington

HITLER'S CRUSADE

Bolshevism and the Myth of the International Jewish Conspiracy

LORNA WADDINGTON

Tauris Academic Studies
LONDON • NEW YORK

Published in 2007 by Tauris Academic Studies,
an imprint of I.B.Tauris & Co. Ltd
6 Salem Road, London W2 4BU
175 Fifth Avenue, New York, NY 10010
www.ibtauris.com

In the United States of America and in Canada distributed by
St. Martins Press, 175 Fifth Avenue, New York, NY 10010

ISBN: 978 1 84511 556 2

A full CIP record for this book is available from the British Library
A full CIP record for this book is available from the Library of Congress

Library of Congress Catalog Number: available

Typeset in Berkeley Oldstyle by Oxford Publishing Services, Oxford
Printed and bound by Thomson Press India Limited
From camera-ready copy edited and supplied by the author

Contents

CONTENTS

Acronyms and Abbreviations

AA	Auswärtiges Amt
ADAP	*Akten zur deutschen Auswärtigen Politik*
AK	Antikomintern
AGD	*Auf Gut Deutsch*
AKND	*Antikomintern Nachrichtendienst*
APA	Außenpolitisches Amt der NSDAP
BBL	Bundesarchiv, Berlin-Lichterfelde
BK	Bundesarchiv, Koblenz
CD	*Ciano's Diary*
CDP	*Ciano's Diplomatic Papers*
DAP	Deutsche Arbeiter Partei
DBFP	*Documents on British Foreign Policy*
DGFP	*Documents on German Foreign Policy*
DKA	Deutsche Kongress Zentrale
DNB	German Press Division
Domarus	*Hitler: Speeches and Proclamations 1932–1945*
FO	Foreign Office
FRUS	*Foreign Relations of the United States*
GDAV	Gesamtverband Deutscher Antikommunistischer Vereinigungen
GPU	State Political Direction
GSWW	*Germany and the Second World War*
Halder-KTB	*Halder: Kriegstagebuch*
Hoover	Hoover Archives, Stanford University
IMT	*International Military Tribunal*
JCH	*Journal of Contemporary History*
KPD	Kommunistische Partei Deutschlands (German Communist Party
LoC	Library of Congress, Washington
NARA	National Archives, Maryland
NSDAP	Nationalsozialistische Deutsche Arbeiterpartei
PAB	Politisches Archiv, Bonn

ACRONYMS AND ABBREVIATIONS

PK	*Propaganda-Kompanien*
PRO	Public Records Office, London
ProMi	Propagandaministerium (ministry of propaganda)
RFP	*Review of the Foreign Press*
RMVP	Reichsministerium für Volksaufklärung und Propaganda
RSA	*Reden, Schriften, Anordnungen*
SDFP	Soviet Documents on Foreign Policy
SHAEF	Supreme Headquarters Allied Expeditionary Force
SS	Schutzstaffel
TBJG	*Die Tagebücher von Joseph Goebbels*
UdSSR	Union Der Sozialistischen Sowjetrepubliken (USSR)
VB	*Völkischer Beobachter*
VfZ	*Vierteljahrshefte für Zeitgeschichte*

Acknowledgements

My chief debt is to Dr Geoffrey T. Waddington and Professor Edward M. Spiers, for their patience, guidance and encouragement during the preparation of this book. My thanks also go to the staff of the various archives and libraries in which I have undertaken the research. I am very grateful for the expert assistance offered by the staff at the various German archive centres, and at the National Archives, London. I have benefited in particular from the expertise of Dr Miriam LeFloch at the Hoover Institute, Stanford University, and Herr Gregor Pikro at the Bundesarchiv in Koblenz. I must thank the late Professor John Erickson for his valuable advice, and also for permitting me to consult his microfilmed records pertaining to the Anti-Comintern Pact. Dr Geoffrey Stoakes was also kind enough to furnish me with material from his private collection of German records. I would also like especially to thank Professor Bernd Martin for providing me with a copy of the Raumer Manuscript. Professors Sir Ian Kershaw, Paul Preston, Wolfgang Michalka, Lothar Kettenacker, John Gooch and Carl Boyd have also offered valuable advice along the way. The advice and comments of Professor Richard Overy proved especially valuable.

I would like to express my sincere thanks to the organizations and institutions that have provided financial support during the preparation of the book. I am especially grateful to the AHRB, both for the original Ph.D. studentship, and for additional funding, which has enabled me to undertake research in Germany. The generous assistance of the German Historical Institute also permitted me to engage in further research at the archives at Berlin-Lichterfelde and Koblenz. A grant from the Royal Historical Society enabled me to consult records at the National Archives of the United States, at Stanford University, and also at the Politisches Archiv des Auswärtigen Amtes, formerly located in Bonn.

The support I have received from friends has also been of great importance to me. I would like to thank the following for offering encouragement: Holly Caulfield, Fanuel Okwaro and Maria di Stefano. Special thanks must go to Dr Lucia Tedesco for help with the Italian translations. The love and support of my children Luis, Kimberley and Luke has been unfailing. I am very grateful for their extraordinary forbearance and good nature.

Introduction

On 1 May 1945, six days before the collapse of the Third Reich, Hamburg Radio broadcast a message to the nation from Grand Admiral Karl Dönitz, commander-in-chief of the German navy since January 1943, and now, following Hitler's suicide on 30 April, the latter's reluctant successor as Führer and Chancellor. After the radio announcer had informed his listeners that Hitler had died 'fighting to the last breath against Bolshevism and for Germany', Dönitz came to the microphone and made the following declaration:

> German men and women, soldiers of the German Wehrmacht, our Führer, Adolf Hitler, has fallen. In deepest sorrow and reverence the German people bows. He recognized the terrible danger of Bolshevism at an early date and dedicated his existence to this struggle. ... His life was one single service for Germany. His action in fighting against the Bolshevist spring-tide was waged beyond that, for Europe and the entire civilized world.[1]

In the circumstances, it is unlikely that these words found any echo save among the most fanatical and deluded Nazi diehards. Indeed, at the point in his address when Dönitz unconvincingly described his predecessor as 'one of the greatest heroes of German history', an unidentified voice broke into the transmission with the remark 'This is a lie.'[2]

Yet, there was an element of truth in what Dönitz said, for Hitler had indeed dedicated, or at least had professed to dedicate, a substantial part of his political career to the fight against Bolshevism, a process that had culminated in June 1941, when, with their ears ringing with propaganda about a historic European mission, the German armed forces launched a breathtaking assault on the Reich's eastern neighbour, and, in so doing, finally

1

unleashed Hitler's wrath on the USSR, the undisputed epicentre of 'Jewish Bolshevism'.

During the 1930s, not least due to his own unstinting efforts and those of his foremost political associates, Hitler's name had became synonymous with the theme of the defence of Germany and Europe against the ideological threat posed by the USSR, and the perceived function of the Third Reich as a bulwark against Bolshevism received considerable approbation from the meek and the great alike. In August 1936, for example, Mrs Louise McNair Crawford, a private American citizen currently resident in San Remo, Italy, felt compelled to make a small financial donation to Hitler, with more to follow, so she promised, in recognition of his role as 'our shield and buckler against Bolshevism'.[3] The following year, one of the most senior figures in the British Conservative Party, the former Viceroy of India and future foreign secretary, Lord Halifax, personally congratulated Hitler on his success in stemming the Bolshevik tide by acknowledging that he had 'not only performed great services in Germany, but also, as he would no doubt feel, had been able, by preventing the entry of communism into his own country, to bar its passage further West'.[4]

In mid-1936, when the outbreak of civil war in Spain sharply focused international attention on the purported Bolshevik threat to Western Europe, the Third Reich redoubled its efforts to advertise itself to the world as the guardian of civilization, a final barrier across the path of this pernicious onslaught against European values and culture. Indeed, with the obvious exception of the Nazi–Soviet Pact of 1939, when Hitler was forced into a transient and exceedingly distasteful accommodation with the USSR in order to realize his immediate goals against Poland, anti-Bolshevism was frequently employed to justify or rationalize a range of German foreign policy initiatives, including unilateral treaty breaches, as in the case of rearmament, the acquisition of major allies, as in that of the Anti-Comintern Pact, and even the destruction of independent non-Bolshevik states, such as occurred in the case of Czechoslovakia.

Thus, in March 1936, as German troops marched into the Rhineland, Hitler was earnestly explaining to the Reichstag, and indirectly to the authorities in Paris, that France, the country whose vital interests had been most immediately affected by the

2

move, had nothing to fear from this latest assertion of German *Gleichberechtigung*. Indeed, the campaign for equality of rights had had 'no harmful effects on the French people', for only 'the Red revolt and the collapse of the German Reich would have dealt the European order and the European economy a blow having consequences which, unfortunately, are virtually beyond the grasp of most European statesmen'.[5] Later in his address, the German Chancellor returned to the theme:

> When today my international opponents confront me with the fact that I refuse to practice this cooperation with Russia, I must counter this assertion with the following: I rejected and continue to reject this cooperation not with Russia, but with the Bolshevism which lays claim to world rulership. I am a German, I love my people and am attached to it. I know that it can only be happy if allowed to live in accordance with its nature and its way. The German people has been able not only to cry, but also to laugh heartily all its life, and I do not want the horror of the Communist international dictatorship of hatred to descend upon it. I tremble for Europe at the thought of what would lie in store for our old, heavily populated continent were the chaos of the Bolshevist revolution rendered successful by the infiltrating force of this destructive Asiatic concept of the world, which subverts all our established ideals. I am perhaps for many European statesmen a fantastic [*phantastisch*], or at any rate uncomfortable, harbinger of warnings. That I am regarded in the eyes of the international Bolshevist oppressors of the world as one of their greatest enemies is for me a great honour and a justification for my actions in the eyes of posterity.[6]

As the case of the reoccupation of the Rhineland amply demonstrates, it would clearly be misguided to suggest that anti-Bolshevism was never used as a tactical weapon in Hitler's armoury. By the same token, it is equally misguided to dismiss anti-Bolshevism as an element of pure convenience for the Nazi leaders, for to do so is fundamentally to misunderstand one of the core concepts at the heart of Nazi ideology.

During the 1936 party rally at Nuremberg, when Hitler, Goebbels and Rosenberg excelled themselves in a series of sustained and vicious attacks on the 'world peril', thus to an extent affirming Göring's recent announcement at a meeting of the German cabinet that war with Bolshevik Russia was inevitable,[7] some commentators, prompted perhaps by the very excesses of the occasion, saw ulterior motives behind the anti-Soviet invective that punctuated virtually every major address delivered by the party leaders. In its issue of 20 September 1936, for example, the *Illustrazione Italiana* ran an article entitled 'Conflict of Religion or German Imperialism?' warning its readers not to permit themselves to be seduced or hypnotized by the German arguments that called for the ostracism of the USSR and the rejection of Bolshevism as a political philosophy.

In itself, Bolshevism certainly constituted a threat, noted 'Spectator', the author of the piece; the recent events in Spain alone testified to that. Moreover, the fact that the Comintern fomented unrest and agitation wherever possible meant that vigilance was essential. The point at which 'Spectator' parted company with the Germans concerned the claims that the USSR represented a threat to Germany itself, for not only did the two states lack a common border, but, it was claimed, the armed forces and industrial capability of the Soviet Union were not sufficient to endanger the German Reich, despite the considerable advances made under the five-year plans.

One instinctively wondered therefore 'whether the Chancellor's apprehensions are justified or whether the whole affair is not a colossal comedy staged to win for Germany's increasingly intensive rearmament the approval of the rest of Europe'. Hitler's 'championing' of Western Europe was certainly suspicious, for National Socialist ideology could hardly identify itself with 'the real authentic Western civilization created by two thousand years of history'. Hitler's aims were 'exclusively national and imperial', the article concluded, and, although Nazi ideology was 'by definition unquestionably anti-communist', its basic function was to serve 'modern Germany's plans', which were 'grandiose and unlimited'.[8]

To some extent the historiography of the Third Reich has followed and mirrored the arguments of 'Spectator' in so far as the function of Hitler's anti-Bolshevism is concerned, with the result

that several commentators have concluded that Hitler used anti-Bolshevism largely as a pretext or cover to disguise his real aims and intentions.[9] Even one of the world's leading authorities on Hitler's foreign policy, Gerhard Weinberg, appears a little uncertain on this issue. In keeping with his focus on Hitler's lust for territorial aggrandisement, and the Führer's eye for the main chance when anything towards that goal might be achieved, Weinberg writes in connection with German policy during the opening phase of the Spanish Civil War that the danger of communism 'may well have influenced Hitler' in his decision to assist Franco. He then immediately dilutes the point by referring to 'important circumstantial evidence' in support of economic motives for intervention.[10]

In contrast, 'intentionalist' historians such as Klaus Hildebrand and Andreas Hillgruber have repeatedly emphasized the importance of ideological factors and anti-Bolshevism in their research,[11] while Jochen Thies has firmly positioned the destruction of 'Jewish Bolshevism' – not, it should be noted, 'Russia' or the 'Soviet Union' – in the sequence of events that Hitler considered necessary to enable him ultimately to launch his bid for world power.[12]

One aim of this work is to engage some of these questions afresh, and, by highlighting the role of anti-Bolshevism – as opposed to *Lebensraum* – to redress a certain imbalance that has been created between these crucial and interwoven components of Hitler's *Weltanschauung*. Hitler himself would not have denied the connection, unless he wished to renounce much of what he had written and said; in fact, during his speech to the German Labour Front at Nuremberg on 12 September 1936 he actually linked the two by first dilating on the primitive nature of Bolshevism before asking his audience to contemplate the prosperity that Germany would enjoy were it one day to possess the Ukraine.[13] The aim of conquering additional *Lebensraum* at the expense of the USSR is certainly key to any understanding of Hitler's external policies, but to view it in isolation, as somehow divorced from the notion of anti-Bolshevism, is as ill-conceived as the idea that the emphasis on *Lebensraum* was simply a cloak designed to conceal the primary aim of combating communism.[14]

In some parts of eastern Europe there was initially considerable confusion about the depth and virulence of Hitler's anti-

Bolshevism, particularly when in the months after 1933 his words were rapidly translated into action. In a serialized article entitled 'Moscow and Hitler', the Estonian journalist Nicolaus Basseches related the Soviet view that Hitler, in his search for a foreign success, had little choice but to declare war on Bolshevism on behalf of the capitalist nations. With the balance of forces in Western Europe ranged solidly against him, and nothing to be expected from Poland, Hitler's strong stance against Bolshevism was in actual fact a means to achieve the revision of the Treaty of Versailles in so far as it limited German armaments and prevented Germany from exercising its rightful influence in Eastern Europe. Poland, it was anticipated, would be an early victim in this process.[15]

Nothing could have been further from the truth, and within nine months Poland and Germany had evidently buried their differences, signed a non-aggression pact and were exploring how they might deepen their collaboration against the USSR. In the German foreign ministry, too, experienced officials, steeped in traditional national-conservative values, and many of them favourable to the Rapallo policy of collaboration with the USSR, were puzzled and alarmed by the rapid and deliberate deterioration of Russo–German relations effected by the Nazi regime after 1933. Ernst von Weizsäcker perhaps spoke for many when he later wrote of his inability to comprehend 'why we should have given our many enemies the advantage of being able to base their policy on the assumption of unwavering German hostility to Russia', for there was 'no dispute between ourselves and the Soviet Union in regard to frontiers, nor did the latter have any perceptible influence on German internal politics'.[16]

Were there a simple explanation for Weizsäcker's bemusement, it perhaps lay in his inability fully to comprehend the phenomenon of Hitler, whose foreign policy was determined not merely by notions of *Realpolitik*, the staple diet of the career diplomat, but also by deep-seated prejudices and other ideological elements. After all, very few at the time could claim to have recognized the profound ideological basis that underpinned Hitler's whole political philosophy, or to have foreseen how that might and did impact on policy. It was the classic mistake made by the German conservatives, who, believing they could manipulate Hitler, succeeded only in handing him control of the state.

The claim that anti-Bolshevism was employed as an expedient is in fact far more appropriate in the case of Mussolini, whose opposition to the threat posed by communism is viewed by a recent biographer as a 'rhetorical trope', which Il Duce 'could turn on and off at will'.[17] Moreover, the Italian leader may well have professed a conviction that the majority of the Bolshevik leaders were Jews, and that Jewish bankers in London and New York financed their secret machinations, but the absence of any deep-seated racial dimension to his political concepts, a fact once bemoaned by Hitler himself,[18] meant that hardly had he finished exposing 'these "Jewish conspiracies" than he was writing in favour of the heavily Jewish revolutionaries of Hungary'.[19] As far as Italian foreign policy is concerned, the history of Italo–Soviet relations, which were relatively cordial until 1936, stands in stark contrast to the systematic campaign Hitler waged against the USSR after 1933. Indeed, as I seek to demonstrate, Italy's gravitation towards Germany from 1935 onwards clearly indicates how the Italians consciously used anti-Bolshevism to interest Germany in a rapprochement following the serious deterioration in Italy's relations with the democracies during the Abyssinian crisis.

Whereas Mussolini's world view may originally have lacked this racial, or at least anti-Jewish, dimension, it is beyond question that it lay at the core of Hitler's beliefs. As Sebastian Haffner relates in his perceptive analysis of Hitler's career, anti-Semitism, the 'first thing to take root in Hitler', soon gave rise to the notion that racial struggle between Aryans and Jews was a 'permanent feature of history'. Whereas the Great Powers were ceaselessly engaged in a noble struggle for survival, which was effectively a struggle for living space, the Jews were the 'spoilsports in this pleasant game', for with their 'internationalism and pacifism, their (international) capitalism and their (equally international) communism they were diverting the "Aryan" nations from their main task, and their main preoccupation, and that is why they had to be removed from the world, and not from Germany only'.[20] Haffner's conclusions about the nonsensical nature of Hitler's racial dogma can readily be accepted, but that does not mean that Hitler was not absolutely serious in his convictions. Geoffrey Stoakes, one of the foremost authorities on the formative years of Nazi foreign policy, has also taken up the theme of the 'international' Jew. He argues that by

1920, thus long before notions of *Lebensraum* or a 'programmatic' foreign policy, indeed at a time when Hitler was thinking in terms of traditional revisionism, the purported 'internationalism' of the Jews, articulated through capitalism and world revolution, was already beginning to define Hitler's *Weltanschauung*. Only through such media, Rosenberg and others had instructed him, could the Jew 'organize, erect and maintain his definitive world-rule'.[21]

To some degree the combination of a virulent anti-Semitism with the notion of hordes of 'Asiatics' descending on Western and central Europe around which Hitler's anti-Bolshevik ideology essentially revolved was paralleled by currents of thought that were already well established within German politics and philosophy. Towards the close of the nineteenth century Germany had been gripped by the so-called 'yellow peril'[22] at a time when, quite coincidentally, several prominent philosophers had left their mark on the growing trend of anti-Semitism witnessed in Germany from the 1880s onwards.[23] Even before the outbreak of war in 1914 had served to unleash a fresh wave of Russophobia in Germany, views and arguments were being advanced across the political spectrum highlighting the Russian tendency towards the 'absorption of individualism', warning of a *'Drang nach Westen'*, and calling for a new *'Drang nach Osten'* in order to reclaim ancient territories. Within a year of the German defeat in 1918 the first calls were heard for a new cultural mission for the German nation designed to stave off the spread of Bolshevism, As Gregory Moore notes, it was the juxtaposition of 'Asiatic Bolshevism' with the 'Oriental Jew' that provided the key to National Socialist perceptions of an elaborate Jewish conspiracy, of which Marxism, with its insistence on 'those eminently Jewish values', internationalism, egalitarianism and pacifism, so antithetical to the *völkisch* ideal, was a key component.[24]

Today, almost ninety years since its outbreak, the revolution that gripped and ultimately transformed the Russian empire into the Soviet Union is generally of little more than academic interest. Unlike the terms 'fascism' and 'fascist', which have been transformed into all-encompassing pejoratives, 'Bolshevism' and 'Bolshevik' have effectively disappeared from everyday usage. For the generation that fought the First World War, however, more so for its leaders, Bolshevism was a new and disturbing phenomenon, for the sudden transformation of a state, itself the size of a continent, into the self-proclaimed centre of world revolution presented a series of fresh problems, for which there appeared to be no obvious remedies. Nowhere was this more evident than in Germany where the cessation of hostilities was attended by the chaos of the 'November revolution' and the subsequent declaration in Munich of the Bavarian Soviet Republic. As so-called workers' and soldiers' councils began to operate in major German cities, individuals and organizations determined to rescue the Reich from the Marxists produced an array of anti-Marxist and anti-Bolshevik literature. As would later become apparent, Goebbels and his acolytes were not above recycling the ideas and arguments deployed by these early German opponents of Bolshevism if their own ends could thereby be served. The work of Edouard Stadtler, one of Germany's foremost pioneers against Bolshevism and founder in December 1918 of the Anti-Bolshevik League, is a case in point.

As a prisoner of war in Russia, Stadtler had gained first-hand experience of Bolshevism which, he claimed, purposefully fostered anarchy to promote its ultimate goal of world revolution. The triumph of Bolshevism, he announced in November 1918, marked the beginning of a struggle between a new all-encompassing 'world danger' and what he coincidentally termed a 'National Socialism'. Backed by funds from wealthy industrialists and financiers Stadtler went on to become a major agitator and propagandist against the internationalist tendencies of Bolshevism in the immediate post-1918 period, arguing that Germany should reject both Marxism and democracy in favour of a 'third way', which would achieve true socialism through a national revolution.[25] Although Stadtler faded into relative obscurity during the 1920s, the Nazis resurrected his anti-Bolshevik message in 1936 with the publication of a collection of his essays, many of which had originated in 1919.[26] How far Hitler may have been influenced by Stadtler in 1919–20, indeed whether he even knew of him, is of course impossible to gauge. Nevertheless, the activities and writings of Stadtler and other like-minded anti-Bolsheviks during those precarious years of German history serve not only to give an indication of the atmosphere in which they operated but might also go some way to explain the later receptivity of large sections of the German population to the anti-Bolshevik message of the NSDAP whose reminders about the red menace may well have touched the nerve of bitter personal experience.

From the outset the Bolsheviks were almost universally derided and despised. Alan Sharpe informs us that for the peacemakers who had gathered at Paris in 1919 Bolshevism represented 'much more than the precepts of Marxism–Leninism. It meant chaos, despair, fanaticism, famine, anarchy and a threat to all orderly government', a fact that goes some way to explain the frustration of the US secretary of state, Robert Lansing, who complained of the delay in finalizing the settlement 'while the flames of Bolshevism eat their way into Central Europe and threaten the destruction of the social order'.[27] Lansing's fears of Bolshevik intentions appear to have been fully justified, not least as the Communist International, the body established in 1919 to oversee the process of world revolution, rejoiced at the worldwide instability that attended the end of the First World War and looked forward enthusiastically to making rapid progress in its work.[28] Shortly after the armistice, with the fighting finally over, there was time at last to peer towards the east and take stock of the tremendous developments in the former Russian empire. To some the next step was obvious. General Haking, chief of the British section of the Armistice Commission, advised his colleagues in late 1918 to stop worrying about the German danger, which had passed, and to work now towards an alliance with 'any people, in or out of Europe, who were prepared to join hands with them to defeat the international power of Bolshevism'.[29] Two years later, Winston Churchill told a gathering of his supporters that, although no one knew what might ultimately emerge from the 'Russian cauldron', it would 'almost certainly be full of menace for Britain', and that consequently, by way of prevention, 'we ought to try and make a real and lasting peace with the Germans'.[30] In 1921 the British government appeared to condone at least the first of Churchill's points by establishing an inter-departmental committee to examine, monitor and combat Bolshevist activities against the empire.[31]

In Germany the organization of workers' councils and the establishment of Soviet-style regional governments after 1918 had been a cause for serious concern among the allies, some of whom were beset by considerable social dislocation and unrest. During the

1920s the fear of a Russo–German rapprochement was cleverly exploited by Stresemann who, by periodically flirting with Moscow, was able to extract concessions from Austen Chamberlain and Briand, for which in other circumstances he might well have had to work considerably harder. Despite the partnership with Russia, which he inherited and subsequently strengthened, Stresemann was too much of a realist to believe that Germany's recovery and future prosperity were in the long term bound up with the USSR, and, placing his faith in the USA, he was already beginning to reconsider his policy towards the Soviet Union in the months before his death in 1929.[32]

Nothing, however, could have prepared the Soviet government for the reorientation of German policy towards the USSR that was introduced after Hitler became chancellor in January 1933. It soon became apparent, even to those unfamiliar with the Führer's writing and proclamations on the subject, that a distinct ideological edge had been imparted to Soviet–German relations by the new appointment that soon began to manifest itself even in the language Hitler chose to employ about the Bolsheviks, those 'noxious microbes' as he described them to the British ambassador in December 1935.[33]

In this study I attempt to place international Bolshevism as defined by Hitler and his associates within an overall international context, and to analyse the role of ideology, diplomacy and propaganda in Hitler's efforts to mobilize support for the policies he intended to pursue against Bolshevik Russia. Although its primary focus is on the international dimension of Nazi anti-Bolshevism, due and appropriate attention has been paid to the origins and development of theories about a Jewish world conspiracy, and to developments in the Jewish question in the domestic German political arena in so far as they impacted on the course of international policy and the origins of the Final Solution. In an attempt to provide a more rounded picture of the German attitude and response to the supposed world conspiracy, some effort has been made to make brief comment as and when appropriate about its plutocratic-capitalist dimension, but the study is primarily concerned with the concept of international Bolshevism as epitomized by the perceived threat emanating from the USSR.

Chapter 1
Hitler, the Jewish Question and the Origins and Development of the 'World Conspiracy' Theory

On the evening of 13 August 1920 Adolf Hitler delivered an address to a gathering of 2000 people in the Festsaal of the Munich Hofbräuhaus in which he posed the simple question: 'Why are we anti-Semites?' At that time Hitler was making a name for himself in Munich and its environs as a skilled orator and agitator whose speeches habitually contained damning references to the influence of the Jews on Germany's recent past. Since joining the Deutsche Arbeiter Partei almost one year earlier he had frequently harangued his audiences in the most violent terms about the misfortunes brought upon the Reich by Jewry,[1] and the two-hour address he made that August evening would prove no exception.

In essence, Hitler explained, a series of fundamental differences between Aryans, or Germans, and Jews, made peaceful coexistence between them impossible. Germans, he argued, accepted work as a moral and social duty to be engaged in for the benefit and advancement of the community; Jews, on the other hand, were work shy, exploitative and obsessively materialistic, and concerned only to profit from the labours of others. Second, whereas racial purity was sacrosanct to Germans, Jews were racial polluters who engaged in unlimited and indiscriminate inbreeding and crossbreeding, with all its lamentable consequences. Finally, whereas a German's inner creative ability produced a vibrant culture that enriched his existence, genuine cultural achievements were beyond Jews, who sought to reduce all art, music and literature to the basest of levels. Building on these arguments, Hitler developed the idea that Jews were parasitic aliens who lacked the qualities that enabled Aryan people to construct, maintain and develop state structures. Jews had thus for centuries lived as nomads, a 'race within other races', a 'state in other states', their aim being to impose their own pitiless dictatorship on unsuspecting host nations, and ultimately to create the conditions for their own domination of the globe. It was therefore the duty of every upright German to oppose Jews, for, as happened wherever a Jew reared his head, there would come a point where Germany would have to make a choice between ejecting the 'undesirable guest' or effectively conniving at its own downfall.[2]

The kind of extreme anti-Semitic invective Hitler espoused on this and other occasions in 1919–20 was commonplace in Germany in the immediate aftermath of the First World War. From 1916 onwards the inability of the German armed forces to achieve a breakthrough on the battlefield had led to increased agitation against Jews throughout the Reich, as people searched for scapegoats to explain the military stalemate and consequent flagging morale on the home front. As German Jews held a considerable stake in big business, the media and finance, areas quickly identified as hotbeds of war-profiteering and defeatism, they were an easy and obvious target. Hitler's message was neither new nor particularly original, for some of his arguments clearly owed a debt to the likes of Georg Ritter von Schönerer, Heinrich Class, Theodor Fritsch and others who popularized anti-Semitism before, during and after the First World War.[3] Yet, in other respects Hitler's address on 13 August 1920 went beyond what had gone before, for it raised the spectre of a global conspiracy orchestrated by international Jewry, which, through a variety of means, notably international finance, Marxism and Freemasonry, sought to establish a Jewish tyranny over the entire globe. For this reason, the speech is indeed of quite 'fundamental' importance, notwithstanding what is generally attached to it as the first surviving full-length record of the future Führer's ideas on the Jewish question.[4] It also constituted his first detailed statement on the international dimension of the Jewish conspiracy, and of the links between Jewish international financiers and the revolution that had transformed imperial Russia into the Soviet Union, whose real masters, as he had argued, was the global 'Alliance israelite'.[5]

As many of the core components of his *Weltanschauung* would show, Hitler's views on the Jewish question largely determined his attitude to international Bolshevism. That much is suggested by the fact that until 1920, by which time he was becoming increasingly familiar with the purported links between international Jewry and the Bolshevik revolution, Hitler had never had much to say about either the Bolsheviks or the October revolution.[6] In his earliest political speeches he focused much more closely on other aspects of Jewry's alleged subversion of Germany, including its complicity in the origins of the war and the subsequent collapse of the Reich,[7] and in particular its supposed links with capitalism and high finance.[8] By mid-1920, however, Hitler had accepted that international Jewry and the Bolshevik revolutionaries were intimately connected, and from that point onwards this linkage, once made, was broken only by his death in 1945.[9] Hitler's attitude to Bolshevism and the related issue of an international Jewish conspiracy thus cannot fully be understood without first assessing the development of his attitude to Jews as a whole. Our first questions must therefore be: how and why did Hitler develop a phobia about Jews, and how does that relate to his understanding of the role of the Bolsheviks in a supposed Jewish 'world conspiracy'?

It is important to register at the outset that Hitler spent his formative years already steeped in the anti-Semitism that had become an integral component of the *völkisch* groups that began to appear in Germany and Austria towards the end of the nineteenth century. Building on existing antipathies to Jewry, and operating in an atmosphere where anti-Semitism was already on the increase, *völkisch* agitators and publicists advocated a strident nationalism coupled with romanticized visions of the German past based on the *Volksgemeinschaft* or 'racial community', which held no place for foreigners or outsiders like Jews. Some, including Eugen Dühring, Wilhelm Marr and, most conspicuously, Housten Stewart Chamberlain, the English publicist and writer who enjoyed Hitler's special esteem, passed beyond nationalism to theories embracing the idea of the superiority of the Aryan race, which, when coupled with agitation against supposed Jewish 'racial inferiors', provided one of the key bases for that brand of extreme racist anti-Semitism that Hitler eventually made his own.[10] At approximately the same time as the *völkisch* movement was beginning to gather momentum, the focus of racist thought in Germany was shifting from that of 'cultural racism', which had its roots in language, history and tradition, to that of a racism focused entirely on 'biological heritage',[11] a process grounded in Social Darwinism and given expression in the pseudo-scientific theories advanced by the likes of Hans Günther, and, most notably, Ludwig Woltmann. According to one commentator, Woltmann's major work, *Die politische Anthropologie*, almost certainly constituted the 'primary source of Hitler's racist convictions'.[12]

Although Chamberlain, Woltmann and others probably did exercise considerable influence over the young Hitler, the latter's claim that his personal experiences and impressions conditioned his anti-Semitism seems plausible. While the autobiographical sections of *Mein Kampf* must be treated with caution, there are grounds to believe that Hitler's years in Vienna between 1908 and 1913, and his reaction to defeat and revolution in 1918–19, marked key stages in the development of his hostility towards the Jews. In Vienna, where he came into much more regular contact with Jewry than he had in Branau and Linz, Hitler professed to have become aware of the distinctive nature of the Jews whom, he quickly discovered, were 'not Germans of a special religion, but a people in themselves'.[13] This crucial identification of the Jews as a race rather than a religious group was a key to Hitler's anti-Semitism, for from it evolved the idea that the 'stateless' Jews undermined and conspired against the national communities they had infiltrated. The claim of the Jews to a common faith was thus no more than a cunning piece of deception, for the 'Mosaic religion' was merely a 'doctrine for the maintenance of the Jewish race'.[14]

This realization was due not only to the distinctive physical appearance of Jews he encountered,[15] but, more importantly, derived from his investigations into their purported and decidedly non-religious activities. Spurred on by a range of anti-Semitic literature, such as Jörg Lanz von Liebenfels's *Ostrara* publications, and inspired by figures such as von Schönerer, and Karl Lueger, the anti-Semitic Christian Socialist mayor of Vienna, Hitler soon detected the complicity of Jews in all forms of 'filth or profligacy', their hand being clearly discernible in prostitution and the slave traffic, as well as in the press, the arts and media, and other aspects of cultural life.[16] Most importantly, the Social Democratic Party, its principles and policies based on the internationalist teachings of Karl Marx, was, Hitler deduced, effectively an instrument of the Jews who had used it to seduce the masses into 'despising their own nationality'.[17] Indeed, social democracy was nothing more than the pathfinder of Marxism, for behind all the commendable slogans calling for workers' rights and an end to exploitation lurked only a 'pestilence, disguising itself as social virtue and brotherly love'.[18] Marxism was thus a vehicle the Jews devised and used to foment social conflict and disintegration, for by deceiving the workers with promises of socialist paradise, and assuring them of the solidarity of the international proletariat, the Jew hoped only to lay the foundations for his own domination of the globe. This not only explained why Marxism was hostile to the preservation of Germanism and contemptuous of nationalism, but also provided the key to its 'disgraceful courting' of Slavic 'comrades', its utter rejection of nationhood and fatherland, and its contempt for morality, religion, education and the authority of law.[19]

On a different level, Jews also conspired to pollute and weaken the German race, sometimes through guile and seduction, sometimes through brutal violation and exploitation, in what Hitler termed a systematic attempt to 'lower the racial level by a continuous poisoning of individuals'.[20] The goal of the Jew in this process, he noted subsequently, was 'the promiscuous bastardization of other peoples, the lowering of the racial standards of the best' in order to establish his rule over the resulting 'racial hotchpotch' through the elimination of the indigenous intelligentsia and its replacement with members of his own kind.[21] The purpose and effects of this process could clearly be seen in Russia, he noted in 1927, where, following the 1917 revolution, Jewish Bolshevik leaders had abolished marriage and replaced it with a random licentiousness with the aim of 'breeding a general inferior human mishmash'. The resulting 'chaotic bastardization' would be so totally lacking in leadership qualities that it would ultimately be unable to survive without the Jews 'as its only intellectual element'.[22] The Marxists' insistence on equality, or rather democracy, and their promotion of pacifism and international brotherhood, complemented this aim as they were essentially designed to suppress individuality, stifle initiative, deny the inevitability of struggle and conflict, and destroy all vestige of culture. As he wrote in *Mein Kampf*, the 'Jewish doctrine' of Marxism rejects aristocratic principles of nature and replaces the eternal privilege of power and strength by the mass of numbers and their dead weight. Thus, it denies the value of personality on man, contests the significance of nationality and race, and thereby withdraws from humanity the premise of its existence and culture. As a foundation of the universe, this doctrine would bring about the end of any order intellectually conceivable to man. And as in the greatest of all recognizable organisms, the result of an application of such a law could only be chaos, on earth it could only be destruction for the inhabitants of this planet. If, with the help of his Marxist creed, the Jew is victorious over the peoples of the world, his crown will be the funeral wreath of humanity.[23]

In a perceptive study of Hitler's political philosophy Rainer Zitelmann makes the important point that Hitler's brand of anti-Marxism bore little relation to the anti-Marxism of the bourgeoisie, indeed it was not even 'directed exclusively against any specific points in the teachings of Karl Marx'.[24] What Hitler found objectionable in Marxism was not its programme for social and economic reform, or its political methods and organization, which he rather admired, but its championing of internationalism, pacifism and democracy, which made it so susceptible to Jewish manipulation. Thus, although in Hitler's eyes Marxism was linked inextricably to Jewry, which constituted its 'spiritual backbone',[25] 'Marxist' or 'communist' were labels that might be attached to any individual, Jewish or Gentile, who consciously or otherwise served international Jewish interests rather than embraced and promoted *völkisch* ideals that aimed at the national rebirth of Germany.[26] This was precisely what he meant when in 1927 he declared that by substituting pacifism for conflict, internationalism for race, and democracy for the individual Marxism was effectively a declaration of war on 'the three basic foundations on which mankind rests'.[27] This message, and variants of it, was a prominent and consistent

17

feature of Hitler's declarations on Marxism during the *Kampfzeit*, and formed an integral part of the evolving Nazi *Weltanschauung*.[28] As he said in February 1930, the NSDAP's 'programmatic basis' was firmly rooted in its approach to the 'racial problem, to pacifism and to internationalism'.[29]

In terms of the development of Hitler's views, the impressions left by his years in Vienna were clearly of considerable significance in forming and consolidating his unique political philosophy. In particular, it seems entirely probable that he had by that stage begun to make some connections between social democracy, or rather Marxism, and Jewry. In Vienna, that 'second Jerusalem' and home to a 'Babylon of races' as he later termed it,[30] Hitler had certainly had far more personal contact with Jewry than before. In these circumstances, and under the impact of the anti-Semitic influences referred to earlier, it is unlikely that he failed to register that the poorer sections of the Jewish community, particularly the so-called *Ostjuden*, mainly political refugees from Russia, were attracted to social democracy. By the time he left for Munich in May 1913 Hitler undoubtedly had a keener appreciation of those 'two menaces', Jewry and Marxism, the combating and ultimately extirpation of which would constitute the key feature of his political mission. As he later told the Bavarian authorities during his trial following the Munich putsch, while he had arrived in Vienna as a 'citizen of the world' he had left it as an 'absolute anti-Semite' and 'a deadly enemy of the whole Marxist world view'.[31]

The First World War did nothing to ease Hitler's anxieties about the progress of Marxism or the Jews' destructive influence. Within six months of its outbreak he was expressing the hope that the conflict would result not only in the final defeat of Germany's external adversaries but also in a spiritual purification of the German Reich. As he wrote to Ernst Hepp, an acquaintance from his Munich days, those of his comrades who had dared to dream of seeing the Fatherland again hoped to return to a land liberated from all foreign influence and finally purged of its own 'inner internationalism', a goal which, he noted tellingly, would be of far greater value than any territorial gain.[32] The future chancellor was thus understandably horrified when, the following year, during a period of convalescence and leave spent in Berlin and Munich, he found precisely the opposite taking place. Hitler was appalled by the degeneration he encountered on the home front where 'the most unprincipled agitators' openly encouraged malingering and cowardice,[33] while the bureaucracies and economy were almost entirely in the grip of Jews. From here it was but a short step to the nightmare vision of a conspiracy, led by an enemy within, driven not by concern for the German national interest but by that inner internationalism of which Hitler had earlier written with such disdain.

It thus comes as no surprise to discover that Hitler readily embraced the *Dolchstosslegende*, the theory of the fatal 'stab in the back', delivered by the Reich's internal enemies, notably the Jews and the social democrats, the so-called 'November criminals' who had wilfully sacrificed the German nation in pursuit of their own perverse internationalist agenda. This preposterous notion not only provided a convenient explanation for the sudden collapse of the Reich in November 1918, but also served as a rallying call for the numerous right-wing, ultra-nationalist, anti-Semitic and *völkisch* groups that proliferated in the immediate aftermath of defeat. Moreover, the *Dolchstosslegende* furnished Hitler with further ammunition in his campaign against the Jews, as too did developments in Bavaria where for a few weeks in spring 1919 Soviet-style workers' and soldiers' councils had seized control in Munich and other major cities.[34] The Jews, Hitler noted in November 1919, in one of numerous articulations of the point, were responsible both for the 'shameful' armistice and for the 'bloody rule of the councils' during the so-called *Räterepublik*.[35] At that fateful juncture, he recalled years later, Germany had 'stood on the brink of Bolshevism'.[36]

The impact of war, defeat and revolution on the development of Hitler's anti-Semitism appears to have altered fundamentally the nature of his attitude to the Jews. As Peter Longerich recently commented, while it is 'highly probable' that Hitler succumbed to anti-Jewish influences during his Vienna years, only from 1918–19 can one speak of the development of 'a programmatic anti-Semitic ideology'.[37] A clear indication of the radicalization of Hitler's position is provided by his celebrated letter to Adolf Gemlich, written in September 1919 in response to a request from Gemlich for clarification on current Reichswehr attitudes to the Jewish question. In a lengthy and revealing response Hitler not only reminded Gemlich of the 'pernicious impact' the Jews had had on Germany, but also called for a 'rational anti-Semitism', the aim of which would be 'the total removal of all Jews from our midst'. Moreover, he also inferred that Jews represented a threat not only to Germany but also to other peoples, referring to them as 'racial tuberculosis of the nations'.[38] In this process of the radicalization of his views on the Jewish question, the alleged complicity of Jewry in the downfall of the Reich in 1918, and in the promotion of the attendant and dangerous revolutionary circumstances, made a profound impression on Hitler, so much so, he implied in *Mein Kampf*, that it determined his political destiny.[39] The Jews, he felt, had impoverished, divided and betrayed the nation, sucked out its lifeblood, wantonly negated the sacrifice made by millions of German soldiers at the front, and, worst of all, delivered the Reich into the hands of ruthless internationalist tyrants.[40] It was a lesson he would never forget; indeed, it was one that would continue to haunt him.

By autumn 1919 Hitler was already conversant with literature and acquainted with circles that purported to have uncovered a Jewish conspiracy based on Jewry's alleged exploitation of international finance and its promotion of worldwide revolution through Marxism. In this context, 1919 was a fateful year not only for Germany but also for Hitler, for at that time he first came into contact with Alfred Rosenberg and Dietrich Eckart, two personalities who undoubtedly helped shape his political *Weltanschauung*. Of the two, Rosenberg undoubtedly exercised the greater influence, for it was he who first instructed Hitler on the Jewish nature of Bolshevism and the relationship between the October revolution and the wider international Jewish conspiracy. Moroever, Rosenberg was able to introduce Hitler to other émigrés and political refugees from former imperial Russia, some of whom, notably Max Erwin von Scheubner-Richter, may have exercised some influence on the future chancellor's perceptions of Bolshevism and its purported Jewish roots. In autumn 1920 Scheubner-Richter founded the White Russian émigré organization *Aufbau*, some of whose members, according to Michael Kellogg, made a significant contribution to the development of Hitler's view of the Soviet Union as a 'Jewish dictatorship'.[41] Here is not the place to engage in a detailed investigation into the origins of Rosenberg's anti-Semitism, but, given his undeniable impact on early Nazi ideology, particularly in connection with the purported conspiratorial activities of the Jews, a brief outline of his ideas would seem appropriate.[42]

Since at least 1917 Rosenberg had been writing and speaking about the threat posed by the international machinations of Jews, arguing that they employed two methods to destroy nations, namely political radicalism, such as Bolshevism, and capitalism. While he had thus approved of the Russian revolution of February 1917, which he had perceived as anti-capitalist in nature, Rosenberg strongly denounced the subsequent Bolshevik revolution of the following October as a Jewish conspiracy, the aim of which was the destruction of Russia as a state. Bolshevism, according to Rosenberg, was nothing more than the 'continuation of Jewish usury by other, more terrible means'.[43] Fearful of the advancing Red Army, Rosenberg fled Estonia in 1918 and eventually settled in Munich, where he soon gravitated into the circle of Dietrich Eckart, a disaffected poet and publicist who shared the conviction that the Jews were engaged in a subversive international intrigue. Blaming Jews for the defeat of the Reich in the First World War, and condemning their influence in the capitalist West where they had furiously agitated for the destruction of Germany both during the war and at the Paris Peace Conference, Eckart claimed that the aim of Jewry was the subjugation of national states, and ultimately Jewish domination of the globe.[44] At the time he met Rosenberg in early 1919, Eckart was already publishing rabidly anti-Semitic views in his own weekly newssheet, *Auf gut deutsch*, to which Rosenberg predictably became a regular contributor.

Rosenberg's first article, a highly polemical essay entitled *Die russisch-jüdische Revolution*, described the calamities the Jews had visited on Russia and concluded with the prophecy that, should the Bolsheviks lose the civil war then raging, not a single Jew would survive the wrath of the incensed Russian population.[45] It was not only in Bolshevik Russia that the Jews held sway, however, for in Rosenberg's view their influence was also discernible in the major centres of international finance. It is difficult to determine to what extent Gottfried Feder, a political theorist associated with the early history of the DAP, influenced Rosenberg's views on this issue. Although Rosenberg periodically denounced 'interest slavery', the term coined by Feder and used frequently in his biting attacks on finance capitalism, his own preoccupation with the Jews and their supposed involvement with high finance long predated his arrival in Germany and thus any knowledge of Feder. Moreover, although both Rosenberg and Feder were associated with the DAP by mid-1919, there were significant differences between the views of the two men. Feder was chiefly preoccupied with the evils of capitalism, and, although he occasionally made anti-Semitic statements, he did not subscribe to Rosenberg's view that capitalism was controlled by world Jewry. He was thus more sympathetic to Bolshevism than Rosenberg, even to the point of endorsing the October revolution, which, he argued, had at least freed the Russian people from capitalist exploitation. Feder certainly exercised enough influence on Hitler to merit a special mention in *Mein Kampf*. In a manoeuvre typical of his political opportunism and unscrupulousness, Hitler mixed the theories of Rosenberg and Eckart about Jewry's control of capitalism with Feder's slogans about 'interest slavery' in order more effectively to vilify the Jews for their supposed manipulation of the world's financial markets, even though Feder had denied that this was the case.

As stated earlier, however, it was to Rosenberg that Hitler owed his greatest debt. Combining his own ideas on the Jewish nature of Bolshevism, Eckart's theories on the Jews' manipulation of capitalism, and Feder's arguments about the role of 'interest slavery', Rosenberg was the first Nazi theorist to articulate the idea of an international conspiracy through which the Jews aimed to influence not only domestic policy within states but also the relations between them.[46] Having exposed the role of the Jews in promoting discord and misery through world revolution and capitalism, Rosenberg's subsequent investigations revealed other strands of the supposed conspiracy, notably in Freemasonry, Jesuitism and, naturally, Zionism.[47] In the early 1920s he spoke and wrote extensively on Britain's support for Zionism, often referring to the Balfour Declaration as a classic example of British appeasement of the Jews.[48] Ironically, he was more approving of the Russians, primarily because of their anti-Semitism, and believed that, as the Jews intrigued against nationalism, a Russia freed from Bolshevism might yet join forces with Germany against the common enemy. He also viewed Russo–German collaboration as desirable in strategic terms, arguing that the postwar European balance of power had pushed Germany and Russia into the same camp. Not only that, but both powers had an interest in the destruction of Poland that had been created at Russian and German expense and was now supported by Jewish politicians in the West. However, he adamantly rejected any notion of collaboration if Russia remained controlled by Bolshevik Jews, fearing that, just as the Bolshevik revolution had been directed by the Jews against the Russian state and the Russian people, a similar fate might well befall Germany. Rosenberg's contribution to early Nazi thinking on the idea of a Jewish world conspiracy should not be underestimated. As one authority observes, it was largely owing to his efforts between 1919 and 1921 that a 'vast web of Jewish intrigue' was uncovered, which in turn served to substantiate the 'suspected collaboration between the Jewish capitalists and Jewish Bolshevism'.[49]

Unlike Rosenberg, Hitler appears to have drawn no connection between the Jews and the Bolshevik revolution prior to 1919, or to have arrived at any independent conclusions about a supposed international conspiracy directed by world Jewry. Having spent the first half of 1919 in various menial capacities in the service of the Reichswehr, he subsequently attended a brief course of instruction in anti-Bolshevism at Munich University as part of his retraining as a propaganda agent and informer whose task it would be to combat sedition among disaffected sections of the German army. Shortly afterwards, after impressing his superiors with his oratorical talents, he was sent to Lechfeld army camp where he instructed the troops on the virtues of nationalism and the terrible dangers of Bolshevism. By that time he was already in personal contact with Dietrich Eckart, and familiar with Rosenberg's views through reading *Auf gut deutsch*. It seems certain that this evolving connection with Rosenberg, whom he eventually met in December 1919, was responsible for the increasing references Hitler made to Bolshevism in his speeches from early 1920 onwards.

The appearance of a German edition of the *Protocols of the Learned Elders of Zion*,[50] also in December 1919, does not appear to have had any profound effect on the development of Hitler's attitude to the Jews or their supposed international machinations, but rather to have confirmed him in the correctness of his own anti-Semitic views. The *Protocols* had in any case been common knowledge in *völkisch* and other right-wing circles for some time, and it is thus unlikely that Hitler had remained unaware of their existence. Hitler's failure specifically to refer either to the *Protocols* or to the menace of international Jewry in his early political speeches was perhaps due to the need at that juncture to concentrate on purely domestic issues in the wake of the disastrous peace settlement.[51] The *Protocols* nevertheless appeared to substantiate what Rosenberg had told him about the conspiratorial plans of world Jewry, and he soon began to incorporate in his addresses the notion of an international Jewish threat. During 1920, possibly due to further reflections on the *Protocols*, but more probably as a result of his deepening acquaintance with Rosenberg, Hitler gradually worked his way around to the latter's theory of the complicity of the Jews in the Bolshevik revolution. By June 1920, having already alerted his audiences to the abominable conditions prevailing in Russia, he was adamant not only that Bolshevism was 'a Jewish affair through and through',[52] but also that the Jewish leaders of Russia were operating in league with the Jewish capitalists of the West in an endeavour to subvert national states and ultimately to erect a Jewish world dictatorship. Moreover, if Marxism was not already sufficiently pernicious as a doctrine, in Soviet Bolshevism, the practical manifestation of Marxism in Russian conditions, a new and important factor had to be recognized, for with the advent of the Bolshevik regime theory had suddenly been turned into practice with the result that 'Jewish Bolshevism' now had at its disposal a ready made resource-laden state virtually on. Germany's doorstep. What could be more threatening in view of the Jew's mission as the 'great agitator for the complete destruction of Germany', the Bolshevization of which was 'conceived only as a preliminary to the further extension of this Jewish tendency of world conquest'.[53] As he explained at his trial in February 1924:

> With us the situation is represented as if here it was merely a question of purely theoretical problems, of views held by a few visionaries or maliciously disposed individuals. No! A world view has won over for its own ends a state, and, starting from this state it will gradually shatter the whole world and bring it down in ruins. Bolshevism, if its advance

24

is not stemmed, will transform the world as completely as in past times did Christianity.[54]

Once Hitler had incorporated the idea of an international conspiracy directed by world Jewry into his political *Weltanschauung* it came to frame many of his attitudes, and determine many of his actions, in both domestic and international affairs following the Nazi assumption of power in 1933. By the early 1920s Hitler had effectively made the Jews responsible for everything detrimental to German interests and well-being, from the peace settlement to the resulting economic privations, from democracy to racial degeneration, and from Marxism to the League of Nations. Worse still was the fact that the Weimar Republic was in the hands of the Jews, either indirectly through the activities of the Jewish 'international bourse bandits' or directly through the control and manipulation by Jewry of Weimar's political elite.[55] If Germany were to have any hope of survival and regeneration, he argued in early 1922, it must free itself from 'this Jew-republic', this 'Jewish democracy', which was nothing more than a 'machine for the destruction of genius'.[56] Even in his last political testament drawn up shortly before his suicide in 1945 Hitler continued to preach 'implacable opposition to the universal poisoner of all peoples, international Jewry'.[57] Having thus unmasked the enemy, and identified him with the cause of Marxism, Hitler relentlessly pursued the 'two menaces' of the Vienna years wherever he found them. The fight had been joined for the soul of the German nation, he declared in 1922. Two worlds had entered into conflict, and an inexorable struggle was now underway between, on the one hand, those elements favourable to national and *völkisch* ideals, and, on the other, the intangible supranational forces of internationalism,[58] that 'inevitable enemy of human advancement'.[59] In the domestic arena the first task of the Nazi movement was thus to win back those workers who had already been infected by the Marxist poison, a process only possible through an 'excess of nationalist fanaticism', which National Socialism alone could deliver.[60] The German worker could not be blamed if bourgeois indifference had driven him towards the Marxists, Hitler argued, for he had been badly served by his political leaders, not one of whom had recognized either the decisive significance of the racial question or the corrosive effects of internationalism.[61] Nor was that especially surprising, given that the parties of the left were nothing more than 'Jewish mercenaries', their bourgeois antagonists simply the 'right-wing of the Marxist groups'.[62]

During the *Kampfzeit* the campaign against Marxism, Jewry and internationalism thus inevitably remained at the forefront of the NSDAP's political programme and propaganda campaign. Building on earlier verbal assaults, Hitler's *Mein Kampf* reverberated with violent denunciations of the Jews;[63] the *Zweites Buch*, though unpublished at the time, and despite its somewhat narrower focus on foreign policy, essentially confirmed the consistency and intensity of Hitler's views on the Jewish menace towards the close of the 1920s.[64] During the 1920s and early 1930s the *Völkischer Beobachter* carried scores of articles on the conspiratorial international machinations of the Jews who, as Hitler reminded the readership in April 1925, had already acquired in Bolshevism and capitalism two instruments with which to facilitate their attainment of world domination.[65] Meanwhile, at grass-roots level, guidelines the party's propaganda leadership issued for use by local and regional speakers routinely recommended works on Bolshevism, Marxism, Freemasonry and the 'Jewish Question' as suitable for addresses and discussion,[66] while Goebbels, having finally cast off his 'National Bolshevik' pretensions,[67] zealously instructed his compatriots on the bond between Marxism and the Jew, that 'rootless ... ferment of decomposition'.[68]

While the more radical strains of Nazi anti-Semitism might occasionally be downplayed for tactical purposes, as when Hitler spoke to foreign newspaper correspondents,[69] the intensity of the onslaught against Marxism remained constant in the years leading up to the Nazi takeover. Between 1930 and 1932, as the NSDAP sought to build on its electoral successes, the agitation against Marxism reached new heights, and hardly any major speech by Hitler passed without some form of attack on the despised 'world plague', as he had referred to it in *Mein Kampf*.[70] Inevitably, Hitler and other senior Nazis frequently held aloft the Soviet Union as the classic and disastrous example of the Bolshevik experiment. In the USSR, Hitler noted in 1929, the 'Jewish-Bolshevik' overlords were 'more firmly in the saddle than ever', their unyielding aim being the destruction of other nations and the erection of a world

26

dictatorship presided over by the self-proclaimed 'chosen people'.[71] Stalin was the 'fanatical champion of Jewish world Marxism', intent, like Lenin before him, on pursuing and exterminating the 'last remnants of Aryan culture' in Russia.[72] Although attacks on the purported Jewish domination of international finance did not disappear completely from the Nazi repertoire, the gaze came increasingly to focus on Russia and Bolshevism, the latter of which he had concluded by 1925, constituted the 'attempt undertaken by the Jews in the twentieth century to achieve world domination'.[73]

Following Hitler's assumption of the chancellorship the Nazis quickly tightened their grip on the German state with dire consequences for their political and racial antagonists. The forces of the left, already decimated by the factionalism and rivalries that had so severely compromised their ability to combat the Nazis during the final stages of the Weimar Republic, quickly faded from view in the months after 30 January 1933. A series of measures undertaken by the NSDAP, notably the Enabling Act of March 1933, coupled with the Gestapo's rule of terror, which prioritized the persecution and incarceration of all known political opponents, meant that any possibility of an organized and effective communist resistance to Nazi rule had practically ceased to exist. Having persistently underestimated the threat posed by the extreme right – even as Hitler was taking office the German Communist Party (KPD) was still firing its main broadsides at the despised socialists – the KPD fragmented and was driven underground, the prospect of any revival of its fortunes becoming ever more remote as the new regime set about restoring German pride, prestige and employment, plus at least a modicum of prosperity, through its rearmament and public works programmes.[74] To be sure, the domestic threat of communism was sometimes played up to foreign governments to justify German hostility towards the Soviet Union,[75] and it would be unwise to take at face value Hitler's statement in 1936 that he and his movement had eradicated all 'Jewish-Soviet ideas' within the borders of the Reich. Nonetheless, despite the KPD's regrouping and the enduring existence of communist cells in Germany, to say nothing of acts of resistance undertaken by individuals, it would be misplaced to speak of any substantial or effective communist resistance to Nazi rule after 1933. As a British visitor to Germany noted in 1936, although there might well be a good deal of communism 'literally underground, for example in the Ruhr mines', it had effectively 'been stamped under for keeps, so far as one can see at present'.[76]

The Jews, too, were made to pay dearly once Hitler assumed the chancellorship. Almost immediately after taking power the Nazis launched a campaign with the specific aim of impoverishing, marginalizing and isolating Jews in German society through a series of punitive measures, including economic boycotts, exclusion from the civil service and the professions, and racial legislation, all played out against a background of appalling intimidation and violence. In its initial phase, the persecution of Jews was intended not only to damage Jewish interests in Germany but also to serve as a warning to international Jewry, which the Nazis held responsible for the violent press attacks that had greeted the new regime's first steps.[77] Public attention was also focused on the alleged complicity of international Jewry in the Reichstag fire, which, according to *Der Stürmer*, was to have been the signal for a general uprising across the Reich. The authorities' timely countermeasures had thwarted this latest manifestation of Jewish-inspired 'Bolshevik world criminality', but the German people must forever remain vigilant against Jews who would inevitably devise 'fresh intrigues and crimes', and who would 'not rest until a new attack on Germany is ready'.[78] This was the kind of message the *Völkischer Beobachter*, *Der Stürmer* and sundry other Nazi publications continually fed the German public.

To be sure, the regime's relentless agitation against communists and Jews in the years before the outbreak of war, which culminated in the *Reichskristallnacht* and Hitler's prophetic warning about the extermination of European Jewry in January 1939, fulfilled a tactical function in terms of domestic politics, but it was primarily driven by genuine fears of racial contamination on the one hand and revolutionary subversion on the other, which could prove to be especially dangerous in time of war or other national emergency.[79] The notorious Nuremberg laws of September 1935 had been designed precisely to meet these threats. By disenfranchizing citizens deemed 'not of German blood' and outlawing marriages and sexual relationships between Germans and Jews, the Nazis hoped not only to prevent what they termed 'race defilement' but also to counter Bolshevik agitation within the frontiers of the Reich.

One of the principal reasons behind the legislation, Hitler told an American journalist, had been the need to combat Bolshevism, for through it the rights of Germans would be safeguarded against destructive Judeo-Bolshevik influences.[80] Using the proceedings of the seventh congress of the Communist International as his justification,[81] the German chancellor announced to the Reichstag on 15 September 1935 that the 'Bolshevist International' had 'resumed its open and methodical revolutionizing', and that in Germany, as elsewhere, it was 'almost exclusively Jewish elements which are at work as instigators of this campaign to spread animosity and confusion among the peoples'. Seeking to take advantage of current international unrest, Jewish circles in Germany appeared to have concluded that the time had arrived 'to set Jewish interests up in clear opposition to the German national interests in the Reich'. The Nuremberg laws were an attempt to combat these designs and to place relations between the German *Volk* and Jewish people on a tolerable footing. 'Should this hope prove false,' he concluded threateningly, 'and intra-German and international Jewish agitation proceed on its course, a new evaluation of the situation would have to take place.'[82]

The struggle against Judeo-Bolshevism was not only proclaimed and played out on the stage of German domestic politics but also increasingly from 1935–36 onwards in the international arena. During those years a series of events beginning with the conclusion of the Franco–Soviet alliance and culminating in the outbreak of a civil war in Spain that came to epitomize the interwar struggle between fascism and National Socialism, on the one hand, and Bolshevism, on the other, brought into ever sharper relief the decisive ideological conflict of the age. Claiming to see in the developments in Spain the beginnings of a fresh onslaught by the 'Jewish Bolsheviks', both within Germany and in the wider world, Hitler warned the party faithful at the 1936 Nuremberg rally not only that attempts to intervene in German affairs conducted by the 'Jewish Soviet authorities' were still continuing, but also that Bolshevism was now seeking 'to draw gradually ever nearer to our frontiers' and that therefore 'we are forced to regard Bolshevism even beyond our frontiers as our mortal enemy'.[83]

As will be demonstrated subsequently, this reference to the need to combat the external threat of Bolshevism was not, as Hitler appears to have wished it to be understood, a timely innovation necessitated by Soviet complicity and intervention in the early stages of the Spanish Civil War. It was a longstanding preoccupation of the National Socialist movement, and one which, since the mid-1920s at the latest, had occupied a central position in Hitler's foreign political plans. By the summer of 1936, with the Bolsheviks and Jews within the Reich contained if not eliminated, the German chancellor was devoting a considerable portion of his energies to what he was accustomed to term the struggle of the civilized world against international Bolshevism, partly of necessity as a result of the developments in Spain, partly because he was moving towards the conclusion of an overtly anti-communist agreement with Japan, and partly because he was gearing himself for a final attempt to cement an alliance with Britain on the basis of common opposition to the red menace. Before examining these and related issues in depth, however, we must first gauge the impact of Soviet Bolshevism and the internationalization of the Jewish menace on Hitler's outlook on foreign affairs during the *Kampfzeit*, and seek to assess the extent to which it conditioned and informed his early conduct of foreign policy as chancellor of the Reich.

Chapter 2
Ideology, *Realpolitik* and Anti-Bolshevism in Hitler's Foreign Policy 'Programme', 1920–33

I n the immediate aftermath of the First World War Hitler's views on international issues were largely informed and shaped by ideas current within the Pan-German League, whose leader, Heinrich Class, has been credited with exercising a considerable influence over Hitler's early outlook on questions of foreign policy.[1] Hitler's international objectives at the time of his introduction to and acceptance of the idea of a Jewish 'world conspiracy' were essentially revisionist and, in so far as they envisaged the destruction of the Treaty of Versailles and the return of the German colonies, were typically representative of those to be found in nationalist circles.[2] Despite the occasional reference to Germany's need for additional living space,[3] there thus appears to have been no readily discernible ideological dimension to his outlook on foreign policy issues.

Hitler also had fixed ideas about which countries the Reich could count among its friends or enemies. Contrary to his later advocacy of an Anglo–German alliance, he was initially hostile to Britain.[4] Associating with the prevailing Pan-German attitude of the time, he viewed Britain as an 'absolute' enemy not only because of its part in the war, but also because of its role in drafting and implementing the Treaty of Versailles. Even in 1919–20, however, Hitler obviously admired and envied British world power, which, he believed, derived its impetus from the strength of British national feeling, a commitment not to tolerate interracial breeding, and a genius for conquest, organization and economic exploitation.[5]

At this stage, in contrast to his overtly anti-British attitude, Hitler was not absolutely opposed to the idea of a future alliance with

Russia. Russo–German enmity had, in his view, been the product of the second Reich's foolish support of Austro–Hungarian ambitions in the Balkans. In view of his developing appreciation of the supposed Jewish 'world conspiracy', it is equally significant that within a few months Hitler began suggesting that it had been the international Jewish press that had prevented a Russo–German agreement before the First World War, a fact that had undeniably contributed to its outbreak.[6] This is one of the first examples where Hitler suggested that the Jews had been responsible for limiting Germany's options and thus weakening its international position even before 1914.

As noted earlier, by 1920, after having made Rosenberg's acquaintance, Hitler accepted that the Jews ruled Bolshevik Russia. He also appeared to share – or perhaps accepted – Rosenberg's ideas on the possibilities for future collaboration between Germany and a Russia freed of the Bolshevik yoke. On 21 July 1920, in keeping with his hostility to Britain and France as the powers chiefly responsible for the peace settlement, and revealing an open mind on a future alliance with a Russia purged of Jewish influence, he declared that Germany's salvation could never come in association with the West; on the contrary, to that end it must seek contact (*Anschluss*) with 'nationalist, anti-Semitic Russia. Not with the Soviet'.[7]

If by 1920 racial ideology had begun to influence Hitler's *Weltanschauung* in so far as future foreign policy was concerned, so too had considerations of *Realpolitik*. France had a special place in Hitler's calculations, for, as a hereditary enemy that had continually sought the destruction of Germany, most recently demonstrated by its policy at the peace conference, France posed the most immediate threat to the integrity of the Reich.[8] These views in turn affected Hitler's perceptions of Italy. Franco–Italian tension following d'Annunzio's occupation of Fiume in 1919 led Hitler to believe that advantages could be gained from exploiting the friction between the two powers, and for that reason he began to consider Italy a possible ally.[9] *Realpolitik* rather than ideology thus determined the role of Italy in Hitler's calculations, and this, moreover, a full two years before the advent of Mussolini and fascism. Anti-Bolshevism appears to have played little or no role in Hitler's initial gravitation towards Italy.

In summary, in the immediate aftermath of defeat a combination of general considerations of *Realpolitik* and pan-German ideology had framed Hitler's outlook. With regard to the USSR, however, his initial views soon began to change with the result that he began to speak increasingly of the threat of 'Jewish Bolshevism'. As this all important question loomed ever larger in his deliberations, and notwithstanding the uncertainty surrounding the sustainability of the Bolshevik regime in the USSR, which was consumed by a bitter civil war, Hitler had by 1921 reduced German foreign policy to a single basic strategy: either an Anglo–German alliance directed against Russia or a Russo–German alliance directed against Britain.[10] By December 1922, as the Bolsheviks finally began to strengthen their grip on power, Hitler's preference for an Anglo–German alliance became clear. In an interview with Edouard Scharrer, co-owner of the *Münchener Neueste Nachrichten*, Hitler openly abandoned the pan-German line and came out strongly in favour of an Anglo–German alliance.[11] Thus, even before the Ruhr crisis revealed the depth of the differences in the British and French approaches to the German question, Hitler believed that Britain viewed Germany not only as a counterweight to French hegemony in Europe, but also as a potential ally against Russia, whose destruction, he candidly admitted, would have to be undertaken 'with England's help'.[12] In this interview Hitler for the first time renounced overseas ambitions that, he calculated, would make Germany attractive to the British as a future ally, and publicly stated that Germany's future *Lebensraum* was to be obtained in the east.

What had caused Hitler to opt for an alliance with Britain against Russia? Was Britain chosen as an ally on its own merits? Did Hitler fall back on a British alliance because he discovered grounds that ultimately forced him to reject Russia? Did the goal of *Lebensraum* in Russia determine his choice of Britain as a future ally? Had Britain been selected for its ideological antipathy to Bolshevism? There is strong evidence to suggest that the choice of Britain was made primarily on the grounds of *Realpolitik*. By the early 1920s there had been a discernible moderation of Hitler's hostile attitude to Britain, not least because the British appeared to oppose French policies towards Germany, notably during the ill-fated Franco–Belgian occupation of the Ruhr in 1923, which has been seen as a turning point in Hitler's view of the British. While he feared the threat that France posed to Germany's territorial integrity, he was certainly aware of the British opposition to French hegemony in Europe, and quick to note the debilitating effect of the Ruhr crisis on the already troubled Anglo–French entente. This was yet another impetus to his idea of Anglo–German friendship, for Britain would be a useful ally against France, Germany's eternal enemy. Having chosen Britain as an ally on these grounds, Russia was naturally rejected, and it would thus be in the east that *Lebensraum* would have to be sought.[13]

Although this appears to be a persuasive argument on the surface, the interpretation is limited, flawed even, because it fails to take the ideological element into account. The evidence suggests that it was not only considerations of *Realpolitik* that led to the choice of Britain as an ally, but also Hitler's increasing obsession with the threat posed by 'Jewish-Bolshevik' Russia. By 1922 he firmly believed that a battle was being waged in Europe between nationalism and internationalism. This was a battle, according to Hitler, 'which began nearly 120 years ago, at the moment when the Jew was granted citizen rights in the European states'.[14] By December 1922 Hitler had been forced to accept the unpalatable fact that the Bolsheviks had won the Russian civil war, and, just as they had consolidated their domestic position, Hitler had adapted himself to the new conditions and consolidated his attitude towards the USSR. As unbridgeable ideological differences now made a Russo–German alliance untenable, Hitler was automatically pushed towards an arrangement with Britain. There is no evidence to suggest that the prospect of acquiring *Lebensraum* in Russia determined Hitler's choice of allies, for only after Hitler had accepted the incompatibility of an alliance with the USSR did he refer regularly to large-scale German expansion in the east. However, what is above all clear is that by 1922 Hitler's doctrines of race and space had converged: 'Jewish-Bolshevik' Russia was the target of future German expansion.

As the 1920s unfolded, traditional considerations of *Realpolitik* continued to influence Hitler's prospective alliance system. His views of France, for example, remained largely consistent, and he continued to believe that France desired the annihilation of Germany in order to consolidate its own hegemony in Europe, a view he would repeat to the point of exhaustion in his writings of the mid-1920s.[15] All the same, *Mein Kampf* and the *Zweites Buch* serve to confirm not only the significance of *Realpolitik*, but also the importance of racial ideology in Hitler's *Weltanschauung*, and it is crucial not to lose sight of this when considering his written observations on foreign policy. As has been demonstrated, it was under Rosenberg's influence that Hitler first identified the Bolsheviks with an alleged Jewish world conspiracy whose goal remained the destruction of all non-Jewish national states.[16] By 1925 Hitler's stance on this issue was clear and unequivocal. *'The fight against Jewish world Bolshevization'*, he wrote in *Mein Kampf*, *'requires a clear attitude towards Soviet Russia. You cannot drive out the Devil with Beelzebub.'*[17]

The ideological dimension of Hitler's foreign policy became clearly evident in *Mein Kampf*. The National Socialist movement, he wrote, had the mightiest task, for it *'must open the eyes of the people on the subject of foreign nations and must remind them again and again of the true enemy of our present-day world'*.[18] He believed it was the duty of Germany and other like-minded powers to confront the 'Jewish-Bolshevik' challenge, and in this respect Britain was an ideal partner. Combined with traditional Anglo–Russian rivalry in the Near East and central Asia, there was an obvious ideological conflict between capitalist Britain and Bolshevik Russia. Whereas Hitler now viewed an alliance with Russia as of no benefit to Germany, Britain, by contrast, was an ideal alliance partner in terms of both ideology and *Realpolitik*. *Mein Kampf* also contains a clear exposition of Hitler's views on *Lebensraum* and racial struggle. Heavily influenced by Social Darwinism, Hitler believed that racial vitality was the key to the health and strength of a nation, and that the principle of the survival of the fittest conditioned the struggle for existence. Taking their cue from this racist viewpoint, his ideas on future foreign policy were closely intertwined with his belief that *'only an adequately large space on this earth assures a nation of freedom of existence'*.[19] In short, the racially superior Germans lacked adequate *Lebensraum*, which Hitler believed was to be found not overseas but in eastern Europe. No longer was it simply a case of removing the constraints imposed by the Versailles settlement; indeed, he believed that the 1914 boundaries meant 'nothing at all for the German future'.[20] Instead, the acquisition of *Lebensraum* in Russia at the expense of racially inferior Slavs was to be the central aim of his foreign policy.[21]

Many of these ideas were recapitulated in the *Zweites Buch*, which was written in 1928 but not published in its author's lifetime. In *Mein Kampf* Hitler had presumed that Britain's determination to maintain the balance of power would automatically make it oppose any French or Russian attempts to achieve hegemony in Europe. In the *Zweites Buch* he sought to explain the obvious contradiction in why Britain would oppose French or Russian hegemony on the one hand, but accept German domination of the continent on the other. Britain, he argued, would only feel threatened if, from its paramount position in Europe, Germany were subsequently to menace its maritime or colonial interests,[22] aims he had already envisaged abandoning in *Mein Kampf*. Indeed, the renunciation of Germany's colonial and naval interests was to be the bait with which Hitler hoped to land the British alliance. His logic was simple: a clear division of interests would leave Britain mistress of the seas and Germany master of Europe.[23] Hitler further reasoned that Germany's search for *Lebensraum* in the east would not affect any vital British concerns; on the contrary, for reasons of both *Realpolitik* and ideology, Britain, he believed, would welcome a German campaign against Russia.[24]

With regard to Russia, the *Zweites Buch* reiterated and embellished Hitler's earlier convictions. Once again he made it clear that only Russia was a suitable target for Germany's future *Lebensraum*.[25] He also reasserted his objections to the idea of a Russo–German alliance, fearing that this would result in the 'complete rule of Jewry in Germany'.[26] Thus, Hitler's perception of Russia, in both his doctrines of race and space, had not changed. He remained convinced that a Russo–German alliance made 'no sense for Germany, neither from the standpoint of sober expediency nor from that of human community'.[27] The future tasks of German foreign policy were clear – to 'free its [Germany's] rear against England and conversely to isolate Russia, as much as possible'.[28]

Any examination of the development of Nazi thought on international questions during the period between the completion of the *Zweites Buch* and the assumption of power is complicated because in these years Hitler did not write anything remotely comparable to *Mein Kampf* or the *Zweites Buch* in terms of value as a historical source. Although it has long been apparent that a number of theories and approaches to foreign policy were current within the NSDAP around the turn of the decade,[29] there had until very recently been difficulties in accessing sufficient and reliable sources on the ideas and attitudes of Hitler himself. Indeed, even at the time the NSDAP's position on the major international questions was a source of some confusion and mystery, and several of the obstacles to a satisfactory analysis applied as much 70 years ago as they do today.

In late 1931, in response to reports of growing anxiety abroad about the aims of National Socialism, the state secretary at Wilhelmstrasse, Bernhard von Bülow, issued a circular summarizing what was known about the Nazi attitude on various foreign policy issues.[30] As far as it was possible to judge from the party programme and the recent utterances of its leaders, he concluded that the NSDAP appeared to have no clearly discernible foreign policy agenda, and based its strategy, if indeed it could so be termed, on a relentless and stinging criticism of the foreign policy of the present German administration. Moreover, in several areas there appeared not only to be uncertainty but also contradiction, for respective Nazi spokesmen took up different positions on the same issue. Nevertheless, Bülow was able to identify some areas where there appeared to be a general consensus on the need for an end to reparations, the thorough dismantling of the Versailles system, friendship with Great Britain and Italy and, significantly from our point of view, the need to combat Bolshevism. In its attitude to the USSR, the state secretary informed his colleagues that the NSDAP had a 'clear and unambiguous line', for the fight against Bolshevism was a 'fixed goal of National Socialist foreign policy'. If nothing else, this statement reveals that by 1931 senior officials in the German foreign ministry were fully aware that anti-Bolshevism was not simply a factor in the Nazi Party's quest for power within Germany but a fixed principle of its intended international policy.

As he had since the early to mid-1920s, Hitler continued to attach great importance to the cultivation of good relations and an eventual alliance with Britain. He believed that the British would value and appreciate a strong Germany, which, having renounced any aspirations to world power, would by virtue of its existence safeguard British interests on the continent.[31] By the early 1930s, however, partly because he had reoriented his views on the relationship between Britain and France, Hitler appeared prepared to make further concessions to achieve an Anglo–German partnership. Chief among these was to be the abandonment of revisionist designs in northern and western Europe.[32] Moreover, there was now considerably less emphasis on the possibility of Anglo–German collaboration against France. To be sure, that element was still present, but Hitler now viewed Anglo–German relations much more from the point of view of a shared ideological antipathy to Bolshevism and the increasing threat posed to Europe by the USSR than from the previously rather limited perspective of a mutual antagonism towards France. Once secured from the threat of any renewed maritime or colonial rivalry with Germany, and assured that the National Socialist regime posed no threat to their most immediate security interests on the continent, Hitler could see no reason why the British should not come to a close working association with Germany on the basis of hostility towards the Soviet Union.

Indeed, that association had now become a vital necessity for both powers because the British, and indeed the French, surely had as much to fear from the red peril as the German fatherland. Moreover, in terms of sheer power politics, the NSDAP saw little distinction between the threat the USSR posed to British interests in India and the Far East and the threat the former imperial Russian regime had presented in previous years.[33] Britain thus had much to fear from Bolshevism not only in Europe but at vital points of its empire, and it was in this connection that a rejuvenated, revitalized and powerful Germany could be of the greatest use to it. When a British journalist asked him what he would demand from England in return for German friendship, Hitler named two conditions: British backing for the cancellation of reparations and, rather more revealingly, the acceptance by Britain of a 'free hand in the east', which would allow Germany's 'surplus millions … a chance to expand into the empty spaces on our eastern frontiers'.[34] Here, too, Hitler demonstrated the essential consistency of his views, for this was simply a repetition of the formula, first articulated in the mid-1920s, of a separation and mutual recognition of German interests in Europe and Britain's interests in the wider world.

Not only that, but Hitler continued to believe that the survival of

38

both countries depended on their collaboration, for it was not possible, he argued, to stand by and permit Bolshevism to conquer Germany and expect the rest of Europe, including the British Isles, to remain uncontaminated.[35] In that sense, Britain needed Germany as much as Germany needed Britain. 'England *also* recognizes the danger Russia presents', he exclaimed to Otto Wagener in autumn 1931. 'England *needs* a sword on the Continent. Thus our interests are the same – yes, we are even dependent on one another. If *we* are overrun by Bolshevism, England falls as well. But together we are strong enough to counter the international danger of Bolshevism. I want to and I must preserve the German *Volk* from the hardship of Bolshevism. That can only be done *with* England.'[36]

Just as Hitler's view of the value and desirability of British friendship remained consistent, so too did his perception of Germany's principal antagonists. In Hitler's view, the salvation of Europe hinged on its ability to mobilize against the dual threat posed by France and the Soviet Union, a process in which Germany, Britain and Italy should take the lead. It had been and remained his conviction, he told an Italian journalist in April 1931, that only such an association could preserve peace and save European civilization from the corrosive influence of a France that was increasingly allowing its blood to be poisoned by the African peoples on the one hand, and from the 'nightmare of Asiatic Bolshevism' on the other.[37]

Nevertheless, although Hitler continued to attack French militarism and reparations policy in public, and despite his concern at their wanton disregard of the most basic principles of racial hygiene, there appears to have been a subtle but significant modification of his attitude to France in or around 1931. This was manifested in a move away from the *Mein Kampf* idea of a war of revenge against Germany's 'mortal foe' towards the possibility of coexistence on the admittedly unlikely basis of France accepting German dominance in Europe. Although the precise reasons for this reorientation remain unclear, the increased emphasis Hitler placed on the consolidation of the Soviet Union under Stalin, particularly following the inauguration of the first five-year plan in 1928, is perhaps not without significance.

The fact that by the early 1930s Hitler had revised his original idea of a war of revenge against France and subordinated that aim to the wider goal of organizing Europe to place Germany in the optimum position from which it could fall on the USSR is certainly suggested by his repeated public renunciation of German aims in Alsace-Lorraine, indeed in western Europe as a whole, and his periodic attempts to arrive at a satisfactory understanding with Paris, both of which, it is important to note, continued long after the period of initial consolidation. It is thus insufficient to view German approaches to France during the early 1930s solely as an attempt to deceive the French, and British, authorities at a time when the Reich was relatively weak and vulnerable. As Klaus Hildebrand noted, there were enough signs in Hitler's policy towards France between 1933 and 1936 to suggest that he was prepared to accept a tolerable relationship with it on the basis of a common front against the USSR, provided France abandoned its interests in eastern Europe and accepted its lot as essentially a second-rate European power whose main focus of activity lay overseas.[38]

Apart from direct public appeals for European, or in the first instance Anglo–German, solidarity against Bolshevism, a further means through which Hitler sought to highlight the international dimension of the red threat was by attempting to anchor the political struggle between the conservative and revolutionary forces within Germany in a wider European or global context. In opposing Bolshevism the National Socialists, unlike their democratic opponents, who were either already intriguing with Moscow or simply too blind to appreciate the dangers, were thus already rendering the international community a considerable service. The threat to other nations, however, was still tangible and imminent. As he told the *Saturday Review* in October 1931, the Nazi movement meant to 'make an end in Germany of the pestilence of Asiatic Bolshevism, which threatens the thousand year-old civilization of Europe and has thrown the incendiary bomb of chaos into every country in the world'. Should the reds emerge victorious in Germany, however, it 'would signalize the beginning of a world catastrophe'.[39]

Although there was naturally a good deal of cheap propaganda to be made from this line of reasoning, it would be unwise to dismiss it as pure rhetoric. Out of the public spotlight, Hitler was no less adamant about the magnitude of the problem and the importance of his self-appointed mission. Indeed, it was largely because the Soviet danger was so great that Germany required allies to confront it. Speaking to a group of German industrialists in Düsseldorf in January 1932, Hitler warned his listeners against underestimating Bolshevism, which was not simply 'a mob ranting about in a few streets in Germany', but 'a world view which is on the point of subjecting to its rule the entire continent of Asia'. The Bolshevik *Weltanschauung* had already conquered an area stretching from central Europe to Vladivostok, and, orchestrated by its Soviet controllers, it intended slowly to 'shatter the world and bring about its collapse'. Indeed, if it were permitted to proceed unopposed, Bolshevism would 'expose the world to a transformation as complete as the one Christianity effected'.[40]

The final method the NSDAP employed in its efforts to spread the anti-Bolshevik gospel to the outside world was to establish contacts abroad. Despite the fact that between 1928 and 1932 the Nazi Party was more an object of curiosity than interest to foreigners, and that as such its opportunities for developing diplomatic and political contacts with representatives of foreign powers were necessarily rather limited, Hitler and his associates made strenuous efforts to forge international links in the years immediately preceding their rise to power. Not surprisingly, in view of the alliance strategy Hitler had devised in the mid-1920s, the powers most frequently targeted in this connection were Italy and Great Britain.

Informal contacts were established with Mussolini as early as 1922 and were further developed as the decade progressed through the use of intermediaries such as Kurt Lüdecke, Guiseppe Renzetti and Hermann Göring.[41] Although the Nazi leader was undoubtedly sincere in his admiration for the Duce, seeing in him and his movement a shining example of the triumph of Italian nationalism,[42] Mussolini appears from the first to have had mixed feelings about Hitler and his followers. There is certainly nothing to suggest that he looked forward enthusiastically to the day when he might confront the USSR in alliance with a National Socialist Germany. For Mussolini's purposes, German nationalism was of much greater practical value when it was mobilized against France rather than against distant and alien Russia. Bolshevism was certainly anathema to the fascists, but Mussolini, lacking any aggressive designs on Soviet territory, and unburdened by Hitler's racial theories that

41

automatically linked the Jews and the Bolsheviks,[43] was rather more defensive in his attitude towards the Soviet Union and its supposed international machinations.

Despite his warm feelings for the Duce and fascism, it was clearly London rather than Rome that in Hitler's eyes held the key to combating the 'Jewish-Bolshevik world conspiracy', and it was partly with the intention of persuading the British of that fact that the NSDAP had a number of propaganda agents, including Hans Nieland, Joachim von Ribbentrop and Eugen Lehnkering operating in Britain during the early 1930s. The most significant party member to visit London during this period was Alfred Rosenberg, who arrived in England in November 1931 with the intention of encouraging understanding for Nazi ideas and emphasizing Germany's role as the first line of defence against the eastern menace.[44] During the course of his visit Rosenberg was introduced to several senior figures, including the secretary of state for war, Lord Hailsham, who later forwarded a record of the conversation to the Foreign Office. Following the habitual denunciation of the French position on disarmament and reparations, the Nazi envoy launched into a lengthy disquisition about the fight against Bolshevism, which he characterized as a matter both for internal suppression by individual countries and a suitable area for large-scale international cooperation. The Nazi Party, he explained, had been established to champion German nationalism and root out communism with its divisive doctrine of class warfare. Externally, enthused Rosenberg, the NSDAP looked forward to 'worldwide cooperation against Russia and the successful defeat of the Russian five-year plan, both on its commercial and on its military side'.[45]

This was not the last the Foreign Office would hear of Rosenberg who returned to London in May 1933 on a further visit with much the same purposes. By that time there had been a marked increase in Nazi propaganda in London, much of which was calculated to exploit British fears of and distaste for the Bolshevik regime in Moscow. Moreover, the British authorities quickly grasped the ultimate purpose of this intensive propaganda activity. Commenting on an MI5 survey of the nature of Nazi propaganda in London towards the close of 1933, the head of the northern department, Laurence Collier, noted how the basic message of the German agents confirmed other reports that had also stressed the 'strong hold which the "Rosenberg policy" of expansion in Russia and the Baltic has on the Nazi leaders – in spite of its inherent fatuity'.[46] Fatuous or not, the combination of German territorial aims in eastern Europe and their political adjunct in the form of an ideological campaign against Bolshevism was set to confound Anglo–German relations over the next few years, and in the process play an instrumental role in driving the two powers ever further apart.

In view of the unprecedented destruction and cost in human life that ultimately resulted from Hitler's actions, it might reasonably be contested that the notion of his having some touching concern to save Europe from the ravages of communism and a consequent desire, predicated admittedly on the assumption that attack is the best form of defence, to organize a system capable of extinguishing the ideological threat posed by the USSR is too ludicrous to entertain. Indeed, according to Kurt Lüdecke, Hitler aimed all along to 'play ball with capitalism and keep the Versailles Powers in line by holding aloft the bogey of Bolshevism', for by so doing he would be able to convince them that a Nazi Germany was the 'last bulwark against the Red flood', which in turn was 'the only way to come through the danger period, to get rid of Versailles and rearm'.[47] On the basis of evidence such as this it has been argued that Hitler's stance against Bolshevism, both within Germany and in the international arena, was essentially a sham.[48] On an emotional level, precisely because of his impact on Europe and the wider world, the portrayal of Hitler as a shallow, self-seeking mega-lomaniac, half mad and devoid of genuine convictions, has an almost compelling appeal. Here too, however, a distinction must be drawn between sincerity and rhetoric, and between objectivity and sentimentality. The idea of mobilizing the European powers behind an Anglo–German front in order to combat Bolshevism was not merely a publicity stunt exercised for the benefit of foreign journalists in the hope of creating a positive impression abroad, but also a recurrent theme of Hitler's private conversations with colleagues such as Otto Wagener, who is patently a more reliable witness than the likes of Lüdecke or Rauschning. Moreover, as demonstrated above, by 1930 an alliance with Britain on the basis of hostility to Bolshevism and in open anticipation of a future conflict with the USSR lay at the core of Hitler's foreign policy calculations.

In view of these factors, it can confidently be asserted that, despite the obvious propaganda mileage to be made from anti-Bolshevism and the portrayal of Germany as a bulwark against the proliferation of Marxist–Leninist ideology, there was a good deal of sincerity behind Hitler's anti-Bolshevik message and the use to which he sought to put it, both within and outside Germany. Because it is impossible to view Hitler's attitude to the Bolsheviks in a vacuum, as if it were simply a device to win votes or a cover for nakedly imperialistic aims and thus entirely divorced from his racial theories, merely strengthens this point. To do so would be to ignore the intimate connection in Hitler's mind between the Bolsheviks and the Jews. Consequently, it would be equally foolish to deny that his racially determined hatred of the Jews and his political rejection of Marx were inextricably connected.

The force of this argument is not at all diminished by Hitler's frequent references to Germany's need for *Lebensraum*, which since 1922 he had determined would be found in the USSR, or by his conviction that Stalin's Russia, irrespective of its ideological identity, was, as the new centre of pan-Slavism, essentially no less a threat to central and western Europe. Nazi territorial aims in European Russia are not somehow separate from but rather complementary to the party's proclaimed mission to extirpate Bolshevism. The essential point to grasp is that no one factor alone can adequately explain Hitler's declared intention to smash the Soviet state. A series of complex and interlinked racial, imperialist and ideological factors, in which a determination to combat the international conspiracy that Bolshevism represented assumed a duly prominent role, conditioned his attitude. This debate, and the issue of the relative importance of imperialism and ideology, which it naturally raises, clearly lies at the core of this study and it is one to which we shall periodically have cause to return.

The general picture that emerges from this analysis of Hitler's attitude to the European powers and the potential role assigned to them in his plans for a crusade against Bolshevism is fairly clear. By 1933 the Nazi leader had plans to cooperate with certain major powers, foremost of which was Great Britain, on the basis of a shared antipathy to Bolshevism and the Soviet Union. By this stage the ideological imperative of Hitler's foreign policy was highly significant, more so than in the mid-1920s when there had been a greater emphasis on power political considerations, which had largely manifested themselves in schemes for an Anglo–German–Italian alliance against France. By 1931–32 Hitler was toying with the idea of an agreement with France on the basis of anti-Bolshevism, and even with the idea of a broadly based anti-Soviet coalition led by Britain and Germany. In this connection his words to Otto Wagener in the early 1930s are highly revealing. Commenting on a remark that Wagener had evidently made to him in connection with the pace of Soviet rearmament, Hitler explained:

What you told me earlier about Russian armaments serves only to make us realize that the sooner we can make up our minds to shatter the universal danger of Russian Bolshevism at its centre of power, the easier it will be got rid of. Furthermore, if Europe is to prevail in the decisive battle with America, it must have the grain, the meat, the wood, the coal, the iron, and the oil of Russia. That is in England's interest as well as in ours, it is in the interest of a United States of Europe! England and Germany are equally threatened. But they are also the backbone of the West, the old world, the cultural source of mankind. And a Europe that stretches from Gibraltar to the Caucasus includes all the spheres of interest of the countries that belong to it in other parts of the world – especially all of Africa, India, the Malayan archipelago, Australia, and New Zealand. Canada will also remain loyal to such a concentration of power, which would otherwise fall to America; and the Arabic family of nations will complete the circle of these United States of the old world. This is the prize we offer England! World peace would be assured for all eternity. No earthly power could sow discord into such a community, and no army or navy in the world could shake such power. *It cannot be that England does not recognize and understand this. In any case, I am prepared, even at the risk of failing to persuade England, to take this road, and I will never betray Europe to bolshevism and Jewry.*[49]

Although Hitler hoped that it would ultimately be possible to interest the British in an alliance based on a common ideological antipathy to the USSR, and thus on an agreed agenda to combat the forces of international Jewry, his latter statements to Wagener demonstrate that he was not entirely convinced of Britain's ability to master its own Jewish problem. Rational considerations of *Realpolitik*, and less tangible notions of ideological solidarity, were thus tempered by fears about the extent of Jewish influence in Britain, which, as a democracy, was especially vulnerable to Jewish infiltration and manipulation. Democracy, Hitler believed, was easily exploited by the Jewish Marxists for their own distinctly undemocratic ends. It was thus 'madness' to imagine that one could counter Jewry's ambitions for 'world conquest' by adopting the 'methods of Western democracy'.[50] As the *Völkischer Beobachter* proclaimed in September 1925, Western parliamentarianism and Russian Bolshevism were the two forms 'in which the present Jewish world conspiracy finds its expression'.[51] Small wonder therefore that Hitler considered the 'decisive influence' wielded in Britain by world Jewry to be a crucial issue determining the future course of Anglo–German relations.[52] For however much he might desire cooperation with the British, such desires must and would come to nothing if the British could not resolve the contradictions between the aims of Jewish international finance and their own national interests. Resolute and ideologically sound allies were required for the fight against 'Jewish Bolshevism', not least as it was in Germany that the 'bitterest struggle for the victory of Jewry' was currently being fought.[53] In this respect it is significant that during the mid-1930s, when Hitler's dream of an association with Britain proved to be an illusion, he explained the failure of his policy not only in terms of Britain's attitude to power politics and its commitment to the maintenance of a balance of power in Europe, but also as a result of Britain's fundamental ideological failings. The German Reich, he hissed in February 1936, was surrounded by 'Bolshevik infested democracies'.[54]

The heated denunciations of 'Jewish Bolshevism' in which Hitler frequently indulged during the 1920s and early 1930s, the repeated warnings against the spread of Bolshevik influence and the clarion calls for international collaboration to combat and ultimately destroy it cannot be characterized as pure rhetoric, the sole or even primary function of which was to drum up support for the NSDAP in its struggle with the communists and the other German political parties. Well might Hitler declare during an exchange with Wagener that he had not taken the road of politics to 'smooth the way for international socialism'.[55] Indeed, in his public speeches and press interviews, in the orders he issued to the NSDAP and in his private conversations everything pointed to the very opposite conclusion. It remained to be seen, however, once the NSDAP swept to power in January 1933, whether these ideas were really the stuff of which practical politics, and ultimately war and conquest, might be made.

Chapter 3

The Reorientation of German *Ostpolitik*: Russia, Poland and the Eastern Pact, 1933–35

Although it might be tempting to assume that the accession of the Hitler regime marked a watershed in Soviet–German relations between the wars, a closer look at the evidence, and in particular at developments during the final phase of the Weimar Republic, suggests that this is not necessarily the case. It is certainly undeniable that the rise of the National Socialists contributed significantly to the sharp deterioration of those relations after 1933, and that within 12 months of Hitler's accession as chancellor the German–Soviet partnership that had been forged during the 1920s had been transformed into an overt and very public mutual hostility. Nevertheless, by the early 1930s there were already distinct signs that the collaboration established at Rapallo in 1922 and confirmed four years later through the Treaty of Berlin had outrun its usefulness and that consequently each party was seeking alternative sources of international support.

Stresemann's successors fully realized what advantages had accrued to Germany through the association with the USSR, not least in terms of the opportunities it had afforded the Reichswehr to engage in illicit rearmament and military training. However, although Soviet–German relations appeared on the surface to remain cordial, Germany's acceptance of the Young Plan and the heightened expectations of further concessions from the West, which it had generated, coupled with Brüning's ill-conceived scheme to turn the post-1929 economic crisis to German advantage, meant that by the turn of the decade German leaders' attention was becoming increasingly focused on their relations with Britain and the USA.[1] As for the USSR, not only was it engaged in the initial phase of large-scale modernization occasioned by the first five-year plan, but Stalin, concerned at the obviously pro-Western stance of the later Weimar cabinets, and with the Nazi threat looming in the background, had already begun to explore how to contain rather than exploit the forces of German nationalism.[2]

It was thus understandable that the advent of the Hitler regime should have produced considerable anxiety in Soviet government circles where the Nazi leaders' anti-Bolshevik and expansionist philosophy was well understood.[3] Despite the efforts of the Wilhelmstrasse to assuage Russian fears in this respect, and in particular to differentiate between the Nazis' persecution of German communists, explained as a purely domestic affair, and the maintenance of amicable relations with the USSR, the Soviet regime found it difficult to reconcile Hitler's public denunciations of the Soviet system, of which his Sportpalast speech of 2 March 1933 was perceived as a particularly offensive example, with Germany's professed desire to remain on friendly terms.[4] This was all the more so given that Rosenberg's *Zukunftsweg deutscher Aussenpolitik* and Hitler's *Mein Kampf*, which contained, in Soviet eyes, the most bitter and most predatory anti-Soviet sentiments ever committed to paper, remained unexpurgated and on open sale.[5] It was up to the Reich government, suggested Karl Radek in an article in *Isvestia* of 22 March entitled 'Where is Germany going?', to demonstrate through its present conduct that it had absolved itself of any and all responsibility for the previous literary productions of some of its members, adding with some point that while the Soviet press had certainly had cause to criticize recent developments in Germany, it had never gone so far as to advocate carving up the German state.[6]

If Hitler's public utterances were sufficient to cause alarm and offence to the authorities in the Kremlin, his private remarks served to demonstrate the essential consistency of aim that lay at the root of his foreign political plans. On the evening of 3 February, less than a week after taking office, the new chancellor addressed senior officials of the German armed forces at the home of the commander-in-chief of the army General von Hammerstein, and instructed them on his plans for the conquest of *Lebensraum* in eastern Europe and its 'ruthless Germanization'.[7] Five days later Hitler announced to his cabinet that all resources for the next four to five years were to be channelled into rebuilding the armed forces on which depended Germany's future position in the world.[8] To those present on either occasion Hitler's words were surely sufficient to dispel any doubts, or indeed hopes on the part of the more conservative minded, that the responsibilities of government would curb the radical nature of the party programme as it had evolved during the *Kampfzeit*. At the very least, Hitler's statements to the military leaders on 3 February indicated that the new administration would not give priority to the promotion or even maintenance of close relations with the USSR, which had since 1922 served the German army so well. Although, as will become apparent, some limited gestures of conciliation were made to the Soviet Union during the first months of Nazi rule, these were never followed up or developed through either regular or unofficial diplomatic channels. Given Hitler's preferred method of conducting his diplomacy through the medium of unofficial intermediaries, and 'man to man' conversations, particularly in his early dealings with Britain, the absence of any such initiatives in his relations with the USSR might be taken as a guide to his sincerity and seriousness in seeking to retain Soviet friendship.

During the early stages of his rule, however, amid talk of preventive war and the largely negative reaction produced abroad by the first measures taken by the regime, Hitler was obliged to tread a cautious path in foreign policy. Reassurance and moderation became the order of the day, even towards 'Jewish-Bolshevik' Russia, the intended target of future German aggression. Thus, partly because it suited him for tactical purposes, partly because of the Soviet reaction to his speech of 2 March, and partly, it would appear, as a consequence of the advice of his foreign minister, Constantin von Neurath, who had been alarmed at the sharp deterioration of relations with Russia since 30 January, Hitler made a half-hearted attempt publicly to reassure the USSR during his address to the Reichstag on 23 March with his passing reference to Germany's determination to 'cultivate friendly relations' with the Soviet Union.[9] Interestingly, guidelines for the section of the speech dealing with Russia had been drafted in the Wilhelmstrasse, where the Rapallo policy had enjoyed much favour, and included a public affirmation, also articulated on 23 March, that the Nazi campaign against communism was a domestic matter and would not affect German relations with other states.[10] Yet, at other points in the speech, where the Wilhelmstrasse had clearly had no input, some uncompromising language about the threat communism posed not only to Germany but, in words reminiscent of the electioneering years, to Europe as a whole appeared to negate these conciliatory messages. For, while the elimination of communism in Germany might be a purely internal affair, it was nonetheless the 'utmost goal of the National Government to stamp out and eliminate every trace of this phenomenon', for 'the outbreak of Communist chaos in the densely populated German Reich would lead to political and economic consequences particularly in the rest of Western Europe, the proportions of which are unfathomable'. Hitler's words of welcome for the Four Power Pact proposal recently advanced by Mussolini in which he registered Germany's willingness to 'cooperate with absolute sincerity ... in order to unite the four great powers, England, France, Italy and Germany in peaceful cooperation to courageously and determinedly approach those tasks upon which the solution of Europe's fate depends' provided another jarring and ominous note.[11]

The Soviet reaction to Hitler's declarations mirrored to some extent the speech itself in that it was both mixed and in some respects contradictory. While the German ambassador in Moscow, Herbert von Dirksen, wrote of a temporary relaxation of tension and Soviet gratification at the distinction that had been drawn between domestic opposition to communism and Russo–German relations,[12] the Soviet press equally drew its own distinction between words and deeds and pointedly asked what positive steps Hitler was prepared to take to translate his sentiments into action. Moreover, attention was also drawn to Hitler's reference to the Four Power Pact, which made it quite clear that the German leader believed that Soviet–German relations had no role to play in deciding the fate of Europe.[13] Any hope that the speech had marked the opening of a new and more conciliatory phase in Soviet–German relations was dashed when, within days, a series of incidents in Germany, largely involving the victimization and arrest of Soviet citizens engaged in commercial enterprises, served to poison the atmosphere further. By early April Dirksen was warning that unless steps were taken to improve the situation a conflict with the Soviet government was inevitable, 'the consequences of which will be *very severe* in a political and economic respect'.[14]

It is in this context that the decision finally to ratify the extension of the Treaty of Berlin, a decision that had been taken in principle almost two years earlier, should be viewed. Alarmed by the drift of Dirksen's reporting, and after a stormy interview on 3 April between the ambassador and the Soviet foreign minister Maxim Litvinov, Neurath raised the ratification issue as a matter of urgency at the cabinet meeting in Berlin on 4 April. While the foreign minister intended this step as a major brake on any further downturn in relations with the USSR, which he persisted in viewing as 'cover for our rear with respect to Poland',[15] for Hitler it was merely an inexpensive act of gesture politics to extricate the Reich from a temporarily difficult situation. As subsequent developments would demonstrate, the chancellor was uninterested in reviving the spirit of Rapallo. Hitler agreed with his foreign minister that the cabinet's decision should not yet be revealed to the Russians, but, unlike Neurath, who feared that such knowledge would strengthen Russia's hand in negotiations over other issues, Hitler wished to avoid giving any impression of concessions to the USSR at a time when Anglo–Soviet relations were still reeling from the Metro-Vickers affair.[16]

Those who may have hoped for a genuine improvement in the atmosphere between Berlin and Moscow from the subsequent ratification of the extension of the Treaty of Berlin on 5 May and the German–Soviet Conciliation Agreement of 1929 were to be sorely disappointed. The following month, during the World Economic Conference in London, the German economics minister, Dr Alfred Hugenberg, produced a memorandum, which, in Soviet eyes at least, not only set out the case for German expansion in eastern Europe but also called on other powers to participate in a crusade against the USSR, which, along with other 'large parts of the east', Hugenberg described as a breeding ground for 'war, revolution and internal decay'.[17] Although the Germans immediately protested that Hugenberg had acted on his own initiative, the widespread opinion was that Hitler had tacitly approved his actions. As Dirksen later reflected, it was difficult to believe that in an authoritarian state a responsible minister would dare take such a step without his superiors' knowledge.[18] The explanation that Hugenberg had allowed Rosenberg to influence him offered cold comfort to the Soviet regime, not least because Rosenberg had recently been appointed head of a Nazi Party foreign policy department, the *Aussenpolitisches Amt der NSDAP*. At the very worst this meant that the individual whom the Germans admitted had been the real inspiration behind Hugenberg's memorandum, and who was already highly suspect to the Soviets in view of his contacts with Ukrainian separatist groups, might soon emerge as the real director of the Reich's foreign policy.[19]

By September 1933 the catalogue of abuse and persecution of Soviet citizens, commercial enterprises and other institutions in Germany, coupled with the sustained contradiction between the Reich government's conciliatory words on the one hand and the hostile acts of its representatives on the other, had convinced senior officials in the Soviet foreign ministry that Germany's leaders were determined not to contribute to an improvement in the situation and had, as Litvinov remarked on 14 September, actively 'entered upon an anti-Soviet course'. Several days later David Stern, head of the German department in the Soviet foreign ministry, made the logical observation to the German chargé d'affaires, Fritz Twardowski, that the only 'reasonable inference' to be drawn from Germany's failure to act on the numerous warnings and complaints that had emanated from Moscow in recent months was to conclude that 'there was simply no interest in having friendly relations with the Soviet Union'.[20]

At a conference of departmental heads held in Berlin on 26 September this bleak appreciation of the situation was all but confirmed when the discussion turned to the current state of German–Soviet relations. On this occasion the state secretary at the Wilhelmstrasse, Bernhard von Bülow, warned that a further crisis point was approaching in those relations, not least because the Soviets appeared finally to have lost patience with the continued German provocation and were now resolved to alter their policy accordingly. One manifestation of this reorientation had been the recent expulsion of German journalists in retaliation for the arrest of Soviet correspondents who had sought access to the trial in Leipzig of the Reichstag fire suspects. Although Bülow was not renowned for his affection for the Russians, or indeed for the Rapallo policy, he nonetheless felt that Germany had nothing to gain from an open breach with the USSR at present, not least in view of economic considerations whose importance for the Soviet–German relationship between 1933 and 1941 should not be underestimated.[21] He thus suggested that, to ease the situation and avert the threatened crisis, it would be advisable to make concessions to the USSR. Most usefully these concessions could take the form of a conciliatory message from the head of the Wilhelmstrasse to the Soviet ambassador, a course of action the Russians had already requested, and, more importantly perhaps, a willingness on the part of Hitler to receive the deputy Soviet foreign minister, Nikolai Krestinsky, who was shortly due to pass through Berlin.

Hitler's response to Bülow's exposition was brief but instructive. The Russians, he averred, would never forgive the NSDAP for having smashed communism in Germany, adding somewhat cryptically that 'the fate of Soviet Russia has been decided by our revolution'. It would, he agreed, be unwise at present to provide the Soviets with a pretext for breaking off relations with Germany and to that end he was prepared to permit Bülow to make some reassuring statements to the Russian ambassador and, 'distasteful though it would be for him', even personally to receive Krestinsky. There should be no illusions, however, for 'German–Russian relations could not in practice be maintained in the long run'.[22]

Indeed, as subsequent developments demonstrated, it soon became clear that they could not even be maintained for the duration. By early October, shortly before the German withdrawal from the League of Nations and the Disarmament Conference rocked the world, a senior Russian diplomat, far from registering any improvement as a result of Soviet representations, pronounced the atmosphere between the two countries 'as bad as one could imagine'.[23] As a result, Krestinsky failed to appear in Berlin on the pretext that because he was insufficiently well versed in the key questions affecting Germany and the USSR, there would be little prospect of a fruitful discussion. Meanwhile, their common hostility towards and fear of Germany drew France and the USSR ever closer together, while on 29 December Litvinov delivered a speech in Moscow sharply attacking Germany, branding it a disturber of the peace and placing it on a par with Japan, Russia's antagonist in the Far East. During a highly charged and in part 'unfriendly' interview on 4 January 1934 the Soviet foreign minister informed the new German ambassador, Rudolf Nadolny, that relations could only be improved if Germany adjusted its policy and 'refrained from what she was now doing'. As matters stood, however, the Soviet leaders had no faith in German sincerity, particularly as they were in possession of material 'that proved that Germany had by no means given up the Ukraine and plans for a crusade'. No doubt certain foreign powers had an interest in fuelling these fears, 'but on the other hand the material was so varied and so unanimous that certain information had to be taken seriously'.[24]

By this point the pattern of wholesale political antagonism on the one hand and limited economic cooperation on the other, which would govern German–Soviet relations over the next five years or so, had been firmly established. The responsibility for this development rested firmly on the German side and thus principally with Hitler who, as Gottfried Schramm rightly emphasizes, deliberately caused and permitted relations with the USSR to 'cool if not to say freeze' during the course of 1933.[25] As the Soviets pointed out on more than one occasion, the nature of the German state under the NSDAP leadership meant that, had the German leader so wished it, the trend towards political hostility and ideological confrontation, inaugurated immediately after Hitler swept to power, could have been reversed overnight. Instead, no genuine effort had been made to arrest the slide into mutual recrimination and acrimony. There had been grudging gestures towards the USSR when the occasion demanded it; in April 1933 Hitler had even received the Soviet ambassador, Leo Khinchuk, to whom he had pledged his continued efforts to maintain Soviet–German relations on a 'permanently friendly basis'.[26] Whatever Hitler promised Khinchuk, however, Soviet–German relations during 1933 and the Nazi leadership's handling of those relations told a different story. A much more reliable guide to German intentions to the USSR than any number of platitudes exchanged between Hitler and a Soviet diplomat were the systematic campaign against Soviet interests in Germany, which, according to a foreign ministry survey of October 1933, had been 'without precedent in the history of Soviet–German relations';[27] the promotion of *Mein Kampf* as the movement's basic creed and the mainstay of education in schools and the army; the encouragement of anti-Bolshevik sentiment to the point of promoting songs calling for war against the USSR among the party's

paramilitary formations; a steadfast refusal to permit any meaning-
ful improvement of the political atmosphere between Berlin and
Moscow; the employment of anti-Bolshevik and anti-Soviet arguments in German dealings with Western powers, and not least the
public references, most notably in Hitler's speech at the Nuremberg
rally on 3 September, to the 'European' nature of Germany's
mission to combat Bolshevism. Clearly, Russo–German relations
were not allowed to plunge such depths as they did in 1933 simply
for the sake of it. There was a clear and positive purpose to all these
developments, each of which must be viewed as intimately connected to a higher goal. As Klaus Hildebrand has argued, it is clear
that statements of the kind made by Hitler at Nuremberg had much
more than a purely 'functional significance'. Indeed, they revealed
that part of his long-term 'programme' sought a basis for agreement
with Italy and the West in order to proceed unhindered against the
Soviet Union.[28]

The tone the Germans set in their relations with the USSR during
the course of 1933 persisted virtually uninterrupted until spring
1939 when each side suddenly found it expedient to accommodate
the other in the Nazi–Soviet Pact. Before that time, despite some
Soviet attempts to engineer an improvement in political relations
through the medium of their economic ties with Berlin, Hitler
showed no interest in altering his fundamentally hostile and
antagonistic attitude to the USSR. As Khinchuk's successor, Jacob
Suritz, informed Litvinov in late 1935, it was futile to hope for any
change in the German attitude because

> Hitler and his entourage are firmly convinced that only if it
> adheres to its anti-Soviet course can the Third Reich realize
> its aims and gain allies and friends. The calculation here
> assumes that the further development of the world crisis will
> inevitably lead to a deepening of the contradictions between
> Moscow and the rest of the world ... I repeat that it's [sic]
> more obvious to me now than at any time before that Hitler
> and his entourage will not voluntarily change their course as
> far as relations with us are concerned.[29]

On the basis of this report Litvinov subsequently submitted a
memorandum to Stalin speaking of the 'utter hopelessness' of any

improvement in political relations and the fact that the NSDAP's campaign against the USSR had now assumed 'Homeric dimensions'.[30] If possible this situation was rendered even more hopeless and, as far as the USSR was concerned, more dangerous the following year when the outbreak of the Spanish Civil War and the conclusion of the Anti-Comintern Pact introduced further elements of crisis and tension into German relations with the USSR, the significance of which will be examined at a later stage of this study. Suffice it to say that if blame were to be apportioned for the breakdown between Berlin and Moscow after January 1933, then the lion's share, if not the entirety, would rest with the German chancellor.

While under Hitler's guidance the development of German policy towards the Soviet Union had hastened and encouraged the demise of the Soviet–German collaboration of the Weimar era, equally radical developments in German relations with Poland completed the reorientation of the Reich's *Ostpolitik*. The pro-Russian trend of German diplomacy during the 1920s had been shaped by prominent groups in the Wilhelmstrasse and the Reichswehr who had focused primarily on the revision of the Treaty of Versailles in eastern Europe. For most Germans the Polish state, much of which had been established on former German territory, was an abomination, a fundamental enemy in all calculations of foreign policy, which would be destroyed as soon as the Reich had recovered its strength.[31] As a consequence, not only were German–Polish relations extremely strained during the 1920s, but influential Germans viewed the Soviet Union, which had suffered substantial territorial loss to Poland, as a natural ally against Warsaw. Indeed, it was this common bond of hostility towards Poland that had to some degree underpinned the Soviet–German treaties of Rapallo and Berlin.

These views, propounded most vociferously by the Prussian Junker caste and the national-conservative elites, stood in stark contrast to those of Hitler, whose Austrian origins, it has been suggested, spared him at least the burden of ingrained hostility towards Poland.[32] Although Hitler's writings of the 1920s contain very few references to Poland, there is in fact no expression of hostile intent towards that country. Indeed, it has recently been suggested that the *Zweites Buch* foreshadows a possible future alliance with the Poles.[33] The central aim of Hitler's foreign policy was the acquisition of *Lebensraum* in 'Jewish-Bolshevik' Russia and its 'vassal border states', among which, given the post-1919 situation in eastern Europe, Poland could hardly be counted. Precariously sandwiched between Germany and the USSR, Poland would necessarily occupy a crucial role in Hitler's plans to organize and launch a war against the Soviet Union. A combination of sheer geographical realities, traditional Russo–Polish enmity, which the recent war and subsequent Treaty of Riga accentuated, and Poland's vigorous opposition to Bolshevism meant that the Poles could either cooperate in or seek to thwart Hitler's aims against the USSR. As events during the summer of 1939 would demonstrate, equanimity on this issue was not a viable option.

Hitler's readiness to place German–Polish relations on a more reasonable basis was to some extent reciprocated by the Polish leader, the staunchly anti-communist Marshal Josef Pilsudski, a man who, in Hitler's eyes, was essential to any plans for a German–Polish rapprochement.[34] In 1930 an emissary from Pilsudski appeared at Nazi headquarters in Munich professing the marshal's sympathy for the nationalist struggle being waged by the NSDAP, but also registering his concern that the 'chauvinism' that inevitably accompanied a process of 'national rebirth' might cause complications if and when the Nazis came to power. To avert such an unwelcome contingency Pilsudski proposed that a Nazi triumph in Germany should be followed by a treaty of peace and friendship between the two nations.

For Poland, the emissary explained, 'Russia posed the greatest danger, since Poland could expect no effective protection against Russia from the Western powers'. Since Pilsudski fully understood this, he had therefore 'turned his eyes toward Germany'.[35] Hitler's response was positive and enthusiastic, for not only would a friendly arrangement with Poland suit Germany's needs on a tactical plane, but it would also symbolize the beginnings of the planned mobilization of the European powers against Bolshevik Russia. Moreover, such an arrangement, it was considered, would not be without effect upon Britain which in turn would help further Germany's broader aims in foreign policy. As Hitler explained to Wagener, a treaty with Poland would be a 'good beginning for our foreign policy' as it would represent the 'first step toward the consolidation of Central Europe. And you will see that England will even then offer us help, in order to remove the universal danger represented by Bolshevism'.[36]

It was thus hardly surprising, and by no means due purely to tactical considerations, that during his first months in power Hitler repeatedly expressed his readiness for improved relations with Poland. For their part, although they were still concerned about the aggressive nationalism of the Nazis, outbreaks of which had caused them particular anxiety during the German election campaigns of 1932, the Poles certainly welcomed the NSDAP's stance against communism, both for its own sake and because it was assumed that the deterioration in Soviet–German relations that was bound to result from the advent of the Hitler regime would finally draw a line under the Rapallo partnership. Indeed, despite rumours of a possible Franco–Polish preventive strike against Germany, by mid-1933 the Poles were becoming increasingly interested in some form of arrangement with Hitler in view of renewed doubts about the value of their French alliance, which France's support for the proposed Four Power Pact had occasioned. This Italian-sponsored scheme threatened not only to marginalize Poland's importance as a European power but also to bind it to the decisions, including those bearing on treaty revision, of a directorate consisting of Italy, Britain, France and Germany. On the German side the need for a measure of reassurance to the other powers following the withdrawal from the League of Nations and the Disarmament Conference in the autumn of 1933 provided the final impetus to a formal arrangement with Poland.

When four weeks later Germany and Poland issued a declaration renouncing the use of force in their mutual relations British analysts questioned whether the move was intended to 'free Germany's hands, so far as Poland is concerned, for a more vigorous policy in Central Europe … or in Russia' or simply to postpone any adventure for a period of years until 'the German domestic situation as regards armaments, finance and economics has been firmly established'.[37] For Hitler a rapprochement with Poland was intended to serve both these purposes, and, with regard to the former, to lay the basis for future collaboration against the USSR. Only four days before the declaration was issued Hitler had told the new Polish minister in Berlin, Jósef Lipski, that he viewed Poland as an outpost against the Bolshevik threat from Asia.[38] Two months later the chancellor expatiated on the importance of improved German–Polish relations, the danger from the Soviet Union and Poland's pivotal role in resisting the Bolshevik onslaught. Poland, Hitler began, had a responsible task in eastern Europe, not least because of the industrial and military dangers posed by the USSR. Blocked by a 'dynamic' Japan in the Far East, Russia would make no headway in that region and would thus 'direct the full impact of its pressure westward'. In these circumstances Poland, as the 'last barricade of civilization in the east' had assumed a 'very momentous' position, so much so that the notion that Germans and Poles were always destined to be deadly enemies should be abandoned forthwith. He had declared to his followers at the outset of his political activities that the Polish nation must be considered a reality that was impossible to eradicate. 'Both nations have to live side by side,' Hitler concluded. There had admittedly been periods during which Germans and Poles had fought each other, but, he stressed, 'at other times we lived in friendship and collaboration'.[39]

The following day Germany and Poland concluded a non-aggression pact, which ushered in a new era in their mutual relations. European opinion was taken aback, having long since regarded German–Polish hostility as a constant feature of the international situation, while in Germany this abrupt reorientation of policy in eastern Europe was met with considerable and voluble hostility on the part of the national-conservatives. For Hitler, however, domestic popularity was never the primary issue; nor indeed, until circumstances dictated it several years later, was Danzig or the Corridor. To his critics the Führer could point to the numerous tangible benefits of an agreement that had effectively cost the Reich nothing. Not only did the pact have considerable value in terms of propaganda, to which end it was represented as evidence of the new regime's peaceful and conciliatory policy, but in strictly power political terms it struck a hefty blow at both French and Soviet ties with Poland, thereby considerably enhancing German security. Beyond these immediate advantages, however, lay the further long-term goal of enlisting Polish support for a policy, which would persist until the early spring of 1939, designed to isolate Soviet Russia and confront it with a formidable combination of powers.

In the official diplomatic exchanges there was no mention of an active German–Polish combination against the USSR, but the non-aggression pact and the new basis for relations that it constituted provided a useful foundation on which to build. Shortly after the pact's conclusion, Poland was already being mooted in Nazi circles as a possible member of the grouping of powers that would eventually emerge as the Anti-Comintern Pact.[40] For the time being it was sufficient that the new warmth in German–Polish relations had radically altered the position in eastern Europe and, in so doing, had given the Soviet leaders further cause for anxiety about Germany's ultimate intentions. Taken together with Hitler's writings in *Mein Kampf* and Rosenberg's fixation on the Ukraine, the evident disappearance of Polish–German hostility caused much anxiety in Moscow where there were fears that the new alignment might seek to exploit any future Russian complications in the Far East.[41] This anxiety would hardly have been diminished by the fact that towards the close of 1933, during the launching of an exhibition celebrating the cultural aspects of Germany's eastern provinces, Rosenberg, who had previously called for the destruction of Poland, had welcomed the fact that those nations that had formerly suffered under the Russian yoke had not only 'nationally and politically emancipated themselves from the communist philosophy of life' but had also 'turned towards Europe', thus once more emphasizing the distinction drawn by the Nazis between 'Bolshevik' Russia and the community of 'European' nations.[42]

The German–Polish non-aggression pact ushered in a transformation of relations between Berlin and Warsaw as complete as the one that had taken place between Germany and the Soviet Union. There were of course still points of tension and difficulty between the former antagonists, but from January 1934 onwards every effort was made, on both sides, to deal with contentious issues relating to Danzig or minority and economic questions in a spirit of friendship and cooperation. In political terms the pact provided an additional stimulus to the developing Franco–Soviet schemes for the containment of Germany, the chief element of which, the proposed Eastern Pact, in turn provided the first fruitful field for German–Polish diplomatic collaboration against Bolshevik Russia. The so-called 'Eastern Locarno', which French and Soviet foreign ministers Louis Barthou and Maxim Litvinov devised during

1933–34, was essentially a scheme to base a multilateral security agreement around a Franco–Soviet alliance directed against Germany. Although Germany was invited to participate in the proposed agreement, which, in view of its fundamental aim made little sense without it, it held no attraction for Hitler, particularly as it was so transparently designed to restrict Germany's freedom of manoeuvre in eastern Europe and thus check any plans for territorial expansion in that region. From mid-1934 onwards, when the proposals were officially communicated to the interested powers, the Germans, backed by Poland, whose leaders were disillusioned with France and fearful of Soviet encroachments, continued to raise objections to the form of the pact when in essence it was the very principle they opposed.[43] As Hitler told Sir John Simon in March 1935, to the German mind the Eastern Pact was superfluous in view of the security arrangements, such as the German–Polish agreement, which already existed between the states of central and eastern Europe. Moreover, the proposed pact was cumbersome and even dangerous as, unlike the Locarno treaties, it was 'intended for a large number of States with unpredictable interests and antagonisms, internal uncertainties and fluctuating Governments'. It might thus engender a 'much larger variety of conflicts', which equally might force him to 'lead the German people to the slaughter for territories in which they had no interest at all'.[44]

Above all, however, the sheer impossibility of entering into any form of mutual assistance arrangements with the USSR, let alone a complicated and cumbersome multilateral security agreement designed to protect the intended victim, ruled out any possibility of German accession to the Eastern Pact. To that extent there was a good deal of sincerity in Hitler's remark to the visiting Polish foreign minister in July 1935 that the German people would for the first time be at a loss to understand him if he, 'whose political career had been taken up with the struggle against Bolshevism, were to conclude a treaty for the protection of the Soviet state'.[45] Although it was obvious that this crucial determining factor could not be articulated with any great frankness during official negotiations, there were enough hints in Hitler's statements to a series of British visitors in early 1935 to demonstrate that any hope of a German signature appearing under the Eastern Pact was quite illusory, and that what he at heart desired was not collaboration with Russia but cooperation against it.

Apart from their cooperation with the Poles over the Eastern Pact, the position of Poland in German schemes against the USSR began to crystallize when, during his visit to Warsaw in early 1935, and on several subsequent occasions, Göring made soundings about the possibility of a German–Polish alignment against Russia.[46] Despite the Polish response being not especially encouraging, Hitler did not abandon his efforts to persuade Poland to join an anti-Soviet combination and in later years Berlin actively sought its participation in the Anti-Comintern Pact. In August 1935, during a general outline of his foreign policy plans, the chancellor spoke of an 'eternal' alliance with Britain, German expansion to the east and the maintenance of a 'good relationship' with Poland, thus registering once more that, if Poland played its part, it had nothing to fear from Germany, but might, by inference, gain substantially from its association with the Reich.[47] That was certainly the impression of the American military attaché in Berlin, Truman Smith, who in November 1935 noted that, provided future German conquests in the USSR were effected on a sufficiently grand scale, it might be possible to compensate Poland with territory in the Ukraine in return for which it might 'cede the Corridor and permit Germany a land empire in northern and central Russia'.[48] These ideas were evidently less fanciful than they might now appear for this was more or less the scheme that Göring had been instructed to suggest to Pilsudski in January 1935.

By that stage the diplomatic revolution in German policy towards Poland and the USSR was complete. The German–Soviet combination of the Weimar era had collapsed, or, to be strictly accurate, had been deliberately laid to rest by the new regime in Berlin. Germany now had a new friend in eastern Europe, Pilsudski's Poland, with which it shared a loathing for Bolshevik Russia and in collaboration with which it eventually succeeded in thwarting the proposed 'Eastern Locarno'. The focus of Hitler's plans for collaboration against the USSR, however, was fixed not so much on the minor powers of the east as on the great powers of western Europe, and concerned principally the British Empire.

Chapter 4

An Anglo–German Vanguard against Bolshevism? Hitler's Quest for British Cooperation against Russia, 1933–35

As has been established from his writings, speeches and conversations during the late 1920s and early 1930s, the idea of Anglo–German collaboration against Bolshevism lay at the core of Hitler's foreign policy plans. This was a subject he invested with great hope, enthusiasm and an increasing sense of urgency in view of the perceived potential for a vast increase in Soviet power after 1928. The success of any such schemes, however, clearly depended not only on his desires and preferences but also on the response they received in Britain. Were the British, as Hitler believed, 'far-seeing' in recognizing the danger represented by the USSR? Were they prepared to play their part in ensuring the 'salvation and preservation of Europe and its culture'? In short, could the British Empire be won over to the idea of collaboration with a National Socialist Germany against the scourge of international Bolshevism?[1]

On the surface, the auspices for such a development, as judged from Berlin at the outset of Hitler's rule, did not appear entirely hopeless. The history of Anglo–Russian (and since 1917 Anglo–Soviet) relations had never been especially happy. Allied now to the traditional Anglo–Russian rivalry in Asia was a deep rooted ideological conflict, manifested in numerous ways but most notably in British intervention against the Bolsheviks during the Russian civil war. It had also played a part in several ugly developments in Anglo–Soviet relations during the 1920s, such as the Zinoviev letter and Arcos raid. Moreover, influential British personalities had on numerous occasions spoken out against the Soviet regime and the threat that Bolshevism, with its proclaimed aim of universal revolution, posed to Germany and the wider world. 'The greatest danger that I see in the present situation,' proclaimed the British prime minister in 1919, 'is that Germany may throw in her lot with Bolshevism and place her resources, her brains, her vast organizing power at the disposal of the revolutionary fanatics whose dream is to conquer the world for Bolshevism by force of arms. This danger is no mere chimera.'[2] Lloyd George's secretary of state for war, Winston Churchill, was equally suspicious of Russia's new rulers and their dangerous ideology. 'If German democracy puts up a fight against Bolshevism and erects a bulwark against this doctrine,' he wrote in the *Daily Express* in April 1919, 'it will take its first step in tandem with the civilized world.'[3]

Ironically, in view of the role he would subsequently play in thwarting Hitler's ambitions, Churchill not only abhorred Bolshevism, as demonstrated by the leading role he had played in the movement for British intervention in the Russian civil war, but by 1930 evidently shared some of Hitler's ideas about how best to deal with it. Speaking to the chargé d'affaires at the German embassy in London in October 1930, the future prime minister gave vent to his dislike of the Soviets whose practice of dumping goods on the world market at prices that undercut their competitors should, he suggested, be challenged by a German–French–British bloc under German leadership. What most alarmed Churchill, however, was the process of rapid modernization inaugurated under the first five-year plan. The 'gradually accelerating industrialization' of Russia was 'a matter of extreme danger for the whole of Europe', which, despite the inevitable setbacks and Russian incompetence, 'could only be halted by the creation of a joint alliance against Russia, comprising the rest of Europe and America'.[4] In common with many of his countrymen, however, Churchill, though vigorously anti-Bolshevik, was also highly suspicious of National Socialism and thoroughly distrustful of Hitler who, he was convinced, 'would seize the first available opportunity to resort to armed force'.[5] Here, in essence, lay one of the dilemmas that would confront Hitler in his dealings with the British during the 1930s. While few people in Britain held any brief for Bolshevism or the Soviet system, their attitude towards it was largely defensive and founded on the desire to stem its advance rather than combine with other powers to destroy it by means of an international crusade. To that extent the perception of Germany as a bulwark against Bolshevism and the protector of Western civilization, to which numerous British personalities gave frequent expression during the 1930s, may well for a time have created a falsely encouraging impression in Berlin, where there was a considerable capacity for misconstruing things English.[6]

Nevertheless, despite this generally defensive attitude to the Bolshevik threat, it would be misleading to suggest that Hitler's warnings and pleas for British collaboration failed to make their mark in some sections of British society. Individuals such as Lieutenant-Colonel Thomas Moore MP and C. G. Grey, editor of *The Aeroplane*, were from very early on enthusiastic supporters of the German leader's stand against the Bolsheviks; so too was the owner of the *Daily Mail*, Lord Rothermere, whose newspaper regularly championed the German cause on a variety of international issues. Thus, in an April 1934 issue of *The Aeroplane*, Grey wrote that if and when Russia began its onslaught 'Germany, backed by British troops on the ground and the Royal Air Force in the air, will probably prove to be quite an adequate defence of Western civilization'.[7]

On similar lines the *Daily Mail* had proclaimed in November 1933 that the National Socialists were Europe's 'guardians against the Communist danger'.[8] Another British peer, the secretary of state for air from 1931 to 1935, Lord Londonderry, was equally persuaded of the role that Germany, with British support, had to play in combating the Bolshevik menace. During his visit to Germany in early 1936 Londonderry was successfully propagandized by Nazi leaders and later recorded his impressions in a book entitled *Ourselves and Germany*. Londonderry doubtless spoke for many people, particularly those on the right of the political spectrum, in confessing to the suspicion that the British Foreign Office appeared to 'condone the associations with communism and Bolshevism through our affiliation with France, while paying but little regard to the robust attitude of Germany, Italy and Japan which whole-heartedly condemn communism and Bolshevism', which was a 'world-wide doctrine which aims at the internal disruption of all modern systems of Government with the ultimate object of what is termed World Revolution'.[9] That being the case,

Londonderry reasoned, in 1938, 'I was at a loss to understand why we could not make common ground in some form or another with Germany in opposition to Communism.'[10]

Even in these cases, however, the emphasis was less on an offensive strategy to eliminate the USSR as the centre of 'Jewish-Bolshevism' than on the importance of Britain and Germany standing shoulder to shoulder to defend western Europe against any possible future onslaught from the east. Few people, and certainly nobody in a position of genuine authority, were prepared to countenance let alone support German domination of eastern Europe, which would be the logical consequence of a victorious German attack on the USSR. If the Germans entertained an ideal in this respect it was most obviously represented by Sir Henry 'Chips' Channon, the Conservative MP for Southend who, clearly intoxicated by the anti-Bolshevik invective that had been the chief feature at the 1936 Nuremberg rally, saw nothing objectionable in the idea that 'we should let gallant little Germany glut her fill of the reds in the East and keep decadent France quiet while she does so.' Harold Nicolson, who recorded these words on 20 September 1936, retorted in a manner that might reasonably be taken to be more typical of the British mentality of the mid-1930s, particularly in view of the reaction Nazi internal policy had produced in Britain, and one that to an extent even helped to determine official British attitudes towards the Nazi regime. 'I say that this may be expedient but that it is wrong,' he wrote indignantly. 'We represent a certain type of civilized mind, and that we are sinning against the light if we betray that type. We stand for tolerance, truth, liberty and good humour. They stand for violence, oppression, untruthfulness and bitterness.'[11]

Despite Hitler's hopes, the general reaction to his assumption of power and the first repressive steps of his regime produced a profoundly negative impression in Britain, so much so that by May 1933 he felt compelled to register his disappointment to the British ambassador that British public opinion towards Germany had deteriorated sharply 'directly he had entered on [sic] office'.[12] Nor was any improvement effected by the visit to London that same month of Rosenberg, whose assurances that the Hitler regime represented a factor for stability and a guarantee against the spread of communism in Europe. This made little impression on the British foreign secretary who instead instructed Rosenberg that

Germany had in the space of two months 'lost the sympathy which she had gained in this country in ten years'.[13] Not only the German ambassador, Leopold von Hoesch, who wrote that the visit had caused British hostility to the new Germany to break out with 'full force',[14] but Rosenberg too appears to have realized the severely detrimental effects of the visit that came to be characterized by a famous incident at the Cenotaph when an enraged British ex-serviceman threw into the Thames the swastika bedecked wreath that the German envoy had laid. Back in Berlin Rosenberg reflected that public opinion had been so obdurately anti-German that he had felt as if he had been 'on enemy territory'. Moreover, according to a British banker with whom he had spoken, there had never been and there still was not any widespread belief in the argument that communism threatened Germany. In the light of his experiences the best course Rosenberg could recommend was that German policy play for time, not least because he had gained from some of his conversations the curious impression that Britain was toying with the idea of waging a preventive war against Germany. The general impression with which he returned was thus overwhelmingly negative and extremely discouraging in view of the kind of progress in Anglo–German relations he and Hitler desired.[15] Reports of Rosenberg's failure, claims Richard Griffiths, caused Hitler to lecture the British ambassador on 11 May on the 'role of the Jews in recent German history, and the need for the British to join in the fight against Communism'.[16]

It was not so much in the official diplomatic arena, however, that Hitler sought to register an impact. Mistrustful of the channels of official diplomacy and suspicious of career diplomats in general, the German leader wished to conduct his soundings personally in meetings with senior British statesmen, and to spread his message through the medium of propaganda abroad. In this way the diplomatic niceties could be dispensed with and the message conveyed clearly and with sufficient force. German propagandists operating in London during 1933, for example, spoke with extreme frankness about the Nazi regime's hostility to Bolshevism, which it was firmly resolved to eliminate, and the future intention to colonize the USSR as German *Lebensraum*. According to German propaganda agents, the pro-Soviet policy General von Seeckt pursued with the aim of avenging defeat in the First World War and visiting German revenge on the western powers had been a colossal mistake as it had been 'based on a miscalculation both to East and West; to the East because no alliance was possible with Bolshevism, which must be all or nothing; to the West because the national triumph of vanquishing the former victors would not in the event entail that re-union of Germanic stock which is the aim of the present regime'.[17]

Special envoys who gained access to senior politicians brought similar messages. For example, Hitler's special emissary and future ambassador in London, Joachim von Ribbentrop, spoke equally openly about Germany's future intentions during a visit to Britain in late 1933. In the presence of Stanley Baldwin on 20 November he outlined the dangers presented by Bolshevism, insisted on the need for an Anglo–German understanding, explained that Germany considered itself a continental country with 'no visions of a world Empire' and, when pressed on the question of exactly where Germany would seek to settle its surplus population, made some 'vague references to Russia'. The general message was thus clear, simple and entirely consistent with the arguments Hitler used in public and private during the early 1930s: Germany and Europe were threatened by Bolshevism; Hitler desired friendship with Britain, whose empire was not threatened by National Socialism and whose cooperation in the fight against communism was both necessary and desirable; and any future German expansion would take place at the expense of the USSR, the ideological enemy of both Britain and Germany. Four days later Ribbentrop told Lord Davidson that 'peace in Europe with a strong British Empire was the only certain defence against the spread of Bolshevism'.[18] To British visitors Hitler was, if possible, even more outspoken about his intentions. In February 1934, for example, he declared to Squadron Leader F. W. Winterbotham that Britain, the USA and Germany should rule the world, and assured his visitor that 'the Germans themselves would destroy the Communists by the conquest of Russia'. All he asked of Britain was that it concentrate on its imperial affairs and 'not interfere with Germany's plans of expansion'.[19]

During 1934–35, as the number of British visitors to Germany increased, more and more prominent Britons were granted interviews with Hitler. This enabled him to spell out in detail his fears about the growing potential of the USSR, the dangers of ideological infection by Bolshevism and the consequent need for solidarity and vigilance. A useful example of the arguments the German leader employed on such occasions is provided by the record of his conversation with Lord Lothian in January 1935. Although France was presently showing signs of political instability, Hitler began, the 'most unstable factor in the situation' was the USSR. When it came to communism, he went on, 'no one knew this question better than he,' for he had 'seen its ravages in Germany and fought it for many years'. Communism was neither one of those philosophies that would simply disappear after a number of years nor a temporary party phenomenon; it was in fact a 'world conquering idea', which might usefully be compared with the great religions. Those who believed it could be confined within state borders were living under dangerous illusions, for it would take root wherever it could find a footing. Bolshevik ideology was only half the problem, however, for one must also take into account the 'might, greatness and power' of the home of communism, Soviet Russia. The sheer size of the USSR, the invulnerability of its industrial centres, its massive population, the richness of its agriculture and its natural resources gave Russia an 'unparalleled capacity to withstand the attack of enemies, however powerful'. When this material power was combined with the communist philosophy, a truly formidable foe would confront one in wartime, particularly given that Bolshevik sympathizers would seek to undermine the home front. To this must also be added the danger posed by Russia's industry, which in ten years' time would have grown to 'enormous dimensions', enabling it to engage in 'devastating' competition and to undermine the economy and culture of those states that had hitherto enjoyed a higher standard of living. 'We should approach this vast economic problem by bringing together States which have a common outlook and interest,' Hitler concluded.

The countries which have relatively the same interests are Germany, England, France, Italy and Scandinavia. They should arrive at some agreement which prevents their nationals from promoting the industrialization of countries such as China and India. It is suicidal to establish industries in the agricultural regions of Asia. From these countries we would do better to take raw materials in return for our manufactured goods. If such an agreement is not reached,

70

> England, Germany and America will lose their export trade.
> Looking far into the future we believe that something like
> this must be done in order to save the civilization which
> these countries have built up.[20]

Despite finishing on a note that concerned not so much the
Soviet Union as the future economic development of the non-
industrialized world, the drift of Hitler's argument was hardly
difficult to fathom and clearly centred on the need for solidarity
between like-minded nations against what he perceived, or wished
others to perceive, as a deadly combination of Soviet military power
and revolutionary communist doctrines.

It was a similar story the following year when Hitler poured out
his anxieties to Lord Londonderry about developing trends in
Soviet politics and the 'growing menace to the world from Bolshevism'. The current situation, he declared in February 1936,
might be compared with the eve of the French Revolution when
those who had warned of the 'impending disaster' that was about to
engulf Europe had been dismissed as 'pessimists and fantasts'. So it
was that he too was now derided in certain quarters for cautioning
against any underestimation of the Bolshevik threat lest Europe and
the world should plunge into 'a catastrophe of the same kind'.
Europe was in a frail and unstable condition, and many states,
including France, were teetering on the brink of internal disorder.
'Against this decay in continental Europe', Hitler continued, 'stands
the extraordinary development of Soviet power'. Territorially
immune from attack, invulnerable to blockade and with its industrial centres located at a safe distance from hostile bombers, the
Soviet nation of 180 million people had turned into the world's
greatest military power. That was not the end of it, however, for the
USSR was also the 'embodiment of an idea', and how 'such ideas
have worked when combined with great strength we know only too
well from the French Revolution'. On the one hand, therefore,
stood a collection of 'distraught insecure governments', faced on
the other by a 'gigantic Soviet block' of enormous strength. 'The
dangers which arise from this are perhaps not clearly recognized by
all, and have not yet come into the light of day with such clarity as
they have here,' Hitler concluded portentously. 'But if this evolution goes any further, if the decomposition in Europe becomes

71

more pronounced, and the strengthening of Soviet power continues at the same rate as hitherto, what will be the position in ten, twenty, or thirty years?'[21]

Hitler's ultimate purpose in delivering this and other such diatribes against the USSR is surely revealed by his final remarks to Londonderry about the dangers of permitting matters to drift until the Soviet threat became so great that it would be impossible to resist. The obvious course of action therefore would be to prevent any further growth of Russian power. In short, either Russia halted its military and industrial development voluntarily, which was clearly unlikely, or a halt would be imposed from outside. It was not of course, as Hitler habitually insisted, Germany's intention to make war on the USSR, but just as he was categorical and reassuring on that point, which, in view of other evidence may safely be dismissed as a palpable untruth, so too was he more often than not vague and imprecise about exactly how the Soviet threat might be combated. In this respect it should be recalled that what Hitler required from Britain was not so much military assistance in his planned onslaught against Russia but, as he had told Winterbotham, a political undertaking not to interfere with his plans. His purpose in lecturing British visitors thus lay more in conveying a sense of urgency and threat with the aim of making any 'preventive' German action against the USSR in the future more palatable and acceptable.

It was not only during unofficial conversations that Hitler warned of the dangers the USSR presented and hinted at the need to make timely preparations for the inevitable showdown with Bolshevism. While those themes appear to have featured more prominently in his discussions with private British visitors to Germany than in exchanges with British ministers and diplomats, at least prior to 1935–36, one should remember that the German priority in official diplomatic dealings with Britain before 1935 was not anti-Bolshevism but rearmament. Without armaments a campaign against the USSR would remain nothing but a pipe dream. It was also easier for Hitler to speak freely and with genuine conviction to a receptive audience of British aristocrats than to the British ambassador who was representative of the career diplomats he so despised. This is not to say, however, that the subject of Soviet Russia and Bolshevism did not feature in Hitler's exchanges with Sir Horace

Rumbold or Sir Eric Phipps, each of whom was convinced that *Mein Kampf* should be taken with deadly seriousness. Rumbold noted in 1933 that Hitler believed that to range Germany alongside Russia against the west, as Seeckt had advocated, would be 'criminal, especially as the aim of the Soviets is the triumph of international Judaism'. Although it was unclear how far Hitler was 'prepared to [go to] put his fantastic proposals into operation', the ambassador believed he could not abandon the 'cardinal points of his programme any more than Lenin or Mussolini' could. Moreover, while acknowledging that since taking office Hitler had been 'as cautious and discreet as he was formerly blunt and frank', Rumbold feared that this was due to his desire to buy time for rearmament, and that it would be illusory to hope for any modification of Hitler's views. Indeed, the foreign policy emerging from Hitler's speeches throughout 1933 was 'no less disquieting' than that laid down in the pages of *Mein Kampf*.[22]

During his first conversation with Hitler, Sir Eric Phipps found himself subjected to a 'long disquisition' on the danger Russia posed to Germany, an observation Hitler chose to couple with vague remarks 'that he sought certain possibilities of expansion in Eastern Europe', and an assurance that he had no intention of solving the Polish Corridor problem by force.[23] Ministers, too, were not spared. The following February Hitler warned Anthony Eden that 'Russia must never be forgotten, because if Russia was not a menace today she would be a very formidable menace tomorrow.'[24]

In early 1935, when the issue of rearmament was effectively buried following the reintroduction of conscription and the announcement of the existence of the Luftwaffe, the German leader signposted to visiting British ministers where he would prefer to deploy his new weapons. In the presence of Sir John Simon and Anthony Eden, at the point in their conversation where the Eastern Pact was raised, he registered his familiar suspicions about the USSR, which, he inferred, might one day fall on Germany. There was an 'aggressive tendency' in Russia and no distinction could be drawn between the doctrines of Bolshevism, which remained the same as they had been 15 years earlier, and the aims of the Soviet government. This dangerous combination of 'Bolshevist doctrine and the political aims of Russia', coupled with Russian military and economic strength, left him with the impression that 'from Russia there was greater probability of war than from other countries'. As for the proposed Eastern Pact, he was certain that Russia's interest in the project was insincere and transitory. Russia's only desire, as he had informed Lothian a month earlier, was to put on a show of solidarity with the European powers that would enable it to concentrate on its difficulties in the Far East. Once that situation had been stabilized, Russia's interest in the Eastern Pact would evaporate. It would be far better therefore, in the German view, to ensure security in eastern Europe by means of bilateral non-aggression pacts such as those that Germany had concluded with Poland. When Eden remarked that, to the British mind, communism appeared to be more of an internal than an international threat, and that even if Russia were dangerous it would surely be better to draw it into an arrangement designed to strengthen European solidarity, Hitler showed his true colours. By his explicit reference to the Russian menace, he explained, he had not meant to suggest that solidarity and cooperation between the European nations was not necessary. In his view, however, Russia was clearly alien to Europe for he was 'firmly convinced that one day cooperation and solidarity would be urgently necessary to defend Europe against the Asiatic and Bolshevik menace'. Having registered the preliminaries during the morning meeting, Hitler pressed his point home that same afternoon with a direct appeal, his most transparent to date during an official conversation, for collaboration with Britain against an unnamed but obvious enemy.

The moment would come when the European nations must stand together. For the time being they were engaged in preventing their own controversies from exploding. But the moment might come when the European nations must stand together, in particular, when Germany and Britain must stand together. ... The German Government wanted agreement with Britain and also with France, but in the case of the latter it was very difficult to dissipate certain misunderstandings; and an understanding with Britain would be a valuable asset ... it might be that even the British Empire might one day be glad to have Germany's help and Germany's forces at her disposal. ... He had outlined a bold idea, but he had wished to put it forward.[25]

These conversations also gave Hitler an opportunity to explain his objections to the Eastern Pact. When the proposals had been formally delivered to the powers in mid-1934 Hitler may well have drawn some encouragement from early indications that the British wished to have nothing whatsoever to do with the project. That much had certainly been implied in a speech delivered by Eden in July in which it was stated that Britain would undertake no further commitments beyond those it had assumed in the original Treaty of Locarno. Moreover, it was reported that the British had made their feelings known to the French foreign minister during his visit to London a few days later, and had in fact 'displayed a hostility towards Russia, the strength of which astonished Barthou'.[26] Shortly afterwards, however, when it became apparent that the British attitude to the Eastern Pact was cautiously positive in view of the contribution it might make to European pacification, and because it would stave off a Franco–Soviet alliance, Hitler's reaction was correspondingly severe. Britain, he was alleged to have told Neurath, was 'betraying Europe' because it was 'recognizing the signature of the Bolsheviks at the very moment when Moscow was stirring up trouble from Amsterdam to San Francisco'.[27]

The meetings in March 1935 thus gave Hitler a chance to state his case and seek to persuade the British that the Eastern Pact would not improve security in Europe, but would, as he put it, 'merely serve to organize war' because it would give the 'appearance of respectability to those who wanted allies'.[28] Perhaps predictably his criticism of the Eastern Pact rapidly degenerated into an attack on Bolshevism and, if only indirectly, a reference to how pleasing he would find collaboration with Britain. No one in Germany had any desire to be rescued by the Bolsheviks, noted the chancellor. Indeed, he was 'more afraid of Russian help than of a French attack'. British assistance he would gladly accept; Bolshevik assistance, on the other hand, never. Indeed, such a prospect was 'about on a par with the Roman Catholic Church wanting to militarise its monasteries and assist Buddhism or Mohammedanism'.[29]

The British reaction to Hitler's warnings about the Soviet Union's strength and intentions, his appeal for an Anglo–German understanding and his statements on the Eastern Pact were not especially encouraging. The conversations had not started particularly brightly as far as Hitler was concerned. Whereas in his introductory statement Simon had noted that of the two methods of organizing the future – general cooperation between the nations or 'a division into two camps, resulting in isolation on the one side, and the formation of blocs' – and had clearly registered a strong desire for the former, Hitler clearly favoured the latter. These opposing strategies could even be discerned in the language each side employed; while the British spoke of 'general cooperation', Hitler was more concerned to establish 'general solidarity' against the USSR. Lacking any 'expansive character', National Socialism was no threat to this solidarity among the states of Europe. Unfortunately, however, 'there were opposed to this political creed a number of other ideas which did not confine themselves spiritually and politically to one people, but deliberately aimed at internationalism and wished to infect others, openly seeking to conquer other nations.'[30]

To what extent these experiences coloured Hitler's view of the prospect of securing British cooperation for his aims against 'Jewish-Bolshevik' Russia is difficult to gauge. Three months later, however, when the Anglo–German Naval Agreement was concluded, Hitler believed he had finally made his breakthrough in relations with Britain and that an Anglo–German alliance was imminent.[31] In view of the political significance the German leader attached to the treaty it is no surprise that even in the forum of negotiations about fleet ratios there should be an unmistakable reference to the common destiny of both nations in the fight against the 'chaos' that was threatening Europe. The only solution to current problems, insisted Ribbentrop, the chief German negotiator, was an Anglo–German agreement that would coordinate the interests of the two powers and through which they would adopt 'a certain common and realistic basic attitude' towards those problems.[32]

Contrary to Hitler's hopes, the Anglo–German Naval Agreement failed to initiate a close understanding with Britain, and by the close of 1935 it was becoming evident that the prospect of such an understanding was as remote as ever. Hitler's annoyance and frustration at this state of affairs was revealed in a tempestuous and significant interview with Sir Eric Phipps in mid-December. The interview, which the British had requested in the hope of discovering Germany's attitude to the possibility of a general European settlement, found Hitler very much out of sorts, in no mood for an exchange of views about the questions that concerned Britain, in which he in any case had no interest, and, most importantly, critical of the British attitude to the USSR. He used the occasion to indulge in a violent denunciation of the Franco–Soviet Pact, which, by bringing Russia 'into the picture', that is by involving it in 'European' questions, had completely upset the balance of power on the continent. Not only that, but the Soviet Union's vast military strength was a direct threat to Germany whose capital city 'might easily in a few hours be reduced to [a] heap of ashes by a Russian air attack'. The German leader was equally unimpressed by recent British attempts to improve relations with the Soviet Union through the medium of possible financial assistance, a move he attributed to a British desire to 'set up' Russia as a 'counterweight to Japan'. Phipps naturally denied any such intention and remarked that as 'we were all living in the same house' it would obviously 'be useless to try and ignore the presence of one inhabitant, viz. Russia'. The British hope was that by negotiating with Russia it might gradually evolve in a more moderate direction, and, according to the ambassador, 'it was possible that she was already doing so'. This, however, Hitler 'hotly and indignantly denied', dismissing Russia as a 'foul and unclean inhabitant of the house with whom the other dwellers should have no political truck whatever'; to his mind the Russians were 'noxious microbes who should be politically isolated'. Russia's attachment to the idea of fomenting world revolution and its widespread subversive activities to that end rendered laughable the notion of any pacts of 'non-interference', for the Soviets were 'continually guilty of the most aggressive and insolent underground interference in the affairs of all civilized States, not excluding the British Empire'.[33]

This obvious annoyance with the British did not mean that he had abandoned all hope of an understanding. Indeed, when the conversation turned to the Anglo–German Naval Agreement, Hitler declared that he had resisted demands from others to press for a 50 per cent ratio of the British fleet in order 'to show beyond doubt his determination to remain on the most friendly terms with us'.[34] Nevertheless, he was undoubtedly annoyed that British policy, far from attuning itself to the idea of Anglo–German collaboration against Bolshevism, was not only tolerant of the French alliance with the USSR but considering rendering assistance to the 'world enemy'.

That this aspect of the matter was of some concern to Hitler appears to be confirmed by his conversation two months later with Arnold Toynbee, the director of the Royal Institute of International Affairs in London, who was asked point blank why Britain was 'so friendly with Russia'. The German leader did not expect an answer to his question, Toynbee recalled years later, for he had only posed it to answer it himself. Sure enough, Hitler then proceeded to develop the thesis he had recently put to Sir Eric Phipps that Britain was seeking to accommodate the USSR through its desire for an ally against Japan. Somewhat astonishingly, given that his own negotiations with Japan for an agreement against Russia were already well advanced, he then made the following declaration:

> But, if you need a friend to help you against Japan, why should your friend be Russia? Why should not I be the friend that you need? Of course, if I was to be your friend in need, you would have to give me back my colonies. But, if you had given me back my colonies, and you then had trouble with Japan, I would give you six divisions and some warships at Singapore.[35]

If nothing else, these remarks, despite their obviously rhetorical nature, might be taken as an accurate measure of Hitler's priorities in seeking political partners against the Soviet Union. For while ultimately it would be possible to fall on Russia without Japanese assistance, the operation would be gravely complicated without first securing some form of accommodation with the British. To that end Hitler now began to consider adapting his policy towards Britain which from 1936 onwards, although it was still geared to the achievement of an understanding based on a common antipathy to Bolshevism, gradually shifted from voluntary concession to a more active phase of pressure and blackmail.

Chapter 5
Anti-Bolshevism and the Mobilization of Allies, 1933–36

B y the start of 1936 it could hardly be contended that Hitler had made any significant headway in his quest to align the major powers in a front against international Bolshevism. Despite the seemingly promising beginnings that had been made with Poland in January 1934, the death of Pilsudski the following year, and the steadfast refusal of the Poles, even while the marshal was still alive, to be drawn into closer cooperation with Germany against the Soviet Union, meant that so far German expectations in that direction remained disappointingly unfulfilled. Equally, in so far as western Europe was concerned, Britain's sustained commitment to a general settlement and failure to acknowledge the political significance of the Anglo–German Naval Agreement served to demonstrate that the path to a partnership with Britain would be far more difficult to navigate than the German leader had initially hoped or believed.

Within 12 months, however, the situation had radically altered and, though progress with London and Warsaw remained problematic, the year ended with Germany having formalized friendships with Italy and Japan, which, in their public manifestations at least, appeared to rest largely on the hostility each of the three powers felt towards the USSR and its global instrument of political subversion, the Communist International. Hitler's original intentions towards and expectations of Italy have already been sketched and will be explored in greater depth in the following pages. First, it seems appropriate to examine the path to the German–Japanese Anti-Comintern Pact of November 1936, which, arguably, furnished the Third Reich with its only credible ally against

Bolshevik Russia before the outbreak of the German–Soviet war in 1941.

Already in the 1920s Hitler had expressed his warm admiration for the Japanese, not least in view of their strident nationalism, invulnerability to the machinations of world Jewry and, in consequence thereof as he saw it, their implacable hostility to Bolshevik Russia.[1] By the early 1930s both he and Rosenberg were in regular contact with Japanese circles in Germany and placed special value on the Japanese army's hostile attitude towards the USSR.[2] By 1932 the contacts established between the Japanese military and the Nazi Party had become a serious concern to Ambassador Obata Yukichi in Berlin,[3] while during the Manchurian crisis the NSDAP was the only German political party openly to support Japan's actions. Not only did Hitler view with approval this expression of the increasingly important role played by the Japanese military in national politics, and its willingness to challenge the established order, he also saw it as a laudable example of a nation vigorously defending its national interests.[4] In this connection there was perhaps more than a tentative link between Hitler's views on race and space and Japan's martial spirit and pursuit of *Lebensraum*. By the time he assumed the chancellorship therefore Hitler had expressed a considerable interest in and admiration for Japan, more so in fact than for any other extra-European country, and, as he clearly had no intention at that time to seek to mobilize it against the Western powers, it can be assumed that his chief preoccupation with Japan was the role it might play in assisting his planned isolation of the USSR. Indeed, Hitler's first initiatives in Far Eastern affairs, coupled with the nature of the discussions that in 1936 resulted in the German–Japanese Anti-Comintern Pact, amply bear out this interpretation.

Nevertheless, Hitler refrained from serious meddling with German policy in the Far East for some time after he came to office, even though White Russians in Berlin greeted the advent of the NSDAP by lauding the resultant German–Japanese containment of the 'Bolshevik colossus', in which sense they had interpreted Japan's recent actions in China.[5] Hitler, however, concentrated on his domestic consolidation and, in a further affirmation of his attachment to an understanding with Britain, even sought to profit from the tension in the Far East by intimating through his propagandists in London a willingness to collaborate against future Japanese aggression.[6] Yet the importance of Japan for his plans against the USSR is clearly confirmed by his instructions to the new German ambassador to Tokyo, Herbert von Dirksen, who was received shortly before his departure to Japan in October 1933. Speaking four days after Germany announced its intention to leave the League of Nations, a step that built a further bridge between Berlin and Tokyo, Hitler authorized the new appointee to negotiate the possible recognition of Manchukuo in return for economic concessions, and stated that he was being sent to Japan specifically to 'effect a consolidation and development of German–Japanese relations' as Japan was 'an important counterweight for us now that relations with the Soviet Union had radically changed'.[7] Whatever his propagandists were saying to the British, therefore, the prospect of cooperation with Japan against Russia was not far from Hitler's mind in late 1933, while from the Soviet Union it was reported that influential circles feared that a German–Japanese political rapprochement was rapidly developing and that Germany 'would utilize the opportunity of a commitment of Soviet means of power in the Far East in order to adjust its own desires for territorial revision at the expense of the Soviet Union'.[8]

Despite Hitler's obvious enthusiasm for Japan by 1933, there were several reasons why prudence prevailed in German dealings with the Far East during the first months of Nazi rule, not least of which, as the army and ministry for foreign affairs urgently advised him, was the importance of the China trade for purposes of rearmament. Nevertheless, Hitler soon began to make overtures to the Japanese through channels other than those provided by Wilhelmstrasse and other bastions of the national-conservative elites. Key to this process was Joachim von Ribbentrop, Hitler's primary foreign policy adviser by 1934 and head of the Dienststelle Ribbentrop, the Nazi foreign policy agency that played the crucial role on the German side in the negotiations that led to the Anti-Comintern Pact. Ribbentrop subsequently testified at Nuremberg that Hitler had discussed with him as early as 1933 whether 'a closer contact with Japan could be established in some form or other', to which Ribbentrop had replied by offering to take soundings on the subject from his Japanese contacts in Berlin. From the outset it was clear what the ultimate purpose of these dealings would be. The question, according to Ribbentrop, was of an ideological nature, and centred on discovering ways and means of winning over other countries to counter communist tendencies.[9]

One of Ribbentrop's Japanese acquaintances, the Japanese military attaché Hiroshi Ōshima – who was highly impressed by Hitler and Nazism and, true to the contemporary spirit of the Imperial Japanese Army, fanatically anti-Russian and anti-Bolshevik – went on to become the key Japanese figure in the negotiation of the Anti-Comintern Pact. During 1934–35 a series of informal soundings took place between Ōshima, Ribbentrop, Hermann von Raumer, the head of the Far Eastern *Referat* of Ribbentrop's Dienststelle, and Friedrich Hack, a shady German arms dealer with a wide range of contacts in the Far East, in the course of which much of the groundwork towards the eventual German–Japanese Anti-Comintern Pact was accomplished. In the summer of 1935 a declaration by the seventh world congress of the Comintern denouncing Germany, Japan and Italy as aggressor nations and aiming stinging criticisms at Britain and Poland, provided these discussions with further impetus.[10] These denunciations not only played into Hitler's hands by arousing hostility towards the Comintern among the very powers Hitler was seeking to enlist against the Soviet Union,[11] but also led to rapid progress in the talks between Ribbentrop and Ōshima over the next few months. Consequently, by late November the Anti-Comintern Pact had been both christened and drafted in its original form. The initial draft of the agreement, drawn up by Raumer, was received with enthusiasm by Ribbentrop and approved by Hitler on 25 November 1935, one year exactly before the pact's formal conclusion. One of the main features of the proposed agreement was that it was hoped that Britain and Poland might be willing to accede to a treaty that, on the surface at least, purported to target communism as opposed to the USSR.

The Soviet authorities, however, who were being kept abreast of developments through their intelligence network, could hardly be expected to see things that way or to accept the distinction implied by the use of the term Anti-Comintern in the communications being exchanged between Ōshima, Ribbentrop and the latter's representatives. Indeed, at the turn of 1935–36 the pace of the German–Japanese negotiations slowed considerably, not least because, whatever cover they had enjoyed over the preceding months, the discussions had recently become known outside the inner circle and had led to considerable speculation in the foreign press about the imminent conclusion of a German–Japanese alliance directed against Russia.[12] In diplomatic circles William Dodd, the US ambassador to Germany, had long since suspected some form of German–Japanese collusion, and in December 1935 he wrote of his 'conviction that there is an entente between Germany and Japan ... based upon the assumption that Germany is bound to make war upon Russia'.[13] Raising the issue with Neurath a few days later, Dodd was assured that Germany would not be drawn into a war with the USSR on Japan's account, but, despite the German foreign minister's dismissive attitude, he too was concerned at the progress of the Ribbentrop–Ōshima talks, about which the Wilhelmstrasse had first heard during the autumn of 1935, and had already registered his objections to any decision in favour of Japan during an interview with Hitler in December.[14] The international speculation about a possible German–Japanese agreement, the representations made by Neurath, and, not least, the desire expressed by Ōshima's superiors for clarification about the state of the negotiations, for which purpose they dispatched a special mission to Germany, combined to stall the negotiations in early 1936,[15] but it would not be long before external developments provided them with renewed momentum.

In spring 1936 the Japanese authorities, impressed by Germany's success in reoccupying the Rhineland and concerned by the probable general strengthening of Russia's position, which would follow from the ratification of the Franco–Soviet Pact, and not least by the Soviet–Outer Mongolian mutual assistance treaty signed in April, appear to have convinced themselves that the time was ripe to take the talks one step further.[16] On 9 June, Hitler received the Japanese ambassador in Berlin, Kintomo Mushakoji, who announced that Japan had great respect for Germany's fight against Bolshevism and that, as a 'spiritually related country', it desired 'the closest cooperation' with the Reich. Hitler, perhaps influenced by recent developments in France where a Popular Front government had taken power the previous month, and encouraged by positive news from Ribbentrop about Britain's growing appreciation of the communist danger, responded with some enthusiasm. The Reich chancellor, recorded Otto Meissner, head of the Presidial Chancellery, was 'happy to take note of this and was prepared for this cooperation', not least as he had 'always considered Europe's only salvation to lie in an uncompromising struggle against Communism'. It was impossible, he averred, to 'reject Communism as an ideology and at the same time maintain friendly relations with Soviet Russia, because in doing so one transplanted the poison of the Bolshevist idea into one's own country'.[17]

The following month Ōshima informed Raumer that the Japanese army wished to supplement the proposed pact against the Comintern with an additional agreement that would provide for neutrality in the event of either signatory becoming involved in war with the USSR. Although Hitler's initial reaction to this suggestion is not known, the outbreak of the civil war in Spain shortly after it was first mooted appears to have sufficed to clinch Hitler's decision in favour of a neutrality agreement, and, indeed, to open up further grand possibilities of collaboration with Japan against Bolshevik Russia. In a revealing interview with Ōshima at Bayreuth on 22 July 1936 the German leader, who had personally summoned the military attaché, agreed without further hesitation to the recent proposal and spoke at length about the danger Russia posed to Europe. Raumer, who was present at the interview, recorded the full drama of the moment and the significance of Hitler's statements. Following reports by Ōshima of the situation in Japan, and its need for *Lebensraum*, the military attaché was set to proceed to address the China problem when Hitler suddenly interrupted him and launched into a heated denunciation of the USSR whose expansionist tendencies represented the greatest danger not only to Germany but also to Europe and the entire Western world. The European continent, he continued:

> was like a mountain valley from whose heights a huge rock is threatening to break off at any moment, plunge to the bottom and bury all life beneath it. It is my view that this danger can be countered in no other way than to split the huge Soviet block into its original historic components. I am therefore determined to do everything I can to hasten and promote this development irrespective of on which flank of the Soviet Union it may occur.[18]

Hitler's statements during this conversation and his subsequent drafting of the celebrated memorandum on the four-year plan were no doubt conditioned primarily by the events in Spain, which not only had a profound impact on him from an ideological viewpoint but also opened up a range of opportunities for the development of German policy towards the USSR.

Although Spain had featured very little in Hitler's foreign policy programme before the mid-1930s, and certainly never in an anti-Bolshevik context,[19] by the summer of 1936 it had of necessity assumed a central position in his calculations. Indeed, even before the outbreak of the civil war there had been some concern in Berlin at the employment by leftist groups of the Popular Front tactic that in February and May 1936 had already resulted in electoral successes for the socialists and communists in Spain and France. It was only natural that Hitler should have viewed with alarm the success of a policy that was clearly designed to establish an anti-German front by reinforcing and extending the Soviet Union's political ties with western Europe. That alarm might well explain why in early May 1936 the Gestapo, having recently concluded an agreement with the Italian police for combating Bolshevism, organized a clandestine mission to Spain through the German foreign ministry, the purpose of which was to observe the progress of communism.[20] The Italians were similarly anxious. In mid-May Mussolini informed Hitler of his grave concern that Spain was 'inclining more and more to the Left'.[21] For the present, however, both Hitler and Mussolini were forced to watch from the sidelines as events took their course. Although Hitler had already decided that anti-Bolshevism would be the main theme of the 1936 Nuremberg rally,[22] there was as yet no direct opportunity to respond to the Bolshevik challenge.

When civil war broke out in Spain on 17 July 1936 there was immediate and widespread concern about the international threat a left-wing victory would pose, and it is in that context that Hitler's famous meeting with Franco's envoys, Johannes Bernhardt and Alfred Langenheim, and his decision to intervene on the side of the rebels, should be considered. The determinants of German policy during the Spanish Civil War have been the subject of sustained historical debate; whereas some have emphasized the military advantages to be gleaned from German intervention, others have cited as especially significant the economic factors, particularly German requirements for Spanish raw materials to assist Germany's rearmament programme.[23] There can be no doubt that German involvement in Spain would bring numerous economic and military advantages, but it was ideology that initially drove Hitler to help the nationalists.[24] Hitler agreed to support Franco within hours of meeting the two German envoys, and the crucial decision had already been taken when he invited Hermann Göring and Blomberg to join in the discussions.[25] According to Bernhardt's account, which stresses Hitler's preoccupation with the threat of Bolshevism, both Göring and Blomberg were initially reluctant to provide Franco with any help at all, and it was only in the face of Hitler's determination that they changed their minds.[26] A few days later Ribbentrop, who felt wary of involvement in the Spanish conflict, was told that Germany could 'in no circumstances tolerate a Communist Spain', for, if France too succumbed to Bolshevism, Germany would be 'finished'.[27]

In the weeks following the outbreak of the Spanish Civil War Hitler continued to emphasize the ideological impetus that had governed his decision to support Franco, treating a string of visitors to Berlin and Berchtesgaden to sustained harangues on the danger of Bolshevik 'contagion' and the inevitability of conflict between those countries that had already fallen victim to Bolshevism and those ruled by authoritarian-bourgeois governments.[28] While the British Foreign Office did not go so far, it was nevertheless admitted that the Spanish Civil War might yet succeed in dividing Europe into two blocs, 'each based on a rival ideology', a prospect that was considered far more worrying than the creation of groups of satisfied and dissatisfied powers, for any such development 'would not merely divide Governments from one another far more deeply than any political dispute, but would also cut across the domestic politics of each individual country'.[29]

Whereas Hitler held that the British were still in a position to choose which path to take in this projected ideological division of the continent,[30] the appearance of the French Popular Front regime in mid-May 1936 had finally put paid to any notion of German collaboration with France on the basis of common opposition to Bolshevism. As unlikely as such a prospect might seem, not least in view of the deep-seated mutual antagonisms between the two countries, there are grounds to believe that tentative hopes of a Franco–German agreement were entertained in Berlin following the handover of power, certainly by some of the new chancellor's advisers, including Ribbentrop, and even by Hitler himself.[31] Although the brunt of Germany's diplomatic effort towards the Western powers had been directed towards Britain, which for Hitler had always been the crucial element in the equation, numerous overtures were made to the French during 1933–35 with a view to exploring the possibilities of a rapprochement that would serve German interests in two ways. First, any perceived thaw in Franco–German relations was bound to agitate France's allies in eastern Europe and, in particular, strike a further blow at the prospects for the Eastern Pact. Second, it clearly made no sense to seek a future conflict with France, if one could be avoided on terms compatible with German aims in eastern Europe. It was partly for that purpose that Hitler showed an interest in holding personal conversations during 1933–34 with senior French politicians, including Daladier and Barthou.[32] Although nothing came of these projects, Hitler's interest in a possible settlement with France did not appear to wane even when Barthou's successor as foreign minister, Pierre Laval, committed his country to an alliance with the USSR in May 1935. The following October Hitler told Laval's personal emissary, Fernand de Brinon, that a French agreement with Germany was indeed possible, but only on condition France abandoned its ties in the East, and especially its association with the Bolsheviks. Europe should unite against the red menace, advised the German chancellor, 'but, as long as France continued "to hinge its policy on what the Russians and their Slav allies do", there was no possibility of agreement'.[33]

How sincere Hitler's repeated professions of friendship for France were by that stage remains an open question. It may well be that the Franco–Soviet Pact had finally damned France in his eyes from the moment it was signed. As he said later, the alliance with Russia had been a sure sign that France was securely on its way to becoming a Bolshevist state.[34] The accession to power of Blum and his associates, and their policy during the opening phase of the Spanish Civil War, certainly convinced Hitler that the French had made their choice on the burning issue of the day, but, unlike the USSR, with its formidable armaments and world revolutionary aspirations, France was no longer considered to pose a serious threat to the Reich. If nothing else, its feeble response to the remilitarization of the Rhineland testified to that. Nor, of course, did it dispose of the *Lebensraum* the National Socialists sought. Hitler's intentions towards France after 1935–36 are certainly difficult to fathom. On the one hand, it is clear that he no longer considered it a particularly significant factor in European politics, a fact that plainly emerged from his conversation with Ciano in October. 'Of France the Führer spoke – as do the other Germans – only superficially and with slight contempt,' noted the Italian foreign minister. 'Some abuse of the Jews who govern her and nothing further. In their opinion France has ceased – at least for the moment – to be an active factor in foreign policy.'[35] On the other hand, there are signs that later, in 1937, he returned to his initial aggressive intentions towards his western neighbour. As Klaus Hildebrand relates, when in October 1937 General Milch told the chancellor of the 'many friendly gestures made to him by French military and political leaders during his visit to Paris, which made him hopeful of a Franco–German agreement, Hitler simply replied: "But one day I will thrash them."'[36]

If by mid-1936 France was as good as finished as far as Hitler was concerned, the new conditions the outbreak of the Spanish Civil War created appeared to rekindle his hopes of basing an Anglo–German partnership on common opposition to Bolshevism. When in early September he received Lloyd George he reiterated his hopes that Britain and Germany could work together against the common menace of Bolshevism, which was not a 'fanatical obsession', but a 'real danger' against which western Europe should unite.[37] 'The obsession with Bolshevism and the menace of Russia,' noted Tom Jones, Lloyd George's travelling companion, 'the danger of Germany finding herself alone and encircled by communistic nations, the imperative need of collaboration with England if Europe is to be saved – we had read it all before, but now heard it with burning conviction from the Führer himself.'[38] While Hitler had experienced considerable disappointment in his relations with Great Britain since the signature of the Anglo–German Naval Agreement, and despite his bewilderment at British policy during the Abyssinian crisis, the events of the summer of 1936 clearly sparked a renewed drive to pursue the possibility of British collaboration in his European schemes. Now, however, it would be pressure rather than concession that would determine his approach to Britain, a point he articulated with great clarity to the Italian foreign minister, Galeazzo Ciano, in October 1936, to whom he spoke of uniting Germany, Japan, Italy, Britain, Poland and Brazil 'under the banner of anti-Bolshevism'.[39]

This use of anti-Bolshevism in Germany's relations with Great Britain during 1936–37 was intended to serve a double function: first to force British cooperation with Germany; second to recruit Britain to the ranks of the anti-Bolshevik powers, thus achieving Hitler's original goals in Anglo–German relations. That Hitler's use of the 'red scare' in both his domestic and international policy was geared towards the achievement not of a series of essentially unrelated aims, such as friendship with Britain and, in domestic terms, the extension of military service to two years,[40] but rather a grand vision is demonstrated by the celebrated memorandum on the four-year plan, which he wrote during August 1936, and his revealing statements at a crucial meeting of the German cabinet less than three months later.

In Hitler's eyes the Spanish Civil War and its impact on the European situation appeared to herald the opening of the inevitable showdown with communism that he had long since prophesied. Such was the essential message of the preamble to his memorandum on the four-year plan, which was drawn up some time towards the end of August 1936.[41] This source is of very considerable significance in discerning Hitler's general outlook and future expectations during the summer of 1936, not least because it is one of the few documents in which the Führer set down his views in writing.[42] Although it dealt primarily with economic issues, the memorandum began with a revealing statement of current and future political factors, which dictated why Germany must be ready for war by 1940. Using the ideological rationale of the 1920s and, influenced by recent events in Spain, warning against the growing threat from the USSR, Hitler outlined his concerns, current evaluations and proposed solution in what the Nazis were wont to call 'world-historical' terms. Since the outbreak of the French Revolution, he began:

the world has been moving with ever increasing speed towards a new conflict, the most extreme solution of which

89

is called Bolshevism, whose essence and aim, however, is solely the elimination of those strata of mankind which have hitherto provided the leadership and their replacement by world-wide Jewry. No State will be able to withdraw or even remain at a distance from this historical conflict. *Since Marxism, through its victory in Russia, has established one of the greatest empires in the world as a forward base for its future operations, this question has become a menacing one.*[43]

Hitler then proceeded to emphasize Germany's position at the vanguard of the Western world in the face of Bolshevist attacks. It was not his aim, he declared, to prophesy the time when the untenable situation in Europe would become an 'open crisis', but it was his conviction that this crisis could not and would not fail to arrive. The collapse of western Europe into Bolshevism would probably be the most 'gruesome catastrophe' that had been visited upon mankind. *'In the face of the necessity of defence against this danger, all other considerations must recede into the background as being completely irrelevant.'*[44]

Assessing the current situation, and in paying particular attention to the relative means of resistance disposed of by the European powers, he continued:

Europe has at present only two States which can be regarded as standing firm in the face of Bolshevism: Germany and Italy. The other countries are either disintegrated through their democratic form of life, infected by Marxism, and thus likely themselves to collapse in the foreseeable future, or ruled by authoritarian Governments whose sole strength lies in their military means of power. ... All these countries would be incapable of ever conducting a war against Soviet Russia with any prospects of success. In any case, apart from Germany and Italy, only Japan can be regarded as a Power standing firm in the face of the world peril.[45]

In the coming conflict with Bolshevism there were thus only two countries Germany could rely on: Japan and Italy. By this stage the Anti-Comintern Pact had essentially been negotiated, and through it Japan had pledged its support against the USSR. At the same time there had been a considerable improvement in German relations with Italy, the other staunchly anti-Bolshevik power mentioned by Hitler, and it is to those developments that we must now turn.

Hitler's original interest in an Italian alliance, which he first mentioned in 1920, revolved exclusively around considerations of *Realpolitik* and was based on the potential exploitation of Franco–Italian differences arising from the Paris peace settlement. For several years thereafter similar considerations would determine Hitler's attitude to Italy, for whose friendship and cooperation he was famously prepared to sacrifice the South Tyrol, much to the disgust of German nationalists, or, as he termed them, 'Jewish-led bourgeois patriots'.[46] The triumph of fascism in Italy in 1922 did not therefore provide the initial stimulus for the pursuit of the Italian alliance that would be such a central feature of Hitler's foreign policy agenda during the 1930s, but it was an important development because it provided him with an ideological platform for Italo–German cooperation. Although the notion of friendship with the Italians had its opponents in the NSDAP, where Italy was viewed as an upholder of the territorial status quo, at least in so far as it concerned Germany, the successful fascist 'March on Rome' demonstrated to Hitler that Italy had triumphed in its own battle against international Jewry, which in turn led him to the conclusion that no state was 'better suited than Italy as an ally for Germany'.[47] As such, the appearance of Mussolini, an event that coincided approximately with Hitler's final rejection of the idea of an alliance with Russia, meant that the first link had been made between the desire for Italian friendship and a future policy based on opposition to Bolshevism.

Mussolini, however, did not share Hitler's view of the international threat Bolshevism posed. As he stated on 23 March 1919, the day the fascist movement was founded, it was a 'typically Russian phenomenon' to which Western civilization was resistant.[48] More seriously, as far as the Nazis were concerned, fascism lacked the vehement anti-Semitism that lay at the core of Nazi doctrine. On the contrary, as the *Völkischer Beobachter* was claiming as late as July 1922, Jewish money had financed Mussolini's movement and Il Duce was little more than a 'hired traitor'.[49] Having already determined on the need for Italian friendship, however, Hitler refused to be deflected and merely noted that Mussolini's struggle against the 'Jewish world hydra' was 'perhaps fundamentally sub-conscious'.[50]

Despite Hitler's hopes that Italy would join Germany's mission to save Europe from the 'nightmare of Asiatic Bolshevism', as he put it to an Italian journalist in 1931,[51] common enmity to the USSR did not feature as a determinant of German relations with Italy between 1933 and 1936. Mussolini had welcomed Hitler's accession to power and for a while there were considerable hopes on both sides that the regimes might be able to effect a close cooperation in foreign policy.[52] At heart, however, the respective aims of any such cooperation were diverse and in some senses contradictory. For while Hitler had a grand vision with distinct end goals in view, Mussolini, for all his dreams of turning the Western powers out of the Mediterranean, was concerned to make piecemeal gains at the expense of Britain and France, and, at the same time, exercise some control over Germany, whose ambitions in southeast Europe he had cause to fear.

It was partly for these reasons, and possibly also because he had succeeded in defeating Bolshevism in Italy, that Mussolini had an entirely different approach to dealing with the Soviet problem. Although his perceptions of the Bolshevik threat had admittedly hardened since the 1920s, Mussolini did not share Hitler's zeal for a policy of confrontation. Indeed, his suspicion of Germany led him in the opposite direction, and until the onset of the Abyssinian crisis he was engaged in a rapprochement with the USSR that was clearly against the Third Reich.[53] In 1933 he advised Hitler not to break with Moscow but to support and copy his own efforts to accommodate Russia, not for any love of the Soviets, but for fear that a German–Soviet breach would lead to a Franco–Soviet combination, which, though primarily directed against Germany, would inevitably strengthen France and have consequent reper-cussions for Italy's position in Europe.[54] Moreover, although he could accept the possibility of a 'Jewish danger', Mussolini also thought Hitler mistaken in provoking international Jewry in a 'head-on collision'.[55] Nazi theorists, particularly Rosenberg, were out of touch with the realities of politics; in private Mussolini was scathing about the racial 'nonsense' Hitler spouted that served only to swell the ranks of his enemies.[56] These differences of opinion, considerable though they were, remained relatively unimportant compared with the Austrian question, which dominated Italo-

German relations to such an extent that it was not until 1936, and then more by chance than design, that anti-Bolshevism became a significant factor in the formation of the Rome–Berlin axis.

In the intervening years Hitler remained undeterred by the coolness in Italo–German relations, confident that the 'mutuality' of ideas between Italy and Germany would eventually bring about a reconciliation.[57] Changes to the European diplomatic scene provided the first openings in this process. These were occasioned by Soviet pacts with France and Czechoslovakia, the Abyssinian crisis, which led to a distinct cooling of relations between Italy and the Western powers and, also to Hitler's advantage, a breach in the Italo–Soviet rapprochement.[58] As Italy's diplomatic isolation increased during the winter of 1935–36, Mussolini became ever further estranged from his former partners in the Stresa Front and almost inevitably more attuned to the idea of an accommodation with Germany. Seizing on what in 1933 he had described to the French ambassador as one of the few areas of common outlook between his own and Hitler's movements,[59] opposition to Bolshevism was now purposefully pushed to the forefront of the agenda in Mussolini's dealings with Berlin. When in January 1936 a visiting German envoy enquired about his view of the Stresa Front, Il Duce responded: 'We have the same enemies, don't we? And Russia! This Russian Army – Bolshevism. Only we two know about it. I and Herr Hitler.'[60] By the following March he professed not only to welcome the idea of a 'front of authoritarian states against the Bolshevik and Jewish democracies', but also made clear that Italy would be willing to enter into 'clear and definite obligations with Germany against France and Russia as well'.[61]

Although Mussolini's main priority at the time was certainly not an association with Germany based on opposition to Bolshevism, it is nonetheless interesting to note that he was becoming increasingly disturbed by the leftist political trends apparent in both France and Spain, and their possible repercussions in international affairs. This is all the more significant given that, generally speaking, Italian foreign policy under the fascists had until this point been determined almost exclusively by considerations of *Realpolitik*. The appearance of the Blum administration in France and the outbreak of the Spanish Civil War inevitably reinforced anxieties about the growth of Bolshevik influence, with the result that by the summer of 1936 there was a distinct ideological dimension to Italian diplomacy. This point was recognized by the German ambassador in Rome, Ulrich von Hassell, who believed that Mussolini's hostility to communism was based partly on ideological considerations and partly on the fear of a growth of French and Soviet influence in the Mediterranean.[62]

The Spanish Civil War was in this sense just the opportunity Hitler had been anticipating to initiate collaboration with Italy on the basis of anti-Bolshevism. In this respect, although Italy and Germany often pursued conflicting and competing policies in Spain between 1936 and 1939, there was absolute sincerity behind Hitler's statement to Ciano shortly after the outbreak of the civil war that by assisting Franco Italy and Germany had 'together dug the first trench against bolshevism'.[63] When Hans Frank, minister without portfolio in the Nazi government, visited Mussolini in September 1936 there was much talk of the need for the two regimes to stand together in the face of the red threat. Through his envoy Hitler assured Il Duce that Germany's actions in Spain were dictated 'solely because of solidarity in the field of political ideas', and he was clearly anxious to impress on the Italians that he considered the Mediterranean a purely Italian sphere of interest. Mussolini, too, stressed that Italy's involvement in Spain was 'an effective proof of our involvement in the anti-Bolshevik struggle'.[64]

The following month, when Ciano met Hitler at the Berghof, the main topics of conversation were Bolshevism and British hostility to the dictatorships, a factor Hitler deliberately played up to impress the Italian foreign minister.[65] Irrespective of his denunciations of Britain on this occasion, it is clear that Hitler placed considerable emphasis on mobilizing Italy against the USSR by early winter 1936. In that sense, in view of Mussolini's smouldering resentment of the British for their part in the Abyssinian crisis, anti-Bolshevism held far more significance for Hitler than for Mussolini as a 'structural principle' of the Axis, as one commentator has termed it.[66] Indeed, far from wishing to alienate Britain, Hitler was about to embark on a renewed effort to seek its friendship. On the very day he received Ciano, the chancellor had also dispatched to London his new ambassador, Joachim von Ribbentrop, who had been instructed to 'get Britain to join the Anti-Comintern Pact' as 'that is what I want most of all'.[67]

The role of anti-Bolshevism in cementing Germany's relations with Italy during 1936 should not be underestimated. It cannot be disputed that there was a more significant development in those relations in that year than those of any other country with which Germany dealt. As the British ambassador to Berlin pointed out in his annual report, this development was 'symptomatic of the year's peculiar characteristic in foreign affairs, namely the increasingly acute division of the powers on ideological lines'.[68] The events in Spain had decisively influenced German cooperation with Italy, concluded Phipps, not least because the outbreak of the civil war had finally alerted Mussolini to the danger represented by the Soviet Union.[69] By mid-November 1936 Italo–German cooperation against Bolshevism had been enshrined in the October protocols, which designated communism the 'greatest danger threatening the peace and security of Europe'. These were formally proclaimed by Mussolini's declaration of the Rome–Berlin Axis, and confirmed by the two powers' recognition of Franco as the legitimate head of the Spanish state.[70]

Meanwhile, on 25 November 1936, Ribbentrop and Ambassador Mushakoji finally signed the German–Japanese Anti-Comintern Pact. Ostensibly directed against the Comintern, the pact contained a secret supplementary protocol that pitched it directly against the USSR. Of those sections of the agreement made public the most significant was Article II inviting other powers to accede to the agreement, which amounted in effect to an invitation to line up against the Soviet Union.[71] This was by far and away the most important aspect of the Anti-Comintern Pact, which, it might be argued, constituted a nucleus around which an anti-Soviet alliance might be built.

Following the ceremony at the Wilhelmstrasse, foreign press representatives were summoned to the propaganda ministry where Ribbentrop read a prepared statement. After reminding his audience of the belligerent declarations that had been made at the Comintern's seventh world congress, particularly its stated aim of 'revolution in all states and the "erection" of a Bolshevik world dictatorship', Ribbentrop discussed the Comintern's activities in Spain. Here he declared that it had 'no other objective than the erection by propaganda and force of a Soviet Republic' from which it would proceed 'further to undermine Europe'. 'Who', he asked rhetorically, 'would be next?' As the present agreement served to demonstrate, Germany and Japan were no longer willing to tolerate the activities of communist agitators and had thus 'gone over to deeds'. The conclusion of the Anti-Comintern Pact, he concluded, represented an 'epoch making event', a 'turning point in the defensive war … against the powers of disintegration', which future generations, even those who had 'not yet appreciated the Bolshevik danger', would surely come to appreciate.[72]

In private, however, there was no emphasis whatsoever on the supposedly defensive nature of German policy towards the USSR, or on the need, provided for by the terms of the German–Japanese agreement, to combat the activities of the Comintern within the frontiers of the Reich. Indeed, quite the contrary, for several weeks before the pact's conclusion Göring had gone so far as to announce to a meeting of the German cabinet that war with the Soviet Union was inevitable.[73] This is not to say that the Anti-Comintern Pact was in any way conceived as a potential military alliance to provide for the contingency of imminent conflict with the USSR, far from it. Nevertheless, through this very public association Germany and Japan had provided an example for others to follow; Italy had made its position clear; in his memorandum on the four-year plan Hitler had decreed that the showdown with Bolshevism was unavoidable. It now remained to be seen what impact this 'epoch making event' would have, and how in particular the other powers would respond to the German–Japanese initiative.

That some form of response was expected is clearly evident from a series of statements Hitler made to a further meeting of the Reich cabinet on 1 December 1936. This remarkable declaration, unknown before the publication of Goebbels's diaries in the early 1990s, provides a revealing insight into the contemporary concerns with Bolshevism, and thus, by inference, the significance of the Anti-Comintern Pact in German diplomacy as 1936 drew to a close. 'Europe is already divided into two camps,' noted Goebbels, paraphrasing Hitler:

> There is no going back. He outlines the tactics of the Reds. Spain elevated to a global question. France the next victim. Blum a convinced agent of the Soviets. Zionist and world destroyer. Whoever is victorious in Spain secures the

prestige for himself. Either way the repercussions are great for the rest of Europe; which explains German military aid. The churches have failed completely. There is danger ahead in France. Germany can only wish that the danger is deferred till we are ready. When it comes, act fast. Get into the paternoster lift at the right time. But also get out again at the right time. Rearm, money can play no role. ... The authoritarian states (Poland, Austria, Yugoslavia, Hungary) are not secure against crises. The only committed anti-Bolshevik states are Germany, Italy, Japan. Therefore agreements with them. England will come over when the crisis breaks out in France. Not a love match with Poland but a reasonable relationship. Enabled us to re-arm. Smaller questions play a subordinate role before the world decision. So disregard them if possible.[74]

Chapter 6
The Mobilization of Propaganda, 1934–36

I f during the early stages of his chancellorship Hitler had been forced to rely on the Wilhelmstrasse for the conduct of German diplomacy, it was a quite different story in the realm of propaganda where the Nazis already had an efficient apparatus that had served them well during the *Kampfzeit*, not least in the domestic struggle against Bolshevism. The establishment in March 1933 of the Reich ministry for public enlightenment and propaganda was a key development in determining the institutional framework for the conduct of German foreign policy during the Third Reich. As subsequent events would demonstrate, few people had a keener appreciation than Hitler and his minister of propaganda, Joseph Goebbels, of the possibilities offered by the conjunction of totalitarian power, which enabled the Nazis to monopolize the instruments of mass communication, and a world eager for information on the views and intentions of the dynamic new regime that had appeared in Berlin.

In view of his subsequent role as one of the most prominent Nazi agitators against the Soviet Union, and indeed one of the party's most committed opponents of Bolshevism, international or otherwise, it is somewhat ironic that until the mid-1920s Goebbels had embraced national Bolshevism, a political philosophy associated with the Strasser faction of the NSDAP, which was essentially pro-Russian and anti-Western in conception.[1] By the spring of 1926, however, he had fallen in completely behind Hitler in questions of future international policy, and now readily accepted not only that Bolshevik Russia intended to 'devour' Germany, but also embraced the *Mein Kampf* thesis of future alliances with Britain and Italy, a combination that only months before he had considered a 'horrible' prospect.[2]

A body of officials fully grounded in the art and techniques of propaganda and veterans of the internal struggle against 'Jewish Bolshevism' staffed the Reich propaganda ministry. Immediately after the *Machtergreifung*, a specially designated division of the ProMi, Abteilung Referat II, charged with combating Bolshevism in both the domestic and international spheres, projected the fight against the red menace onto the world stage. According to the head of the new department, Eberhardt Taubert, the fight against Bolshevism had from the outset constituted an 'unmistakable guideline' of the policy and propaganda carried out by the ProMi.[3] Starting from the premise that Bolshevism was directed by the Jews, who saw the new Germany as the chief obstacle to their ultimate goal of world revolution, the ProMi propagated the idea that a 'life and death struggle' with Bolshevism could not be avoided, and in that connection sought especially to highlight the colossal military power of the USSR with which it aimed to pursue its ambitions. On a more proactive plane, the ProMi set itself the goal of constructing a world movement against Bolshevism of which Nazism, the 'political antithesis' of Bolshevik ideals, would be the natural leader. By thus taking the fight to the Bolsheviks, Germany not only hoped to win friends abroad, but, in time, to 'assume leadership of a powerful [*gewaltig*] global force' dedicated to the extirpation of international Bolshevism. To all intents and purposes, Taubert recalled in 1944, these aims had effectively set the ProMi on its own collision course with the USSR.[4]

In 1933, at a time when the Reich was not only particularly vulnerable politically and militarily but also keen to advertise its peaceful aims, it was impossible overtly to promote anti-Bolshevik, and thus anti-Soviet, ambitions through a state agency, let alone one of the regime's main ministries. One of Taubert's first acts was thus to merge the major German anti-communist organizations into a single unit, the Gesamtverband Deutscher Antikommunistischer Vereinigungen (GDAV) or, as it was subsequently renamed, the Antikomintern, a body which, though ostensibly privately financed and functioning independently of the Nazi regime, constituted an integral division of the ProMi, whence it received its funding and operational directives. Goebbels admitted as much in December 1936 when, in response to confusion in the party about the status and purpose of the Antikomintern, he wrote a circular communication describing it as a body, which, 'for reasons of camouflage, appears to the outside to be a private association, but which is in reality an agency of my ministry', the main purpose of which was to build 'a world anti-Bolshevik movement under German leadership'.[5]

The director of the Antikomintern, Dr Adolf Ehrt, was a publicist and writer, who, in Alfred Rosenberg's words, was not only one of the Reich's 'leading authorities on communism and Bolshevism', but also an individual who had made a 'significant contribution to the struggle against Marxism in Germany'.[6] In 1930 Ehrt published his first book, *Ein deutscher Todesweg*, in which he sought to alert the German people to the wholesale degeneration of economic and cultural life that had resulted from Bolshevik rule in the Soviet Union. Attracted by the anti-Bolshevik stance of the NSDAP, Ehrt joined the party in March 1932 and subsequently published further books in quick succession, each a stinging attack on Bolshevism, some of which were clearly aimed at audiences outside Germany.[7] In 1933, as part of his work as head of the newly inaugurated GDAV, he wrote an account of Bolshevik complicity in the Reichstag fire, which was published shortly before the trial of van der Lubbe and his associates. Quite in keeping with the ProMi's conception of its anti-Bolshevik functions, the book, entitled *Bewaffneter Aufstand*, concluded with the message that the 'destruction of the Communist International is a task for all the nations of the Christian and civilized world'.[8]

Surviving personal papers of Antikomintern officials suggest that its work held considerable appeal for young idealists. The average age of a sample of 20 employees was 29,[9] with many, including Ehrt, having been born in Russia where, according to one authority, they had gained their own 'decisive impressions' of the Bolshevik revolution.[10] Due to the nature of its operations and the wholesale destruction of its files in an allied air raid in 1943, it is difficult to reconstruct with any precision the range and nature of the Antikomintern's activities, but two documents drawn from the files of the Aussenpolitisches Amt der NSDAP, both written by Georg Leibbrandt in the autumn of 1934 provide an insight into its early work. The Antikomintern's essential aims, he noted on 2 October, were to advertise the dangers of Bolshevism to the world and to counter the machinations of the Comintern. In its foreign operations the Antikomintern neither employed agents to work abroad nor sought to establish offices in foreign countries. It aimed instead to forge links with similar agencies and organizations through which it could disseminate its propaganda, largely in the form of exhibitions, books, brochures and articles.[11] Recent Antikomintern successes, Leibbrandt continued, included mounting an anti-Bolshevik exhibition in Norway and providing advice and assistance to the Japanese ministry of the interior, which had wished to establish its own organization for combating Bolshevism. There had also been a considerable advance for the Antikomintern in Switzerland where it had helped to establish two anti-Bolshevik bodies, the Pro-Deo Commission, which was effectively managed by the Antikomintern from Berlin, and a Geneva based committee that had agitated strongly against the proposed entry of the USSR into the League of Nations.[12]

Leibbrandt's second memorandum, dated 10 October 1934, gave details of the Antikomintern's plans for the immediate future, particularly those involving cooperation with the Pro-Deo Commission. These included a series of exhibitions to be mounted in Scandinavia, the Baltic states, Poland, Holland, France, the USA and Greece, a further special operation in France, where anti-Bolshevik forces had requested assistance to establish their own organization in opposition to the 'governing Jewish Masonic clique', and a series of publicity campaigns dedicated to exposing the atrocities committed by the Soviet regime against its own people, including its policies of deliberate starvation and forced labour.[13]

By early 1935 the Antikomintern had an extensive network of connections throughout Europe. In the early stages of its activity it appears to have placed particular emphasis on cultivating links with Poland, which is hardly surprising given the Polish attitude to the USSR, and, in particular, the recent developments in German–Polish relations that had been partially designed to facilitate future political cooperation against Bolshevism. This work consisted of exchanging material with Polish anti-communist organizations, including mutual translations of important works and exhibition pieces,[14] orientation visits by Antikomintern representatives to investigate the nature and extent of anti-communist activity in Poland and explore the possibility of joint initiatives,[15] and visits by leading officials, including one by Ehrt to Warsaw in May 1936.[16]

In late 1935, alongside other initiatives already taken as part of the ongoing thaw in Italo–German relations since the early summer,[17] discussions took place with an emissary from Rome with a view to initiating a degree of Italo–German cooperation against Bolshevism. According to Mussolini's envoy, identified as Insabato in the Antikomintern's record of the discussions, Russia's anti-Italian attitude and the strong anti-fascist propaganda put out by Moscow as a result of Italy's invasion of Abyssinia had shaken Il Duce's Russian policy. In the light of these developments Mussolini had charged Insabato to contact the Antikomintern with a view to forming a block between Germany, Italy, Hungary and Poland directed against the USSR and Czechoslovakia.[18]

One organization with which the Antikomintern enjoyed close relations in the 1930s was the Entente internationale contre la Troisième Internationale, a Geneva-based agency headed by Theodor Aubert, which counted among its numerous anti-Soviet activities the delivery of a lengthy document to the League of Nations protesting against the proposed admission of the USSR.[19] The Entente internationale assisted Ehrt and his colleagues in several important ways, not only in furnishing the Antikomintern with vast amounts of anti-Bolshevik literature, but also in more practical ways, such as in April 1935, when, on the eve of the League council meeting to discuss recent German breaches of the Treaty of Versailles, Aubert arranged for every delegate to receive an Antikomintern brochure detailing the threat posed to all European countries by the Red Army.[20]

The Antikomintern's activities included the provision of assistance to fledgling anti-communist organizations, like the one Senator Milan Popovic established in Yugoslavia in January 1936, and to more mainstream political organizations like Leon Degrelle's Rexist Movement in Belgium. Following consultations with the Wilhelmstrasse it was agreed to supply the new 'Yugoslavian Anti-Marxist Committee' with an Antikomintern official, a Yugoslav national delegated to assist and advise the new body during its first months of activity. Within three months arrangements had been made for Popovic to visit Berlin to deliver a lecture on conditions in Yugoslavia.[21] As far as relations with Degrelle are concerned, the Antikomintern appears to have made its first contact with the Rexist leader through one of its senior officials, Alfred Gielen, who visited Brussels in October 1936. During a discussion between Gielen, Degrelle and the latter's propaganda expert, René Lust, it was agreed that the Antikomintern should supply anti-Bolshevik material to the Rexists and also arrange the shipment to Brussels of an exhibition, a prospect that had appealed to Hitler and Goebbels when it was mooted in the course of Degrelle's recent visit to Germany.[22]

Publicity was a major activity of the Antikomintern. Its press division, headed by Rudolf Kommoss, produced two publications, the bi-monthly *Antikomintern Nachrichtendienst* (*AKND*), an English language version of which started to appear in late 1934, and the *UdSSR-Dienst*, which appeared thrice weekly, covering up to the minute developments in the Soviet Union largely for German domestic consumption. It also monitored and supervised the appearance of anti-communist articles in German newspapers and magazines, the preparation and dissemination of propaganda in languages other than German, and the provision of anti-Bolshevik material to the political leadership for the purposes of speech writing.[23] Each *AKND* bulletin followed a similar format and consisted of easily digestible items covering various aspects of communist activity in Europe, and inevitably pointing to the USSR as both the font of all evil and a vivid reminder of the catastrophic results of Bolshevik tyranny. Familiar targets included the desperate social and economic conditions obtaining in the USSR, the Comintern's attempts to subvert the political process in various European states, and the formidable nature of the Soviet armed forces. Each issue carried a section entitled 'The Comintern at Work', which detailed all known activities undertaken by communist groups or individuals throughout Europe, including meetings, demonstrations, and acts of violence and sabotage, as well as outlining the measures taken to combat such activities.

Following the outbreak of the Spanish Civil War in July 1936 Spanish issues inevitably took centre stage in Antikomintern publications, and none more so than in the *AKND* bulletins, which, in compliance with the general direction of German diplomacy at the time, also carried articles on the heightened danger Bolshevism posed to Britain. Nevertheless, the *AKND* still managed to devote a considerable number of column inches to purely Soviet issues;[24] during 1938–39 it became if anything more overtly anti-Soviet in several respects. Additions to the format included two new regular sections, 'Russia Today' and 'Moscow Overseas', the purpose of the former being to bring home to the readership on a regular basis the plight of the average Russian citizen, while the latter sought to expose Stalin's manipulation of the Popular Front movement, the aim of which was to sneak 'into the ranks of those who for one reason or another are discontented' in order to create the 'revolutionary situation necessary for the Bolshevist upheaval'.[25] Hoping to exploit the offence caused to the religious-minded by the Bolshevik promotion of atheism, the *AKND* also ran a series of articles on the machinations of the 'Godless International', which, so it was claimed, was determined to impose atheism on societies already paralysed by class struggle, thus serving the basic Bolshevik objective of the 'annihilation of all religion'.[26]

Apart from the regular output of the *AKND*, the Antikomintern's main publicity effort in 1936 related to a collaborative international work entitled *Der Weltbolschewismus*. This 500-page volume, published in early 1936, and two and a half years in preparation, consisted of articles detailing the Comintern's activities in regions as far flung as the South Pacific and Turkestan, and in countries as diverse as France and Outer Mongolia.[27] Its main purpose was to expose the Comintern's work in a brief, clear and accessible form, and to indicate what measures were being taken around the globe to combat it. Whatever the publication's merits, it clearly stimulated some interest. For example, shortly after its appearance the German minister in Rome, who had recently been in negotiations with Peter Ledit, a Jesuit priest who published his own anti-Bolshevik newsletter, the *Lettres de Rome*, requested several copies of the French and Italian editions of *Der Weltbolschewismus*, which he thought might usefully be distributed in Vatican circles.[28]

Several contributors to the volume attended a major conference organized by the Antikomintern at Feldafing in Bavaria in November 1936. The six-day event provided a forum for representatives of European and non-European countries to pool their experiences of the operations of Bolshevism; it also provided a platform for the leaders of the Antikomintern to advise on measures to counter it. As a sign of the importance the German authorities attached to the event, Goebbels and Taubert not only put in appearances but also held a reception for the delegates at the

Rathaus in Munich. In his brief address to the conference Taubert sounded a familiar note:

> Today we no longer stand alone in our fight against Bolshevism. ... To combat it effectively, it is necessary for all the healthy forces of the world to come together. Bolshevism is fundamentally interested in spreading war and confusion. ... The fight against Bolshevism is not a fight for the maintenance of culture in one's own land, but a fight for world peace.[29]

The main result of the gathering at Feldafing was the decision to hold a future world conference against Bolshevism, for the purposes of which a standing committee was set up under the chairmanship of the Swedish delegate, Nils von Bahr.[30]

Antikomintern activities have received scant attention in literature on German propaganda in the 1930s. Apart from a rather dismissive analysis by Walter Laqueur, which seeks to downplay if not ridicule its work, virtually nothing of note has appeared in English. In his assessment of the Antikomintern, Laqueur makes some curious observations. At one point, for example, he suggests that the organization's 'true aim' was 'not to denounce the Soviet Union but to gain support in the West for Nazi policy', as if somehow the two activities are not obviously and intimately connected.[31] He is, moreover, well off the mark in suggesting that Ehrt and his colleagues were not genuinely anti-Bolshevik in outlook.[32] In one of the few attempts by German historians to assess the Antikomintern's work, Hans-Adolf Jacobsen is similarly sceptical of its significance, writing that, although it engaged in a great deal of activity, it could hardly claim to have scored any 'major successes'.[33] Yet, such successes could hardly be expected from what might justifiably be termed a 'grass roots' organization that worked patiently and unspectacularly towards its goal. Ehrt and his colleagues were surely unlikely to set the world alight with their investigations into 'colonial Bolshevism' or their support for the 'International Women's League against War and Bolshevism',[34] but these examples are indicative of the diversity, range and nature of the Antikomintern's efforts to spread its message as far and wide as possible.

If the Antikomintern operated quietly and methodically behind the scenes, Hitler and his close political collaborators never tired of declaring their hostility to Bolshevism and Soviet Russia from public rostrums the length and breadth of Germany, especially after 1935 when German propaganda against Bolshevism and the Soviet Union became increasingly strident and confrontational. Hundreds of speeches the chancellor and his colleagues made in the 1930s contained damning references to the incompetence of the Bolsheviks as administrators, their persecution of their own people, their hopeless mismanagement of the economy, industry and agriculture, and, of course, their preoccupation with armed might and notions of world revolution. Since Hitler's speeches and proclamations were widely reported in the world press, the simple medium of the spoken word constituted an effective source of anti-Bolshevik propaganda for the Nazi regime.

No attempt will be made here to analyse even a fraction of these speeches in so far as they concerned anti-Bolshevism. True to Hitler's maxim about the effectiveness in propaganda terms of ceaselessly repeating one point to drive home the essence of the message, Nazi pronouncements on Bolshevism were invariably predictable, verbose and repetitive. The tone of the anti-Bolshevik propaganda being put out by the Nazi regime by the mid-1930s can be conveyed by a brief examination of the 1936 Nuremberg rally, the annual gathering of the party faithful, and, in the wake of the Olympic Games, more than ever something of a showcase to the outside world. Coming so soon after the outbreak of the Spanish Civil War, there was a general expectation that the key speeches would be directed against Bolshevism, but, as the British embassy in Berlin reported on 23 September, 'the extent of the attacks and their violent and pointed, and in fact provocative, nature' had 'exceeded all expectations'.[35]

In an important address that subsequently appeared in pamphlet form,[36] Goebbels criticized western European politicians for their 'fatal lack of insight into the nature and structure of international Bolshevism'. It was a colossal mistake to view Bolshevism as an 'outlook on life', he warned, when it was in fact a 'pathological and criminal kind of madness', devised, maintained and manipulated by the Jews, who aimed to destroy European civilization and replace it with 'a Jewish-international world regime that would subject all

106

nations to their power'. Following a lengthy exposition of the means by which the Bolsheviks intended to achieve this goal, the Reich propaganda minister turned inevitably to the events in Spain, a challenge that was 'a matter of concern to the whole world'. The outbreak of civil war in a western European country, a conflict that had been engineered by Bolshevik agitators, was the most urgent signal to date that Bolshevism was 'no longer a problem that can be dealt with by those who theorise about the various outlooks on life', but had become an issue of 'grave concern for statesmen all over the world' It was they, continued Goebbels, who would

> have to tackle this problem unless they wish to become responsible for the future development which – because of their negligence – will push Europe into the most severe crisis and eventually into ruin. The problem of Bolshevism as it faces Europe today is a question of to be or not to be. Here and now the souls of men are ranged on the one side or the other. A definite side will have to be taken either against or in favour of Bolshevism and all consequences resulting therefrom will have to be accepted.[37]

It was no longer sufficient to counter the Bolsheviks with demonstrations of 'well-staged moral disapproval', he continued, and the German nation could feel proud of unmasking the 'Jewish wire-pullers', and, indeed, of having identified the Jews as the originators and manipulators of international Bolshevism. 'Bolshevism must be exterminated if Europe is to regain its normal state of health', he announced frankly, for to dally with it would spell 'ultimate ruin'. The ruthlessness of the Soviet regime served as a warning to all, as did the Soviet war machine and Stalin's aggressive intentions towards Germany and western Europe. Already the terrors of Bolshevism had reached the Iberian peninsula, where the present chaos and destruction were but part of a 'well-laid plan to make the civil war started by Bolshevism in Spain develop into an international conflict'. Bolshevism, Goebbels announced by way of conclusion, was:

> an infernal pestilence which must be eradicated and which it is the duty of everyone, conscious of his responsibilities, to

assist in removing. It is not merely oratory when we Germans appeal to all the nations of the world to combine in order to meet this menace if they do not wish to be drawn into a terrible and incalculable fate. Germany has given the signal for this world struggle. ... May the world follow Germany's example. ... May they do so before it is too late, for the danger is approaching everywhere. ... For the Red enemy of civilization is at work in every country. The whole world is in danger. Therefore there must be no more vacillation. We must be ready to meet the danger at the decisive hour.[38]

On 14 September, the conference closing day, Hitler spoke in virtually identical terms in an address, which, in Max Domarus's words, was 'for the most part a reiteration of the imminent threat to the world posed by Communism'.[39] In his proclamation to the party on 9 September the Führer had already set the tone for the proceedings by justifying the recent increase in compulsory military service from one to two years through reference to the strength of the Red Army and the relentless agitation of 'Bolshevik wire-pullers' who, from their 'international Jewish revolutionary headquarters in Moscow' were redoubling their efforts to engulf the continent. 'We have learned from the experiences of the last eighteen years,' noted the chancellor.

We know what is the fate of the nation that, without force of its own, depends on foreign justice or even dares to hope for assistance. We see around us evil times to come. What we preached for years about the greatest world danger of the end of this second thousand years of our Christian era is becoming a terrible reality.[40]

He could never come to terms with Bolshevism, which, in its first act after gaining power, habitually liberated the 'scum of humanity', he declared on 14 September. Bolshevism was a ruinous plague, a fomenter of world unrest, its leaders the 'international disseminators of strife'. These were only some of the grounds that separated National Socialists from communists. The ideological antagonisms between the two could never be reconciled for they were in essence

108

'two worlds which do grow but farther apart from each other and can never unite'.[41] For hours, reports Domarus, 'he continued along these lines', 'as if he intended to march against Russia within days'.[42]

The extreme anti-Bolshevik tone of the 1936 party rally provoked substantial comment from foreign observers. The US ambassador in Berlin thought that the 'extraordinary and searching' statements about Bolshevism senior Nazis had made might even 'make it difficult for the Soviet Embassy to remain in Berlin'.[43] Dodd was closer to the mark than he could have realized on this point, for on the eve of the rally Hitler had expressed the hope that the forthcoming verbal barrage would prove so intolerable to Stalin that he would break off diplomatic relations.[44] Contrary to his ambassador, who misguidedly believed that the declarations made at Nuremberg had been driven by a desire for prestige,[45] the US military attaché was convinced that the anti-Bolshevik invective had had a quite specific and different purpose. The denunciation of communism, he wrote, was 'aimed at achieving for Germany the leadership of a still unborn anti-Communist European front'; the general tenor of the Nuremberg gathering being 'Hitler's first blow in forging a great and powerful anti-Communist block'.[46]

British observers came away with similar impressions. The German people, noted the consul general in Munich, were being 'taught to believe that Soviet Russia and international Jewry wish to attack and destroy them'. The world, they had just been told, was already divided on ideological grounds between weak democracies on the verge of succumbing to Bolshevism, and strong totalitarian states that rejected any form of compromise with that pernicious and poisonous doctrine. 'Implicit in this teaching', noted St Clair Gainer, 'is the belief, nay even the hope, that one day force will decide the issue between the two ideologies'.[47] Commenting on these observations, Orme Sargent believed that the recent German verbal assaults on the Soviet Union had been designed not only to 'inspire the average German with a crusading zeal', but also to rally European states around a German-led anti-Bolshevist movement in order ultimately to 'secure the benevolent neutrality, or even the active cooperation, of the democratic States, if and when a direct conflict with Russia ensues'.[48]

Although the effects of any propaganda campaign are notoriously difficult to assess, there can surely be little doubt about the motives behind National Socialist Germany's invective against Bolshevik Russia. Taken together with German intervention in Spain and the imminent conclusion of the Anti-Comintern Pact, the violent harangues delivered against Moscow in September 1936 were clearly intended as a component in a sustained effort to isolate and ostracize the Soviet Union and its Bolshevik masters. Whatever the impact of their activities as propagandists, one could hardly accuse Ehrt and Taubert, still less Goebbels and Hitler, of failing to publicize not only the threat of international Bolshevism, but also their intention to take the offensive against it. It now remained to be seen where others stood on this crucial issue. One thing, however, was certain. As Goebbels announced at a top secret briefing of the German press in November 1936, National Socialism and Bolshevism could not coexist in the long run; one of them must finally disappear; Germany, declared the Reich propaganda minister, stood now on the verge of 'a great historical conflict'.[49]

Chapter 7
The Failure of Hitler's Anti-Bolshevik Appeal, 1936

Marked by solemn declarations of solidarity between the German and Japanese signatories, and launched in a blaze of publicity expertly managed by the Reich propaganda ministry, the Anti-Comintern Pact inevitably sent reverberations throughout Europe and beyond. To many conservative elements across the continent, the signature of an agreement designed specifically to undermine the activities of the Moscow-inspired Communist International must have seemed timely and propitious, if only because Spain was already engaged in a vicious civil war, which, in the eyes of numerous contemporary observers, represented a struggle to the death between the forces of order and chaos.[1] Coming so shortly after the Nuremberg rally, where Hitler and his colleagues had spoken of the unbridgeable ideological divisions that separated communism from the civilized world, the agreement seemed to herald the opening of a major propaganda offensive against Bolshevism and even, in the words of the *New York Times*, to have realized finally the German chancellor's dream of a 'worldwide anti-Communist bloc, prepared by agreements with Austria and Italy, and now reaching from Burgos, Spain, to Tokyo'.[2]

By itself, however, the Anti-Comintern Pact represented very little. As the *Manchester Guardian* noted on 26 November, the substance of the treaty had been widely anticipated, and its conclusion had thus done little more than 'register the present state of German–Japanese relations, made particularly cordial by a common hatred of Communism'.[3] Even the secret protocol, to those who knew of it, had a hollow ring, for, notwithstanding the reservations each power had inserted to preserve its freedom of action, the state of Germany's and Japan's relations with the USSR hardly required a formal declaration of neutrality in the event of either becoming involved in a conflict with their declared ideological adversary. The Anti-Comintern Pact would thus only assume significance, both for its own sake and in terms of the purpose for which the Germans had designed it, if it succeeded in making a positive impact on the major powers, and especially, in view of Hitler's aims and desires, if Britain, Italy and Poland chose to associate themselves with it.

In its original form it was difficult to see how the Anti-Comintern Pact could aspire to 'defend European civilization', as Ribbentrop's representative, Dr Theodor Böttiger, had announced to international press representatives gathered at the Reich propaganda ministry on 25 November.[4] Few, in any case, took that supposed objective seriously. As would rapidly become apparent, the Anti-Comintern Pact provoked a wide range of reactions quite different from those Hitler anticipated and desired. Generally it was viewed with varying degrees of hostility, suspicion and reserve; several commentators saw it simply as a blind for the future expansionist ambitions of Germany and Japan, the former in central Europe, the latter in China; perhaps, ventured one imaginative mind, it would provide the basis for a partition of the Dutch East Indies between Germany and Japan.[5] Within a year of its signature the pact had changed character completely and, by the time of Italy's accession in November 1937, it had assumed a specifically anti-Western orientation, which clearly bore little relation to its original impetus.

Ironically, the country with the greatest cause for alarm at the conclusion of the Anti-Comintern Pact, the USSR, adopted a relatively relaxed attitude to it, not least because information the Soviet intelligence service supplied confirmed that the agreement, including the secret protocol, had done little more than formalize the obvious. Secure in this knowledge, the Soviet reaction amounted to a concerted effort, through the press, public declarations and diplomatic channels, to point out the threat of a German–Japanese combination not to themselves but to others. Even before Ribbentrop and Mushakoji had signed the agreement, *Isvestia* carried a leading article claiming that the forthcoming pact, which was set to constitute 'one of the most pernicious elements of the international situation', was essentially a conspiracy against world peace cloaked in meaningless anti-Bolshevik jargon. As such, it was merely 'the latest development on that preparation of world war which constitutes the main historic function of fascism'. In these circumstances, peace loving nations were surely called upon 'as never before' to work together to provide and ensure collective security for all.[6] Litvinov spoke in similar terms to the eighth congress of Soviets, which met in Moscow towards the end of November, adding a special reproach for Mussolini, who, after a decade of 'highly proper' relations between Italy and the Soviet Union, suddenly appeared to have discovered that communism was after all a threat to the existing world order.[7] By late December, when it had become clear that the Anti-Comintern Pact had failed miserably in its purpose of attracting additional signatories, the Soviet ambassador in London told Eden, somewhat unconvincingly, that the USSR, confident of its ability to fight on two fronts if necessary, was 'not at all apprehensive' about the agreement. On the other hand, Maisky continued, the mere fact of a German–Japanese alliance might well encourage the signatory powers to act with less restraint towards others; and in that respect there was indeed considerable anxiety in Moscow about 'what fate might befall Czechoslovakia'.[8]

The Soviet Union's foremost European ally, France, governed since May 1936 by a Popular Front administration, took a similarly dim view of the Anti-Comintern Pact, which the leftist press immediately decried as a 'monument to hypocrisy and a danger to peace'. Though less outspoken, Le Temps, the leading French broadsheet hardly renowned for its love of communists, was no less critical of the agreement. Although it was the duty of all countries to fight revolutionary communism on their own soil, ran a leading article on 26 November, the danger inherent in transferring this 'elementary duty of defence' to the international plane was that it would inevitably lead to a division of Europe on ideological lines.[9] According to the Paris correspondent of The Times, French opinion held that the German crusade against communism, now enshrined in the Anti-Comintern Pact, was nothing but an exploitation of ideological prejudice for material gain. In that connection attention was drawn to Hitler's reference at the recent Nuremberg rally to the vast riches of the Ukraine, which had 'merely confirmed French suspicions that it is not so much what Soviet Russia is, as what Soviet Russia has, that engages German attention and ambition'.[10]

The smaller democratic states in western and northern Europe were equally unimpressed with the new German–Japanese association. While in Belgium it was anticipated that the Anti-Comintern Pact would serve no purpose other than to encourage the formation of opposing ideological blocs, a point well illustrated by the *Libre Belge*, which saw in it little more than a riposte to the Franco–Soviet alliance, the Dutch minister in Berlin, Count Limburg-Stirum, spoke for many of the minor powers when he expressed concern lest the signatories use the pact to legitimize their interference in the internal affairs of other countries.[11] Equally, the *Stockholms-Tidningen* reflected a view heard in many quarters, namely that the Germans and Japanese would surely find it difficult to 'persuade the world that they are so seriously threatened by Communist revolutionary activities that they need each other's assistance to avert the peril'. Sweden's basic position on the possibility of its alignment with any bloc of powers had recently been made clear by the statement of its foreign minister, Rickard Sandler, that Sweden had 'no reason to buy foreign assistance at the price of her independence'.[12] The Finnish attitude was much the same, not least because of Finland's strong attachment to the so-called 'third European bloc', the group of democratic powers that looked to Britain for leadership within the framework of the League of Nations. The British minister in Helsingfors reported on 28 November that moderate opinion in Finland 'entirely disapproved' of the Anti-Comintern Pact, which was regarded as unnecessarily provocative towards the USSR, a particularly telling judgement in view of Finland's own intense hostility to the Soviet Union. As if to stress the point, the Finnish Academic Karelian League immediately cancelled the proposed visit to Finland of Dr Adolf Ehrt, head of the Antikomintern organization, who had been invited to address an audience on the menace of Bolshevism.[13]

By virtue of their geographical, diplomatic and economic situation the reaction of the states of central Europe to the Anti-Comintern Pact was necessarily cautious. More than most the central Europeans had felt the force of Hitler's insistence that the Spanish Civil War had divided Europe into two ideological blocs, if only because they effectively constituted the line of division. On the one hand, increasingly dependent on German trade and mindful of the changes to the strategic balance occasioned by the remilitarization of the Rhineland, on the other fearful of antagonizing the USSR, the events of 1936, particularly the developments in France and Spain, had caused a good measure of unease in central Europe, a fact Hitler was clearly intent on exploiting to the full. One week before the signature of his treaty with Japan the Führer received the Austrian state secretary, Guido Schmidt, to whom he explained his general conception of the European situation in the following terms:

> The historical element of the present and the near future is the fact that in Bolshevism a philosophy with aggressive military tendencies has been created. ... The Bolshevik idea is attempting to dominate the world. ... We shall not and cannot detach ourselves from our European community; for that reason I cannot face with indifference the danger of catastrophes in our neighbouring countries. ... Central Europe is seriously menaced by Bolshevism, and I have been trying to convince the countries of Central Europe again and again that we have no aggressive intentions, but only that of warding off Bolshevism.[14]

The Germans did not seem especially anxious to secure Austria's accession to the Anti-Comintern Pact, though it is understandable that this intention was mooted in the British press in view of the 'gentlemen's agreement' recently arrived at between Berlin and Vienna.[15] It was precisely because of that agreement, however, that Hitler was relatively unconcerned about Austria's position on the Bolshevik menace. The agreement provided for a coordination of Austria's foreign policy with that of Germany and because it marked a further important stage on the evolutionary road to *Anschluss*, once achieved, it would automatically make the question redundant. Besides, having secured an agreement with Schuschnigg that served his purposes for the present, Hitler may have thought it tactically inadvisable to push the Austrian chancellor in a direction that his rival, Prince Starhemberg, only recently expelled from the cabinet following a fierce power struggle, was known to favour. In that sense, though powerless to prevent it and despite the advantages of his agreement with Schuschnigg, Starhemberg's fall might be interpreted as running contrary to the Führer's anti-Soviet plans.

As recently as April 1936 the prince had remarked to an associate that 'in order to conduct the common fight against Bolshevism and in order to know on which side Austria stood if a conflict broke out', he intended to seek an agreement with Germany.[16]

From other states in central and southeast Europe considerably more was expected.[17] The Hungarians were not only Germany's natural allies against Czechoslovakia but also vehemently anti-communist, anti-Slav and anti-Semitic, so their support for the Anti-Comintern Pact, which the press assumed likely, might reasonably have been anticipated. In fact, in recent conversations, including one with Hitler on 24 August, the Hungarian regent, Admiral Horthy, had appeared fully to share the German view of the Bolshevik peril and the need for like-minded countries to unite against it.[18]

Welcoming the declaration of the Rome–Berlin Axis as a positive development for Hungary, Horthy's foreign minister, Kálmán de Kánya, went so far as to declare to Ciano only days before the Anti-Comintern Pact was signed that 'Hungary is always willing, even in the international field, to take up a position openly alongside the anti-Communist states'.[19]

In practice, however, that proved not to be the case. So long as the USSR did not try to influence events beyond its borders, the Hungarians preferred a Soviet to a tsarist regime in Moscow, for the latter, they feared, 'might become the rallying point and at the same time the instigator of brutal and uncoercible Panslavism [sic]'.[20] It was more serious that Hungary seemed unable to subordinate its local rivalries to the greater goal. With the notable exception of its agitation against Czechoslovakia, which as an ally of the Soviet Union was in any case destined to perish, Hitler disapproved of Hungary's propensity to 'get lost in matters of minor political importance'. He understood the Hungarian mentality completely, he told Guido Schmidt, but Germany too had been compelled 'to make a serious renunciation with a view to loftier political reason', a duty he regarded as 'something like a collective responsibility for Europe'. He thus 'did not consider it opportune if Budapest now raises claims for revision in every direction', more especially since 'Rumania and Yugoslavia are more important to me as outposts against Bolshevism than if they were weakened by war or threats of war'.[21] The following month Hitler repeated these points to

Nicholas de Kozma, the Hungarian minister of the interior. 'I perceive that Europe is moving toward a gigantic conflict', he began on familiar lines, 'and in preparation for this development I am attempting to oppose Bolshevism with a common front'. To that end he had already secured understandings with Italy and Japan, and he was now seeking to recruit the states of central Europe, not least because, compared with 'this impending world catastrophe, all other problems are dwarfed'. It was time to drop petty rivalries, for, in view of the Bolshevik menace:

> it must be our aim to forge a Central European bloc that would include beside Italy and ourselves, Austria, Hungary, Rumania, Poland, Yugoslavia and also the Baltic States. It would be a very good thing if we were to concentrate on this aim and postpone other aspirations until later. What is decisive is political success.[22]

The Romanians, to whom similar arguments were put,[23] were focused equally sharply on revisionism, not least on the part of Hungary, whose leader had described them to Ciano as 'jackals',[24] and it was not so much fear of Bolshevism as the anxieties thus generated that lay behind King Carol's approaches to Hitler in the autumn of 1936. As far as the antagonism between Russia and Germany was concerned, Romania, far from wishing to take sides, sought to maintain a balance between the two, an aspiration that met with some success until well into 1940.[25]

Of all the continental powers, with the possible exception of Italy, the Germans primarily looked to Poland for support in their efforts to construct a front against the USSR. Following the auspicious start that had been made through the non-aggression treaty of 1934, the Anti-Comintern Pact naturally brought this issue once more into sharper focus. In what was presumably a preliminary sounding of Polish opinion only a few days before the signature of the Anti-Comintern Pact, the German ambassador in Warsaw, Helmuth von Moltke, who had received his instructions directly from Hitler, told the Polish foreign minister, Josef Beck, that the Führer hoped for a continuation of the German–Polish understanding, one of the 'basic tenets' of German foreign policy as he described it, not least because of the need for a common defence against the 'progressive Bolshevization of Europe'. Beck's reply, however, was disappointing, and mirrored in all essentials the negative response given three months earlier to a Japanese suggestion that Poland might wish to participate in an eventual agreement directed against communism. Naturally Poland shared the German chancellor's attitude, Beck assured the ambassador, but 'Poland's geographical position forced her to exercise a certain restraint in order to avoid diplomatic complications with her Eastern neighbour.'[26] The inspector general of the Polish armed forces, Marshal Rydz-Smigly, repeated as much to von Moltke on 25 November. When their conversation turned to events in Spain, thus providing von Moltke with the opportunity once more to broach Hitler's views on the Bolshevik danger in Europe, Rydz-Smigly 'displayed a keen interest and stated that he took the same view on this question and could not understand how certain countries – he was obviously referring to Britain – failed to recognize the full extent of the danger'.

In matters of national defence each country had to take its own interests into account. This explained why Germany was able to pursue a more stridently anti-Bolshevik policy than Poland, which was 'forced to observe greater restraint on account of her long frontier with Soviet Russia'. The concluding assurance that 'Poland would never be found in the Bolshevik camp' must have come as cold comfort to Hitler whose purposes would hardly be served by Warsaw's passive-defensive attitude towards the USSR.[27] It nonetheless appeared to be confirmed when two days later the Poles issued a formal declaration dismissing the possibility of their acceding to the Anti-Comintern Pact, 'however great the temptation might be'.[28] Although the possible accession of Poland remained a subject of discussion between the Germans and the Japanese until 1939, the Polish leaders, conscious of their vulnerability vis-à-vis the USSR, could not be moved from the position they adopted in November 1936, a fact that ultimately sealed their fate.

In Britain, which since the 1920s had been the most crucial factor in Hitler's planned mobilization of the powers against Russia, and thus the area in which he was most anxious to succeed, the reaction to the Anti-Comintern Pact was perhaps the greatest disappointment of all, particularly given that the express purpose of Ribbentrop's mission as ambassador to London was to secure a

British signature to the treaty. Although the outbreak of the Spanish Civil War had encouraged Hitler to hope that Britain might yet be persuaded of his view of the Bolshevik threat, the policy of non-intervention pursued by London caused a considerable amount of alarm in Berlin where it was interpreted as a symptom of increasing Bolshevik influences.[29] By September 1936 Hitler had grown increasingly critical of British blindness to the 'red menace', a fact he demonstrated during the Nuremberg rally with his cutting reference to 'Robinson Crusoe island',[30] so much so that the future of Anglo–German relations was effectively seen to depend on Britain's attitude towards developments in Spain. As Basil Newton, chargé d'affaires at the British embassy in Berlin, wrote to Eden on 3 September, there were already signs of disappointment in Nazi circles with regard to relations with Britain:

> not only because Anglo–German friendship has made so little progress, but because the reality of the Bolshevik peril cannot apparently be brought home to the average English-man. It is, however, felt that events are rapidly leading to a division of Europe into Bolshevik and anti-Bolshevik camps. When this situation arises, England will have to make her choice, and, it is hoped, the correct choice.[31]

In this atmosphere Ribbentrop arrived in London on 25 October, two days after the Anti-Comintern Pact had been initialled, hopeful, though perhaps not over confident, that his mission might succeed.[32] The anti-communist message, however, and the emphasis the new ambassador placed on the need for an Anglo–German combination to combat it, found few supporters in Britain. The unfortunate public denunciation of Bolshevism Ribbentrop delivered at Victoria station on the day of his arrival alienated even moderate opinion, while in official circles the idea of an ideological crusade found no echo whatsoever, not least because sanctioning and supporting any such initiative would automatically signify a renunciation of the 'general settlement', which remained the central British goal in Europe. Far from encouraging cooperation with Germany, the Anti-Comintern Pact met with considerable suspicion in both the British press and Whitehall, where, despite a tendency to ridicule the agreement as being both unnecessary and, as far as

Japan was concerned, entirely counterproductive, there was a general suspicion that it was at least as inimical to the interests of the British Empire, particularly in the Far East, as it was to those of the USSR.[33] Indeed, this attitude ran so deep that even before the Anti-Comintern Pact had time to make an impact the Germans were producing reassuring articles in their press disclaiming any intention to impair Anglo–Japanese relations and insisting, on the contrary, that Germany favoured improved relations between Britain, Italy and Japan, which could only work for the benefit of Europe as a whole.[34] Nevertheless, the condemnatory tone of the official British communiqué hardly boded well for German hopes of recruiting Great Britain to the ranks of the Anti-Comintern powers. 'So far as the British Government are concerned,' it read, 'we have explicitly deprecated any tendency to divide the world into conflicting camps, especially on ideological grounds, and our policy continues to be to promote as far as possible friendly relations between all nations.'[35]

Despite the fanfares that marked the launch of the Anti-Comintern Pact, and contrary to the hopes entertained in Germany and indeed Japan that it would arouse considerable interest among other powers, it was clear that within weeks of its signature the German–Japanese treaty had proved an abject failure. Not only did the vast majority of European states greet it with reserve and suspicion, but even Italy and nationalist Spain, with whom Germany was ostensibly cooperating in the Spanish Civil War, could hardly be said to have reacted with particular enthusiasm. Indeed, the attitude of Mussolini and Franco, coupled with the relatively lukewarm reception accorded the Anti-Comintern Pact by Japanese opinion, where there were anxieties about its effect on relations with Britain and the USA, considerably weakened its impact.

Naturally, both Il Duce and the Caudillo professed to welcome the pact as a significant advance in the fight against Bolshevism, but neither appeared to be in any hurry to join its ranks. Approached by the Germans on this issue in early 1937, Ciano parried the overture with assurances that Italy was exploring the possibility of its own separate agreement with Japan.[36] For his part Franco, who was in any case engaged in unspoken competition with Hitler for the leading role in the European crusade against Bolshevism,[37] surprised the Germans by moving closer to Italy, with which in

November 1936 he signed a secret agreement that appeared to preclude any similar arrangement with Germany. From the German perspective it was incongruous in view of recent events, notably the conclusion of the Anti-Comintern Pact and recognition of Franco as the undisputed head of the Spanish state, to discover from the protocol of the Italo–Spanish treaty that Mussolini and Franco were 'united in the common fight against communism, which at this moment is threatening the peace and security of Europe more than ever',[38] yet to find both somewhat apathetic about the prospect of joining Germany and Japan in the same struggle.

Reviewing the international situation as the year drew to a close, a senior official in the British Foreign Office went so far as to suggest that the Anti-Comintern Pact, which had clearly failed in its original purpose, represented a political victory for the Soviet government, a conclusion which, in view of the evidence, is difficult to contest. With his crusade against communism, noted Orme Sargent:

> Hitler has already secured a little success with his Japanese treaty, but it is a very fragile success and unless it is extended it looks as if the effect will soon wear off. Hitler must be said to have definitely failed in his original project, which was to pose as the saviour of European civilization and to rally Europe round him.[39]

Chapter 8
Politics and Propaganda in the 'Year of Awareness', 1937

Although it was clear by the end of 1936 that the Anti-Comintern Pact had failed to arouse significant international support for Germany's mission to protect the civilized world from the perils of Soviet communism, that failure does not appear to have deflected Hitler from his original purpose, or indeed to have diminished the prominence accorded to anti-Bolshevism in German diplomacy and propaganda. Such was the concentration on that issue at the turn of the year that the US ambassador in Berlin could write to the secretary of state that 'practically all of Germany's political energy and effort expended in pursuit of her foreign policy [is] now centred in anti-communism'. The Christmas holidays, Dodd explained, had given the German political leadership ample opportunity to comment on 'the most important phase of Nazi foreign policy at the moment'. On Christmas Eve, for example, Rudolf Hess had made a radio broadcast praising Hitler's foresight and rationalizing the Anti-Comintern Pact and Rome–Berlin Axis as 'new and important steps to make Germany and the world secure against Bolshevism', while seven days later it had been Joseph Goebbels's turn to applaud the German and Japanese governments for their 'untiring and consistent' resistance to Bolshevik machinations.[1]

The general tenor of the messages Hess and Goebbels broadcast was repeated in Hitler's proclamation to the NSDAP that marked the beginning of its fourth year in power. 'The Führer issues a marvellous new year call to the Party,' enthused the Reich propaganda minister on 2 January 1937. 'Relentless struggle against Bolshevism.'[2] Intended largely for internal consumption, this procla-

122

mation, which spoke of a world 'more than ever menaced by the shadow of a severe international peril', and emphasized Germany's consequent role as a 'bulwark of European culture and civilization',[3] largely set the tone for much of the propaganda that issued from Berlin over the following months. The German campaign against Bolshevism, which, as Hess had suggested, had achieved a certain cohesion by virtue of Berlin's friendships with Rome and Tokyo, now passed from deeds to a greater concentration on persuasion and propaganda, for which there are essentially two explanations. First, the initial reaction of Britain, Poland and Italy to the conclusion of the Anti-Comintern Pact demonstrated that none of the major powers Germany had envisaged as potential recruits to the agreement was yet prepared to consider that option seriously, a fact that made it advisable to tread warily for the time being and to avoid any undue heavy-handedness at the diplomatic level. Second, as John Fox argued in his study of German Far Eastern policy in the 1930s, for the time being the mere existence of the Anti-Comintern Pact was deemed sufficient for Hitler's immediate purposes in that it not only created an international counterbalance to the USSR but also acted as a further means of pressure on the British to fall into line with his plans.[4]

One should nevertheless be wary of attaching undue weight to the Anti-Comintern Pact's tactical function. Indeed, the contemporary evidence suggests that, while the British attitude towards Bolshevism certainly perturbed him, at the beginning of 1937 the same issues that had led to his revelations at the meeting of the German cabinet on 1 December 1936 still dominated Hitler's thoughts. General Kühlenthal, the German military attaché in Paris, had endured three hours of conversation with Hitler following the annual military attachés' conference held in Berlin over the Christmas period. 'It is the Comintern and all its works which seems to obsess Herr Hitler to the exclusion of all else,' he informed his British counterpart shortly afterwards, 'and it is to counter the Comintern that he made the agreement with Japan', an explanation which, perhaps surprisingly, the British Foreign Office accepted at face value. 'As regards his obsession over the Comintern,' noted Rumbold on 20 January 1937, 'I think no one has ever doubted that as far as he himself is concerned it is quite genuine.'[5]

Shortly afterwards the British received what appeared to be a further sign of Hitler's sustained preoccupation with Bolshevism from their own military attaché in Berlin, Colonel Elliot Hotblack, who reported details of an illuminating conversation that had recently taken place between the Führer and an unnamed officer of the German General Staff. Discussing his experiences during the war the officer had remarked how surprised he had been when his regiment, which he had previously considered absolutely reliable, had suddenly embraced the communist philosophy. In reply, Hitler professed to have heard of many such episodes. Indeed, such was the impression they had made on him that, although 'the main-spring of his policy was to protect the German nation against the Bolshevik contagion', he still nevertheless found it 'extremely difficult to judge the state of such a disease, and he doubted if he would be able to trust completely a generation that had been infected in the years before he came to power'. In present circum-stances, however, it was not so much the German internal situation that perturbed him as the foolishness of the Western democracies, which had committed the 'unpardonable crime' of admitting Russia, and thus Bolshevism, into the League of Nations. He was not, he claimed, in the least concerned for the democracies themselves, 'since if they became infected by Bolshevism they thoroughly deserved it', but he feared the 'spread of the disease in the same way that influenza epidemics spread across Europe from one country to another'.[6]

It was not only Hitler and his closest political collaborators, how-ever, who were busying themselves in the first weeks of 1937 with the problems presented by Bolshevik Russia. On 27 January the chancellor and his propaganda minister attended a meeting at Bendlerstrasse at which General von Blomberg, the Reich war minister, made a detailed presentation of a Wehrmacht case study covering the contingency of hostilities between, on the one hand, Germany and its 'fascist allies', an interesting ideological twist on what was presumably a purely military question, and, on the other, the USSR, Czechoslovakia and Lithuania. 'A massive feat of organiz-ation', noted Goebbels approvingly, 'calculated down to the last detail'.[7] That afternoon, possibly inspired by the theme of Blom-berg's address, Hitler spoke at length on German rearmament, the current strength of the Soviet Union, and its unswerving goal to force through world revolution. He hoped to have a further six years to complete his preparations, he announced over lunch, but he would not fail to grasp a favourable opportunity should one present itself earlier. In any case, Germany was growing in strength as each day passed, a fact that certainly did not escape the Russians, whose own 'hysterical' activities simply served to swell the ranks of Germany's friends, notably in the cases of Romania and Yugoslavia, and especially in that of Poland.[8]

Three days later Hitler made his customary address to the Reichstag, speaking for just under three hours and concentrating for a considerable part of that time on the situation in Spain and, inevitably, on the wider context of the Bolshevik threat both to the Reich and to the wider international community. A crucial feature of this speech, already reflected in Hotblack's report, was the German leader's obvious irritation with the failure of the British to grasp the wider significance of what was happening in Spain, which in turn he considered symptomatic of their dangerous misreading of the Bolshevik phenomenon as a whole. 'At issue here is not a special form of life indigenous to, let us say, the Russian people,' he declared.

> Rather it is the Bolshevist goal of world revolution. The fact that the honourable Foreign Secretary Eden refuses to see Bolshevism as we see it is perhaps related to Great Britain's location, perhaps to some other experiences of which we have no knowledge. I do, however, hold that we speak of these things not as theoreticians, one cannot accuse us of being insincere in our conviction. For Mr Eden, Bolshevism is perhaps something sitting in Moscow; for us, however, Bolshevism is a plague against which we have been forced to defend ourselves in a bloody fight, a plague which has attempted to make of our country the same desert it has made of Spain. ... National Socialism did not seek contact with Bolshevism in Russia; rather, the Jewish international Muscovite Bolshevism attempted to penetrate Germany! And it is still attempting to do so today! And we have fought a difficult battle against this attempt, upholding and thus defending not only the culture of our Volk, but perhaps that of Europe as a whole in the process.[9]

125

Hitler's recent biographer, Ian Kershaw, notes that the German leader made no less than 26 major speeches during 1937 in the course of which 'past achievements were lauded, grandiose future plans proclaimed' and 'the horrors and menace of Bolshevism emphasized'. It was, as Kershaw notes, a time to take stock, to keep a 'watchful eye on the changing world situation'. He also notes importantly that in the Führer's numerous proclamations 'there was no conflict between propaganda and ideology', for the chancellor 'believed what he was saying'.[10] As had been his practice in the past, Hitler did not fail in the course of many of these proclamations to point to the revolutionary plans of his ideological enemies, to declare his solidarity with like-minded nations in opposing communism and, most importantly, to warn others of the threat that faced them from Moscow.

He also continued to instruct and advise foreign visitors on the Bolshevik danger. Shortly before the outbreak of the Sino–Japanese war, for example, Hitler received a delegation of senior Chinese personalities, headed by the minister of finance, Dr Kung, and instructed them on the world revolutionary aims pursued by Russia.[11] Two weeks later it was the turn of Hisashi Ishida, a senior official of the Japanese judiciary, to listen to Hitler's denunciations of the Soviet Union, the 'enemy of Germany and mankind ... with whom there was no possibility of compromise'.[12]

In 1937 there was a different emphasis in some of Hitler's pronouncements on Bolshevism, extending from the straightforward denunciation of the Comintern and USSR to the broader question of Germany's alliance policy, with particular reference to Great Britain. Britain's apparent indifference to the threat posed by Bolshevism, already a feature of Hitler's speeches by late 1936, became a recurrent theme during 1937 in both his public and private statements. Despite his surprise at Britain's policy during the Abyssinian crisis, which he judged as weak and muddled, and the repeated failure of his overtures to London, most recently in the form of Ribbentrop's mission as ambassador, Britain was still a preferred ally against the USSR in the first months of 1937. It increasingly became apparent, as was only logical in view of his ultimate aims and the essentially anti-Soviet purpose of his planned understanding with London, that Britain's view of the events in Spain came to dominate his own attitude towards Anglo–German

126

relations. Speaking to Lord Lothian in May 1937, Hitler frankly outlined his priorities and preferences, professing incredulity at British indifference to what was happening in Spain, and expressing the somewhat coded hope that Britain might yet 'do something more positive to assist the people of Spain'.[13]

In view of the unmistakable thrust of Hitler's remarks it would be unwise to take at face value his assurance during the same conversation that the divergence in view between Britain and Germany over Spain need not represent an insurmountable barrier to an Anglo–German understanding. Indeed, his violent reaction the following month to Britain's refusal to take part in a naval demonstration off Valencia in response to an alleged Spanish republican torpedo attack on a German warship operating in the Mediterranean reveals far more about his preoccupations than the platitude served up to Lothian.[14] Hitler was not the only German leader to wonder at Britain's evident detachment from the Bolshevik danger. In July Göring told the British ambassador that Germany could not afford to see the Bolsheviks established in Spain as it had then to be feared that 'their influence would spread to France and Germany would find herself in the intolerable position of being surrounded by countries taking their cue from Moscow'.[15]

Goebbels too was not idle in this respect. In early February 1937, in the wake of Hitler's criticisms of Eden, the Reich propaganda minister joined issue with the British foreign secretary at a mass rally of 40,000 people in Hamburg. Contemptuously dismissing the desire expressed by Eden not to see Europe divided into two camps, he warned that there was already 'a nation of 180,000,000 people at the frontiers of Europe whose leaders are resolved to draw the other nations into the whirlpool of anarchy'. Alluding to Hitler's September 1936 reference to 'Robinson Crusoe Island', Goebbels further warned that even an island could not remain isolated from the inevitable struggle between communism and the forces of order. There must be no doubt whatsoever that the Soviets desired war 'because they know that only through war can they advance the world revolution'.[16] Some days later he returned to the charge. On 12 February he proclaimed:

> If the Bolshevists conduct propaganda against Germany throughout the world, we shall organize the same sort of

propaganda against them – and we know how to do it. ...
When Mr Eden says 'Let us not divide Europe into two
camps,' I say with the Führer that it has happened already ...
the time is past when one could say 'I am neither pro- nor
anti-Bolshevist.' One has to show one's colours.[17]

Goebbels proved to be as good as his word. On 31 March 1937 he
issued a comprehensive set of guidelines governing future propaganda activities relating to the fight against Bolshevism. The general
focus of German policy, began the Reich propaganda minister, was
the struggle against 'world Bolshevism'; and German propaganda's
main task was to highlight and amplify that fact. Following the
Nazi seizure of power in 1933 Bolshevism in Germany had been
rapidly eradicated, but this did not mean that the danger had been
extinguished. Germany's fight against Bolshevism after 1933, he
noted, had been transferred to the world stage, to the extent that
the task of German propaganda was now not merely to educate the
German people to believe that communism was their deadly enemy,
but also to 'demonstrate to the world that it is the enemy of all
peoples and nations'.

Turning to the form and nature of Bolshevism, Goebbels
denounced it as a purely Jewish doctrine, invented and orchestrated
by Jews, the aim of which was to foment chaos and engineer world
revolution in order ultimately to bring into being 'a world state
under Jewish leadership after the example of the Soviet Union'. For
National Socialists these were self-evident truths; any other
interpretation was simply misguided. Bolshevism was not a specifically Russian phenomenon and Stalin could not be described as the
leader of the Russian people. On the contrary, Bolshevism knew no
state boundaries and had no national identity. It was a 'Jewish'
phenomenon through and through. Accordingly, Stalin was simply
the instrument the Jews used to enslave the Russian people. It was
equally incorrect to say that Bolshevism had abandoned the goal of
world revolution, for world revolution lay at the very core of
Bolshevik doctrine. Bolshevism was not an 'idea' or a 'world view';
it was a form of 'organized crime'. As such, it had to be combated,
and to that end German propaganda must draw attention not only
to the appalling conditions the Bolshevik system imposed on
Russia, but also, with a view to mobilizing further support for the

'united front of anti-Bolshevik states', at whose head stood the German Reich, by stressing the danger of world revolution.[18]

The international anxieties the Spanish Civil War generated provided Goebbels with an excellent focal point upon which to concentrate Germany's anti-Bolshevik propaganda during 1937. The ProMi essentially ran two operations in Spain between which there appears to have been a considerable degree of overlap in terms of activity, but relatively little cooperation or coordination. The first of these, the Sonderstab Köhn, was named after its head, Willi Köhn, a ProMi functionary who had formerly operated as the ministry's representative in South America. It was established in late 1936 at the insistence of Goebbels, with support from Hess and Bohle, to provide political education and propaganda opportunities for the Spanish rebels. As Helmut Michels notes, Köhn's organization was at least partially designed to compete with the Wilhelmstrasse and German war ministry in their dealings with Franco, largely because of Goebbels's conviction that civil servants and soldiers would hardly be in a position to appreciate the ideological dimension of the conflict.[19] The Sonderstab's activities included monitoring the republican press and radio broadcasts, advising Franco's supporters in the same areas, supplying material for use in nationalist propaganda, and offering translation services for German propaganda publications, notably the Antikomintern's *Nachrichtendienst*, which might prove useful to Franco's cause.[20]

The Antikomintern began a long involvement with the Spanish Civil War almost immediately after its outbreak by dispatching a special emissary to Lisbon where, with the assistance of the Portuguese authorities, he arranged for news about developments across the border to be broadcast over the radio and otherwise disseminated by organs of the Portuguese propaganda authorities. This was followed in October 1936 by the publication of the first edition of a special fortnightly Spanish language newssheet, the *Informaciones Antibolcheviques*, subsequently renamed the *Boletin de Informaciones Antikomintern*. Early the following year a special Antikomintern office was established in Salamanca from which a variety of initiatives sprang before its dissolution following Franco's victory in March 1939. These included the collection, collation and distribution of material for general propaganda purposes in Spain, Germany, Latin America, the United States and other European countries, and ranged from exhibitions, publications and radio broadcasts to the compilation of a photograph archive for use by the press and in other anti-Bolshevik literature. The Salamanca agency was also involved in the production of placards, posters, postcards and leaflets, which were either dropped over republican-held areas or distributed in regions retaken from republican forces in an attempt to drum up support and enthusiasm for the nationalists, essentially by describing how appalling conditions had once been and might yet become again unless vigilance was maintained.[21]

The Antikomintern was also the driving force behind a series of special initiatives in Spain ranging from furnishing advice to Franco's director of propaganda at the fighting fronts, the aptly named Major Morales, interrogating International Brigade prisoners held in nationalist concentration camps, the purpose of the exercise being to build up a picture of international involvement in Spain, down to monitoring Soviet press coverage of the civil war and cataloguing refugee accounts of conditions behind the lines.[22] Moreover, apart from its inevitable collaboration with the ProMi, the Antikomintern also worked with other party agencies on Spanish issues, notably Bohle's Auslandsorganisation, which helped finance Antikomintern operations in Spain, and the Dienststelle Ribbentrop, which was keenly interested in the Antikomintern's anti-Bolshevik material, some of which, relating specifically to Soviet involvement in Spain, Ribbentrop personally requested for use at sessions of the London-based Non-Intervention Committee.[23]

Reflecting on its activities in Spain, the Antikomintern looked back with some satisfaction on its achievements. At the outset it had set itself two goals: first, to supply nationalist Spain with material on which to base its anti-Bolshevik propaganda and, in so doing, to create a permanent centre for anti-communist agitation in Spain; second, to engage in extensive anti-Bolshevik propaganda abroad using the events in Spain as a central point of reference. By 1939 the Antikomintern judged it had been successful on both counts; not only had it been widely accepted that the USSR was responsible for the Spanish Civil War, but Spanish nationalist propaganda was centrally rooted in anti-communist arguments, in consequence of which German anti-Bolshevism had received widespread publicity and recognition.[24]

In general, the Antikomintern's work in Spain between 1936 and 1939 appears to have been very similar to, if more extensive than, that of the Sonderstab Köhn, for both organizations supplied the rebels with considerable amounts of literature, 2500 items alone in the case of the Antikomintern, and other propaganda materials. In some ways, however, it is clear that the Antikomintern's work held the greater significance. It had a greater variety of operations in Spain and in early 1938 the Spanish ministry of the interior absorbed the Salamanca office and restructured it along the lines of the Antikomintern central bureau in Berlin. From February 1938 onwards this new agency ran a news service called 'Servicio Antimarxista', and, in a bid to cement ties with Berlin, there followed shortly afterwards discussions towards a formal agreement between the ProMi and Franco's propaganda specialists in the *Delegacion para Prensa y Propaganda*.[25]

Moreover, whereas Köhn's activities were confined to Spain, the Antikomintern was able to exploit the Spanish situation to make propaganda abroad. Its extensive archive of Spanish material provided a source of reference for the German press and formed the basis of numerous German and foreign language publications about Spanish conditions and, inevitably, Soviet culpability, godlessness, terrorism and brutality.[26] Some of this material was incorporated in a major Antikomintern publication on the Spanish Civil War, the *Rotbuch über Spanien*, which was specifically designed to demonstrate that the Bolsheviks had engineered the outbreak of the war in Spain, and contained not only graphic depictions of red atrocities, but also a good deal of evidence documenting the scale and nature of Soviet intervention.[27]

The Antikomintern requested that maximum press coverage be given to the *Rotbuch*, which was widely distributed throughout the various echelons of the NSDAP.[28] It was launched at a press conference on 21 June 1937 attended by Taubert, Rudolf Kommoss, head of the Antikomintern press section, and the chargé d'affaires at the Spanish embassy in Berlin. In his account of the proceedings the DNB correspondent clearly grasped the essential purpose of the *Rotbuch*, which, despite its obvious focus on Spain, was intended to convey a much broader message. 'It is not a civil war in the original sense of the word which is currently tearing Spain apart,' ran his report, 'It is not simply a case of Spaniard fighting Spaniard there, but of a people defending itself against the onslaught of a world revolutionary power.'[29] Following an initial publication run of 50,000, a further 50,000 copies were produced within three months of the book's launch and, according to an Antikomintern review of its activities in Spain, the *Rotbuch* was not only valuable in itself as a comprehensive guide to Soviet complicity in the Spanish Civil War but also served as the basis for many other anti-Bolshevik publications both in Germany and abroad.[30]

Despite its official title, and, indeed, Georg Leibbrandt's definition of its essential purpose,[31] the Antikomintern had never functioned as the Third Reich's counterpoise to the Moscow-based Communist International. From its inception the emphasis had been less on the promotion of National Socialism than on the pursuit of Bolshevism in general, the fundamental aim being to mobilize the German and other nations for the coming showdown with the Soviet Union rather than to cross swords directly with Georgi Dimitrov and his acolytes.[32]

To be sure, *AKND* bulletins and other Antikomintern publications inevitably and frequently targeted the Comintern, but that was only one aspect of the organization's activities, which, as its work in Spain demonstrates, were considerable and diverse. One might reasonably assume that the situation that developed in Spain after 17 July 1936 provided a perfect scenario for a clash between Ehrt and Dimitrov, and the bodies they headed, but ironically nothing of the sort happened. In fact, a profound weakening of the Comintern's position during 1936–37, both internationally and in the Soviet Union, meant that the Antikomintern was in some respects better coordinated and effective of the two organizations.

Already, well before the outbreak of civil war in Spain, and if only in terms of its image abroad, the Comintern appeared to have lost some of its radical edge by adopting a Popular Front strategy at its seventh congress in Moscow in the summer of 1935. This did not mean that it had abandoned its basic goal of world revolution, but the tactical shift it made towards cooperating with other workers' parties and the bourgeoisie undeniably diluted the force and credibility of the Comintern's clarion calls for mass uprisings against the established order, which had in any case fallen on deaf ears across the European continent. This was nowhere more apparent than in largely rural Spain where the Comintern's heavy-handed approach, coupled with its promotion of 'inappropriate and sectarian' tactics and policies, only succeeded in weakening the Spanish Communist Party and hastening its marginalization during the 1920s and early 1930s.[33]

When the initial disturbances broke out in July 1936, the Comintern was taken completely by surprise. Moreover, it viewed the prospect of a protracted armed struggle with some reserve, for while the domestic situation in Spain was thought to be developing favourably from a revolutionary perspective, conditions were not yet ripe enough to give any potential uprising a reasonable chance of success. Nevertheless, Dimitrov began to mobilize the Comintern for action and, in August–September 1936, the first moves were made to assist the republicans with funds and advisers, and to organize counterrevolutionary forces in the shape of the famous International Brigades. Before long, however, the Comintern's work in Spain effectively ground to a halt. Not only was its own communication network in the Iberian peninsula fragmented and unsynchronized,[34] which hardly augurs well in a war with numerous and shifting fighting fronts, but Stalin's attitude and actions also undermined and destroyed the prospects of a Comintern success in Spain.

Franco's rebellion presented the Soviet leaders with a dilemma both from the ideological point of view and from that of practical politics, for while, on the one hand, it represented an opportunity to fight 'fascism' and assist like-minded revolutionaries, whose enemies were being openly supported by Germany and Italy, on the other it threatened to involve the USSR in untimely international complications. Rejecting Litvinov's advice to shore up the Soviet defence system by seeking to extend collective security, Stalin chose to tread a wary path at first, and was anxious not to antagonize either the Western powers or Germany for fear of repercussions in eastern Europe. If anything, by the turn of 1936–37 the Soviet leader seemed interested in exploring the possibility of improving relations with the Nazis and, with this in mind, the head of the Soviet trade delegation in Berlin, David Kandelaki, made a further approach to the president of the *Reichsbank* and German minister for economics, Hjalmar Schacht.[35]

This cautiousness in Soviet foreign policy was regrettable from

the Comintern's point of view, for it hardly smacked of revolutionary zeal, but it paled into insignificance compared with the
decimation the 'Great Terror' of the mid-1930s wrought within the
organization. Within weeks of the show trials of Zinoviev and
Kamenev opening in August 1936, the witch hunt for 'Trotskyist'
deviants had spread to the Comintern, leading ultimately to what
one authority termed a 'genocide' within its ranks.[36] Although the
Comintern had already been shaken by a wave of arrests and
denunciations in the early 1930s, it had escaped relatively intact
and unscathed. It would not be so lucky during the 'Great Terror',
however, when it is estimated that more than two hundred of its
officials and tens of thousands of foreign communists and political
émigrés living in Russia fell victim to Stalin's paranoia. Thus, in
Spain, where it might have expected to meet an opponent fiercely
committed to a diametrically opposed cause, the Antikomintern
found itself confronted by a fratricidal and terrorized adversary in
considerable disarray, whose functionaries were too paralysed by
the fear of denunciation, and thus too concerned with their own
affairs, to offer a sustained and vigorous resistance to its anti-
Bolshevik message.[37]

Latin America was another important area of Antikomintern
activity during 1937, with links either forged or further developed
with Uruguay, Venezuela and Brazil in particular. The year also saw
a good deal of coverage in the Antikomintern's *Nachrichtendienst* of
Latin American issues, with a series of individual articles covering
Argentina, Brazil, Mexico and Bolivia, followed in December by an
alarmist piece supposedly revealing Bolshevik plans to destabilize
the whole of South America.[38] By 1936 the Antikomintern had
already secured what appears to have been its first real foothold in
that part of the world with the establishment of an 'anti-communist
office' in Montevideo, which the Uruguayan authorities sponsored
and approved, and the Antikomintern furnished with funds and
extensive propaganda materials.[39] From this base, argued Ehrt's
close collaborator, Alfred Gielen, it might eventually be possible to
coordinate an anti-Bolshevik campaign across the whole of South
America and, ultimately, to 'integrate the Latin American states into
the anti-Soviet front under our leadership'.[40]

Although this aspiration proved wildly optimistic, the Antikomintern had a further opportunity to influence the Uruguayan cam-

paign against Bolshevism the following April with the creation of the *Frente Anticommunistica Nacional* and an immediate request for literature and other resources from Antikomintern headquarters in Berlin. In Venezuela, where a similar anti-communist organization had been founded in 1936 in response to the planned merger of several leftist parties, progress was more limited. However, through contacts established between the Antikomintern and the Venezuelan general-consul in Berlin, Dr Trujillo, moves were undertaken to forge links between the German and Venezuelan press, quite clearly, in the German case, in the hope of exercising anti-Bolshevik influence in Caracas. By 1938, after consultations between the Antikomintern and a representative of the Venezuelan regime, Señor Ortega-Martinez, Berlin was supplying substantial amounts of anti-Bolshevik literature to the latter who in October was appointed director of the *Centro de Colaboración y Servicio Social*. Antikomintern communications described this body as the 'official anti-Communist office of the Venezuelan Government' and, as in the cases of Uruguay and Brazil, it was heavily dependent on the Antikomintern for material.[41]

It was in Brazil that the Antikomintern's greatest hopes lay. It was where the brunt of its South American activity was engaged, but where ultimately it encountered its most bitter disappointments. Contemporary documents indicate that the Antikomintern first showed an interest in Brazil after the failure of the communist uprisings in the northern provinces in November 1935. Following this a good deal of progress was made, or at least claimed, in both promoting anti-Bolshevism *per se* and, more importantly, in ensuring that German influence was paramount in the nature and direction of anti-communist propaganda. Not only were Antikomintern publications translated into Portuguese for distribution in Brazil and serialization in provincial newspapers, but the organization was also centrally involved in launching a weekly anti-communist newspaper, simply called *Anti-Komintern*. Its first edition appeared in late May 1937 following lengthy negotiations with the Brazilian ministry of propaganda.[42]

A further important development in Brazil, which the Antikomintern assisted, came five months later with the establishment of the 'Brazilian League for the Protection of Society against Communism'; it held its first mass rally in Rio de Janeiro on 31 October. The

founding of this organization, noted Dohms, corresponded precisely to the original intentions of the Antikomintern in its dealings
with Brazil, and could therefore be considered 'a complete success
for our work'.[43] By the close of 1937 the Antikomintern had good
grounds to be satisfied with its work in Brazil; even the head of
state, General Getúlio Vargas, had requested its assistance in
connection with an intended series of radio broadcasts on anti-
Bolshevism.[44]

Nevertheless, all this positive activity failed to translate into any
political advantage. The Brazilians were quite prepared to avail
themselves of Antikomintern material and to receive instruction on
the techniques of propaganda, but this was designed only to
enhance their own role as the champions of anti-Bolshevism among
the South American states. Although the possible accession of
Brazil to the Anti-Comintern Pact remained a subject of discussion
in Berlin, and a prospect in which the Japanese showed considerable interest, Vargas had no intention whatsoever of becoming
party to the agreement. Brazil, like other Latin American countries
that were opposed to Bolshevism, found that the new character of
the Anti-Comintern Pact following the accession of Italy made
association with it a less attractive prospect because of the probable
reactions in Britain and the United States.

Apart from its considerable activities in Spain, which absorbed
most of its energies, and the expansion of its initiatives in South
America, the Antikomintern continued to be engaged with the
promotion of anti-Bolshevism in western Europe, to which purpose
it organized several exhibitions held in foreign capitals, including a
fairly successful event in Britain in February 1937.[45] More importantly, especially in view of the general aims of German diplomacy,
and with particular reference to policy towards Britain, the
Antikomintern echoed through its *Nachrichtendienst* the concerns
that German political leaders continued to express about the
Bolshevik threat to the British Empire. In its June 1937 issue, for
example, it carried an article entitled 'Red Imperialism Threatens
India', accusing Moscow of seeking to exploit the successes of the
Congress Party, and naming the president of the Indian National
Congress, Pandit Nehru, a 'puppet of Moscow'. India was not
immune to the menace of Bolshevism, warned the article in conclusion, and it was to be hoped that the increasingly obvious signs

that it was being prepared for revolution would soon 'open the eyes of the authorities to the seriousness of the situation'.[46]

In its final major venture in 1937, namely the organization of the world's first anti-communist congress, the Antikomintern experienced a considerable setback. At the Feldafing meeting, which the Antikomintern had organized in November 1936, it was decided to establish an office to coordinate preparations for a larger public gathering through the various international anti-Bolshevik organizations with which the Antikomintern maintained regular contact. Although the subsequent 'Organization Bureau for the First Anti-Communist World Congress' was ostensibly unaffiliated to any state, evidence from Antikomintern files reveals that it was effectively an adjunct of that body and all along secretly run by the Germans.[47]

Due to the paucity of documentation it is impossible to discover the nature and extent of the preparations that were in fact made for the planned congress. Indeed, from the statements the chairman of the 'Organization Bureau', Nils von Bahr, made in April 1937 in a supposed press 'interview' – in reality a written statement he simply delivered to the Associated Press and DNB offices – it might almost be inferred that holding the congress was secondary to the aim of publicizing the cause, which, in view of the elaborate preparations envisaged, would inevitably be assured.[48] Indeed, the planned 'world congress' suffered the same fate as the 'First Ibero-American Anti-Communist Congress' in that neither was ever convened.[49]

At first glance this seems curious given that by the spring of 1937 progress appears to have been more than satisfactory. In March Taubert had informed the Wilhelmstrasse that Hitler had already given his approval for the congress to go ahead;[50] the following month the Antikomintern launched a new publication, the *Contra Comintern*, the first issue of which carried von Bahr's aforementioned press statement, once more delivered in the form of an interview, advertising the fact that the preparatory work was proceeding apace.[51] Within three weeks, however, Hitler had evidently not only withdrawn his support but insisted that the Congress take place outside Germany and that no German government agency should attend it.[52]

The reasons for this decision cannot be established with any certainty, but they are likely to be connected with Hitler's personal doubts about the reliability and discretion of some of the individuals involved in the congress scheme, which was largely being run by low-level party functionaries.[53] Perhaps, more importantly, he was also frustrated at the unprecedented amount of political infighting that had followed the signature of the German–Japanese Anti-Comintern Pact in 1936. These bitter disputes, involving mainly the foreign ministry, Gestapo, APA and Dienststelle Ribbentrop, were fought over issues of authority and competency, and centred on two related problems. The first was the question of who exercised supreme authority in the conduct of Germany's anti-Bolshevik activities, which extended even to the point of bickering about who was responsible for translating into Russian speeches made by party leaders at the 1936 Nuremberg rally.[54] The second was a problem caused by the conduct of von Raumer when, in pursuit of an Italian accession to the Anti-Comintern Pact, he had visited Rome in February 1937 and engaged in negotiations with the Italian leaders without informing the German ambassador. Both Hassell and Neurath were understandably enraged at this development, and the ensuing dispute had a further edge to it given that Ribbentrop and Neurath were diametrically opposed on the whole issue of the Anti-Comintern Pact.

Typically, Hitler preferred to impose compromise solutions that satisfied no one and only ensured that the same problems would re-emerge later. Thus, in so far as the rivalry between Neurath and Ribbentrop was concerned, the chancellor forbade von Raumer to undertake any further initiatives along the lines of his visit to Rome, yet by the same token continued to support Ribbentrop in his anti-Bolshevik activities. To ensure no further confusion on the broader issue, he appears also to have revived an idea that had first occurred to him in the autumn of 1936 to make Rosenberg his 'Commissioner against World Bolshevism'. This much is implied in Neurath's statement to Raumer on 23 April 1937 that in future the 'combating of communism and Russian Bolshevism is to be done through Reichsleiter Alfred Rosenberg'.[55] Although subsequent developments demonstrate that an official appointment to this effect was never made, it would be characteristic of Hitler to have silenced Neurath's protests through a suitable inference that it might be. Several months later, Rosenberg and Ribbentrop were still engaged in fairly acrimonious discussions on the precise delineation of their respective spheres of activity in connection with the fight against Bolshevism.[56]

On the diplomatic front the German campaign against Bolshevism appeared to receive a considerable boost in November 1937 when Italy finally acceded to the Anti-Comintern Pact. Already earmarked as a prospective partner against the Bolsheviks while the original agreement was being negotiated, Italy had first been approached on this question in February 1937 when, on Ribbentrop's instructions, Raumer had visited Rome to sound out the views of Mussolini and Ciano. Their reaction was discouraging to say the least. Clearly with one eye on the possible development of the agreement just concluded with Britain concerning the status quo in the Mediterranean, the Italians professed to be interested in the German proposal but stalled Raumer's approach with a series of reservations, which, according to Ciano, could nevertheless be sorted out over the following months. At the same time the Japanese had approached the Italians with the idea of a separate bilateral Italo–Japanese treaty on the lines of the original Anti-Comintern Pact. When in the autumn of 1937 this latter agreement appeared likely to materialize, Ribbentrop, by that time thoroughly disillusioned with the idea of an Anglo–German understanding and hoping to construct an alliance principally against Britain, seized the initiative and swiftly arranged for Italian accession to the German–Japanese treaty.[57]

The international reaction to this widely predicted development was almost uniformly negative, not least as it was interpreted as having transferred the focus of the Anti-Comintern Pact from the Soviet Union to the Western powers, particularly Britain. As the US ambassador to Tokyo, Joseph Grew, put it, anti-communism was merely a 'banner' under which the dissatisfied powers were aligning themselves. As a result of the new combination the threat to Britain was 'very real and immediately apparent upon reflection that with the addition of Japan to the Rome–Berlin Axis the lifeline of the British Empire is threatened from the North Sea through the Mediterranean and beyond Singapore'.[58] As was only to be expected, the Germans hotly denied any such intention, Göring even going so far as to explain to Henderson that the very involvement of the German ambassador to London surely demonstrated that the British had nothing to fear, to which Henderson could only reply that 'it was a mistake to keep harping on about Communism in England where it was comparatively innocuous.'[59]

By the time of Italy's accession to the Anti-Comintern Pact Hitler was forced to admit this latter point, which he typically explained in terms of the advances made by Judeo–Bolshevik influence in London.[60] The autumn and early winter of 1937 was indeed a time of considerable disappointment and frustration for the German leader whose plans to recruit both Britain and Poland to the Anti-Comintern Pact had badly misfired. Recognizing that, with Britain in particular, little was now to be done, a new note had featured in Hitler's ritual diatribes against Bolshevism during the 1937 Nuremberg rally, where his denunciations of democracy recalled to mind earlier musings about the instruments employed by the Jews in their attempts to impose their own dictatorship on the world. As the American ambassador in Berlin put it, for all the invective against Bolshevism, the 1937 party rally had seen:

> as much time … devoted to criticism of democracy as to criticism of communism, [with the result that] whereas in the beginning Nazi creed envisaged only a conflict between Bolshevism and National Socialism, the scope of political interests opposed by a united fascism has broadened and now rather clearly encompasses not only communism but democracy as well.[61]

Time would tell what impact these developments would have on the future course of German foreign policy, and in particular whether the attacks on democracy denoted any weakening in, or indeed broadening of, the German commitment against Bolshevism. It is surely significant that by the winter of 1937–38 Hitler, Ribbentrop and an influential section of the NSDAP all seemed more preoccupied with Britain rather than Russia.[62] Perhaps now Hitler's crusade against Bolshevism would finally be revealed in what many considered to be its true colours: as a tactical smokescreen to confuse and confound the supporters of the status quo, behind which lay nothing more than a programme of German territorial conquest.

Chapter 9
The Ebb and Flow of Anti-Bolshevism, 1938–39

During the period 1938 to 1941, the years of the Nazi regime's greatest foreign and military triumphs, some of which were achieved in partnership with the despised Soviet Union, it might plausibly be argued that, despite all the denunciations, appeals and warnings against the supposed Bolshevik threat, Hitler finally revealed himself as the supreme opportunist in matters of diplomacy, although that in itself need not necessarily preclude an ideological dimension to his foreign policy. Indeed, it might appear that from the winter of 1937–38 onwards the German campaign against Bolshevism ground to an abrupt halt. This was because on the one hand a series of unexpected crises arose that had to be addressed and on the other the failure of German policy towards Britain meant that Hitler was forced to adjust his original intentions towards that power. Yet, a strong case can also be made to demonstrate that, although anti-Bolshevism *per se* undeniably took a back seat in comparison with the emphasis attached to it in earlier years, especially, in the context of 1938–39, in relation to considerations, however insincerely advanced, of national self-determination, it was used periodically for tactical purposes, notably during the Munich crisis, in pursuit of the broader aim of positioning Germany for what in 1940 Hitler reputedly termed the 'great and real task – the conflict with Bolshevism' in which – self evidently – ideological factors played a significant role.[1]

Part of the problem in placing anti-Bolshevism in the general context of German policy, and of Hitler's long-term aims during the years 1938–39, is the significance that is justifiably accorded to the meeting he held with his senior military and diplomatic advisers at the Reich Chancellery on 5 November 1937, the so-called Hossbach Conference.[2] I naturally do not intend to dispute the general importance of that gathering for any understanding of Hitler's ultimate aims for Germany in Europe or the means through which, in certain eventualities, he would seek to achieve them. Nevertheless, due to the central position the Hossbach Conference occupies in the historiography,[3] coupled with the fact that during 1938–39 Hitler undeniably had to adjust to a series of events not entirely of his own making, other aspects of German policy can become obscured, overshadowed or even ignored.

The central question arising from the Hossbach Conference in the context of this study concerns Hitler's failure at any point in the proceedings to refer specifically to Bolshevism and other issues relating to ideological struggle, and his silence on the planned seizure of vast tracts of land in the USSR. Given the purpose of the conference, however, or rather the way Hitler's monologue developed according to the record, these failings can hardly be considered particularly surprising, precisely because he was speaking about the realization of his immediate aims, namely the preliminary objectives that had to be secured before the real quest for *Lebensraum* began, and the risks that Germany could afford to run in pursuit of them. Despite the omission of any reference to Bolshevism, the Hossbach Conference demonstrated nothing if not the consistency of Hitler's view that Germany required large-scale territorial expansion to secure its future, for which the absorption of Austria and Czechoslovakia, the chief focus of Hitler's remarks, would be necessary prerequisites. In this sense any specific reference to the USSR or to the ideological bases of the envisaged conflict with Russia would have been superfluous. They would probably only have further alarmed Neurath, Blomberg and Fritsch who were already sufficiently anxious about Hitler's assessment of the probable reaction of Britain and France in the event of German aggression in central Europe. Moreover, from Hitler's statement that Germany, having improved its strategic situation, would proceed to solve the *Lebensraum* problem by 1943–45 at the latest, it is not as if they could have been left in any doubt about the scale of what was intended, or that they could have interpreted the totality of his aims as being limited to the annexation of Austria and Czechoslovakia.

In this context it is important to note that both before and after the events of 5 November the Führer reinforced his message about the plague of Bolshevism, the folly of those who underestimated it and, almost now as an afterthought, the need for European solidarity against it. During his closing speech at the Nuremberg rally on 13 September, for example, Hitler reiterated and reinforced much of what his propaganda minister had said in his own address, which, in the eyes of one German journalist, had marked the onset of the 'final struggle' with Bolshevism, the destruction of which remained Germany's 'world mission'.[4] Both Goebbels and Hitler were undeniably critical of democracy in their speeches, but it is crucial to note that the criticisms were linked to the continued failure of the Western powers to acknowledge the extent of the threat facing them and their failure to appreciate Germany's services as a bulwark against the USSR. In the circumstances, this was clearly a reference to Britain.

Congratulating his movement on its success in making the Reich immune from Bolshevik infiltration, Hitler noted how this had set Germany aside from the 'supposed' victors of the First World War who had since fallen victim to 'the creeping poison of internal dissolution'. It was as well that Germany was strong in present circumstances because, with Italy, it stood at the forefront in a struggle against a 'veritable world sickness', a 'plague which devastates whole peoples'. Hitler was highly critical of the 'wilful blindness' of those who continued to deny or ignore the threat from Moscow and, in terms redolent of the preamble to his memorandum on the four-year plan of August 1936, stated that much as the democracies might like to wash their hands of communism, 'concern themselves with Communism they must one of these days' otherwise their political systems would 'in one way or another ... fall in ruins'. Europe constituted a community of nations, he averred, and it would stand or fall as such in the face of the 'poisonous infection' of Bolshevism. Having set down its roots in Russia following its decimation of the Germanic elite, 'Jewish Bolshevism' had established 'a base of operations and a bridgehead from which it can attempt further conquests'. As such, the problem was thus 'no longer confined to Russia'; it had become a 'world question which must be determined in one way or another'. Germany was not about to permit the progress of Bolshevism to

143

destroy it politically and economically – nor should other countries, warned Hitler, appearing once more to urge the European
states to stand together in the face of the mounting dangers.
Germany, he continued, had no wish to isolate itself; on the
contrary, it was anxious to cooperate with those who similarly
aspired to the development of a true European community. By the
same token, however, the Reich categorically refused to be 'united
with those whose programme is the destruction of Europe and who
make no secret of that fact'.[5]

The German chancellor's New Year proclamation to the NSDAP,
issued from Munich on 1 January 1938, in which he proudly
referred to the improvement that had been effected in the world
position of the Reich since 1933, echoed these latter points.
Germany, with its powerful friends – an unmistakable reference to
the triangular Anti-Comintern Pact – had helped to create 'an
international element of self-confident order', which stood in sharp
contrast to the 'meanderings of those dark powers which Mommsen
once described as the enzyme of decomposition for all peoples and
all states'. It was, he declared, 'this new framework of true
cooperation between the peoples which will ultimately be the
downfall of the Jewish-Bolshevist world revolt!'[6] A short time
earlier, in a conversation with Goebbels about the purges currently
taking place in the USSR, Hitler had given an intimation of the
pivotal role to be played by Germany in this process. Stalin must be
mentally sick, he exclaimed *en route* to Munich. 'Crazy! Otherwise
there is no explanation for it all. Has to be exterminated.'[7]

Before the Blomberg–Fritsch crisis and a series of developments
in Austria necessarily engaged his attention,[8] and notwithstanding
the different focus of his statements at the Hossbach Conference,
Hitler seemed as preoccupied with the threat of Bolshevism as ever.
In conversations with the Polish foreign minister, Josef Beck, and
the Yugoslavian minister president, Milan Stoyadinovich, on 14 and
17 January respectively, he expatiated at length on the subject of
communism and Russia; to Stoyadinovich in particular he had
criticized the British for their short-sighted indifference to the peril
of Bolshevism.[9] Having weathered the storm created by the
Blomberg–Fritsch affair, and with German designs on Austria
brought one step closer to realization by the Berchtesgaden Agreement, Hitler would be given a further reminder of the scale of his

original miscalculation about Britain and the possibility of an Anglo–German alliance when on 3 March the British proposed a colonial settlement in return for guarantees of Germany's commitment to appeasement in Europe.[10] After registering his barely concealed contempt for any such idea, Hitler proceeded forcefully to assert Germany's right to dominate central Europe, highlight the military danger posed by the Soviet Union, insist on the futility of all attempts to cooperate with the USSR, and finally to castigate the Western powers for their failure to respond to his past offers of friendship, which had been geared towards a 'unification of Europe without Russia'.[11]

Eight days after this conversation took place the German army rolled into Austria. The details of the *Anschluss* need not detain us here, not least because it has already been established that in the case of Austria the Nazi political leadership perceived anti-Bolshevism as having at best a negligible influence on the development of the evolutionary solution of the Austrian question, which Hitler had favoured since 1934.[12] According to the German government the *Anschluss* was, to all intents and purposes, a 'family affair' in which people of a common blood and heritage were united, thereby rectifying one of the most glaring and unjust denials of self-determination to have emerged from the 1919 peace settlement.[13]

During the crisis that culminated in the Munich Agreement in September 1938 the Germans again focused their attention on the denial of self-determination to the Sudeten German minority, which, under the Treaty of Versailles, had been incorporated into Czechoslovakia. Shortly after the *Anschluss*, which had created a new strategic balance in southeast Europe distinctly inimical to Czech security, Hitler received the leader of the Sudeten Germans, Konrad Henlein, and instructed him to use the grievances of his followers to create a crisis in Czechoslovakia that would ultimately provide Germany with a pretext for armed intervention.[14] As had recently been the case with Austria, nationalist aspirations would thus again provide an ideal cover under which to take the first preparatory steps towards the conquest of *Lebensraum* in Russia and the concomitant annihilation of 'Jewish Bolshevism'. What made the Czechoslovakian case different from that of Austria, and what in effect transformed it into a major international crisis that brought Europe to the brink of war, was first the fact that

Czechoslovakia was a formidable military power in its own right, and thus both a threat to Germany's eastern flank and a barrier to its eastward expansion, and second that it was an ally of both France and the Soviet Union.

In view of the events of the summer of 1938, it might easily be assumed that Hitler harboured a particular dislike for Czechs, which partly explains the relish and enthusiasm with which he plotted against and ultimately destroyed their country. Yet such an impression is barely substantiated by an examination of the contemporary evidence. Brigitte Hamann, for example, has found that, apart from one incidental remark to his close friend August Kubizek, 'no other anti-Czech utterances are documented from Hitler's Vienna years'.[15] Similarly, in the future chancellor's writings of the 1920s, Czechoslovakia is hardly mentioned save for one passing reference in the *Zweites Buch* to its position as France's ally. The point was made not so much to highlight a distinct threat to the Reich from southeast Europe, but to demonstrate once more that Germany's 'most dangerous enemy' was France, as 'she alone, thanks to her alliances, is in a position to be able to threaten almost the whole of Germany with aircraft'.[16] It is perhaps worth noting that this military factor also applied to Poland, with which Hitler sought and for a time achieved a reasonable working relationship rooted in opposition to Bolshevism. Indeed, this is not the only similarity to be drawn between the position of Poland and Czechoslovakia in German calculations, for both also contained large German minorities and were clearly important in geostrategic terms in view of Hitler's aims in Russia. Moreover, it should be recalled that in the early 1930s it was Poland rather than Czechoslovakia that had first taken fright at the growth of German nationalism by concluding in 1932 a treaty of non-aggression with the Soviet Union. By that time Hitler had already mentioned Czechoslovakia in the context of a German-led economic bloc against the USSR.[17] Before the Czechs effectively sealed their own fate in 1935 by entering into a military alliance with Russia, there are indeed signs that Hitler was at least prepared to explore the possibility of an arrangement with Czechoslovakia not dissimilar to the one he was to achieve with Poland.[18]

Whatever Hitler's original intentions *vis-à-vis* Czechoslovakia, there can be little doubt that the alliance President Masaryk signed with Stalin within two months of the reintroduction of conscription in Germany primarily determined that power's position in his calculations after the spring of 1935. Hitler rarely found himself in complete agreement with his career diplomats, but even he is unlikely to have questioned their characterization of the Czech–Soviet alliance of 16 May 1935 as being 'unilaterally and exclusively directed against Germany'.[19] More importantly, especially in view of the Franco–Soviet Pact, which had been concluded two weeks earlier, France, Russia and Czechoslovakia now constituted, in the words of Richard Meyer, head of the Wilhelmstrasse's eastern European division, 'a single political and military instrument'; as such, the Czech–Soviet treaty was an event of 'decisive importance' for Germany. By virtue of their alliance with Russia, the Czechs had 'assumed a heavy political responsibility and have created a serious danger', for they would now 'necessarily become involved in any conflicts arising in the East'.[20] Indeed, the dangers inherent in the new arrangements were apparent for all to see, not least as shortly after the conclusion of its alliance with the USSR the international press began to refer to Czechoslovakia as a 'deployment zone' for Soviet forces, particularly the Soviet air force, in the heart of central Europe.[21]

The evocative image of Czechoslovakia as a 'Soviet aircraft carrier' was a veritable gift for the Nazi regime and, from mid-1935 onwards, it was exploited on every conceivable occasion. Such was the emphasis placed on the issue in Berlin that, following a short visit to the German capital in early 1936, Ernst Eisenlohr, the German minister to Prague, told Masaryk's successor, Edouard Beneš, that

> in every Government office I entered, every conversation I had started with the phrase 'Czechoslovakia is the aircraft carrier of Soviet Russia'. In the press and in private conversations the fear was repeatedly expressed that Czechoslovakia was making ready airfields for the Russian Air Force and was building factories for the repair of Russian aircraft, and that a Russian squadron was already stationed there.[22]

Unsurprisingly, given the general anti-Bolshevik tenor of the speeches at the 1936 Nuremberg rally, this aspect of the European situation received ample comment from the Nazi leaders in their addresses to the rank and file of the NSDAP. 'The Bolshevists state that they are conducting a campaign against militarism,' Rosenberg had declared on 9 September, but this was hardly borne out by the fact that on the western frontier of the USSR the 'Jewish managed Soviet army', buttressed by its alliances with France and Czechoslovakia, was waiting for revolutionary conditions to develop in the west that would permit it finally to launch its 'attack on Europe'.[23]

Hitler made the same point more succinctly during his speech to the Reichstag on 30 January 1937. The Franco–Soviet and Czech–Soviet treaties, he declared, had simply delivered 'Central Europe to Soviet Russia as the field of play for its gigantic forces'.[24] Nevertheless, the concern of the Nazi regime about the extent of Soviet ideological influence in Czechoslovakia remains difficult to determine, not least because, irrespective of the scale of its supposed political subservience to Moscow, the Czech state, if it refused to accept German dictation, had to disappear purely on geostrategic grounds in view of the future quest for *Lebensraum* in Russia. Ideological considerations did, however, play a role in the development of German policy towards Czechoslovakia during the mid-1930s, and especially at the time of the Munich crisis of 1938. The archives reveal that by early 1936 reports assessing the attitudes of the main political parties in Czechoslovakia towards communism were finding their way to the Reich Chancellery via the Berlin based *Sudetendeutscher Dienst*. What use was made of this information is unclear, but at the very least it surely provided further ammunition for the Nazi propaganda machine.[25] In 1937 the Antikomintern also apparently planned to establish a 'Czechoslovak League for Defence against Bolshevism', which, according to Eisenlohr, would operate primarily under German influence and the promotion of which 'even in this country would undoubtedly be in our interests'.[26]

For their part the Czechs, fully alive to the blow dealt to their security by the reoccupation of the Rhineland in March 1936, vainly sought a rapprochement with Germany in the months that followed. The Czech authorities were subsequently at great pains to profess their dislike of the Soviet connection, even to the extent of offering to cooperate with the Gestapo to eradicate communist propaganda on their territory.[27] Czechoslovakia would 'strive in the future for the greatest integrity towards Germany', Beneš had told the Austrian minister in Prague in November 1937. 'Her close relations with Russia, which were always being thrown in his teeth, had nothing whatsoever to do with any similarity of ideologies', but 'arose from the necessity of the balance of power in Europe and from the realization that Russia represented a political reality, regardless of the regime which was in the saddle there'.[28] Any such assurances were destined to fall on deaf ears in Berlin where, long before Hitler made his intentions explicit at the Hossbach Conference, the idea that Czechoslovakia's days were numbered had been freely expressed, notably by Göring to Malcolm Christie, a former British air attaché to Berlin and confidant of Sir Robert Vansittart.[29] By the beginning of 1938, with the aggressive intentions expressed at Hossbach already incorporated in a crucial revision to existing military plans concerning Czechoslovakia, it was simply a question of when, not if, Germany would pick its moment to move against Prague. As Gerhard Weinberg writes, the opinion expressed by the German ambassador to Rome that Hitler would require a few months to 'digest' Austria before proceeding to tackle Czechoslovakia is 'probably an accurate reading of Hitler's time schedule at the beginning of April 1938'.[30]

In view of the considerable force that attached to the case of the Sudeten minority, German dealings with the other great powers over the spring and summer of 1938 were largely concerned with emphasizing the principle of self-determination and its wrongful denial to the German-speaking population of Czechoslovakia. At the same time they lent support to Henlein who set out his case during a public speech at Karlsbad on 24 April.[31] Ironically, before the 'May crisis' persuaded Hitler to set 1 October 1938 as the latest start date for a military strike against Czechoslovakia,[32] it was Britain and France rather than Germany that seemed intent on raising the spectre of Bolshevism in connection with the Czech Sudeten dispute, thereby hoping to exercise a restraining influence in Berlin on the basis that only the communists stood to benefit from a European conflict.[33] Despite Ribbentrop's attempts to highlight the futility of the Runciman mission by castigating the Prague government as being 'strongly influenced by Bolshevik ideas' and, as such, 'the real obstacle to the pacification and peaceful settlement of Europe',[34] German diplomacy did not lay particular emphasis on Czechoslovakia's ties to the Soviet Union during the summer of 1938.

Following Hitler's meeting with Chamberlain at Berchtesgaden, which, contrary to Hitler's aims, at least left the way open for a negotiated settlement, the Wilhelmstrasse and Nazi press shifted emphasis and, while continuing to stress ethnic aspects, brought anti-Bolshevik factors increasingly to the forefront. On 17 September, for example, following a question from Mussolini about the precise nature of German aims in the current crisis, Ribbentrop, characteristically skirting the enquiry, proceeded to inform the Italian ambassador that there was 'no doubt that, with chaos increasing in Czechoslovakia, the Bolshevik element was gaining ground, just as in Spain', and for that reason 'the necessity arose of achieving an immediate radical solution'.[35] The French ambassador in Berlin, André François-Poncet, noted a distinct change in the attitude of the German press during the week separating the meetings at Berchtesgaden and Godesberg, during which time, he informed Bonnet on 22 September:

> The Reich press has ceaselessly maintained that Moscow and the Communists were, more and more, the real inspiration and instigators of Czechoslovak policy, that Czechoslovakia had thereby become a peril, a red peril for Europe, and that finally M. Beneš, as the instrument of Bolshevism and the discredited and suspect head of a country in the process of complete disintegration, was no longer a partner with whom one could do business.[36]

Even in the aftermath of Munich, or perhaps because of it, the Germans continued to refer to Czecho-Slovakia, as it was now known, as an outpost of Bolshevism. Speaking on the second anniversary of the German–Japanese Anti-Comintern Pact, Ribbentrop announced that, like Spain and China, Czechoslovakia had been 'another point of departure for world revolution, but here too Bolshevik intentions had been nipped in the bud by the iron determination of the Führer'.[37] Following the seizure of Prague Hitler could not resist a reference during his speech of 28 April 1939 to the role of the former Czechoslovakia, which had been, 'no other than to prevent the consolidation of Central Europe' in order to 'provide a bridge to Europe for Bolshevik aggression'.[38] Years later, as if to emphasize the depth of the bond that united Czechoslovakia and the USSR, he would reflect that it would be the Czechs who would be most put out by the decline of Bolshevism 'for it is they who have always looked with secret hope to Mother Russia'.[39]

If for the most part German diplomacy had downplayed the anti-Bolshevik factor in handling the Sudeten crisis, the same certainly cannot be said of the Nazi propagandists who, in 1938, produced numerous publications, largely under the auspices of the ProMi and APA, devoted to Czechoslovakia's ties with Bolshevik Russia.[40] Most prominent among these was a 70-page essay by Hans Krebs, a senior figure in the Reich ministry of the interior, simply entitled 'Prague and Moscow', which appeared as volume 7 of *Bolschewismus*, the long-running series edited by Georg Leibbrandt of the APA. As the title suggests, Krebs's essay purported to expose the numerous links between democratic Czechoslovakia and the USSR, but the real message was contained in the brief foreword by Krebs's chief, Wilhelm Frick. 'Prague and Moscow', he wrote, not only demonstrated the dangers to which Germany and Europe were exposed as a result of the 'Czech–Bolshevik war preparations', but also highlighted the need for firm and rapid action to bring an end to a situation that was a constant source of European unrest and, moreover, made German people the victims of foreign hatred. The oppression of the Sudeten German minority, which had been carried out with 'Hussite hatred and Bolshevik blood lust', clearly demonstrated the danger posed to peace, order and central European culture by the alliance between Moscow and the Czech state.[41]

Beginning with an introduction to the historical ties between the Czechs and pan-Slavism, Krebs took his readers through a series of rather repetitive chapters dealing *inter alia* with the links between pan-Slavism and Bolshevism, the origins of the Czech–Soviet mutual assistance pact, the scale of subsequent military collaboration, the activities of some 400 Bolshevik or Bolshevik inspired organizations, groups and clubs in Czechoslovakia, and the operations of the 'League of Friends of the Soviet Union', notably its promotion of visits by Czech nationals to the USSR, which the Soviet authorities exploited to prepare Czechoslovakia for its role as the 'springboard of world revolution' in central Europe. The

Czech foreign minister may have described Czechoslovakia as a bulwark against Bolshevism, noted the author, but as the 'bridge to the Bolshevization of Europe', it was in fact the very opposite.[42] Some crude graphics accompanied Krebs's text, including a series of postage stamps depicting Soviet tanks, infantry and aircraft, which carried heroic captions affirming Russia's commitment to Czechoslovakia and celebrating the strength of the Red Army. Also included was a map, supposedly drawn up by Czech imperialists before 1914, in which two-thirds of the Second Reich had been either directly absorbed into a 'Greater Slavic Empire' or reconstituted in a new Habsburg empire. Almost inevitably the pamphlet contained a map of Czechoslovakia detailing the locations of Soviet airfields – with names given in Russian for added effect.

In a further publication, *The Betrayal of Europe*, a 200-page book hastily thrown together in the offices of the Antikomintern in the aftermath of the 'May crisis', Karl Vietz explored similar themes. No longer able to suppress the seven-million foreign nationals living in their state, and realizing that the injustices meted out to these unfortunates represented a challenge to their co-nationals (*Muttervolk*), Vietz argued that the Czechs had been forced to seek allies and had found a willing partner in the USSR. In return for Moscow's aid in suppressing the ethnic minorities incorporated in the Czech state, Prague had made available its territory to the 'world enemy' as a gateway into the heart of Europe. The consequences of this catastrophic folly were threefold: first, ethnic groups that the Czechs had oppressed had been delivered to the Bolshevik terrorists and threatened with the destruction of their national identity; second, Czechoslovakia's neighbours, Germany, Hungary and Poland, had been forced to endure on their borders not only a 'seat of Bolshevik pestilence' but also an advanced deployment zone for the Soviet armed forces; third, Europe in general had suffered from the existence of Czechoslovakia, which sought to sabotage any policy aimed at promoting peace, and which, through its very existence, constituted a permanent threat of conflict. 'The betrayal of Europe', wrote Vietz, was thus at the heart of the Czech mission in Europe.[43]

Throughout the Czech crisis the focus of the European powers had been fixed on the perceived grievances of the Sudeten German minority in Czechoslovakia and the possibility of a major conflict arising from the resulting tensions between Berlin and Prague. It was on that basis that the crisis had arisen and, to all outward appearances, it was on that basis that a settlement was finally reached. Yet, German diplomacy, and to a greater extent German propaganda, had not lost sight of the capital to be made from Czech ties to the Soviet Union in the pursuit of aims that ultimately had a much greater goal than the reunification with the Reich of 3.5 million so-called *Reichsdeutsche*. In so far as the destruction of Czechoslovakia, effected in March 1939, was a crucial step on the road to conflict with Russia, and thus the eradication of Soviet Bolshevism, the use of anti-communism alongside self-determin-ation during 1938–39 had been a significant factor in what Hitler later called a triumph for 'propaganda in the service of an idea'.[44]

That Hitler was inwardly unconvinced of that triumph was demonstrated by his hostile reaction to the Munich Agreement, which left him both determined to destroy what remained of Czechoslovakia as soon as a favourable opportunity arose and deeply resentful of British interference in a question that, to his mind, had always been an exclusively German concern.[45] Munich had deprived the Führer of the control of Czechoslovakia he needed to achieve his longer-term goals. Above all else, he believed that Britain's actions had thwarted his plans. With this latest evidence of Britain's opposition to his European ambitions fresh in his mind, Hitler was forced to consider the possibility that, contrary to his original intentions, he might have to fight Britain, or at least force it to drop its interest in continental affairs, before he even-tually moved east for the struggle with Bolshevik Russia.[46] In these circumstances the position of Poland, which Hitler previously conceived of as a desirable component in an anti-Soviet alliance, assumed added significance. If he were to proceed first against the West, it was vital to secure Germany's eastern flank, not least because the Polish alliance with France was still technically oper-ational. Alternately, should it be possible to move east without a prior conflict with Britain and France, Poland would have to be squared. As Gerhard Weinberg observes, to fulfil his programme in eastern Europe Hitler 'needed either Poland's acquiescence or that country's destruction; any truly independent Poland would be a bar to his aims; and in the immediate future he especially wanted Poland quiet while he settled with England and France'.[47]

It is in this context that Germany's efforts after Munich to persuade Poland to join the Anti-Comintern Pact should be understood. From 1934–35 until the autumn of 1938 those efforts had had as their principal purpose the recruitment of Poland as an ally against the USSR;[48] and it is in that sense that Hitler's remarks to Beck, referred to earlier, and his warm reference to Polish–German collaboration in his speech of 20 February 1938 are to be interpreted.[49] In the negotiations that followed Munich, however, from Ribbentrop's conversations with Lipski in October–November 1938, through Hitler's reception of Beck in Berlin in January 1939, to Ribbentrop's visit to Warsaw later that month, the Germans were essentially requiring Poland to accept the status of a satellite, a condition that would be demonstrated through concessions over Danzig and the Corridor and, more importantly, by its immediate accession to the Anti-Comintern Pact.[50]

It was clear when Ribbentrop met Lipski on 24 October 1938 that the Poles were unwilling to comply with these German wishes. Despite its hostility to the USSR and its superficially cordial relations with Germany, Poland remained determined to maintain a balance between its neighbours. It hoped that by not leaning too heavily towards one, it would not antagonize the other. Following a steep rise in German–Polish tension at the turn of the year, and notably under the impact of Hitler's seizure of Prague in mid-March 1939, Poland accepted a guarantee of its territorial integrity from Britain and, in so doing, effectively sealed its own fate. By revealing itself as an accomplice of Britain, as Hitler viewed it, Poland had made its choice, thus answering in a roundabout way the fundamental question the German–Polish negotiations had posed in the previous six months. Although for a time afterwards he appears to have clung to the hope that the Poles would ultimately yield to German pressure, it was clearly necessary to make plans for a military solution, a contingency that Hitler addressed on 3 April 1939 when he issued the directive for *Fall Weiss*, the German plan for an attack on Poland, according to which the German armed forces were to be ready for action at any time after 1 September.[51]

Seven weeks later Hitler spoke to his senior military personnel at the famous conference of 23 May 1939 and instructed them on the purpose of the coming conflict with Poland. In essence, the Führer repeated the basic point he had made at the Hossbach Conference

18 months earlier to the effect that Germany's economic problems could only be solved by the conquest of lands adjacent to the Reich. In the present dispute with Poland therefore, 'it is not Danzig that is at stake'; rather, it is 'a matter of expanding our living space in the East'. There would be no repetition of the Czech crisis, he warned. 'This time there will be war. Our task is to isolate Poland. Success in isolating her will be decisive. ... It must not come to a simultaneous showdown with the West.'[52]

Having taken the decision to proceed militarily against Poland, Hitler's main concern in the summer of 1939 was how to ensure British non-intervention in the forthcoming conflict. The most effective way to achieve this objective was to deprive Britain of the means effectively to come to the assistance of Poland, which, in the circumstances, amounted to forestalling British efforts to secure an alliance with the USSR in which London had been engaged since May. The story of the ensuing 'race to Moscow' has been told many times and need not be repeated here. Although some of the recent research on Soviet policy in 1939 has tended to emphasize Stalin's preference until fairly late in the day for an association with the Western powers,[53] compelling reasons ultimately led the Soviets to choose alignment with Berlin. The essential arguments had been well summarized in late July during a conversation between Julius Schnurre of the Wilhelmstrasse's economic policy department and Georgi Astakhov, counsellor of the Soviet embassy. 'What could Britain offer Russia?' asked Schnurre rhetorically.

> At best participation in a European war and the hostility of Germany, hardly a desirable end for Russia. What could we offer as against this? Neutrality and keeping out of a possible European conflict and, if Moscow wished, a German–Russian understanding on mutual interests which, just as in former times, would work out to the advantage of both countries.[54]

On the basis of this logic Germany and the USSR were able to find ground for an agreement that shocked the world.

Chapter 10

Towards Barbarossa and the 'Final Conflict with Bolshevism', 1940–41

F or Hitler, the pact Ribbentrop signed with Molotov on 23 August 1939 represented no more than an exercise in *Realpolitik* with the limited function of deterring Britain from assisting Poland and, by the same token, ensuring the latter's rapid elimination by the German armed forces. The German chancellor never saw it as a turning point in the Reich's foreign policy, as Ribbentrop and others appear to have hoped.[1] Although the Nazi–Soviet treaty brought numerous political and economic benefits to Germany, Hitler was uncomfortable with the ideological volte-face the new arrangement with Russia implied and over the coming months clearly struggled to come to terms with it. Even before the negotiations with Moscow were concluded he made a frank admission of his inner feelings to Carl Burckhardt, the League of Nations high commissioner, who visited him at Berchtesgaden on 11 August. In what Burckhardt described as the 'most extraordinary statement' of their conversation, Hitler exclaimed:

> Everything I undertake is directed against Russia. If the West is too blind or too stupid to realize this, then I shall be forced to come to an understanding with the Russians, strike at the West, and, after its defeat, turn with all my concerted force against the Soviet Union.[2]

Two weeks later, despite the clear advantage the German–Soviet non-aggression pact had afforded him in eastern Europe, the

156

Führer essentially repeated the point, complaining bitterly to the British ambassador that it had been 'England which had forced him into agreement with Russia'.[3]

Although ideological stalwarts such as Rosenberg professed profound shock and amazement at what they perceived to be a fundamental betrayal of Nazi principles,[4] Hitler's subsequent attitude towards the rapprochement with Moscow demonstrates quite clearly that their concern was unfounded. In the summer of 1939 strategic and political necessities had dictated a radical course of action to achieve short-term goals. In such circumstances ideological issues, however weighty, had to be pushed into the background. 'The question of Bolshevism is momentarily of secondary importance,' noted Goebbels on 24 August. 'The Führer also considers it to be shedding its skin. But what does all that matter? We are in a tight spot and, like the devil, have to eat flies.'[5] As these sentiments imply, the Nazi–Soviet Pact did not signify any far-reaching ideological compromise on Hitler's part. On 29 August he remarked that he was 'in no ways altering his fundamental anti-Bolshevist policies; one had to use Beelzebub to drive away the devil; all means were justified in dealing with the Soviets, even a pact such as this'.[6] Nearly three months later a certain Dr Grimm, a Wilhelmstrasse lawyer and Nazi propaganda agent with reputedly excellent connections to Hitler and Ribbentrop, told a friend of Frank Walters of the League of Nations Union of a meeting that had taken place on 22 November during which Hitler had explained his apparent ideological volte-face as a necessary if distasteful measure to secure the vital interests of Germany.[7]

On 23 November, in a secret speech to 200 of his most senior military commanders, Hitler again betrayed his inner feelings about the USSR, concentrating this time on the strategic implications of Soviet policy for future German ambitions. Although the essential purpose of the address was to rationalize opening an offensive in the west, it was clear that the question of the Soviet Union was not far from the chancellor's thoughts. Russia was no danger to the Reich at present, he declared, but it still had 'far-reaching goals' in the Baltic, the Balkans and the Persian Gulf that conflicted with German interests. 'We can oppose Russia only when we are free in the West,' he candidly announced, adding that should the Soviets ever renounce internationalism, which had for the moment admittedly 'retired to the background', it would only be replaced by pan-Slavism.[8]

This characterization of the Soviet Union as a state in pursuit of national interests might well indicate that Ribbentrop's enthusiastic endorsement of Stalin and his regime had not been entirely without impact on Hitler's views in the autumn of 1939. Stalin was 'no longer the international Bolshevist', the Führer told Sven Hedin in March 1940, but 'showed himself as an absolute Russian nationalist' who was 'following exactly the same natural policy of Russian nationalism as the Tsars'. One feature of that policy had been the search for an ice-free port, which partially explained why Russia had been fighting Finland for the best part of four months.[9] Although official German support for the USSR during the 'winter war' had hardly reflected the mood of German public opinion, which was overwhelmingly pro-Finnish and had made the Germans extremely unpopular throughout Scandinavia, Hitler appears to have understood Stalin's policy in so far as it was intended to realize a long-coveted objective of Russian foreign policy.[10] Several months later the German leader may have spoken of the 'gallant Finns',[11] but his attitude to their fate at the turn of 1939–40 appears to have been largely one of indifference, if not *Schadenfreude*, in view of their former support for the League of Nations and their rejection of German proposals for a non-aggression pact in the summer of 1939.

In tandem with this acknowledgement of Stalin's promotion of Russian nationalism, however, came considerable anxiety about the potential repercussions of such a development for Germany and Europe. The fact that Stalin might have broken free from his internationalist masters in no way diminished the Bolshevik menace, for, as Hitler later explained, the Soviet leader knew full well how to exploit Bolshevism for his own purposes. In early 1942 the Führer told a gathering of his colleagues: 'Stalin pretends to have been the herald of the Bolshevik revolution. In actual fact, he identifies himself with the Russia of the Tsars, and he had merely resurrected the tradition of pan-Slavism. For him Bolshevism is only a means, a disguise designed to trick the Germanic and Latin peoples.'[12]

Mussolini, who had been so appalled by the Nazi–Soviet treaties of August–September 1939 that he had dispatched a letter to Berlin imploring the Führer not to abandon his crusade against Bolshevism,[13] had already been instructed on these lines during the meeting of the two dictators at the Brenner Pass on 18 March 1940. It was true that the USSR had recently experienced a 'modification of the Bolshevist principle in the direction of a nationalist Russian way of life', Hitler explained, and since Litvinov substituted Molotov as Soviet foreign minister in May 1939 there had been a distinct change in Moscow's attitude to Berlin. Nevertheless, although Bolshevism might have discarded its 'Muscovite–Jewish and international character' and 'assumed a purely Slavic–Muscovite' complexion, that should not be taken to mean that 'this, too, might not prove dangerous for Germany'.[14]

At the turn of 1939–40 Hitler indulged in an interesting reflection on recent developments and trends in the Soviet Union that might have led him to these conclusions. 'The Führer finds the Russian question very interesting,' noted Goebbels on 29 December 1939.

> Stalin is a typical Asiatic Russian. Bolshevism has cast out the Western European leading stratum which alone could render this huge colossus capable of action. It is a good thing that this is no longer the case today. Russia remains Russia, no matter who may govern it. We can be happy that Moscow is preoccupied. We will know what to do to prevent a Bolshevik encroachment into Western Europe.[15]

Bolshevism, Hitler declared two weeks later, was the political system at present best suited to the Slavs. Left to their own devices the Russians were in any case incapable of achieving anything better. Although Stalin was arguably 'a modern Ivan the Terrible, or, if you like, even a Peter the Great', Russia was essentially governed by a bunch of 'incompetent Slavs'. From the German point of view that was no bad thing, Hitler continued, for it was much better to have as one's neighbour a weak partner rather than a powerful ally. 'If all the treaties that had ever been concluded had been kept,' he concluded prophetically, 'then humanity would have ceased to exist.'[16]

These revealing insights into Hitler's view of Stalin, Russia and Bolshevism at the turn of 1939–40 certainly suggest that, although

Hitler might have accepted that Stalin had embraced nationalism, he saw him as no less a threat to German interests, not least because he might seek to harness the forces of pan-Slavism and Bolshevism in pursuit of an aggressive foreign policy. During the early part of the 'phoney war' Hitler's attitude towards the USSR, never especially positive, had certainly undergone a transformation. Whereas on 1 October 1939 Goebbels had found the chancellor 'convinced of Russia's loyalty', ten weeks later he found him 'very sceptical towards Moscow'.[17] Notwithstanding the inherent distaste Hitler presumably felt at the prospect of collaboration with his mortal enemy, several reasons might explain the fluctuations in Hitler's attitude. Foremost among these was perhaps the continued activities of the Comintern, about which Rosenberg kept him informed,[18] the outbreak of the Russo–Finnish war, which could clearly be interpreted as an attempt to profit while Germany was preoccupied elsewhere, and the repeated Soviet requests for concessions in the technical, economic and territorial spheres, all of which he steadfastly refused.[19]

Before the German victory in the west the Nazi–Soviet rapprochement had certainly worked to the general satisfaction of both parties, but from Hitler's perspective it would be wrong to see in it anything more than a strictly business arrangement. Although the respective propaganda machines sought to highlight the newfound friendship between Berlin and Moscow, the facts of the situation were somewhat at odds with that picture. In particular, the Germans had encountered considerable Soviet obstruction and suspicion during the negotiation of the economic agreement concluded in Berlin on 11 February. Although this agreement represented to the Germans 'a wide open door to the East', they had found the negotiations 'difficult and lengthy', and characterized by 'ever-present distrust' on the part of the Russians.[20] The operation of the economic agreement after February 1940 was equally troublesome. In several respects the Russians appeared intent on making difficulties, and only relaxed their attitude following demonstrations of German military power in Scandinavia and western Europe.[21] Of particular concern to the Germans was the Soviet Union's withdrawal of certain facilities at Basis Nord, the naval base near Murmansk that Russia had made available for German vessels operating in the Barents Sea. Hitler's reaction to

160

this move on the very eve of the German invasion of Denmark and Norway does not appear to have been recorded, but he is surely unlikely to have been impressed.[22]

The tone of Hitler's public statements about his association with Moscow was never especially friendly, and left a distinct impression that relations, though correct, could hardly be described as cordial. Hitler described the Nazi–Soviet agreements in generally negative terms as being instrumental in thwarting the desire of the Jews and the 'plutocratic statesmen of the West' to embroil Russia and Germany.[23] Moreover, Hitler made no attempt to deny in his public addresses that Germany's goal remained the acquisition of *Lebensraum*, not in Africa, but, as he vaguely termed it, in those parts of 'Central Europe' that had been 'cultivated, civilized and economically developed by us Germans' – an interesting choice of phrase given Hitler's views on the earlier role of Germanic elites in consolidating and governing the Russian state.[24]

With the fall of France in June 1940 the Nazi–Soviet Pact lost much of its strategic value to Germany and, almost overnight, the Wehrmacht's triumph gave an entirely new complexion to German relations with Russia. There remains considerable debate about what Hitler intended to do with his victory in the west, and in particular about how it shaped his intentions towards the Soviet Union and the future conduct of the war against Britain.[25] For a moment the sheer scale of his achievement may well have left even the Führer with no clear idea of how to proceed, a possibility that might go some way to explain the apparent inconsistencies between some of the statements he is reported to have made at the time. Albert Speer, for example, overheard Hitler remark to Keitel in late June 1940 that in comparison with the western campaign a military adventure against the USSR would be like 'a child's game in a sandbox'.[26] A few days later, speaking to the commanders of Army Group A, Hitler is alleged to have expressed the expectation that Britain would now be prepared to conclude a reasonable peace settlement that would free his hands for the 'great and real task – the conflict with Bolshevism'.[27] Within weeks, however, the German leader had evidently changed the emphasis, if not the direction, of his thoughts. 'The war in the west has ended,' he reportedly pronounced.

France has been conquered, and I shall come, in the shortest possible time, to an understanding with England. There still remains the conflict with the east. That, however, is a task which throws up world-wide problems. ... One might perhaps tackle it in ten years time; perhaps I shall leave it to my successor. Now we have our hands full for years to come to consolidate and digest what we have obtained in Europe.[28]

Evidence from the recently revised edition of the Goebbels diaries unfortunately sheds little fresh light on these issues; indeed, if anything, that the entries for May and June 1940 reveal signs of irritation with rather than hostility towards the USSR would tend to support the argument that Hitler was at best undecided about how his future policy towards the USSR might unfold.[29] Sustained collaboration with Stalin, however, which Ribbentrop and Wilhelmstrasse advised and which had its supporters in the German military elites, was the path Hitler was least likely to tread. As he told Mussolini in March 1940, his association with Russia had been forced upon him by 'bitter necessity' and, irrespective of the needs of the moment, the USSR remained an 'absolutely alien world' with which one could never be on terms of genuine friendship. Russia, he remarked revealingly, was 'only the protection for the rear'.[30] Following a sharp deterioration in German–Soviet relations occasioned by Stalin's ultimatum to Romania, itself prompted by the speed and scale of the German triumph over France, Hitler became increasingly suspicious of Soviet intentions and, more importantly, appears to have readjusted his focus on Russian issues away from pan-Slavism and back to purely ideological concerns. 'Russia will always remain alien to us,' noted Goebbels following a conversation with Hitler on 8 August 1940. 'We must erect an insurmountable wall between ourselves and Moscow. After all, Bolshevism is still world enemy number one. At some point we will come into conflict with it as well. The Führer is of the same opinion.'[31]

Despite the conflicting nature of the evidence on Hitler's attitude and intentions towards the Soviet Union in the immediate aftermath of the western campaign, contemporary witnesses and commentators are in broad agreement on the following points: (a) the German leader hoped for and expected a compromise peace with

Britain in summer 1940; (b) he found himself facing a strategic dilemma when it was not forthcoming; (c) he was anxious and outraged by Soviet actions in the second half of June when Stalin both overstepped the mark under the terms of the Nazi–Soviet Pact by laying claim to Bukovina, which was not covered by the secret protocol to the German–Soviet treaty, and threatened to ignite the Balkans with his demand for Bessarabia, with all that implied for the supply of oil and other raw materials to the Reich from Romania and Yugoslavia; and (d) it was generally accepted among the German elite that the eastern question would have to be tackled at some point in the future.[32]

A revealing insight into thinking at the highest level of the German leadership in mid-July 1940, by which time the prospects of a British capitulation had significantly diminished, is provided by a confidential briefing from the propaganda ministry, which issued the following information for the guidance of editors of Germany's leading newspapers:

> Germany's views about the possibilities of a political peace ... involved Britain withdrawing from Europe, i.e. from the continent and the Mediterranean and agreeing to a complete revision of the colonial sphere in Africa. Until the soundings were broken off, the Führer was of the opinion that sooner or later Germany would have to work together with the healthy section of the British people and therefore that it was not appropriate to destroy the whole [British] empire, since this would simply mean that the Russians, the Japanese, and the Americans could secure an easy inheritance which is not in our interest. In the Führer's view sooner or later the racially valuable Germanic element in Britain would have to be brought in to join with Germany in the future secular struggles of the white race against the yellow race or the Germanic race against Bolshevism.[33]

When later that month the realization finally sank in that Britain was not prepared to negotiate, and a sober assessment had been made of Stalin's recent moves in the Balkans, not to mention his earlier transgressions in Finland and Lithuania,[34] Hitler rapidly concluded that all his problems could be solved by risking everything on a lightning military campaign against the USSR, the logic of which he explained at a military conference at the Berghof on 31 July. Britain, he reasoned, was holding out because it was hoping for assistance from not only the USA, but also primarily from the USSR. 'If Russia drops out of the picture,' he continued 'America, too, is lost for Britain, because elimination of Russia would tremendously increase Japan's power in the Far East'. Russia had been shocked by the speed and scale of the German victory in the west and, despite the evident rebuff Stalin administered to the new British ambassador, Sir Stafford Cripps, it was suspected that London and Moscow were still secretly talking to each other. 'All that Russia has to do is to hint that she does not care to have a strong Germany,' reasoned Hitler, 'and the British will take hope, like one about to go under, that the situation will undergo a radical change within six to eight months.' Ill-equipped and unwilling to launch an invasion of the British Isles, the German chancellor decided to turn east on the basis that the elimination of Russia would shatter any remaining British hopes. General Halder, chief of the army general staff, noted: '*Decision: Russia's destruction must therefore be made a part of this struggle. Spring 1941.*'[35]

Two days before this conference took place, Alfred Jodl, chief of the high command's operations staff, had conferred with General Warlimont and other military leaders to whom he had disclosed the Führer's intention to launch a surprise attack on the USSR to rid the world 'once and for all' of the pestilence of Bolshevism. Warlimont and his associates were horrified, their shock and consternation made all the greater by the further revelation that the operation against Russia was to proceed even if Britain had not been defeated beforehand. There were strong objections to the prospect of a two-front war, and puzzlement over why an attack on the USSR was even contemplated in view of the benefits the association had brought to Germany, particularly in terms of the delivery of raw materials. According to Warlimont, Jodl could only respond to these points by repeating Hitler's view that, as a collision with Bolshevism was inescapable, it was better to face it while Germany was strong.[36]

Unable to account for Hitler's decision in terms of grand strategy, and clearly anxious to explore other options, notably the possibility of striking Britain at the periphery of its empire as outlined in a memorandum by Jodl on 30 June,[37] the Atlantic–Mediterranean–African option the German navy advanced[38] and the *Kontinental-block* idea Ribbentrop strongly favoured,[39] Russian experts in the Wilhelmstrasse and senior German military figures explained it at the time and later in terms of the ideological roots of his foreign policy. Gustav Hilger believed that Hitler had convinced himself that destiny had summoned him to make an end to Bolshevism and not to rest until he had secured Germany's *Lebensraum*.[40] Warlimont agreed. Hitler's determination to turn against Russia had from the outset been 'unconditional and unalterable', he later wrote. 'The real background to his decision undoubtedly lay in his permanent, deep-rooted and deadly hatred of Bolshevism.'[41] General Lossberg told von Herwarth that Hitler had issued orders for an all-embracing plan to invade the USSR based on the following assumptions: 'first, that the Soviet Union was getting stronger every year, and would finally be a mortal danger for Germany; second, that Hitler's readings of the laws of history indicated to him that anyone who succeeded him would be a weaker man than himself'. On this basis the chancellor had therefore concluded that 'the best and probably the only opportunity to destroy the Soviet Union and the Communist system was at hand.'[42]

In view of its profound significance for the course and outcome of the Second World War, the determinants and effects of the German invasion of the Soviet Union have featured prominently in the historical research relating to that conflict. Invariably, there have been different and widely divergent explanations of Hitler's extension of hostilities in June 1941, and a heated debate has been generated about the timing of and reasons for his decision to break with Stalin. In turn, this has fuelled a further debate about the connection between the launching and course of the German–Soviet war and the origins and implementation of the 'Final Solution'.[43] In what remains one of the most authoritative accounts of Hitler's policies during 1940–41, Andreas Hillgruber argued in the mid-1960s that there were essentially four motives driving Hitler to attack the Soviet Union, namely the desire to eliminate 'Jewish Bolshevism' and exterminate the European Jews; the acquisition of *Lebensraum*; the subjugation and enslavement of the Slavs; and the creation of a continental Germanic empire from which it would be possible to wage later wars in order to achieve world power status.[44]

With his basic hypothesis that Hitler's decision can be explained within the framework of the foreign policy programme the Nazi leader devised in the 1920s, Hillgruber set the tone for much of what has flowed since from the pens of those who attribute the break with Russia primarily to ideological and programmatic factors.[45]

For some commentators, on the other hand, the German leader's actions appear to have had little direct connection with any such ideologically determined programme. Hansjoachim Koch's research into the Führer's deliberations during the summer of 1940, for example, has led him to conclude that Hitler's attitude to the Soviet Union in the wake of the western campaign was not determined in the slightest by his long coveted aims of territorial aggrandisement, but by the increasing friction with the USSR in northern Europe and the Balkans, areas that were essential either for the defence of the Reich or as springboards for a future invasion of the USSR.[46] In the early 1990s considerable attention was focused – and in consequence considerable controversy aroused – on the dubious notion that the German attack on the USSR was essentially a preventative strike designed to protect the Reich and its recent conquests from an invasion long planned by Stalin and his colleagues, although a detailed study of Soviet policy by Gabriel Gorodetsky has critically discredited this thesis.[47] More recently, work by German historians has focused on the economic imperatives underpinning the launch of Operation Barbarossa. Christian Gerlach, for example, categorically dismisses the notion that the campaign against the USSR was an 'ideological luxury', arguing that the German attack was an attempt by Hitler to escape the strategic impasse created by his failure to defeat Britain, a 'last resort' in effect, and concomitantly an essential attempt to secure the resources of the USSR for the inevitable struggle with the Anglo-Saxon powers.[48] Rolf-Dieter Müller finds himself broadly in agreement with at least the second of these hypotheses, arguing that Barbarossa's primary function was to safeguard and improve the economic position of the German Reich.[49]

The balance of the wider debate would presently tend to confirm Gerd Ueberschär's observation that Hitler's decision to attack Russia 'can in no way be explained in a monocausal manner by the political situation in 1940, but should be assessed in the context of his "Eastern Program", elaborated before 1933, for the conquest of *Lebensraum* in Europe'.[50] Ideological, racial, political and strategic motives, some longstanding, others a product of the European situation in mid-1940, prompted a decision in principle to break with Russia. Events during the remainder of the year, notably the gruelling and unproductive round of negotiations that took place during the November 1940 visit to Berlin of Vyashalev Molotov, the Soviet foreign minister, then consolidated and confirmed that decision. That the breach would come was not in question; and in that sense whichever factor appeared to dominate at any given time is not of crucial importance. However, as the military opponents of a conflict with Moscow believed, a core conviction driving Hitler was his desire to destroy Bolshevism, be that in its former 'international' guise or in the new national variant that Stalin had exploited to German detriment in Finland and Romania.

In the course of his frequent expositions on the unwelcome developments in Soviet policy after June 1940, particularly in relation to southeast Europe, Hitler habitually mixed power political reasoning with a basic underlying ideological message. Soviet pressure on Romania, applied in the form of a demand for Bessarabia and Bukovina presented to Bucharest only days after the collapse of France, had been dangerous enough in view of the importance of Romanian raw materials, notably oil, for the German war economy. When Hungary and Bulgaria followed suit and, prompted by the Soviet move, tabled their own claims against Romania, the entire region was threatened with the outbreak of a general conflict from which Russia alone stood to benefit. For months afterwards the sudden emergence of this crisis, which was fraught with danger for the Reich, and its eventual resolution in late August through Axis, or rather German, arbitration in the form of the Second Vienna Award, continued to trouble Hitler. As he informed the Hungarian minister in Berlin on 10 September, his main concern had been to ensure that Romania did not collapse, for in that eventuality 'the East', a somewhat euphemistic term for what was clearly meant to be understood as Russia, would have extended its influence into the region with unforeseeable consequences. It had also been crucial to make a timely and decisive intervention before others, notably the Soviets, were able to take advantage of the situation. Indeed, had Russia attempted further interference in

167

the affair, Hitler continued revealingly, an armed clash with Germany would have been inevitable, for, in the final analysis, 'two worlds which were basically deadly enemies, came into collision here'. Any such conflict would have exposed the entire Balkan region to the 'danger of infection' by Bolshevism, a prospect that would have confronted Germany with 'difficult problems', irrespective of its desire not to jeopardize its 'friendly relationship' with the USSR.[51]

Hitler's juxtaposition of power-political and ideological factors in his explanation of the Romanian crisis to Sztójay was characteristic of his handling of the Russian problem in the last months of 1940, indeed until the launching of Barbarossa. Although on some occasions, notably when speaking to a gathering of his senior military personnel at the Berghof in early January 1941,[52] ideological issues were consciously relegated to the background in favour of more sober military and political considerations, the German leader frequently combined smouldering resentment at Soviet encroachments in Romania, and purported anxieties about the growing threat the USSR posed to Germany, with concern at the evidence of renewed Bolshevik agitation in southeast Europe, indeed even within the Reich. Ribbentrop recalled that during his numerous discussions with Hitler on the future of Soviet–German relations after the western campaign, the Führer focused his criticisms of Russian policy on the build-up of Soviet forces on the German border, the 'aggressive' Russian mentality towards the West, and the alleged communist propaganda activities of the Soviet trade delegation to Berlin.[53] In November 1940 the new Romanian leader, Ion Antonescu, was instructed on the continuing threat posed by Bolshevism to Romania and the need to stem the 'Slavic tide', while in the same breath Hitler expatiated about the warnings he had recently issued to Molotov about Germany's determination to uphold its guarantee to Romania, issued as part of the Second Vienna Award, and its refusal to tolerate further Soviet aggression against Finland.[54]

A similar tendency was noticeable in Hitler's remarks to the Bulgarian minister president, Bogdan Filov, in January 1941. A German defeat, Hitler prophesied, would be even more catastrophic for the continent than it had been in 1918, for at that time there had been 'no big third party in the background ready to profit from the situation, as the Soviet Union would now'. If the Axis were beaten in the present war, Europe would cease to exist, and for that reason 'all countries of continental Europe had an interest in seeing Europe preserved through a German victory'. It was the responsibility of each country to guard against contamination by the red peril. Germany had studied Bolshevism and its methods, Hitler warned, with particular reference to the ravages unleashed by Russia in the Baltic states, and had concluded that the Bolsheviks remained incapable of any 'constructive effort'. Wherever they surfaced they brought hunger and distress, and destroyed all vestige of cultural life. If Jewish and Russian commissars were permitted to run amok in the Balkans, torturing and murdering their opponents, and thus stifling all opposition, 'it would indeed be a disaster'. Hitler was gratified to find a 'growing comprehension of this situation, especially in Hungary where, in recognition of the fact that Europe's fate was at stake, they were showing the greatest cooperation in helping to transport the German troops to Rumania'.[55]

Private statements made by Hitler and by the internal directives he issued in the months leading up to 22 June 1941 appear to have amply borne out these observations. As the maintenance of secrecy and the effective use of diversionary tactics were paramount considerations for the German leadership in its attempts to ensure the advantage of surprise, there was naturally no reference made even to the remotest possibility of war with the USSR in German propaganda, which Goebbels, kept in ignorance of the planned campaign against the USSR until late March 1941, continued to direct against the British 'plutocrats'.[56] Similarly, in diplomatic conversations, even with his closest allies, Hitler was careful to give nothing away, and, although it was impossible to conceal that there were frictions with Moscow, every effort was made to downplay their significance. Thus, although Germany was ready for any eventuality in its relations with Russia, and 'would not hesitate a second to take the necessary steps in case of danger',[57] the Reich did not wish a breach, for Stalin was a 'shrewd and cautious fellow' and, as long as he was alive, 'Russia would certainly not attempt anything against Germany'.[58]

Away from the public forum and the diplomatic arena, however, it was an altogether different story. As if to highlight the extraordinary nature of the conflict that was about to be embarked upon, a series of directives and orders additional to the regular military preparations was issued during the first half of 1941, which clearly underlined the ideological imperative of the struggle. When in late February a draft document entitled 'Guidelines in special fields concerning Directive no. 21',[59] which detailed some of these measures, including the treatment of the civilian population and prisoners of war, was forwarded to Hitler, he immediately returned it to Jodl who was ordered to make substantial revisions. 'The impending campaign is more than a clash of arms,' insisted the Führer, 'it also entails a struggle between two ideologies. To conclude this war it is not enough, given the vastness of the space, to defeat the enemy's forces. ... The Jewish-Bolshevik intelligentsia, as the oppressor in the past, must be liquidated.'[60]

Later that month, during a meeting with senior army personnel, Hitler reviewed his goals in the forthcoming campaign, which, he assured his audience, would be 'very different from the war in the west'. In the course of what Halder described as a 'crushing denunciation of Bolshevism', Hitler characterized the future struggle as a clash of ideologies in which there could be none of the customary comradeship between combatants, for the communist was 'no comrade before or after the battle'. The Reich was about to engage in a war of annihilation. 'If we do not grasp this,' Hitler continued, 'we shall still beat the enemy, but thirty years later we shall again have to fight the Communist foe.' With this in mind, German soldiers were to steel themselves for the coming tasks, prominent among which would be the 'extermination of the Bolshevist commissars and of the Communist intelligentsia'.[61] These intentions were later enshrined in the infamous 'Commissar Order' of 6 June, which decreed that, as the enemy would hardly 'act in accordance with the basic principles of humanity or international law', Bolshevik political commissars were to be terminated 'immediately with a weapon', whether they offered resistance or not.[62]

Moreover, the orders transmitted to the invading force, comprising Wehrmacht units, SS formations and the notorious Einsatzgruppen about the treatment of Jews were sufficiently ambiguous to permit, indeed encourage, large scale atrocities, including mass executions, even if the general focus had not yet

170

shifted to a 'Final Solution' based on industrial murder.[63] The ideologically motivated measures that were to be implemented against political opponents and Jews found considerable resonance in army circles where, despite the Rapallo partnership of earlier years, there was little love lost for the Bolsheviks, or the Jews, particularly among the younger officers.[64] As von Reichenau reminded the troops on 10 October 1941, the fundamental purpose of the operation was to effect the 'complete annihilation of the false Bolshevistic doctrine of the Soviet State and its armed forces', for this was 'the only way to fulfil our historic task to liberate the German people once and forever from the Asiatic-Jewish danger'.[65]

As the moment for the attack on Russia approached, Hitler appeared almost to hesitate at the magnitude of what he was undertaking, conscious, no doubt, that there was a considerable element of gamble involved in Barbarossa, irrespective of all the confident forecasts of Soviet military weakness and ineptitude. 'I feel as if I am pushing open the door to a dark room never seen before,' he is alleged to have remarked on the eve of the invasion, 'without knowing what lies behind the door'.[66] In the circumstances, a degree of uncertainty and trepidation was perfectly understandable. The German armed forces, under the political direction of the National Socialist Party, were about to embark on a military adventure that for Hitler would mark the culmination of two decades spent plotting and preparing for the inevitable showdown with Bolshevism. Admittedly, the onslaught against the USSR would be launched in conditions entirely different from those he had originally envisaged and hoped for, and to which end he had pursued his foreign policy more or less in accordance with a programme tabulated during the 1920s until the disappointments of 1936–37 had forced him to tread a different path. Despite the undeniable importance of those military and political factors in determining the timing of the break with Russia during 1940–41, and despite his hopes that the collapse of the USSR would bring him the partnership with Britain he had always craved,[67] the underlying ideological impulse for the German invasion of the USSR should not be marginalized.

The day before his troops poured across the Soviet–German border Hitler wrote to Mussolini finally informing him of the momentous developments that were about to engulf eastern

Europe. Although the German leader could hardly be credited with exercising any particular candour in his dealings with Il Duce, the letter concluded with sentiments, some of which clearly came from the heart. Mindful perhaps of Mussolini's January 1940 communication, which had implored him not to break with his anti-Bolshevik principles, Hitler wrote of the 'irksome' partnership with the USSR, which had been at odds with 'my whole origin, my concepts, and my former obligations'. Now that the die was cast, he concluded, 'I am happy ... to be relieved of these mental agonies'.[68]

Chapter 11
The Primacy of Ideology: Anti-Bolshevism in the Context of the 'Endlösung', 1941–43

In the weeks that followed the launching of Operation Barbarossa Hitler approached a state of euphoria as his armed forces smashed through the Soviet defences and rolled ever deeper into the USSR. The rapid advance of the Wehrmacht, and the substantial damage it was able to inflict on the Russians in the initial stages of the campaign, appeared to suggest that the prediction of an early victory had been fully justified. Less than three weeks after the invasion began the Führer announced triumphantly to his propaganda minister that the Soviet Union was practically beaten. To be sure, some tough fighting still lay ahead, but the pounding the Red Army had already taken meant that in military terms at least Bolshevism was a spent force.[1]

Despite the sweltering confines of the 'Wolf's lair', his headquarters at Rastenburg in East Prussia, Hitler was in excellent spirits during the early phase of the Russian campaign, frequently joking with his secretaries and holding forth to the inner circle about the glorious future that lay ahead of the Reich.[2] At mealtimes he sat opposite a wall across which was draped a huge map of the USSR, which, as Christa Schroeder recalled, often provoked animated outbursts against the Soviet Union and the iniquities of Bolshevism.[3] During one such outburst, on the night of 11–12 July, Hitler reaffirmed his belief in the inseparability of Bolshevism and Jewry: Bolshevism was 'Christianity's illegitimate child,' he announced; both were 'inventions of the Jew.'[4]

In confident expectation of an imminent Soviet collapse, Hitler began to turn his attention to new tasks and challenges, some arising directly from the breathtaking advance of German forces in Russia, others rather less tangible, but, in Hitler's mind at least, no less real and compelling. At first glance there would seem to be little discernible connection between smashing 'Jewish Bolshevism' in European Russia and the growing likelihood of a conflict with the USA. For Hitler, however, who remained steeped in the belief that Bolshevism was but one manifestation of Jewish 'internationalism', the provocative nature of US policy since mid-1940, most recently demonstrated by the US occupation of Iceland, had confirmed his suspicions that the American president, Franklin Delano Roosevelt, was himself an assiduous servant of international Jewry. As he wrote to Mussolini on 20 July 1941, America, 'thanks to her Jewish leadership' was not only the antagonist of both Europe and East Asia, but would also one day reveal itself as the 'most dangerous enemy' of the British Empire, whose present leaders were blinded to this inescapable fact due to their own 'narrow-minded stupidity'.[5]

Only a few days before writing these words Hitler had received the Japanese ambassador and, in one of his most revealing statements of that momentous summer, urged Japan to fall on Russia, whose defeat would finally enable the combined might of Germany and Japan to be brought to bear against the USA in the decisive struggle for world supremacy.[6] At other points not far removed in time from his conversation with Ōshima, and redolent of his past dreams of an Anglo–German alignment, the chancellor predicted that Churchill would suddenly fall from power, following which Britain, gripped by a massive wave of anti-Semitism, would be the first to join the ranks in 'Europe's struggle against America'.[7] Whatever form that confrontation might take, and with whomever Germany was partnered, be it Britain, Japan or both, the prerequisite for opening the struggle with the USA was, as he had emphasized to Ōshima, the final and irreversible defeat of the Soviet Union.

As close as that objective seemed in mid-July 1941, its achievement would inevitably confront the Reich with staggering logistical problems, if only due to the sheer vastness of the territory Germany now occupied and administered. Apart from a general desire to exploit for German benefit the vast economic resources of the

Soviet Union, the implications of the successful execution of Barbarossa had hardly been thought through in their entirety. As a result of the Wehrmacht's advance, hundreds of thousands and soon millions of civilians were uprooted or automatically incarcerated in the ever-expanding 'occupied territories'. This situation, which from the German perspective deteriorated with every additional village taken, coupled with the nature, ethnicity, race and religion of the indigenous population of European Russia, inevitably opened up the racial issues that lay at the root of Nazi ideology and, in particular, the question of what was to be done with Soviet Jewry.

Before examining the significance of that question for this study, namely the relationship between the ideological impetus for Operation Barbarossa as a campaign designed to eradicate 'Jewish Bolshevism' and the origins of the 'Final Solution', it seems advisable briefly to sketch some of the main developments in the Jewish question in so far as it had conditioned German domestic politics since the autumn of 1935 with the promulgation of the Nuremberg laws. Despite that legislation having caused widespread offence and protest, notably in the democratic world, there was no slackening in pace or reduction of intensity with regard to the various schemes under discussion for the persecution of the German Jewish community. To be sure, during 1936, with all eyes on the Berlin Olympics, which provided the regime with a unique opportunity to demonstrate to the world its splendour, achievements and respectability, there was considerable concern for Germany's public image and this certainly affected the rate and severity of anti-Semitic outbursts and atrocities. Behind the scenes, however, plans proceeded apace to introduce additional measures designed to accelerate the social, political and economic marginalization, emasculation and impoverishment of German Jews and, in the perverse *credo* of the Nazi state, to offer further protection to the German people against the possibility of racial contamination.

Indeed, although 1936 appeared a relatively quiet year in terms of the Jewish question, developments in foreign politics conspired not only to prepare the ground for further crippling economic exploitation of the German Jews, but arguably to lay the foundations for the transformation of the 'Jewish problem' from one of largely domestic concern to one of truly international dimensions.[8] In short, with his strategic position greatly strengthened by the reoccupation of the Rhineland, and with the prospect of conflict with the Soviet Union brought sharply into focus by the outbreak of the Spanish Civil War, Hitler was both able and obliged to concentrate his energies on preparing the country for external aggression and foreign conquest. This was the essential purpose of the four-year plan, Hitler's memorandum on which had not only outlined the prospect of a major conflagration arising in the foreseeable future pitting the Reich against Bolshevik Russia and 'worldwide Jewry', but also, with a view to the possible machinations of Jews in wartime – even a second 'stab in the back' – provided for the expropriation of all Jews through the provision of a law making 'the whole of Jewry', not solely German Jews, liable for any damage inflicted on the 'German economy, and thus the German people'.[9]

Once German foreign policy had moved into its initial phase of active aggression during 1938–39, with the annexations of Austria, the Sudetenland and finally the rump of Czechoslovakia, the Jewish question inevitably became internationalized. In annexing these territories, Germany nominally assumed responsibility for Jewish citizens of other sovereign nations, and this, long before the momentous numbers involved during the conquests of 1940–41, soon resulted in complications. Indeed, immediately following Munich the Jewish question had become a practical foreign-policy problem, in this case encumbering German relations with Poland, because of the decision to expel forthwith all Polish Jews from the Reich. While the treatment meted out to the Jews in Germany had already resulted in serious international consequences, particularly with regard to the United States, and was about to do so again as a result of the Reichskristallnacht, the dispute with Poland in late autumn 1938 marked the first occasion on which the Jewish question spilled over into German relations with a friendly state and, moreover, at that stage one that was still being considered as a potential ally against 'Jewish Bolshevik' Russia.[10]

After the Reichskristallnacht, inevitably explained as a response to the intolerable provocations of 'world Jewry',[11] the statements of Hitler and other senior Nazis on the Jewish question became positively menacing. Within three months of the pogrom Hitler had threatened the Jews with destruction in revenge for their treachery in November 1918,[12] Göring had promised a 'showdown' with Jewry should the German Reich become embroiled with foreign powers,[13] and Ribbentrop had spoken of the need to suppress Germany's 'sworn enemies', the Jewish 'vermin'.[14] Most famously, in a speech to the Reichstag on 30 January 1939, Hitler made a chilling prophecy that has justifiably been viewed as a seminal statement on the road to the 'Final Solution'. 'If the Jewish international financiers inside and outside Europe succeed in involving the nations in another war,' declared the chancellor, 'the result will not be the Bolshevization of the world, and with it a victory of Jewry, but the annihilation of the Jewish race in Europe.'[15]

When war broke out between Germany and the Western powers in September 1939 the fate of the Jews thus already hung in the balance. During the invasion and early stages of the occupation of Poland, violence against Jews perpetrated by the SS and isolated Wehrmacht units, though widespread, was largely sporadic and uncoordinated, partially as a result of the initial concentration against the Polish intelligentsia.[16] In the wake of the western campaign, which brought Belgian, Dutch and French Jews under German control, the Nazi leadership began seriously to consider a plan, first mooted in 1937–38, to solve the 'Jewish problem' by transporting all European Jews to the French colony of Madagascar. This proposal, succinctly formulated in a memorandum of 3 July 1940 by Franz Rademacher of the German foreign ministry, had the added advantage of using the European Jews effectively as hostages, or, as Rademacher put it, 'as a pledge for the future good behaviour of the members of their race in America', at a time when increasingly disquieting noises were being heard from the other side of the Atlantic in relation to the progress of Nazi arms in Europe.[17]

With the extension of the war to Russia in June 1941 the magnitude of the 'Jewish problem' increased to a colossal degree for two main reasons. First, given the scale of the operation, huge numbers of Jews would be bound to fall into German hands. Second, as already noted, the ideological nature of the war, which was understood and accepted in large measure by the Wehrmacht, and the sanctioning in advance by the German leadership of the most brutal and inhumane modes of conduct, made it likely that no quarter would be given to the Jews, irrespective of their putative activities as partisans or political commissars. This is certainly some way removed from the idea that the invasion of the USSR, with its declared aim of extirpating Bolshevism, was intimately bound up with the timing and reasons for the decision to move from the planned mass deportations of Jews eastwards in the wake of victory over the USSR to the 'Final Solution' of their physical annihilation. Nevertheless, the undisputed ideological impetus underpinning Barbarossa, the acceptance by the invading force of the apocalyptic nature of the conflict, their own cooperation and participation in the genocide, the deployment of the Einsatzkommando, the recruitment of local support for anti-Jewish measures – all these and more serve to demonstrate that the fate of Soviet Jewry after 22 June 1941 was effectively sealed as long as German forces occupied tracts of Russian territory.

These important questions aside, any concentration on Bolshevism, and its links with so-called international Jewry, leads naturally to an examination of the association, freely drawn by Hitler and advertised volubly by Goebbels after June 1941, between Soviet Bolshevism on the one hand and Anglo–American 'plutocracy' on the other, and the related conclusions the Nazi leadership drew about the Jewish international conspiracy, of which Bolshevism had always been the primary but not the only focus. While the Nazi–Soviet Pact had governed German relations with the Soviet Union, Hitler and Goebbels had essentially side-stepped the contentious issue of their previous denunciations of 'Jewish Bolshevism' through the simple expedient of altering their public terminology, transforming Jews into 'plutocrats' and Bolshevists into 'capitalists'.[18] No sooner had German troops crossed the Soviet–German demarcation line, however, than the verbal attack on Judaism and Bolshevism and the assertion of intimate links between the two was reignited with added vigour. Finding themselves now at war with Britain and the USSR, German propagandists suddenly revealed the link between capitalist 'plutocracy' and 'Jewish Bolshevism', thus rediscovering the old fable of the joint direction of world affairs by international Jewry through its manipulation of Bolshevism and international finance.[19]

More significantly perhaps, particularly in view of what Hitler had said to Ōshima on 14 July 1941, the attack on Judaism was not principally aimed at British but at American 'plutocracy'. Indeed, only two days after Barbarossa got underway the ProMi-Informations-dienst released an article purporting to demonstrate the links between Bolshevism and 'plutocracy' by exposing how a group of New York-based Jewish exiles, each a veteran and leader of the 1905 Russian revolution, had actually financed the Bolshevik revolution of 1917. Claiming to base these revelations on contemporary records, in particular on a memorandum penned by the head of intelligence at the French embassy in Washington, the article provided details of how this clique of failed subversives had drummed up financial, political and other support from leading Jewish circles in the USA.[20]

With respect to Jewish influence in Britain, it was less the financing of revolution in Russia than the tireless efforts of Jewry to encircle the Reich that attracted the attention of Goebbels and his colleagues. In an undated piece, possibly written before the onset of Barbarossa, the ProMi pundits drew what they considered to be interesting comparisons between the Jewish role in Britain in the years before 1914, and again before 1939, concluding that, as Jewish influence was so prevalent in the British diplomatic and military elites, to say nothing of its domination of the media, it was essentially the Jews who had led the drive to encircle the Reich on both occasions.[21] Before long the Germans inevitably turned their focus on the 'marriage' between London and Moscow, pointing to the historical links between Jewry and Bolshevism in Britain[22] and, as an indication of Britain's subservience to the Comintern, its connivance with the Soviet Union in the invasion of Iran.[23] By declaring war on Germany in September 1939, it was held in December 1941, Britain had already shown its colours, deflecting the Reich from its real mission of protecting Europe and the world against 'Moscow's Jewish-Bolshevik nihilism'.[24]

As relations between Germany and America continued to deteriorate, most obviously because of incidents in the Atlantic culminating in Roosevelt's 'shoot on sight' order of September 1941, German anti-Bolshevik and anti-Semitic propaganda came increasingly to focus on the United States. Already, on 4 July, a significant day in the American calendar, the Antikomintern's *UdSSR-Dienst* had done its best to spoil the independence celebrations by running an article on why America's 'Jewish plutocrats' were to be counted among the most enthusiastic supporters of Bolshevism. In response to claims that all previous attempts to draw connections between Anglo-Saxon 'plutocrats' and Soviet Bolsheviks had been nothing but the slanderous inventions of anti-Semites, the article claimed that, irrespective of the undeniable lessons of history, which demonstrated the link amply, it was obvious to all that capitalism and Bolshevism complemented one another perfectly. Capitalism and 'plutocracy', it was argued, simply prepared the way for Bolshevism. Thus, capitalism and 'plutocracy' promoted the concentration of wealth and power in the hands of a small elite while the masses sank ever deeper into despair, suffering from hunger, exploitation, sickness and sundry other miseries associated with poverty and unemployment. In this atmosphere of helplessness and desperation Bolshevism was able to flourish until such time as its Jewish controllers ignited the revolutionary fire.

As evidence for these ideas, the article quoted the statements of an unnamed but 'powerful' Jewish New York banker who, in conversation with a former French diplomat had admitted quite openly that capitalism and Bolshevism were two 'poles' in the hands of an axis controlled by international Jewry. The source was equally candid about the aim of this seemingly unlikely alliance. Israel, he declared, was a nation like any other, whose elements, although dispersed throughout the globe, were united by the bond of a common race. The Jews were a 'League of Nations', to which every nation belonged, a fact that bestowed on the Jews the right to unite them all. 'We are accused of being destructive elements,' he concluded, 'but that only applies to a certain transitional stage. Today we are the smallest common factor among the nations. One day we will unite them all under one rule.'[25] One week later the Antikomintern warned its readers not to be duped into believing that America's recent rejection of a request from Moscow to represent Soviet interests in Vichy France was a sign that there were limits to how far Roosevelt was prepared to go in collaborating with the 'agents of subversion and chaos'. The reality of the situation was revealed, claimed the article, by an examination of the composition of Roosevelt's 'Jewish Bolshevik' staff and advisers whose task it was to 'create the conditions for a world revolution designed to secure Jewish world domination'.[26]

Shortly after Churchill's meeting with Roosevelt at Placentia Bay,

Newfoundland, in mid-August 1941, which spawned not only the Atlantic Charter but a warm message to Stalin promising support and material for the Soviet Union's fight against the Nazis, national distinctions were dropped entirely in a *UdSSR-Dienst* article entitled 'Jews of All Countries Unite!' The article described a radio broadcast from Moscow on 25 August about a meeting of prominent Jews held the previous day, the essentially Jewish nature of the occasion being underlined by the fact that the transmission had gone out in Yiddish. The essence of the message was that prominent Jewish writers, academics, artists and other individuals had congregated in the Soviet capital specifically to make an 'unprecedented cry for help ... aimed at Jews throughout the world', exhorting them to fight 'fascism', which 'threatens *them* with annihilation, *not the Soviet Union, notice*, but the *Jewish people*'.[27]

The significance of this meeting, or rather the significance allegedly attached to it at the highest level of the Nazi leadership, may well, argues Tobias Jersak, prove to be a key factor in our understanding of the reasons for and timing of the decision to annihilate European Jewry. From his investigation into the interaction of Hitler's conduct of war policy and the progress of plans towards a final solution to the Jewish question, Jersak concludes that events in August 1941 provided the impetus for genocide. The implications of the Placentia Bay summit, the Atlantic Charter and the joint message to Stalin, coupled with the slowing of the advance in Russia, as well as fear of an internal crisis and potential 'stab in the back' by a Jewish enemy called to arms by the international masters of Britain, the USA and the Soviet Union, meant that Hitler's plans and timetable had been thrown into complete disarray. Having based his calculations on achieving a final solution to the 'Jewish problem' and engaging in a possible confrontation with the United States only after the successful Blitzkrieg against the USSR, developments in August 1941 signified that Hitler's enemies had wrestled the initiative from his hands and combined in a common assault on the Reich. This was, however, not merely a case of Britain, the Soviet Union and the United States uniting against him, for the unifying element between British 'Jewish plutocracy', American 'Jewish high finance' and Soviet 'Jewish Bolshevism' was all too plain to see. From this analysis, and from measures taken subsequently in the autumn of 1941, including the decision finally to force German Jews to wear the Star of David, coupled with renewed anxiety about a crisis on the home front reminiscent of 1918, Jersak postulates that the decision to murder the European Jews was essentially a reaction on Hitler's part to a perceived declaration of war on Germany by international Jewry.[28] That being the case, Hitler would prove to be as good as his word when he had prophesied in the Reichstag in January 1939 that if Jewry caused a further world conflagration then the ultimate result would be the destruction of the European Jews.

Whatever Barbarossa and the reactions it provoked had done to Hitler's aims and intentions on the Jewish question, the euphoric mood that gripped the German leadership in the summer of 1941 was dissipated by a series of military reversals and setbacks, the culmination of which was the launch of a Soviet counter offensive in December that repulsed the German advance and threatened the Wehrmacht with a chronic strategic reversal. These events naturally shook Hitler, for they effectively signalled the failure of the Blitzkrieg against Russia and left Germany facing the prospect of a war for which it was not prepared. Despite the stabilization of the front, Hitler was still clearly troubled when Goebbels saw him on 20 March 1942. Although he professed to have clear objectives in view for the coming campaigns against the Bolshevik forces, he had already begun to hint at a limitation of his aims in Russia, and had even spoken of the possibility of a 'hundred years' war in the East'. 'I am shocked by the impression made upon me by the Führer on this occasion,' noted the Reich propaganda minister. 'I have never seen him so serious and deflated as today.'[29] A different emphasis was also evident in Hitler's speech at the Berlin Zeughaus on 15 March, for although the German leader had threatened the Bolshevik forces with 'utter destruction' in the coming offensives, he had also stated as Germany's war aim not the extirpation of Bolshevism, but the holding of the 'Bolshevik colossus ... at a remote distance'. In keeping with his ideological fixations, Hitler also used this occasion to highlight the fundamental responsibility of international Jewry for the war, alerting his audience to the collusion between 'Jewish wire-pullers who, spread throughout the globe, hoped to destroy the whole of Europe in a coordinated attack, a conspiracy which unites democracy and Bolshevism in a community of interests'.[30]

However, this is not to say that the military setbacks suffered in December 1941 any way permanently demoralized Hitler; indeed, much of the evidence detailing his attitude during 1942 reveals him as supremely confident of victory, even when the tide had clearly turned against Germany in the autumn of that year.[31] Nor does it denote any significant weakening of his commitment to combat Bolshevism, a subject on which he continued to lecture his allies on lines that had become too familiar to warrant repetition here. Nevertheless, although military affairs inevitably preoccupied Hitler at that time, which the surviving records of his political discussions with foreign statesmen and diplomats amply demonstrate,[32] it is also evident that he was gradually retreating into an ideological cul-de-sac, which only served to highlight the vicious impulses that underpinned his whole *Weltanschauung*. One explanation of this certainly lies in the simple fact that, having overrun huge areas in the east, Hitler was now in a position to perpetrate atrocities against the Jews and other alleged racial undesirables on an unprecedented scale. The renewed primacy of ideological factors was also conditioned by the addition of America as a formal enemy of the Reich following the German declaration of war on that country on 11 December 1941. Hitler had always suspected the influence of the Jews on American policy, and his decision to fight the USA most certainly had an ideological dimension to it.

Numerous commentators, including Hitler's more authoritative biographers, have argued that after 1937, and certainly following the outbreak of war, ideological issues became paramount in Hitler's deliberations and decision-making.[33] Nothing illustrates this better than his growing preoccupation with the Jewish question in and especially after 1941, when, as Jersak plausibly argues, the systematic annihilation of European Jewry gradually subsumed all notions of a coordinated strategy for the execution of war policy.[34] In much the same way, the fight against Bolshevism, for so long the central ideological principle of Nazi foreign policy, became absorbed by the wider struggle against world Jewry. Although one might contest Jersak's at present rather ambitious claim that the decision to proceed to organized industrial genocide was taken on the basis of events in mid-August 1941, not least because Hitler did not seem unduly anxious about the Atlantic Charter,[35] the extensive measures the regime took in late 1941 and 1942 systematically to prepare and implement the 'Final Solution', tend to emphasize the basic point that ideology, and within that definition anti-Semitism, was coming increasingly to the fore in Hitler's deliberations.

That Hitler made repeated references in and after 1941, in public and private, to the January 1939 'prophecy' about the extermination of European Jewry is an illustration of his preoccupation with the 'Jewish problem'. Already, in his speech of 30 January 1941, in what has plausibly been seen as a direct warning to the United States,[36] the German chancellor declared that if Jewry succeeded in bringing the 'other world', namely the USA, into the war, thus transforming it into a world conflagration, it would mean the end of the Jews in Europe.[37] In the months following the onset of Barbarossa, the 'prophecy' and, indeed, its unfolding fulfilment, was mentioned numerous times in the inner circle,[38] while during 1942 Hitler made four separate references to it in addressing the Reichstag and other public gatherings.[39] He was no less restrained in private. 'World Jewry will suffer a great catastrophe at the same time as Bolshevism,' noted Goebbels following a meeting with the chancellor in mid-February 1942.

> The Führer once more expressed his determination to clean up the Jews in Europe pitilessly. There must be no squeamish sentimentalism about it. The Jews have deserved the catastrophe that has now overtaken them. Their destruction will go hand in hand with the destruction of our enemies. We must hasten this process with cold ruthlessness. We shall thereby render an inestimable service to a humanity tormented for thousands of years by the Jews.[40]

As Goebbels confirms a year later, and as the appalling facts demonstrate, this was no transient preoccupation; in May 1943 Hitler was once more demanding that anti-Semitism 'again become the focal point of our spiritual struggle'.[41] That same month he decreed that German propaganda should further concentrate its efforts on exposing Jewry as the cause and catalyst of the world conflagration. This, he believed, would not only find an echo abroad, leading others to question the wisdom of tolerating Jews in their midst, but also inspire the party old guard that had hitherto been left cold by propaganda drives on issues such as the creation of the 'new Europe'.[42]

By that stage Hitler's capacity for self-delusion in the face of an increasingly catastrophic military situation on the eastern front appeared to know no bounds. After Stalingrad the German leader had decided to put his faith in 'total' warfare, convinced it would be Germany's salvation, even though arguably by that point and certainly after the catastrophe at Kursk in July 1943, with its tremendous losses in terms of materiel and personnel,[43] Germany was in the long term incapable of fighting even a defensive war. Gradually, the exhortations to struggle on against the Bolshevik hordes became devoid of either impact or meaning; after 1943 they were aimed at an ever dwindling audience as one by one Germany's European allies in the struggle against the USSR either deserted it or were overrun by the Red Army. Yet there can be no doubting either Hitler's personal commitment to the cause or the significance of those ideological convictions that contributed so extensively to his own ruination. On Heroes' Remembrance Day in March 1943, only weeks after the surrender of the Sixth Army at Stalingrad, he continued to propagate the essential message that had underpinned his actions since the summer of 1941, and upon which the fundamental features of his political philosophy had always been based:

> What is becoming increasingly clear to us is that the conflict in which Europe has been engaged ever since the First World War has gradually assumed the character of a struggle which can only be compared with the greatest historic events of the past. A pitiless and merciless war has been imposed upon us by world Jewry. If we are not able to halt these elements of destruction at Europe's frontiers, then they would lay waste to the whole continent. ... Whether English or American newspapers, parliamentarians, popular speakers, and literary men demand the destruction of our children, the sterilization of our male youth, and so on as their primary war aim, or whether the Bolsheviks without further ado slaughter whole nations, men, women and children, it is one and the same thing. For the ultimate driving force in each case is the eternal hate of that accursed race which for

thousands of years has, as a true scourge of God, so flogged the people until, in times of self-contemplation, they once more turn on their tormenters. ... I repeat the prophecy I have already made: at the end of this war it will not be Germany or her allies who will have fallen prey to Bolshevism, but those countries and peoples who, by delivering themselves ever more into the hands of Jewry, will one day collapse and succumb to the Bolshevist poison.[44]

Chapter 12
Goebbels, the Antikomintern and the Propaganda Onslaught against Bolshevism, 1941–43

W hile Hitler and his military commanders waited in anticipation for the decisive military breakthrough in the weeks after the launching of Operation Barbarossa, it fell to the German propagandists to explain to the German people and, indeed, the people of occupied and neutral Europe, the rationale and justification behind the assault on the USSR. Goebbels's immediate priority after the onset of hostilities was to provide clarification – of sorts – to a bemused continent and, in particular, to the German nation. At his press conference on 22 June 1941 the Reich propaganda minister announced that the 'criminal faithlessness' of the Bolshevik regime was especially to be highlighted in the press to drive home the point that the attack on Russia was no 'simple about-turn', but an expression of the essence of National Socialism, which was thereby returning to those fundamental principles that had inspired it: 'the struggle against plutocracy and Bolshevism'.[1]

The *Völkischer Beobachter* opened the campaign on 23 June with a broadside that contained many strands of the propaganda that would be employed during the first few weeks of Barbarossa. Under the headline 'Moscow's Desire for Bolshevik Chaos Proves Stronger than Political Reason', the *VB* claimed to provide documentary proof of Soviet treachery, which included the intensified agitation of the Comintern, an extensive Soviet espionage network in Germany, Russian collusion with London and, inevitably, the Soviet military build-up and threat posed to Europe by the Red

Army.[2] These various justifications for the German attack on the USSR were sometimes juxtaposed with stories of Bolshevik atrocities and abomination, presumably in an effort to maximize their effect. Thus, three weeks into the campaign the VB insisted that in combating 'Jewish Bolshevism' the Reich was waging a war of 'moral humanity against spiritual desolation, against the decline of public morals, against spiritual and physical terror, and against criminal policies whose makers sit on mountains of corpses'.[3]

Prior to the launching of Barbarossa, the ProMi had prepared an extensive and confidential guide for use by those involved in public speaking that detailed the general guidelines to follow and arguments to use when dealing with the German–Soviet conflict.[4] While they were instructed to make no reference to the prospective fate of the German conquests, so as not to arouse undue hopes, speakers were given three essential tasks in this area. The first, a common theme in early Nazi propaganda during the eastern campaign, was to stress the treachery of the Soviet Union and its collusion with Britain, with which it had been secretly conniving at Germany's destruction.[5] Speakers were to emphasize that following the defeat of Russia Britain would once more become the focus of Germany's attention, a rather neat way of communicating to the public that the anticipated defeat of the USSR did not mean the end of the war. Second, the eastern campaign was to be portrayed as Germany's fight against a plot hatched by the British to exterminate Germany by uniting Jews, democrats, Bolsheviks and reactionaries. Finally, and most importantly, speakers were to stress the inevitability of final victory.

In the main it would appear that these guidelines were adhered to in the early phase of the Russian war. In a review of the German media's coverage of the campaign compiled one month after the attack, the Foreign Research Press Service, an adjunct of the Royal Institute of International Affairs, detected some differences of emphasis in the propaganda emanating from Berlin. Although by no means silent on ideological issues, German domestic propaganda tended initially to rationalize the attack by stressing the growing military threat posed by the USSR. In its external propaganda, on the other hand, the ProMi laid much more emphasis on the notion of an ideological crusade. Thus, in its release of 27 June, which did not feature prominently in the German press, the DNB claimed that what had begun as the 'battle of Germany against Moscow' had rapidly become the 'crusade of Europe against Bolshevism'. The DNB further claimed that Germany had received a European mandate for its actions, and that in the present conflict Europe, having at last 'found herself', was defending everything that in the 'struggles, labours, and creative efforts of a thousand years, she has made the central point of all human culture and civilization'. Inspired by National Socialism, Germany had taken up the fight against Bolshevism to 'defend the basic principles of human society', the only alternative to which was subjugation to a system that aimed at nothing less than 'Bolshevik world dominion'.[6]

From this general standpoint of European solidarity against the common enemy, German propaganda developed some interesting characteristics to accommodate local conditions. To the Portuguese, for example, the Germans unsuccessfully attempted to portray the onslaught against Bolshevism as a Christian crusade against atheism, while to the Danes communism was described as the deadly enemy of the ideals of the Scandinavian people.[7] To the Czechs, on the other hand, the German propagandists magnified the threat of a Bolshevik assault on Europe, and drew a distinction between the Bolshevik tyrants and their long-suffering victims, the Russian people.[8]

As 1942 opened, Goebbels and his propagandists faced not only the problem of how to incorporate the war against the United States into their propaganda, but also the repercussions of the military setback on the Eastern Front, which, as Goebbels freely admitted, necessitated fundamental changes in the nature and direction of the Reich's propaganda campaigns.[9] One area of German propaganda that saw a marked intensification after 1941 was Britain's supposed collusion with Bolshevism, with the German press instructed to highlight not only British receptivity to Bolshevik ideology,[10] but also to brand Britain's plan to deliver western and central Europe to Bolshevism after victory over Germany as a shameless betrayal of European culture.[11] As the year had begun under the impression of Eden's visit to Moscow, Goebbels instructed that the smaller European countries, particularly those under German occupation, must be made to understand that Britain was determined to 'surrender the European continent to Bolshevism'; in this way they must also be forced to accept that a 'European defensive front' was required against Bolshevism and all others who conspired to betray European culture.[12]

By mid-1942, however, a lull had occurred in Germany's anti-Bolshevik propaganda, partly due to Goebbels's concern that it might be having a detrimental rather than a positive effect. He was concerned, for example, that the constant reference to Bolshevism as a coherent doctrine had invested the Soviets with ideals that inspired them to acts of 'fanaticism and heroic resistance'. In his terms, of course, it was not heroism at all, but 'the primitive animal instincts of Slavdom organized into resistance by ferocious terror'. The secret of Russian resistance lay in the fact that the 'Slav mentality has allied itself with an infernal Jewish "education"', the result of which was Bolshevism.[13] Moreover, after the experiences of the winter of 1941–42 the Reich propaganda minister was understandably so wary of raising German hopes following the start of the summer offensive that by mid-July he wanted a 'brake' put on reports from the Eastern Front, not least because the fluctuating fortunes of the military operations could never capture the essence of Germany's mission. 'This struggle cannot be comprehended by the military experts since it is essentially an ideological conflict,' he complained, 'and no one can know whether the Russians will not once again very soon face us with a few more million men.'[14] There were also organizational complications because the army in the east had its own *Propaganda-Kompanien*, which sometimes caused problems for Reich-based propaganda agencies. In June 1942, for example, the Antikomintern complained that material being sent back to Germany by the *PK*s was too restricted by topic and recommended it be widened in scope so that it might be deployed throughout Europe to better effect.[15]

Nevertheless, German propaganda was clearly enjoying some success in the neutral states, certainly enough to annoy the British minister in Lisbon, Sir Ronald Campbell who, in early June, sent to London a scathing review of the Portuguese press, some of which had clearly fallen for the German line. As Alfredo Pimenta wrote in the *Voz* newspaper on 8 May, the hour was approaching

> when the sword of justice of Lohengrin will deal the final blow, for which all Europe is waiting, at the Moscow dragon, which has not yet been destroyed only because of the

sacrilegious and nefarious help that the Russians are receiving in an attempt to bring about a victory that would be a catastrophe and would be the overthrow of Europe.[16]

During the Soviet–German conflict the Antikomintern was able to base its activities primarily on what might be termed the 'practice run' it had had during the autumn of 1936 when the Wehrmacht manoeuvres had been based on the contingency of a war with Russia. During the manoeuvres the Antikomintern had functioned as it expected to in the event of a genuine German–Soviet conflict, and in so doing had worked out a programme of propaganda measures for use as a 'weapon of the armed forces', as Taubert later put it. Nevertheless, the 1936 experience was useful only to a point because the propagandists' activities, like those of the diplomats, were essentially determined by the Reich's military fortunes. In that sense one can readily understand Taubert's point that the propagandist was never an initiator but always cast in a support role and, as such, able only to represent events, not shape them. The activities of both the ProMi and the Antikomintern were, moreover, complicated following the launching of Barbarossa because numerous other agencies became involved in the dissemination of propaganda in the occupied territories, which meant that the nominally responsible agencies faced some serious and disruptive competition.[17]

The Antikomintern's chief role in the early phase of Barbarossa, for which it had created the Dienststelle Vineta, a special staff of translators and native speakers of Russian and other eastern languages, was to explain to the Russian population that Germany perceived as its principal enemy its own 'Jewish-Bolshevik oppressors'. To that end the Antikomintern had also equipped Wehrmacht units with leaflets, brochures, placards, recordings and films designed to reinforce the message that Hitler was not to be feared as a conqueror but welcomed as a liberator. In this way, Taubert recalled, the opening phase of the Russian campaign was quite different from other military operations in that the propaganda was quite literally to accompany rather than follow the invading force.[18] A further function of the Antikomintern in the early stages of Barbarossa was to highlight the appalling conditions of Soviet workers and the total absence of cultural life in the USSR

191

in an attempt to demonstrate the socially debilitating effects of the relentless Bolshevik drive to arm the country. As far as records for 1942 permit a judgement to be made, the Antikomintern appeared to be in active collaboration with anti-Bolshevik agencies in occupied, non-belligerent and neutral countries, and continued to fund exhibitions, publications and film shows in occupied and neutral Europe.[19] Taubert and his Antikomintern colleagues were centrally involved in promoting the 'Sowjet Paradies' exhibition, which ran in major German cities in the first half of 1942. This combination of displays, decrepit artefacts from the USSR, films, posters and a wide range of literature depicting the horrors of life in the Soviet Union not only emphasized the links between Jewry and Bolshevism, but also made a special point of drawing a distinction between the Bolshevik tyrants and the long-suffering Russian people who were being 'ruthlessly sacrificed for the goals of the Jewish world revolution'.[20]

After the onset of Operation Barbarossa the emphasis the Antikomintern placed on the purported links between Bolshevism and Jewry became much more pronounced than had hitherto been the case. To be sure, such linkages had not been unheard of prior to the attack on the USSR, but, as Jeffrey Herf has noted, it was only in mid-1941 that the Antikomintern joined forces with specific anti-Semitic agencies in a concentrated drive to emphasize the importance of the Jewish question in the ideological struggle against the USSR.[21] The campaign was only a few days old when the Antikomintern published a 130-page booklet entitled *Warum Krieg mit Stalin?*, the essential message of which could be gleaned from the illustration that adorned the front cover.[22] This depicted a figure, a characteristic Nazi Jewish stereotype complete with sunken eyes, a large hooked nose, thick lips and his hair in ringlets, dressed in Soviet military attire, crawling with dagger in hand through a trail of skulls, presumably those of his previous victims. With a menacing grin on his face the assassin was stealthily advancing on an unsuspecting German soldier, the intention clearly being to convey the impression of Jewish-Bolshevik treachery against the Reich and to substantiate the German thesis of a premeditated Soviet strike.

Warum Krieg mit Stalin? covered many of the issues common to earlier Antikomintern publications, including the aggressive intentions of the Soviet Union, the destructive activities of the Comintern and Bolshevik mismanagement of the economy, but its most important feature was the new prominence given to the role of world Jewry as the common denominator in the conflicts into which Germany had been forced in September 1939 and again in June 1941. 'Created by Jews, the Soviet Union is also today run by Jews', proclaimed the author at the start of a lengthy chapter that purported to expose the crucial positions occupied by Jews at every echelon and in every area of activity of the Communist Party and the Soviet state.[23] Thus, the Jews dominated the political life of the USSR, the Red Army, the Soviet economy, the press, science and the cultural arena. Lists of Jews prominent in each of these spheres coupled with statistics intended to demonstrate the staggering ratio of Jews in positions of authority relative to the total number of Jews in the Soviet Union were provided to support the central point that as an essentially Jewish state the USSR was and always had been an enemy of the Reich. Such anti-'Semitic' as opposed to anti-'Bolshevik' propaganda would become a central feature of the Antikomintern's activities as the German–Soviet conflict progressed; in this way Taubert and his colleagues played an important part in the generation and dissemination of propaganda relating to the war in the east, the essential purpose of which was to supply a 'public justification for mass murder'.[24]

The relative lull in the anti-Bolshevik activities of both the ProMi and Antikomintern during 1942 stood in stark contrast to the fresh propaganda offensive occasioned by the Allied landings in North Africa in November and the German reversals in Russia, which culminated in the capitulation at Stalingrad. As the battle for Stalingrad drew to a close, the British Foreign Office, which had continued to monitor German propaganda, noted that the Germans were in the process of hurriedly disinterring 'that long buried corpse which they call the "Bolshevik bogey"'.[25] In contrast to the confident tone that had characterized German propaganda at the time of the Wehrmacht's military successes in the summer of 1941, when a stridently upbeat momentum had been maintained, the chief feature after Stalingrad was the emphasis on the need for the European nations to pull together not, as generally in earlier times, to cooperate in a crusade against Bolshevism but to collaborate in the defence of the continent.

Goebbels announced the opening of the new offensive to his senior colleagues on 12 February 1943, only days before he was to exhort the masses gathered in the Berlin Sportpalast to wage 'total war' on Germany's enemies.[26] The struggle against Bolshevism must become the dominant and 'all-pervading' theme of German propaganda in the coming months, he declared, not least because the recent military reversals had generated fear among the neutrals and heightened the sense of allegiance towards the Reich felt by Germany's friends and allies.[27] Göring had already struck the first note to this effect in his speech on 30 January 1943, the tenth anniversary of the handover of power and only days before Paulus surrendered to the Russians, by referring to Germany's historic role as the continent's defensive bastion against invaders from the east, a role that was now all the more crucial because 'for Bolshevism, Europe is a jumping-off ground', while for Russia it represented nothing more than a 'mere appendix'.[28]

Before long the impact of this line of language, plus the intensified anti-Bolshevik propaganda carried out simultaneously throughout Europe, was making itself felt. On 22 February the special issues committee of the ministry of information and the political warfare executive met to discuss a paper that highlighted the fact that German propaganda about the 'Bolshevik bogey' had reached 'a new crescendo' in the aftermath of Stalingrad. A notable feature of this propaganda was the assertion that even if Germany managed to keep the Soviet armies at bay, the USSR would continue to pursue its aim of spreading Bolshevism throughout Europe by subversive means in order to 'disintegrate countries from within'. In that respect the Germans drew a sharp distinction between the physical threat to those states that lay across the advance of the Red Army, and the less tangible, though no less real, ideological threat to the countries of western Europe.[29]

These and other themes were subsequently taken up by the *Polish Fortnightly Review*, the official organ of the London-based Polish government in exile, which noted how Goebbels had 'gladly snatched at every reference to Polish–Soviet affairs' to demonstrate the alleged designs on Poland commonly attributed to the USSR. German propaganda was exploiting the Polish–Soviet problem throughout occupied Europe, both in the press and in radio broadcasts, as an example of the annexationist tendencies of the

USSR not towards an opponent but towards one of its allies and, moreover, at a time when it was still far from certain of victory. In addition, by tolerating this state of affairs the British were demonstrating how lightly they took their obligations to the Poles. In words that may well have returned to haunt them, the authors of the article accused the Germans of seeking to create in the minds of their audience the impression that Britain and the USA were impotent in the face of Soviet demands, and that therefore 'no European State can count on effective help against the Soviets on the part of the Anglo-Saxon world'. What this amounted to, it was argued, was a cynical attempt by the Nazis to sow discord among their opponents to conceal anxiety about their own position, and an effort to undermine faith in the 'great moral principles for which Great Britain and her allies are fighting'.[30]

In these circumstances, the discovery of the atrocity the Russians had perpetrated at Katyn played directly into Goebbels's hands. 'The discovery of 12,000 Polish officers, murdered by the GPU, is being brought into play in our anti-Bolshevik propaganda in the grandest manner', he noted enthusiastically on 14 April.[31] 'How the Katyn incident will develop further I cannot say at the moment. But it is my intention to transform it into a political affair of the very highest order,' he continued three days later.[32] Accordingly, the German press was instructed to cover the story in all its gruesome details, to expose the 'naked reality' of this 'Jewish-Bolshevik crime', and to expose as a naïve fallacy the assurances of the British and Americans who had insisted that Bolshevism had undergone significant changes since the days of the revolution.[33]

Katyn provided Goebbels with his last major coup against the Soviet Union before military developments in the summer of 1943 thrust the German propaganda machine onto the defensive. Nevertheless, the indefatigable propaganda minister was resolved to the end to make as much mileage as possible out of the 'Bolshevik bogey'. With that aim in view he continued to support the efforts of the Antikomintern to promote anti-Bolshevik, anti-Soviet and anti-Jewish sentiment throughout Europe, approving, for example, the considerable sum of 222,750 Reichsmarks for a series of anti-Bolshevik propaganda initiatives in France,[34] and 137,800 Reichsmarks for a mobile exhibition in Greece.[35] Somewhat perversely hoping to profit from the string of Soviet victories against the

Wehrmacht from mid-1943 onwards, and perceiving cracks in the alliance between the Anglo-Americans and the USSR, in late 1943 Goebbels geared himself for a further titanic effort. 'I am organizing a new and great anti-Bolshevik campaign for our entire domestic and foreign propaganda apparatus,' he noted on 16 November. 'With the Soviet military successes as its basis, this campaign will amount to a further attempt to really give the European and enemy states the creeps. There is no way that they should be released from their fear of Bolshevism'.[36]

Sure enough, within days a draft document had been produced, proudly headed 'European Anti-Bolshevik Propaganda Action', which envisaged a propaganda campaign of very sizeable proportions, unfolding in three stages, and incorporating *inter alia* massed 'spontaneous' demonstrations, a European radio offensive against Bolshevism in which leading anti-Bolshevik campaigners from across the continent were to take the microphone, and a designated day to mark the anti-Bolshevik struggle in which the European nations were involved.[37] How successful any of these measures were in galvanizing support for the German cause is difficult to ascertain, but it is a measure both of Goebbels's tenacity and the strength of his convictions that in an ever deteriorating situation he continued to be driven by the desire to take the offensive against the 'Jewish-Bolshevik' enemy.

Chapter 13

Occupation and Cooperation: Russians and Europeans against Bolshevism, 1941–43

I n all probability Hitler had convinced himself by June 1941 that he would be rendering Europe a vital service by destroying the Soviet Union, whose purportedly aggressive intentions, as he stressed on several occasions, had been a significant factor in his decision to act.[1] This was clearly an obvious point to score in public, not least as a means of drumming up support for the campaign in important neutral states such as Turkey, where there was no love lost for Russia, either Bolshevik or otherwise.[2] Moreover, it was also a useful means of settling German opinion, where the notion of a collective struggle against a familiar adversary might succeed in offsetting some of the confusion that had been created by the sudden opening of a new phase of the conflict. It was thus no surprise when in his address on 22 June the Führer especially emphasized that his purpose in beginning hostilities in the east was not the 'protection of single countries' but the 'safeguarding of Europe and thereby the salvation of all'.[3]

Yet, the notion of a new European order arising from the defeat of Russia was by no means a purely tactical device. Following the expected collapse of Bolshevism, Germany would certainly dominate the continent, but a select group of other nations might share in the benefits of its victory if they chose to do so, especially the Nordic countries, Holland, and, curiously, Greece, in belated recognition of its valiant struggle against Italy.[4] When Count Ciano visited him at Rastenburg in October 1941, Hitler noted with satisfaction how the eastern campaign, which by that time had been joined by volunteer contingents from a number of countries, including Italy, had engendered 'a feeling of European solidarity'. This development he deemed to be of great importance for the future, especially in view of a possible clash between Europe and the United States. As the German chancellor explained:

> A later generation would have to cope with the problem of Europe–America. It would no longer be a matter of Germany or England, of Fascism, of National Socialism, or antagonistic systems, but of the common interests of Pan-Europe within the European economic area with her African supplements. The feeling of European solidarity, which at the moment was distinctly tangible, even though only faint against the background of the fighting in the east, would gradually have to change generally into a great recognition of the European community.[5]

Vague though these statements might be, it would be rash to dismiss them as idle rhetoric simply because they originated with Hitler. As early as the 1920s he had envisaged the possibility of a conflict between a German-led Europe and the United States of America. Now, with the prospect of the domination of the continent a distinct possibility, it should perhaps come as no surprise that this issue began to resurface in his thoughts. 'Europe', he further explained to the Italian foreign minister, 'held together by Germany in the north and Italy in the south', would be favourably placed to meet a challenge from the United States, not least in view of America's internal decomposition and the looming economic crisis that threatened it. Provided the Russian campaign was brought to a successful conclusion, and thereby the east 'placed in the service of the European idea', Europe would prevail in any struggle with 'the ridiculously half-civilized America'.[6]

The development of relations between the new Europe and the United States was, however, an issue for the future. For the moment, although selected European peoples would be permitted to prosper under the new order, others would be decidedly less fortunate. The Russian émigrés would certainly not be welcomed back. Not only had they done nothing for their homeland, but the simple fact was that 'Russia had been conquered with German blood for the protection of Europe *against* Russia'.[7] When shortly after the German invasion of the USSR the Russian Grand Duke Vladimir, then living in exile at St Briac in France, forwarded to Hitler a proposed proclamation calling on all Russians to cooperate with the Wehrmacht in their liberation from Bolshevism, he was immediately and sharply rebuffed. The proclamation, Ribbentrop wrote to Abetz, would hinder rather than assist the German war effort in that it would provide the Bolsheviks with an opportunity to claim that 'Russia was now threatened by the return of the old Tsarist feudalism'.[8]

There was of course never any question that the war Hitler unleashed in June 1941 was being fought for German ends and that the benefits accruing to other nations, though significant, not least the final exorcism of the red peril, were essentially incidental. During the 1930s Hitler had never portrayed Germany's mission in Europe as anything other than a defensive bulwark against Bolshevism. Now, with his armies swarming towards Leningrad and Moscow, he was hardly likely to share his prize, particularly with states that had at best reacted with lukewarm support for the original Anti-Comintern Pact. When in mid-July 1941 a Vichy French newspaper suggested that the assault on the USSR was 'Europe's war', and thus ought 'to be conducted for Europe as a whole', Hitler was appalled by this latest manifestation of Gallic impudence. In the course of the conference at which this issue was discussed, the Führer clearly outlined his intentions and the tactics he would employ to implement them. 'In principle we have now to face the task of cutting the giant cake according to our needs,' he explained, the order of priorities being 'first, to dominate it; second, to administer it; and third, to exploit it'. In pursuit of these goals Germany would disguise its real aims in the Soviet Union through the simple expedients of avoiding superfluous declarations, emphasizing that the Reich had been forced to a military decision, and posing as a liberating force; it made no sense to 'make people into enemies prematurely and unnecessarily'. The Germans would thus 'act as though we wanted to exercise a mandate only', but it must be clear 'to *us* ... that we shall never withdraw from these areas'.[9]

These predatory designs soon brought the Germans into conflict with those who genuinely hoped for liberation from Bolshevism. In the Ukraine, for example, the establishment in September 1941 of the civilian administration under Erich Koch, who, according to a postwar account based on the experiences of both Germans and Ukrainians, demonstrated no intention of enlisting the help of the Ukrainians in the fight against Bolshevism, effectively destroyed the friendly relationship that had been established between the Wehrmacht and the indigenous population. As an early victory was expected, it was felt that Ukrainian participation in the struggle would serve only to complicate German aims in the Ukraine, especially in so far as these concerned its economic exploitation, for which the 'most stringent measures' were envisaged.[10] Already by October 1941 the information that was reaching London about the nature of the German occupation led the Foreign Office to comment on the 'grave psychological mistakes' the Germans had made in handling the conquered population, for 'their methods can only serve to rally the Russian people round the [Soviet] regime'.[11] The thoroughly inappropriate nature of German policy and propaganda in the occupied territories was similarly highlighted by two collaborating Soviet officers who complained that it was simply not enough to stress the deprivations Bolshevism had inflicted on the Russian people. By late 1942 this repetitive and uninspiring message was becoming increasingly ineffective, not least as Soviet prisoners of war and the inhabitants of the occupied territories generally held that rule by Germany, far from being a liberation, was altogether a 'bad bargain'. In contrast to the sterile monotony of German propaganda, Stalin, who had reintroduced religious freedom and curtailed the activities of the political commissars, had 'taken the trumps out of Germany's hands'.[12]

Those in control of the Reich's propaganda campaign in the east would not necessarily have disagreed with this diagnosis. Goebbels realized that the organizational chaos of German policy in the occupied territories was having a most detrimental effect on the battle for people's minds. In April 1943 he commented on the failure to exploit Vlassov's separatist army more effectively, which he held to be symptomatic of a fundamental flaw in the whole approach to the Russian war. 'One is shocked at the absolute lack of political instinct in our Central Berlin Administration,' he noted in this connection. 'If we were pursuing or had pursued a rather more skilful policy in the East, we would certainly be further on there than we are.'[13] The Reich propaganda minister was certainly no friend of the Russian people, but he was not above admitting that mistakes had been made in the German conduct of the war; nor was he blind to the fact that a wiser occupation policy might have yielded significant results. Commenting on Vidkun Quisling's observations on the German campaign in the east, Goebbels clearly agreed that it would be both possible and desirable to mobilize large sections of the Russian population against Stalin if only 'we knew how to wage war solely against Bolshevism, not against the Russian people. Therein lies the only chance of bringing the war in the East to a satisfactory end.'[14]

Goebbels's' colleague, Eberhardt Taubert, placed the responsibility for the hopeless conditions in the east squarely on the shoulders of Alfred Rosenberg, who had been appointed minister for the occupied territories shortly after the launching of Barbarossa. Taubert pointed out that Rosenberg had not only blamed the Jews for Bolshevism, but also the Russian people for tolerating it. Due to impurities of blood, the Russian had, in Rosenberg's view, a 'natural affinity to the destructive ideologies of Bolshevism'. It might be, Taubert continued, that Rosenberg had not fully thought out the consequences of his actions, but that did not excuse his whole notion of the Russians as *Untermenschen* being the product of a false conception. Moreover, Rosenberg had possessed insufficient strength of character to rectify his mistake once the detrimental effects had become apparent.[15] Although Taubert's diatribe against Rosenberg is understandable, if only for the obstacles the incompetent Reichsleiter placed before the German propagandists in the east, it might yet be a little harsh on a man who in March 1942 was warning against any reference to the occupied territories as German 'colonial territory', as this greatly annoyed the local populations and played directly into the hands of the Soviet propagandists.[16]

To what extent Goebbels and his propagandists helped encourage the formation of volunteer corps from occupied Europe is impossible to determine. It is beyond doubt that the appeal of anti-Bolshevism struck a chord with a considerable number of individuals from Spain to Slovakia, and from Norway to Greece, for by the close of 1941 more than 43,000 volunteers were fighting in Russia for the German cause. German propaganda naturally made a great play of these units, which were the most obvious manifestation of their much proclaimed theme of 'European solidarity', and the ProMi sponsored Wehrmacht magazine, *Signal*, regularly featured heartening articles on the Bolshevik danger and necessity for European unity against it. Readers of *Signal*, which was produced in 20 languages and became the biggest selling magazine in Europe between 1940 and 1945, hitting a peak circulation of 2.5 million in 1943, were reminded after 22 June 1941 of the collective nature of the struggle against the USSR by articles such as Giselher Wirsing's 'We, the Europeans' which argued *inter alia* that Europe was not a geographical but a 'spiritual conception'.[17]

There was, however, another dimension to the volunteer corps that did not necessarily work to German advantage, namely the notion that the dispatch of 'volunteers' to the Russian front obviated any involvement of the respective state in the struggle against the USSR. Germany had already experienced something along these lines in the case of Finland, which, though fighting alongside Germany against the Soviet forces in northern Europe, did not class itself a *bona fide* ally in pursuit of the same objectives. To the Finns, who, like others, were wary of drawing upon themselves the odium of Britain and the USA, Bolshevism was certainly anathema, but by a calculated use of definitions they succeeded in avoiding too close an association with German war aims, and thus later with German atrocities. In essence, Finland was fighting a 'parallel war', or rather a 'continuation war' in which its primary aim was to reverse the Treaty of Moscow, which in March 1940 had brought an unfavourable conclusion to its conflict with Russia. Finland was thus not Germany's ally against the USSR, but its 'co-belligerent', and its soldiers were 'comrades-in-arms'.[18]

Spain was another case in point. The Spanish 'Blue Division' is perhaps the best known of all the volunteer units to have fought alongside the Germans in Russia and, in view of the German role during the Spanish Civil War and the extreme anti-communist character of Franco's dictatorship, support from Madrid might have been expected in return. Sure enough, on 22 June 1941, the Spanish foreign minister, Ramón Serrano Suñer, having noted with the 'greatest satisfaction the beginning of the struggle against Bolshevist Russia', informed the German ambassador of Spain's desire to 'send a few volunteer formations of the Falange to participate in the fight against the common foe'. This gesture of solidarity was naturally being made 'independently of the full and complete entry of Spain into the war beside the Axis, which would take place at the appropriate moment'.[19]

Behind these grand words lay the reality that Spain was crucially dependent on Britain and the USA for its food and other vital supplies, meaning, in effect, that considerations of survival determined its foreign policy. In the circumstances of 1941 that depended to a much greater extent on maintaining reasonable relations with the Anglo-Americans than on a German success in distant Russia. The Blue Division, therefore, despite the undoubted ideological commitment of many of its members, was a useful means through which Spain could balance between its supposed solidarity with Germany and the practical requirements of feeding its population. Serrano Suñer admitted as much during a further interview with Stohrer on 25 June, for when the latter requested a public declaration that Spain was 'in a state of war with the Soviet Union', he was told that such a step would most probably be answered by a declaration of war on Spain by Britain, and possibly by America, the repercussions of which would be 'detrimental to Germany during the Russian campaign'.[20] A week later the Spanish foreign minister told the *Deutsche Allgemeine Zeitung* that present circumstances were limiting Spain's contribution to the defence of Western civilization to a position of 'strict moral belligerency'.[21]

Although the number of volunteers committed to the German cause by the end of 1941 might be considered impressive, a further consideration to be borne in mind is that for every Frenchman, Spaniard, Dutchman and Belgian who enlisted to join the fight against Bolshevism, there were countless others who welcomed the German–Soviet conflict for an altogether different reason. It did not take an advanced knowledge of military strategy to realize that Germany might well find itself in an increasingly precarious position if the campaign in the USSR were not swiftly concluded, not least due to the coming change in the Russian climate, the failure to defeat Britain and, importantly, the disturbing developments in American policy. Indeed, unless a rapid and decisive victory could be guaranteed, the notion of a two-front war went against all military logic, irrespective of meteorological conditions, and was a course of action that Hitler had discounted in his writings of the 1920s. It is in this sense, and with one eye on American potential, that his oft-quoted remark to Jodl in late 1940 to the effect that Germany must solve all its problems by the close of 1941 should be interpreted.[22] Hitler's inability to subdue Britain had provided the strategic rationale for the attack on the USSR, the calculation being that the collapse of Russia would have a decisive effect on the future policies of both Britain and the United States, for with the resources of the Soviet Union at his disposal, he would be able to sustain the German war machine even if Britain, supported by America, continued to fight on.[23]

Conversely, the failure to defeat Russia in a lightning strike would at the very least complicate Germany's position. That these issues had already begun to trouble Hitler at an early stage of the Russian campaign is indicated by his remarks to Goebbels in mid-August 1941 when, after absolutely discounting the idea five weeks earlier, he spoke of a possible peace settlement with Stalin. Should the Soviet leader offer a compromise, Hitler announced, he would certainly consider it, but only on the basis of huge territorial annexations and the total emasculation of the Red Army, without which Bolshevism would no longer be a danger to the Reich. If Bolshevism were thus driven back into 'Asiatic Russia', it could develop there as it wished, for it would then be of little interest to Germany.[24]

By the autumn of 1941 it had become clear that, despite the dazzling successes, the key strategic objectives had not been reached. And, in all probability, this did not elude the representatives of the various powers who had congregated in Berlin towards the end of November 1941 for the ceremony to mark the renewal and extension of the Anti-Comintern Pact. German diplomacy had necessarily been more concerned with the ongoing Japanese–American negotiations since the spring of 1941 and, with Ribbentrop's field of manoeuvre in Europe already severely restricted by the launching of Barbarossa, the Wilhelmstrasse was provided with a welcome opportunity to make its own contribution to the success of the war in the east. This particular diplomatic initiative, however, gave little cause for celebration, for the powers Germany was especially interested in persuading to accede to the pact, notably Portugal and Turkey, refused to act on German overtures. The various receptions and interviews provided platforms for Hitler and Ribbentrop to explain the progress of the war against Russia to visiting dignitaries, and to indulge in the usual recriminations and accusations against the Bolsheviks, but, all in all, the meetings achieved little apart from giving Hitler the opportunity to wax lyrical about the concept of 'European solidarity'. As he explained to the Danish foreign minister, the renewal of the Anti-Comintern Pact, the accession of new states and the exchanges between the foreign ministers and diplomats were all 'indications of a new Europe that was slowly emerging'. At the same time, Hitler left his listeners in no doubt about their collective responsibility on the one hand and the magnitude of the debt they owed Germany on the other.

> Germany was fighting on the eastern front because she stood there. If she did not stand there another power would have to fight there. We have been fighting this tremendous battle against the constantly onrushing East for one and a half thousand years. Earlier there were the Huns, the Tartars and the Mongolians; today it was Bolshevism that had mobilized the whole of Asia against Europe. ... Germany, having borne the greatest blood burden in this struggle and again bearing it this time, was fighting for herself, but at the same time she was fighting for the whole of Europe. If Germany had not recovered and prepared herself for this great struggle, these Bolshevik-Asiatic hordes would have rolled across Europe like a wave.[25]

Despite the extravagant coverage of this event in the German press,[26] this was in effect the first and only demonstration, and a modest one at that, of European solidarity in the fight against Bolshevism at the level of high diplomacy. As has already been mentioned, the possibilities for German foreign policy had been curtailed by the outbreak of war with Russia, and in these circumstances the military situation inevitably conditioned German diplomacy during 1942–43. The initiatives undertaken by the Wilhelmstrasse consisted largely of efforts to keep the anti-Soviet alliance intact while at the same time exercising pressure to extract the maximum military commitment from each ally. Thus, the flurry of diplomatic activity at the start of 1942 saw a concerted effort to secure additional military contributions from Hungary and Romania, not least by reminding them of their roles in the 'European community of fate against Bolshevism', while taking every care to keep them apart in their territorial dispute arising from the Second Vienna Award.[27] In the case of the neutrals an attempt was made to frighten Turkey into a closer relationship with the Axis by revealing to the authorities in Ankara the purported demands of Stalin who, during his meeting with the British foreign secretary in December 1941, was said to have requested the cession to the USSR of Constantinople and the Dardanelles. In connection with this the Turks were also reminded that in its present struggle Germany was 'liberating Europe and thereby Turkey also from centuries' old Russian pressure'.[28] In the difficult question of Bulgaria's attitude towards the Soviet–German war, the Germans were wise enough to appreciate the difficulties presented by the pro-Russian disposition of the Bulgarian people, but nevertheless sought to persuade King Boris of the need to break off diplomatic relations with Moscow, not least as the maintenance of a Soviet mission in Sofia provided Russia with a focus for its espionage operations against the Reich in the Balkans.[29]

If the possibilities for German diplomacy had been restricted during 1942, they were effectively rendered non-existent under the impact of the Allied landings in North Africa in November 1942 and the German reversal at Stalingrad two months later, following which the neutral and non-belligerent powers became even less amenable to German wishes. The case of Spain serves to illustrate this point well, for, despite his repeated declarations of solidarity with the German cause, Franco remained exceptionally wary of antagonizing the Anglo-Americans upon whose continued goodwill the welfare of his country effectively depended. A warning note was sounded for the Germans in February 1943 when the issue of Spain's attitude towards communism and the possible enlargement of the Blue Division became the object of political in-fighting in Madrid in a dispute between the foreign ministry and the General Staff. During an interview with the German ambassador, the Spanish foreign minister Francisco Gómez-Jordana explained that his suspension of a propaganda drive against communism was because the army had inadequately prepared it. This explanation did not fully satisfy von Moltke who felt that other considerations had determined Gómez-Jordana's attitude, notably his desire not to cause further offence to the allies.[30] Two months later Gómez-Jordana gave a speech in Barcelona in which he claimed to understand that the warring parties, by which he meant Germany and the Anglo-Americans, wished to achieve a 'total victory', but in the same breath asserted that such attitudes were hardly consistent with the interests of the European 'family of nations', not least as the longer the war went on the greater the possibilities became for the advancement of international communism.[31] After the German defeat at Stalingrad the Spaniards redoubled their efforts to find the basis of a compromise between Germany and the West, which was a hopeless enough undertaking even before the respective announcements of 'unconditional surrender' and 'total war' at the beginning of 1943.

Some time before the military reversals Germany suffered at the turn of 1942–43, it had been noted in the British Foreign Office how in the course of recent speeches by Hitler, Goebbels, Göring and Ribbentrop 'the pretence of a united Europe gladly cooperating with victorious Germany [has] dropped completely into the background'.[32] After Stalingrad, although German propaganda had, as detailed earlier, resurrected the 'Bolshevik bogey' to panic the European nations into compliance with German wishes, the initial effect was dramatic but short-lived as the hopeless strategic position of the Reich became more apparent. In any case, Hitler's private thoughts on the prospective role of other European nations in opposing the Bolsheviks were hardly conducive to fruitful collaboration. Only the Germans were capable of offering sustained resistance to the Soviet Union in Europe, he announced to a gathering of senior party leaders in early May 1943. The experiences of the previous winter had demonstrated all too clearly the shortcomings of Germany's allies; from now on, only German troops would be deployed on the Russian front. Once the war had been brought to a successful conclusion it would be time to dispense with all the 'rubbish' that remained of the smaller European states, and proceed to organize and unite the continent, another task of which Germans alone were capable.[33]

Two years later it was not the unification of Europe but its division, and with it the division of Germany, that preoccupied the leaders of Britain, the United States and the Soviet Union who, after years of bloody conflict, had finally shattered the once formidable power of the Third Reich. The new conditions inevitably brought new problems and, indeed, fresh antagonisms as the strains within the wartime alliance began to take their toll. First at Yalta, then at Potsdam, Anglo-American negotiators experienced at first hand Soviet truculence, duplicity even, as Stalin sought to press home the advantages he enjoyed as a result of the tremendous achievements of his armed forces. The victory over Hitler was certainly a genuine cause for celebration in Moscow, London and Washington, and in countless other cities across Europe and overseas. Already, however, there were signs of further trouble on the horizon. As General Patton remarked on the day of the German surrender, 'They ["tin soldier politicians in Washington"] have allowed us to kick hell out of one bastard and at the same time forced us to help establish a second one as evil or more evil than the first. We have won a series of battles, not a war for peace.'[34]

Overview and Epilogue

I n this study I have examined the origins, nature, function and development of international Bolshevism as a determining factor in Germany's external relations during what might, for the purposes of this book, be considered four distinct stages of the Third Reich's foreign policy. During the first stage, encompassing the years from Hitler's assumption of the leadership of the NSDAP until the handover of power, the notion of international Bolshevism as an integral part of a Jewish-led 'world conspiracy' was assimilated relatively swiftly into the movement's political philosophy, and had emerged by 1933 as the ideological leitmotiv of the regime's foreign policy and external propaganda programme. In the second stage, which ran from Hitler's accession as chancellor until the winter of 1937–38, an attempt was made to configure international alignments and influence world opinion with a view to isolating the Soviet Union in preparation for the destruction of 'Jewish Bolshevism' and the conquest of living space in the east. During the third stage, from 1937–38 until 1940, Hitler's plans went seriously awry, notably with regard to his original intentions towards Great Britain and Poland, so much so that in September 1939 he found himself in the grotesque circumstance of being at war with two powers earmarked as potential allies against Bolshevik Russia, with whom he had been compelled to conclude a pact of non-aggression. In the final stage, beginning in June 1941, Hitler finally launched his ideologically determined attack on Bolshevism, a decision that not only represented the climax of years of planning and preparation, but one that also had profound repercussions for the fate of European Jewry.

Throughout this book the emphasis has been on the offensive and crusading aspect of Hitler's campaign against international Bolshevism, which in large part explains the decision to cease coverage in mid-1943 following the German defeats at Stalingrad and Kursk.

Stalingrad was a colossal setback, in comparison with which the stalling of the German advance in late 1941 paled into insignificance, but it was Kursk that marked the end, or the beginning of the end, of Germany's offensive potential, thrusting the Wehrmacht back onto its heels to stage one of the longest fighting retreats in history. As one leading authority on the history of the Second World War has noted, it was at Kursk that the military initiative finally passed to the Soviet Union, whose forces had soon succeeded in crossing the river Dnepr at several points, thus breaching what Hitler had insisted would constitute the 'final rampart against Bolshevism'.[1]

It would be wrong to suggest, however, that after 1943 the Nazi regime lost its focus on the rapidly advancing peril from the east, notwithstanding the looming prospect of an Allied invasion of 'Fortress Europe', which finally became reality on 6 June 1944. Indeed, in many ways the magnitude of the military reversals and the increasingly tangible threat to the Reich, coupled with the collapse of Germany's European allies during 1943–44, meant that in some ways the focus on the red threat was even sharper and more compelling than ever. Anti-Bolshevism was in any case too ingrained in the political make-up of Hitler, Goebbels and other Nazi stalwarts to be downgraded in the order of priorities as Germany was forced onto the defensive.

For Hitler, whose views and actions have inevitably been the main focus of this study, the scourge of Bolshevism had always been inextricably linked to the wider danger presented to Germany and the world by the machinations of international Jewry. That fact alone is indicative of the profound significance of anti-Bolshevism as a determinant of his political actions. Despite his ever-dwindling military options after 1941, Hitler insisted that there could never be any compromise with the Bolsheviks. When following the collapse of Italy in 1943 Ribbentrop had approached him, not for the first time, with the suggestion of a negotiated settlement with Stalin, the Führer had revealed his unwillingness and inability to countenance a negotiated end to the conflict with Russia with the remark: 'You know, Ribbentrop, if I settled with Russia today I would only come to grips with her again tomorrow – I just can't help it!'[2] In this respect, despite repeated pleas from a variety of quarters, there would be no change until the bitter end.[3] In increasingly rare public addresses, he left no doubt about the focus of his attentions. Thus, in his final speech, broadcast to the nation on 30 January 1945, the Führer referred, inevitably, writes Ian Kershaw, to a 'Jewish-international world conspiracy', 'Kremlin Jews', 'Asiatic Bolshevism', and the now imminent 'storm-flood from inner Asia'.[4] As his political testament demonstrates, his preoccupation to the last with international Jewry, the 'universal poisoner of all nations', was neither rhetoric nor simply an attempt to drum up support through the use of familiar pejoratives for a cause many already considered hopeless.[5]

Just as Hitler continued to stress the fight against Bolshevism in public and in private, so too did Goebbels's propaganda machine continue its attacks on Bolshevism after the setbacks of 1943. Following Stalingrad, Goebbels had first directed his attention to a revival of the familiar 'red bogey' line of argument, in which connection he managed to score a number of minor successes lasting well into 1944. Pro-Nazi, or at least anti-Bolshevist, regimes, such as those of Salazar and Franco, tended to peddle the German line in this respect, with the Spanish 'fascist' newspaper *Arriba*, for example, carrying an article in April 1944 appealing for the belligerents to find a basis for a settlement, while insisting that any proposals must originate with the West for fear that Russia, its imperialist designs now clearly unfolding, would seek to impose 'an Asiatic peace'.[6] At the same time the German propagandists did not abandon their direct assaults on Bolshevism and the Red Army, so much so that in May 1944 Ribbentrop's press chief, Paul Karl Schmidt, felt it necessary to assure his Japanese acquaintances that the recent violent attacks on Bolshevism, which highlighted Germany's determination to destroy communism for the sake of the whole of Europe, did not mean that the Reich authorities 'had the hidden intention of effecting a compromise with Britain'.[7]

As the ring tightened, following further Soviet military successes in 1944–45, Goebbels was forced to focus increasingly on the domestic front in an effort to move the German people to a last heroic, if futile, defence of their homeland and the principles of National Socialism. In these endeavours he was actually obliged to tone down some of the more extreme anti-Bolshevik propaganda for fear that the idea of capitulation to the Western Allies might tend to look attractive in comparison.[8] At the other end of the spectrum he clearly had to inspire a terror and loathing of the Red Army if he were going to be able to galvanize resistance to its advance. When in February 1945 complaints were heard about the graphic descriptions of Soviet atrocities in East Prussia, which the ProMi had recently issued, the Reich propaganda minister dismissed them out of hand. As he noted on 10 February:

> If we do not keep the German people fully informed of the atrocities perpetrated by the Soviets, we run the risk that a good many people will come to the conclusion that the Soviets are not at all as bad as we have always made them out to be, and the power of resistance gradually falls away. We must let the facts speak for themselves. If in doing so a certain shock effect is produced, then that cannot be avoided; indeed, in one sense it is necessary.[9]

Following the Soviet breakthroughs at the turn of 1944–45, Goebbels effectively found himself in the same position as Ribbentrop in that each man controlled a huge apparatus for the dissemination of advice and information, but, as the Allied victories continued to pile up, there were simply fewer and fewer people left to listen.

The same effectively applied to Alfred Rosenberg, the party ideologue who, despite his relative marginalization after 1933, had first been responsible for instructing Hitler in the ways of the 'Jewish international conspirators'. In the later years of the war, long since events had negated his role as minister for the occupied eastern territories, Rosenberg contented himself with contributing a series of articles to the *Völkischer Beobachter* on the folly of British statesmanship, itself decimated by Jewish finance, which worked hand in glove with the 'Bolshevik-Jewish leadership', for delivering the continent to the ravages of the Red Army. For that despicable deed, Churchill must surely go down as 'the symbol of the greatest act of betrayal of European history and of the European continent'.[10] Germany, by contrast, was seeking to defend not just the Reich, but the whole of Western civilization. As he proclaimed on 14 October 1944, one hundred years to the day since the birth of Nietzsche, the 'European *Kulturbürger*' was being overwhelmed by a once-dammed destructive fanaticism from the East; a fanaticism which, notably in alliance with Jewish-Western Marxism, has shaken not only Germany but the entire European continent, to its foundations. If therefore we are proud that National Socialist Germany alone still defends this old Europe today, we can proclaim, somewhat differently from Nietzsche in the nineteenth century, that today we are the 'good Europeans', for this is a right for which we have struggled honourably.[11]

Hitler's world view, shaped by personal observations and experience and refined through his encounters with individuals such as Rosenberg, emerged as a compound of ideological and power-political considerations that combined to create what has been called, with considerable justification, a programme for the foreign policy that in broad outline he sought to pursue during his years as chancellor. After 1933 it can clearly be seen how Hitler sought to steer a course that corresponded essentially with the programmatic ideals of the 1920s. The ideological dimension of the programme, which was refined to take account of changing world conditions after 1928, was manifested in two ways: the pursuit of alliances with those great and middle powers that shared his antipathy for the USSR, and would thus conceivably have little objection to its destruction by Germany; and anti-Bolshevism *per se*, manifested, for example, in the dismantling of the Rapallo relationship with Russia after 1933, and German policy during the Spanish Civil War. After 1935 German diplomatic efforts to pursue the programmatic goals in relation to the USSR were loudly supplemented by the activities of the German propaganda ministry, which established the Antikomintern in an attempt to mount a wide-ranging, centralized and coordinated campaign against Bolshevism. The problems in reconstructing the work of the ProMi, and in particular the Antikomintern, have been referred to at an earlier stage of this study, but even from the limited records that have survived it is apparent that the anti-Bolshevik activities of both organizations, particularly in the years 1935–37, were varied and considerable.

In certain areas, as in France between 1933 and 1936, Hitler demonstrated that there was a degree of flexibility in his ideological framework, for, although there were questions that encumbered Franco–German relations from the ideological perspective, he was prepared at least for a time to consider the possibility of an association with France on the basis of anti-Bolshevism. Moreover, the success of the programme, and Hitler's ability to pursue it with conviction and vigour, depended on his retaining the initiative, which, to a considerable extent he succeeding in doing until 1937. In one obvious case, namely that of the Nazi–Soviet Pact, he was forced temporarily to compromise his principles in order to solve an isolated and immediate problem. Yet, despite this glaring exception to the rule, the essential force of Hitler's remark to Burckhardt in August 1939, only days before the German chancellor authorized the treaty with Stalin, that everything he undertook was directed against the USSR, held good throughout his period as chancellor, even during the era of the Nazi–Soviet Pact.

Towards the close of 1937, when it had become clear that Britain and Poland were not prepared to play the roles allotted to them and, indeed, that the Anti-Comintern Pact had failed in its function to raise support for the isolation of Russia, Hitler readjusted his priorities and fixed a loose timetable for action at the Hossbach conference, following which he became enmeshed in a series of internal and external crises, which necessarily shifted the focus temporarily away from ideological issues. Nevertheless, it should not be forgotten in this connection that the destruction of Czechoslovakia, Poland and France during 1939–40 was undertaken with a greater goal in view, that of seeking to create favourable conditions for the ultimate showdown with Bolshevism. During this period the focus of German propaganda also shifted to align with the immediate requirements of German diplomacy and, from mid-1939 onwards, propaganda of any complexion directed against the Soviet Union virtually ground to a halt.

In 1941, when Hitler finally turned against the USSR, ideology, diplomacy, propaganda and vicious racism were collectively brought to bear against 'Jewish Bolshevism' in the shape of the orders issued for the conduct of the war in the east, the attempted mobilization of other powers and volunteer units against the USSR, the various anti-Jewish and anti-Bolshevik campaigns Goebbels orchestrated, and finally the onset of genocide against Soviet Jewry and other hapless unfortunates. The German crusade against the

USSR was indisputably an ideological conflict first and foremost, an uncompromising fight to the finish between bitter and irreconcilable enemies. As Hitler remarked on 2 April 1945:

> If we are destined to be beaten in this war, our defeat will be utter and complete. Our enemies have proclaimed their objectives in a manner which leaves us no illusions as to their intentions. Jews, Russian Bolshevists and the pack of jackals that follows, yelping at their heels – we know that none of them will lay aside their arms until they have destroyed and annihilated National Socialist Germany and reduced it to a heap of rubble. In a ghastly conflict like this, in a war in which two so completely irreconcilable ideologies confront one another, the issue can inevitably only be settled by the total destruction of one side or the other. It is a fight which must be waged, by both sides, until they are utterly exhausted.[12]

Hitler's aim to destroy Bolshevism as a political force, an ambition that can be traced back to his earliest political activities, is sometimes referred to in the literature on the origins of the Soviet–German war almost as a subsidiary determinant of Operation Barbarossa; sometimes it is virtually overlooked; sometimes it is labelled a convenient cover for a policy of naked imperialism. Yet, as I have sought to demonstrate in this book, it lay at the very heart of Hitler's political philosophy. The destruction of international Bolshevism has to be viewed in the context of and in conjunction with the so-called 'Jewish problem' and the much vaunted quest for *Lebensraum* in eastern Europe. These concepts must be considered parallel with and complementary to one another; it is futile and misleading to seek to disentangle them, as if they exist independently of one another.

Shortly before his death, when the quest for *Lebensraum* was a distant memory, and anti-Bolshevism a sentiment capable of firing only the most fanatical of his followers, Hitler peered into the future and saw, in much the same way as British and American planners were beginning to see, a new conflict on the horizon. Four weeks before his death, he announced:

215

With the defeat of the Reich and pending the emergence of the Asiatic, the African, and, perhaps, the South American nationalisms, there will remain in the world only two Great Powers capable of confronting each other – the United States and Soviet Russia. The laws of both history and geography will compel these two Powers to a trial of strength, either military or in the fields of economics and ideology.[13]

Two months later, Ribbentrop, who in October 1945 would have the gall to wish the Western powers better luck than Germany had enjoyed in handling the Soviet Union,[14] was questioned about Hitler's reaction to Stalin's annexation of Bessarabia and northern Bukovina in June 1940. The former foreign minister, who, in stark contrast to the nervous wreck who took the stand at Nuremberg, appeared relatively relaxed and assured during his interrogation by political officers of the Supreme Headquarters of the Allied Expeditionary Force (SHAEF), one British, the other American, spoke of certain 'arrangements' that Germany had arrived at with Russia during the negotiations of August–September 1939. When asked whether these arrangements had not in fact catered for the annexation of Bessarabia by the USSR, Ribbentrop made a simple reply, with 'a smile and an expression of mock embarrassment', to which might well have been added a touch of *Schadenfreude* because the Anglo-Americans now faced the problem of how to contain the Soviet colossus in central Europe. 'Must I answer that question?' he enquired innocently, 'After all, Russia is one of your allies.'[15]

Notes

Introduction

1. *News Chronicle*, 2 May 1945.
2. Ibid.
3. Public Record Office [hereafter PRO], GFM34/458, McNair Crawford to Hitler, 28 August 1936.
4. *Akten zur deutschen Auswärtigen Politik 1918–1945*, Serie D (1937–1941) vols I–XIII, eds J. S. Beddie et al. (Baden-Baden, Frankfurt am Main, Bonn, Göttingen, 1950–1970) [hereafter *ADAP*, D] I, no. 31, record of a conversation between Halifax and Hitler, 19 November 1937.
5. M. Domarus (ed.) *Hitler: Reden und Proklamationen 1932–45. Kommentiert von einem deutschen Zeitgenossen.* 2 vols (Munich, 1965) [hereafter Domarus] I/2, 7 March 1936, speech to the Reichstag, p. 585.
6. Ibid., p. 587.
7. *The Trial of the Major War Criminals before the International Military Tribunal.* Proceedings, vols I–XXIII. Documents in Evidence, vols XXIV–XLII (Nuremberg, 1947–49) [hereafter *IMT*] XXXVI, doc. 416-EC, Niederschrift des Ministerrates am 4 September 1936, pp. 489–91.
8. National Archives and Records Administration, Maryland [hereafter NARA] State Department Decimal File 762.00/117, *Illustrazione Italiana*, 20 September 1936, enclosed in Bullitt to Hull, 22 September 1936. In a similar vein see *Foreign Relations of the United States: Diplomatic Papers* (Washington, 1952–1959) [hereafter *FRUS*] 1937, I, Cudahy to Roosevelt, 26 December 1936, p. 25. The US Military Attaché in Berlin, on the other hand, felt that the speeches made at the Nuremberg rally were 'neither rant nor bombast', but had been 'skilfully constructed to fit into the general line of the coming German foreign policy'. NARA, 762.00/138, Smith to Hull, 1 October 1936.
9. See A. Bullock, *Hitler: A Study in Tyranny* (London, 1962) p. 489; J. L. Heineman, *Hitler's First Foreign Minister: Constantin Freiherr von Neurath, Diplomat and Statesman* (Berkeley, 1979) p. 160; R. W. Whealey, *Hitler and Spain: The Nazi Role in the Spanish Civil War 1936–1939* (Kentucky, 1989) pp. 28–9.
10. G. L. Weinberg, *The Foreign Policy of Hitler's Germany*, vol. 1. *Diplomatic Revolution in Europe, 1933–36* (Chicago, 1970) p. 289.

11. The most important works in this respect are: K. Hildebrand, *The Foreign Policy of the Third Reich* (London, 1973) and A. Hillgruber, *Hitlers Strategie: Politik und Kriegführung, 1940–41* (Frankfurt am Main, 1965).

12. J. Thies, *Architekt der Weltherrschaft: Die 'Endziele' Hitlers* (Düsseldorf, 1980) p. 61.

13. *Reden des Führers am Parteitag der Ehre 1936* (Munich, 1936); 'Der Führer auf der vierten Jahrestagung der Deutschen Arbeitsfront', 12 September 1936, pp. 55–6.

14. On this aspect see D. Eichholtz, '"Grossgermanisches Reich" und "Generalplan Ost"', *Zeitschrift für Geschichtswissenschaft,* 28 (1980) pp. 834–41, here pp. 835–6.

15. Politisches Archiv des Auswärtigen Amtes, Bonn [hereafter PAB] R83395, Reinebeck to AA, 25 April 1933.

16. E. von Weizsäcker, *Erinnerungen* (Munich, 1950) p. 231.

17. R. J. B. Bosworth, *Mussolini* (London, 2002) p. 275. Alan Cassels appears to share this view, seeing Mussolini as a 'professional anti-bolshevik'. See A. Cassels, 'Was there a Fascist Foreign Policy? Tradition and Novelty', *International History Review,* 2 (1983) pp. 255–68, here p. 257.

18. E. Wiskemann, *The Rome–Berlin Axis: A Study of the Relations between Hitler and Mussolini* (London, 1949) pp. 28–9.

19. Bosworth, *Mussolini,* p. 133.

20. S. Haffner, *The Meaning of Hitler,* trans. E. Osers (London, 1988) p. 84. Previous quotations from pp. 81–2.

21. G. Stoakes, *Hitler and the Quest for World Dominion: Nazi Ideology and Foreign Policy in the 1920s* (Leamington Spa, 1986) pp. 70–1.

22. This curious phenomenon is analysed in H. Gollwitzer, *Die gelbe Gefahr: Geschichte eines Schlagworts. Studien zum imperialistischen Denken* (Göttingen, 1962) and U. Mehnert, *Deutschland, Amerika und die 'gelbe Gefahr': Zur Karriere eines Schlagworts in der Grossen Politik, 1905–1917* (Stuttgart, 1995).

23. On this see the recent article by O. Heilbronner, 'From Antisemitic Peripheries to Antisemitic Centres: The Place of Antisemitism in Modern German History', *Journal of Contemporary History,* 35 (2000) pp. 559–76.

24. G. Moore, 'From Buddhism to Bolshevism: Some Orientalist Themes in German Thought', *German Life and Letters,* 56 (2003) pp. 20–42, here pp. 40–1.

25. The activities of Stadtler and other German opponents of Bolshevism during the latter stages and immediate aftermath of the First World War are examined in some detail in K.-U. Merz, *Das Schreckbild: Deutschland und der Bolschewismus 1917 bis 1921* (Berlin, 1995).

26. See E. Stadtler, *Bolschewismus als Weltgefahr* (Düsseldorf, 1936). The volume contains updated versions of Stadtler's 1919 publications *Der Bolschewismus und seine Überwindung* (Berlin, 1919), *Der kommende Krieg: Bolschewistische Weltrevolutionspläne* (Berlin, 1919) and *Weltkrieg, Welttragödie und Weltbolschewismus* (Berlin, 1919). Material on Stadtler, including original application forms to join his 'Vereinigung zur Bekämpfung des Bolschewismus', is available at the Hoover Institution, Stanford University [hereafter Hoover], German Subject Collection, box 1, 'Gegen Bolschewismus und Terror'.

27. A. Sharpe, *The Versailles Settlement: Peacemaking in Paris, 1919* (London, 1991) p. 154.

28. K. E. McKenzie, *Comintern and World Revolution, 1928–1943: The Shaping of Doctrine* (London, 1963) p. 45.

29. A. J. Mayer, *Politics and the Diplomacy of Peacemaking: Containment and Counter-revolution at Versailles, 1918–1919* (London, 1968) p. 754.

30. *The Times*, 16 February 1920.

31. PRO, WO32/5728, summary of a report of the Committee's initial meeting, 26 June 1921.

32. For an early indication of Stresemann's suspicions of Bolshevism see *Gustav Stresemann: His Diaries, Letters and Papers*, ed. and trans. E. Sutton, vol. II (London, 1937) Stresemann to the former Crown Prince Wilhelm, 7 September 1925, pp. 504–5.

33. *Documents on British Foreign Policy*, Second Series, eds E. L. Woodward et al. (London, 1947–1984) [hereafter *DBFP*, 2] XV, no. 383, Phipps to Hoare, 16 December 1936.

Chapter 1

1. In one of these addresses Hitler spoke of his 'inexorable determination' to extirpate Jewry 'root and branch'; on another he is alleged to have demanded the 'murder' of the Jews. On a further occasion, having freely admitted that his speech was inspired by racial hatred, he asked rhetorically how one might defend oneself against the Jews, leading to cries from the audience of 'String them up! Strike them dead!'. See *HSA*, no. 91, Diskussionsbeitrag auf einer NSDAP-Versammlung, 6 April 1920; ibid., no. 103, 'Das deutsche Volk, die Judenfrage und unsere Zukunft', Rede auf einer NSDAP-Versammlung, 31 May 1920; ibid., no 112, 'Der Jude als Arbeiterführer', Rede auf einer NSDAP-Versammlung, 24 June 1920.

2. Ibid., no. 136, 'Warum sind wir Antisemiten?', Rede auf einer NSDAP-Versammlung, 13 August 1920.

3. For summaries of the ideas of Class and Fritsch, and an assessment of their impact on Hitler, see Stoakes, *Hitler and the Quest for World*

Dominion, pp. 31ff. Detailed information on von Schönerer's views and Hitler's receptivity to them can be found in B. Hamann, *Hitlers Wien: Lehrjahre eines Diktators* (Munich, 1996) *passim*, especially pp. 337ff. See also Hitler, *Mein Kampf*, p. 107f.

4. Hence the title of R. Phelps's article, 'Hitlers grundlegende Rede über den Antisemitismus', in VfZ, 16 (1968) pp. 390–420. On the significance of the address see also Kershaw, *Hitler: Hubris*, pp. 152, 650, note 99; E. Jäckel, *Hitlers Weltanschauung: Entwurf einer Herrschaft: Erweiterte und überarbeitete Neuausgabe* (Stuttgart, 1981) pp. 59–60.

5. *HSA*, no. 136, 'Warum sind wir Antisemiten?' Rede auf einer NSDAP-Versammlung, 13 August 1920.

6. Kai-Uwe Merz notes that Hitler's first reference to Bolshevism in a political address came in February 1920. See Merz, *Das Schreckbild*, p. 462. The notes for the address, which referred to 'Bolshevism on the march', are in *HSA*, no. 80, Rede auf einem DAP-Sprechabend, 9 February 1920. In *Mein Kampf* Hitler referred only fleetingly to the Bolshevik revolution in October 1917, recalling how at the time he had speculated about the probable effects of the Russian collapse on the military situation. See Hitler, *Mein Kampf*, pp. 214–15.

7. See in particular *HSA*, no 65, 'Brest-Litowsk und Versailles', Stichworte zu einer Rede, 11 November 1919; and ibid., no 87, 'Die Wahrheit über den "Gewaltfrieden von Brest-Litowsk?" [sic] und den sogenannten "Frieden der Versöhnung und Verständigung von Versailles"', Rede auf einer NSDAP-Versammlung, 4 March 1920.

8. See, for example, ibid. no. 60, 'Sozial- und wirtschaftspolitische Schlagworte', Rede im Reichswehr-Aufklärungskommando, 25 August 1919; ibid., no. 69, 'Deutschland vor seiner tiefsten Erniedrigung', Rede auf einer DAP-Versammlung, 10 December 1920; ibid., no 73, Diskussionsbeitrag auf einer DAP-Versammlung, 16 January 1920.

9. Note in this connection, however, the transformation in Hitler's view of Stalin by 1940. See R. Zitelmann, *Hitler: Selbstverständnis eines Revolutionärs* (Hamburg, 1987) pp. 440ff, and below pp. 211ff.

10. F.-L. Kroll, *Utopie als Ideologie: Geschichtsdenken und politisches Handeln im Dritten Reich* (Paderborn, 1998) pp. 50–1.

11. E. H. Vieler, *The Ideological Roots of German National Socialism* (New York, 1999) p. 63.

12. Ibid., pp. 72–3. Daniel Gasman, on the other hand, stresses the role of the *völkisch* thinker Ernst Haeckel in shaping Hitler's racist views, although one recent commentator has taken considerable issue with Gasman's findings, considering his focus on Haeckel 'too blinkered', and stressing the range of influences acting on Hitler at the time. See respectively D. Gasman, *The Scientific Origins of National Socialism: Social Darwinism in Ernst Haeckel and the German Monist League*

(London, 1971) pp. 159ff; and R. Weikart, *From Darwin to Hitler: Evolutionary Ethics, Eugenics and Racism in Germany* (New York, 2004) pp. 216ff. See also below, note 16.

13. Hitler, *Mein Kampf*, p. 60.
14. Ibid., p. 165.
15. This is not to say that Hitler refrained from insulting Jews even in respect of their appearance, or on grounds of personal hygiene. See ibid., pp. 59–61.
16. Ibid., pp. 61–3. On Liebenfels and *Ostrara*, the society he founded in 1905 dedicated to the promotion of Aryan values, and from which flowed a considerable racist literature, see Vieler, *Ideological Roots of German National Socialism*, pp. 74ff. On the impact of Lueger during Hitler's Vienna years see Hitler, *Mein Kampf*, pp. 58–9, 107ff, 133; Hamann, *Hitlers Wien, passim*, especially pp. 393ff; Kershaw, *Hitler: Hubris*, pp. 33ff.
17. Hitler, *Mein Kampf*, p. 61.
18. Ibid., p. 40.
19. Ibid., pp. 39–41.
20. Ibid., p. 357.
21. *Hitlers Zweites Buch*, p. 221.
22. Ibid., p. 222.
23. Hitler, *Mein Kampf*, p. 59.
24. Zitelmann, *Hitler: Selbstverständnis eines Revolutionärs*, p. 439.
25. *HSA*, no. 634, interview with Hans Lutz, 25 April 1924.
26. Hence his insistence that the German bourgeoisie was essentially Marxist because it stood for and supported 'parliament, democracy, the rejection of battle, internationalism and the rejection of race'. See *VB*, 27 April 1927. Without wishing to dwell here on semantic issues, the terms Communism and Marxism appear to have been largely interchangeable as far as Hitler was concerned, whereas Bolshevism, in the early years at least, was used to denote the physical manifestation of Marxism in Russian conditions. On occasion he used all three terms to signify the same thing. See, for example, Domarus, I/2, 15 February 1936, speech to representatives of the German motor industry, p. 576.
27. *RSA*, II/1, no. 96, 'Der Nationalsozialismus als Weltanschauung, der Marxismus ein Wahnsinn!', Rede auf [einer] NSDAP-Versammlung in Munich, 2 April 1927.
28. See, for example, ibid., III/2, no. 7, Stellungnahme zu einem Vermittlungsverfahren wegen Hochverrats, undated but written sometime between September 1929 and March 1930.
29. Ibid., III/3, no. 13, Aussage vor dem Landgericht München I, 4 February 1930.

30. *HSA*, no. 96, 'Politik und Judentum', Rede auf einer NSDAP-Versammlung, 27 April 1920.
31. Ibid., no. 605, Vor dem Volksgericht: Erster Handlungstag, 26 February 1924. It should perhaps be noted that Hitler arrived in Vienna shortly after the publication of a virulently anti-Semitic book by Rudolf Vrba, *The Revolution in Russia*, which not only linked the Jews with social democracy, but also 'conjured up the dangers of a Jewish world conspiracy'. Hamann, *Hitler's Wien*, pp. 490–1. Whether Hitler knew of this work is unknown.
32. *HSA*, no. 30, Hitler to Ernst Hepp, 5 February 1915.
33. Hitler, *Mein Kampf*, p. 210.
34. Hitler's political leanings and activities at this crucial juncture remain a mystery. It has several times been suggested that he inclined to the left. See, for example, Kershaw, *Hitler: Hubris*, pp. 118ff; Zitelmann, *Hitler: Selbstverständnis eines Revoutionärs*, p. 415. On the German revolution and the *Räterepublik* see U. Kluge, *Soldatenräte und Revolution: Studien zur Militärpolitik in Deutschland 1918–19* (Göttingen, 1975); Ulrich Kluge, *Die deutsche Revolution: Staat, Politik und Gesellschaft zwischen Weltkrieg und Kapp-Putsch* (Frankfurt am Main, 1985); M. Seligmann, *Aufstand der Räte: Die erste bayerische Räterepublik vom 7 April 1919* (Grafenau, 1989).
35. *HSA*, no. 65, 'Brest-Litowsk und Versailles', Stichworte zu einer Rede, 13 November 1919.
36. *RSA*, IV/2, no. 91, Rundfunkrede, 11 December 1931. Hitler's proposed broadcast was prohibited by the Prussian authorities. The text of his address appeared two days later in the *New York American*. For Hitler's retrospective assessment of the danger posed to Germany by 'Jewish Bolshevism' in 1918–19, and the measures then implemented to safeguard the nation, see ibid., III/2, no 85, 'Politik der Woche', *Illustrierte Beobachter*, 19 October 1929.
37. P. Longerich, *The Unwritten Order: Hitler's Role in the Final Solution* (Stroud, 2003) pp. 28–9. In this respect see also P. Burrin, *Hitler and the Jews: The Genesis of the Holocaust*, trans. P. Southgate (London, 1994) pp. 28ff.
38. *HSA*, no. 36, Hitler to Gemlich, 5 September 1919.
39. Hitler, *Mein Kampf*, p. 225.
40. Ibid., pp. 211–12, 223–5.
41. M. Kellogg, *The Russian Roots of Nazism: White Émigrés and the Making of National Socialism, 1917–1945* (Cambridge, 2005) p. 2. Aside from Scheubner-Richter himself, Kellogg highlights the influence purportedly exercised over Hitler by another prominent *Aufbau* member, Colonel Fedor Vinberg. As a devoutly religious person who saw National Socialists as upholders of Christianity and who, paradoxically,

had been suspected of having an improper relationship with Tsarina Aleksandra Romanov, Vinberg sounds an unlikely mentor for Hitler. Indeed, the evidence for Vinberg's alleged influence over Hitler in the early 1920s is hardly compelling. Kellogg implies that 'detailed ideological discussions' with Vinberg had convinced Hitler by late 1922 that the USSR was a 'Jewish state' (p. 230). It is clear from other sources, however, that Hitler was persuaded of the role of Jewry in the Bolshevik party, and thus in the governance of the USSR, long before this. For a more balanced assessment of the impact of White Russian émigré circles on Hitler in the early 1920s see Stoakes, *Hitler and the Quest for World Dominion*, pp. 126ff.

42. For an indication of Rosenberg's attitude to the Jews in mid-1918, see his essay 'Der Jude', published in A. Rosenberg, *Schriften und Reden*, vol. 1 (Munich, 1943) pp. 34–67. There are some interesting comments on the genesis of Rosenberg's ideas on Jewry in Kroll, *Utopie als Ideologie*, pp. 118ff. On Rosenberg in general see R. Cecil, *The Myth of the Master Race: Alfred Rosenberg and Nazi Ideology* (London, 1972). Rosenberg's political philosophy is closely examined in F. Nova, *Alfred Rosenberg: Nazi Theorist of the Holocaust* (New York, 1986). See also J. Baur, *Die russische Kolonie in München 1900–1945: Deutsch-russische Beziehungen im 20. Jahrhundert* (Wiesbaden, 1998) pp. 270ff.

43. A Rosenberg, *Pest in Russland: Der Bolschewismus, seine Häupter, Handlanger und Opfer*, ed. G. Leibbrandt (Munich, 1937) p. 41. The first edition of this book appeared in 1922.

44. On Eckart see M. Plewnia, *Auf dem Weg zu Hitler: Der 'völkische' Publizist Dietrich Eckart* (Bremen, 1970). There is a brief discussion of the views of Eckart and Rosenberg, and their contributions to *Auf gut deutsch* [hereafter *Agd*] in Merz, *Das Schreckbild*, pp. 432ff. For a contemporary indication of Eckart's attitude to the Jewish question see above all his article 'Das Judentum in und ausser uns', *Agd*, 17 January 1919. 'Das Judentum' became a long running series in *Agd*.

45. A. Rosenberg, 'Die russisch-jüdische Revolution', *Agd*, 21 February 1919. See also, A. Rosenberg, *Schriften aus den Jahren 1917–1921*, intro. H. Baeumler (Munich, 1943) pp. 342ff.

46. In this connection see especially A. Rosenberg, 'Judenheit und Politik', *Agd*, 13 June 1919.

47. See Stoakes, *Hitler and the Quest for World Dominion*, pp. 13ff.

48. See, for example, his essay 'Der Zionismus' in Rosenberg, *Schriften aus den Jahren 1917–1921*, pp. 261–3. In 1921 Rosenberg wrote a booklet entitled *Der staatsfeindliche Zionismus* (second edition, Munich, 1938) which was solely concerned with the Jews' alleged infiltration of British politics.

49. Stoakes, *Hitler and the Quest for World Dominion*, p. 12.

50. The text of the Protocols can be examined in *Protocols of the Meetings of the Learned Elders of Zion: Translated from the Russian Text by Victor E. Marsden* (London, 1948). Hitler's acceptance of the Protocols as proof that the whole existence of the Jews was based on a 'continuous [*fortlaufenden*] lie' can be found in Hitler, *Mein Kampf*, p. 337.

51. Stoakes, *Hitler and the Quest for World Dominion*, p. 34

52. *HSA*, no. 105, Rede auf einer NSDAP-Versammlung, 2 June 1920. The following month Hitler linked the 'Jewish-Bolshevik' domination of Russia with a direct threat to the Reich, and warned his compatriots to shun social democracy as the vehicle through which the Jews were seeking to destroy German nationalism in order to replace it with their own Marxist 'internationalist exploitation'. Ibid, no. 121, 'Spa, Bolschewismus und politische Tagesfragen', Rede auf einem NSDAP-Sprechabend, 21 July 1920. Bolshevism, Goebbels later averred, was 'the most devilish infection the Jews can bring upon a people'. See *Das Reich*, issue of 20 July 1941.

53. Hitler, *Mein Kampf*, p. 703.

54. *HSA*, no. 605, Vor dem Volksgericht. Erster Handlungstag, 26 February 1924.

55. Ibid., no. 362, 'Graf Lerchenfeld', Rede auf einem NSDAP-Sprechabend, 20 February 1922. As early as April 1920 Hitler had claimed that the Weimar administration was not led by the will of the people but by 'Jewish gold'. See ibid., no. 92, Schlusswort auf einer NSDAP-Versammlung, 9 April 1920.

56. Ibid., no. 368, 'Der Klassenkampf ein Börsenbetrug', Rede auf einer NSDAP-Versammlung, 1 March 1922; ibid., no. 374, Rede auf einer NSDAP-Versammlung, 2 April 1922.

57. Bundesarchiv Koblenz [hereafter BK], N1128/23, Das politische Testament Adolf Hitlers, 29 April 1945.

58. *HSA*, no. 393, 'Freistaat oder Sklaventum'. Rede auf einer DAP-Versammlung, 28 July 1922.

59. *RSA*, III/2, no 7, Stellungnahme zu einer vermittlungsverfahren wegen Hochverrats, undated but written at some point between September 1929 and March 1930.

60. *HSA*, no. 634, interview with Hans Lutz, 25 April 1924; ibid., N[achtrag]21, Rede auf einem deutschen Tag, 7 October 1923.

61. Ibid., no. 387, Rede vor dem Nationalen Klub 1919, 29 May 1922.

62. Ibid., no. 178, 'Der völkische Gedanke und der Partei', Aufsatz, 1 January 1921.

63. Hitler, *Mein Kampf, passim*, especially pp. 329ff.

64. Hitler, *Zweites Buch, passim*, especially pp. 220ff.

65. *VB*, 27 April 1925. See, as representative examples of other articles, 'Die zionistisch-bolschewistische Weltverschwörung', *VB*, 29 September

1925; 'Marxismus und Judentum', *VB*, 18 September 1926; 'Die Herrschaft der Börse ist Demokratie', *VB*, 12/13 June 1927; 'Der Völkerbund als Werkzeug der Welt-Freimauerei', *VB*, 20 July 1928; 'Wie ganz Juda zusammenarbeitet', *VB*, 30 October 1929; 'Die Verschwörung des Weltjudentums', *VB*, 30 April 1930. An analysis of these and similar articles would be superfluous in the context of the present study. In accordance with Hitler's maxim that the most effective propaganda consisted of a few points repeated over and over again, the articles, despite their differing titles, essentially registered the simple point that the Jewish race aspired to dominate the globe, in pursuit of which objective it used international high finance, revolution, internationalist doctrines and movements such as Marxism, Freemasonry and Jesuitism, Zionism, democracy and all manner of political deception and subversion.

66. Parteileitung der NSDAP. Propaganda Abteilung, *Propaganda* (Munich, 1927) p. 39.

67. On Goebbels's mid-1920s dalliance with the concept of 'National Bolshevism' see below p. 131.

68. 'Heil Moskau!' *Der Angriff*, 21 November 1927, reproduced in J. Goebbels, *Der Angriff. Aufsätze aus der Kampfzeit* (Munich, 1941) pp. 236–8.

69. See, for example, *RSA*, III/2, no. 119, Interview with the *New York American*, December 1929; ibid., IV/1, no. 8, Interview with *The Times*, 14 October 1930. Hitler also employed guarded terms about the Jews in his dealings with German industrialists, whose support he courted, preferring for obvious reasons to highlight the political and economic threat represented by Marxism. See A. Hitler, *Der Weg zum Wiederaufstieg* (Munich, 1927), and below p. 58.

70. Hitler, *Mein Kampf*, p. 170.

71. *RSA*, III/2, no. 16, 'Politik der Woche', *Illustrierte Beobachter*, 30 March 1929.

72. Ibid., III/3, no 14. 'Politik der Woche', *Illustrierte Beobachter*, 8 February 1930.

73. Hitler, *Mein Kampf*, p. 604.

74. On the fate of the KPD following the *Machtübergabe* see S. Bahne, 'Die Kommunistische Partei Deutschlands', in E. Matthias and R. Morsey (ed.) *Das Ende der Parteien 1933* (Düsseldorf, 1960) pp. 655–739; E. D. Weitz, *Creating German Communism, 1890–1990: From Popular Protest to Socialist State* (Princeton, 1997) pp. 280ff. As a measure of the success of the Nazis in decimating the KPD leadership after 30 January 1933, Beatrix Herlemann notes that of the 422 senior KPD officials active at the start of Hitler's chancellorship, only 13 remained working in the German underground by August 1935. See B. Herlemann,

'Communist Resistance between Comintern Directives and Nazi Terror' in D. E. Barclay and E. D. Weitz (eds) *Between Reform and Revolution: German Socialism and Communism from 1840 to 1990* (New York, 1998) pp. 357–71, here p. 362.

75. See, for example, Neurath's comments to his British counterpart recorded in *DBFP*, 2/XV, no. 486, Eden to Phipps, 27 January 1936.

76. Ibid., 2/XVII, appendix I, memorandum by Vansittart, 10 September 1936. On the issue in general see, A. Merson, *Communist Resistance in Nazi Germany* (London, 1985).

77. *TBJG*, I/3/ii, 31 March, 3 April 1933.

78. 'Der Schuldige', *Der Stürmer*, no. 10, March 1933. On a similar theme see 'Die Geheimpläne gegen Deutschland enthüllt', ibid., no 34, July 1933, which, citing the *Protocols of the Learned Elders of Zion* as evidence of conspiratorial intentions, argued that the Jews 'must be exterminated from the face of the earth'. Edited by the notoriously anti-Semitic Gauleiter of Nuremberg, Julius Streicher, *Der Stürmer* was probably the most rabidly anti-Semitic publication to appear in Germany before the outbreak of war in 1939. Although some of its content verged on the pornographic, *Der Stürmer* did not neglect to highlight the international dimension of the Jewish menace or the bond between Jewry and Bolshevism, unsurprisingly marshalling the most spurious of arguments in the process. In 1934, for example, the fact that an Amercian academic had criticized Hitler's persecution of the Jews and his suppression of the communists was offered as 'forcible proof that the Jews work hand in hand with Communism'. See 'Wer herrscht in Amerika?' *Der Stürmer*, no. 36, July 1934. On Streicher see R. L. Bytwerk, *Julius Streicher: Nazi Editor of the notorious anti-Semitic Newspaper Der Stürmer* (2nd edn, New York, 2001). For a detailed account of the coverage of the Jewish question and the Jewish 'world conspiracy' in the more prominent Nazi publications, especially the *Völkischer Beobachter*, see W. Meyer zu Uptrup, *Kampf gegen die 'jüdische Weltverschwörung': Propaganda und Antisemitismus der Nationalsozialisten 1919–1945* (Berlin, 2003).

79. In this latter connection note Hitler's comment to Adolf Wagner in June 1937 that all Jewish doctors would be prohibited from practising medicine in the event of war. See Saul Friedländer, *Nazi Germany and the Jews*. Volume 1. *The Years of Persecution 1933–39* (London, 1998) p. 226. The desire to stifle Jewish influence was not restricted to Hitler and the Party radicals. In March 1936 Ribbentrop's assistant, Professor Count von Dürckheim-Montmarin, told A. L. Kennedy of *The Times* that the Nazi regime aimed to 'exclude the Jews from influencing the national life – either in politics or education'. While the Jews would be permitted to earn a living, 'they [namely the Nazis] do not want them

either to mislead youth in universities or to corrupt public life or to diminish Germanism'. See G. Martel (ed.) *The Times and Appeasement: The Journals of A. L. Kennedy, 1932–1939* (London, 2000) 3 March 1936, p. 197.

80. *VB*, 28 November 1935.
81. The seventh Comintern Congress, which had taken place in Moscow in July 1935, had castigated Germany for its aggressive intentions. See Bundesarchiv Berlin-Lichterfelde [hereafter BBL], NS43/51, 'Beschluss des Politbüros der WKPB vom 4 August 1935'.
82. Domarus, I/2, 15 September 1935, speech to the Reichstag, pp. 536–7.
83. *Reden des Führers am Parteitag der Ehre 1936*, 'Die Schlussrede des Führers auf dem Kongress', 14 September 1936, pp. 69–70.

Chapter 2

1. See Stoakes, *Hitler and the Quest for World Dominion*, pp. 51ff. On Class and the Pan-German League see R. Chickering, *We Men Who Feel Most German: A Cultural Study of the Pan-German League, 1886–1914* (London, 1984); A. Kruck, *Geschichte des Alldeutschen Verbandes* (Wiesbaden, 1954).
2. For representative early pronouncements by Hitler on foreign policy issues see *HSA*, no. 66, 'Brest-Litovsk und Versailles', Rede auf einer DAP-Versammlung, 13 November 1919; ibid., no. 87, 'Die Wahrheit über den "Gewaltfrieden von Brest-Litowsk?" [sic] und den sogenannten "Frieden der Versöhnung und Verständigung von Versailles', Rede auf einer NSDAP-Versammlung, 4 March 1920; Phelps, 'Hitler als Parteiredner', no. 4. Speech at the Hofbräuhaus-Festsaal, 27 April 1920.
3. See *HSA*, no. 141, 'Betrogen, verraten und verkauft', Rede auf einer NSDAP-Versammlung, 5 September 1920.
4. See, for example, ibid., no. 69, 'Deutschland vor seiner tiefsten Erniedrigung', Rede auf einer DAP-Versammlung, 10 December 1919.
5. On this see Phelps, 'Hitler als Parteiredner', no. 3. 'National-sozialistische [sic] Deutsche Arbeiterpartei im Hofbräuhaus-Festsaal am 17 April 1920'.
6. Ibid. In September 1920 he accused the Jews of fanning the flames of war. Ibid., no. 15, 'Versammlung der Nationalsozialistischen Deutschen Arbeiterpartei München im Hofbräuhausfestsaal am 22 September 1920, abends 8 Uhr'.
7. *HSA*, no. 121, 'Spa, Bolschewismus und politische Tagesfragen', Rede auf einem NSDAP-Sprechabend, 21 July 1920. See also ibid., no. 124, 'Spa-Moskau-oder Wir?', Rede auf einer NSDAP-Versammlung, 27 July 1920.

8. Phelps, 'Hitler als Parteiredner', no. 3. 'National-sozialistische [sic] Deutsche Arbeiterpartei im Hofbräuhaus-Festsaal am 17 April 1920'.

9. *HSA*, no. 118, Rede auf einer NSDAP-Versammlung, 6 July 1920.

10. Ibid., no. 305, Rede auf einer NSDAP Versammlung, 21 October 1921. Notably, Hitler reasoned during this speech that Germany was now confronted with exactly the same choice it had faced *vis-à-vis* Russia and Britain before 1914.

11. BBL, R43I/2681, E. A. Scharrer, 'Bericht nach Hitlers persönlichen Ausführungen', December 1922, p. 4.

12. Ibid.

13. This view is supported by Axel Kuhn and Klaus Hildebrand. See Kuhn, *Hitlers aussenpolitisches Programm*, pp. 70ff; Hildebrand, *Foreign Policy of the Third Reich*, pp. 19ff.

14. *HSA*, no. 393, 'Freistaat oder Sklaventum?' Rede auf einer NSDAP-Versammlung, 28 July 1922.

15. See Hitler, *Mein Kampf*, pp. 696, 699, 763–5, 766; Hitler, *Zweites Buch*, *passim*.

16. Hitler, *Mein Kampf*, pp. 184–5. See also pp. 69–70, 356, 750–1. In a speech delivered on 27 February 1925 Hitler identified as the 'clear and simple' goal of the NSDAP 'the struggle against Marxism and the spiritual carrier of this world pestilence and scourge, the *Jew*'. RSA, I, no. 6, 'Deutschlands Zukunft und unsere Bewegung', Rede auf [einer] NSDAP-Versammlung, 27 February 1925 (emphasis in the original).

17. Hitler, *Mein Kampf*, p. 752 (emphasis in the original).

18. Ibid., p. 724 (emphasis in the original).

19. Ibid., p. 728 (emphasis in the original).

20. Ibid., p. 738.

21. Ibid., p. 154.

22. Hitler, *Zweites Buch*, pp. 163–6.

23. According to Hitler, even before the First World War, Germany should have renounced 'her senseless colonial policy … her merchant marine and war fleet', and 'concluded an alliance with England … thus passing from a feeble global policy to a determined European policy of territorial acquisition on the continent'. Hitler, *Mein Kampf*, p. 753.

24. As we shall see, Hitler continued to express his fears of the Bolshevik threat and often spoke of an Anglo–German–Italian union against Bolshevism. See, for example, *RSA*, IV/2, no. 84. Interview with *Sunday Graphic* and *Sunday News*, 5 December 1931; ibid., V/1, no. 66. Interview with Carlo Scorza, 29 April 1932.

25. Hitler, *Zweites Buch*, pp. 102, 155.

26. Ibid., p. 153.

27. Ibid., p. 159.

28. Ibid., p. 102.

29. Although Hitler's attitude to Russia was clear, his anti-Russian, pro-British policy was not without its critics. In the early 1930s a circle of prominent Nazis (including Göring and Reventlow) wanted to remove Rosenberg's influence from the formulation of Nazi foreign policy. It was believed that if Rosenberg were frozen out then it would be easier to move the NSDAP in the direction of a pro-Russian policy and thus away from Hitler's preferred German–British–Italian understanding. BK, ZSg. 133/42, unsigned memorandum, 30 July 1931. Göring's love–hate relationship with Russia was exemplified by his declaration in November 1931 that while he 'greatly admired the Soviet system ... he detested the Soviet doctrine'. *DBFP*, 2/II, no. 302, notes of a conversation between Mr Yencken and Captain Göring, 24 November 1931.

30. *Akten zur deutschen Auswärtigen Politik 1918–1945*, Serie B, 1925–1933, vols I–XXI, eds H. Rothfels, W. Bußmann et al. (Göttingen, 1966–1983) [hereafter *ADAP*, B] XIX, no. 105, Bülow circular, 8 December 1931.

31. *RSA*, IV/1, no. 8. Interview with *The Times*, 14 October 1930. See also ibid., III/2, no. 119. Interview with *New York American*, December 1929; ibid., no. 124. Interview with *Daily Mail*, 25 September 1930.

32. See Wagener, *Hitler: Memoirs of a Confidant*, p. 230.

33. *DBFP*, 2/II, no. 302, notes of a conversation between Mr Yencken and Captain Göring, 24 November 1931.

34. *RSA*, IV/1, no. 111, interview with *Daily Express*, 1 May 1931.

35. Hitler frequently spoke of his fears of the nightmare scenario that one day the Bolshevist menace could spread so that the 'Red Flag flew from Vladivostock [*sic*] to the English Channel'. In the battle against the international threat posed by Bolshevism the NSDAP was a 'vital necessity' not only to Germany but also to Britain and Europe. Ibid., no. 1, interview with *The Times*, 2 October 1930. For similar views see ibid., IV/2, no. 15, interview with Reuters, July 1931; ibid., no. 91, *Rundfunkrede*, 11 December 1931.

36. Wagener, *Memoirs of a Confidant,* p. 157 (emphasis in the original). See also p. 173.

37. *RSA*, IV/1, no. 110, interview with *Il Popolo d'Italia*. The concept of 'Asiatic Bolshevism' employed here by Hitler and dating back in National Socialist terminology to the early 1920s established rather a neat link between the racial and political dimensions of his anti-Bolshevik ideology. This may have been specifically designed to make the maximum impact on and elicit the maximum capital from the racial and political prejudices of his audience both inside and outside Germany.

38. K. Hildebrand, *German Foreign Policy from Bismarck to Adenauer: The Limits of Statecraft*, trans. L. Willmot (London, 1989) pp. 121–49. See also F. Knipping, 'Frankreich in Hitlers Aussenpolitik 1933–1939', in M. Funke (ed.) *Hitler, Deutschland und die Mächte: Materialien zur*

Außenpolitik des Dritten Reiches (Düsseldorf, 1976) pp. 612–27. Hitler even mentioned the idea of an accommodation with France to the Italian press – a significant point given that he had hitherto deliberately stressed the common enmity felt towards France. *RSA*, IV/2, no. 87. Interview with *Gazzetta del Popolo*, 6 December 1931. See also ibid., no. 99, Interview with *Christian Science Monitor*, 22 December 1931.

39. Ibid., no. 56. Article in *Saturday Review*, 24 October 1931. This article entitled 'Germany at the Crossroads' subsequently appeared in Spanish and Italian newspapers.

40. Domarus, I/1, 27 January 1932, speech to the Industrieklub, p. 77. Hitler also sought to highlight these aspects in newspaper articles, open letters and, significantly, in his communications with senior officials of the German army, where there was considerable support for the Rapallo policy of collaboration with the USSR. See *RSA*, IV/1, no. 15, '"Das Telegramm Hervés und Deutschland", Erklärung', 26 October 1930; ibid., no. 24, '"Deutschland und Frankreichs Abrüstung", Erklärung', 7 November 1930; ibid, V/2, no 15, '"Nationalsozialistische Weltauffassung gegen Ideenlosigkeit und Dilettantismus": Schreiben an Franz von Papen', 16 October 1932. On the military aspect, see Hitler's letter to von Reichenau of 4 December 1932 published in A. Adamthwaite, *The Lost Peace: International Relations in Europe 1918–1939* (London, 1980) pp. 131–6.

41. *RSA*, IV/3, no. 16, interview with *La Stampa*, 31 January 1932. See also J. Petersen, *Hitler-Mussolini: Die Entstehung der Achse Berlin-Rom 1933–1936* (Tübingen, 1973) pp. 24–6, 44–8.

42. See, for example, *RSA*, V/2, no. 4, interview with *Il Tevere*, 4 October 1932.

43. In June 1932, in a conversation with Prince Starhemberg, the Austrian Heimwehr leader, Mussolini condemned the Nazis' virulent anti-Semitism as 'stupid and barbarous'. See Prince Starhemberg, *Between Hitler and Mussolini: Memoirs of Ernst Rüdiger Prince Starhemberg* (London, 1942) p. 24.

44. See *ADAP*, B, XIX, no 105, Bülow circular, 8 December 1931; H-A. Jacobsen, *Nationalsozialistische Aussenpolitik, 1933–1938* (Frankfurt am Main, 1968) pp. 73–5; F. W. Winterbotham, *The Nazi Connection* (London, 1978) pp. 30ff.

45. PRO, FO371/15217/C9862, FO minute, 31 December 1931. The conversation had actually taken place on 4 December.

46. Ibid., FO371/16751/C10679, minute by Collier, 13 December 1933.

47. K. Lüdecke, *I Knew Hitler: The Story of a Nazi who Escaped the Blood Purge* (London, 1938) p. 422.

48. As a representative example see W. Laqueur, *Russia and Germany: A Century of Conflict* (London, 1965) pp. 158–9.

49. Wagener, *Memoirs of a Confidant*, pp. 173–4 (emphasis in the original).
50. Hitler, *Mein Kampf*, p. 413.
51. *VB*, 17 September 1925.
52. Hitler, *Zweites Buch*, pp. 174–5. See also p. 223.
53. Ibid., p. 223.
54. E. M. Robertson, 'Zur Wiederbesetzung des Rheinlandes 1936', *VfZ*, 10 (1962) pp. 178–204, here p. 194, memorandum by Hassell, 19 February 1936.
55. Wagener, *Memoirs of a Confidant*, p. 165.

Chapter 3

1. G. Hilger and A. G. Meyer, *The Incompatible Allies: A Memoir-History of German–Soviet Relations, 1918–1941* (New York, 1971) pp. 250–1; M. Lee and W. Michalka, *German Foreign Policy 1917–1933: Continuity or Break?* (Leamington Spa, 1987) pp. 112ff. A useful and recent general overview of German–Soviet relations during the Weimar and Third Reich eras is A. M. Nekrich, *Pariahs, Partners, Predators: German–Soviet Relations, 1922–1941*, ed. and trans. G. L. Freeze (New York, 1997).
2. J. Haslam, *The Soviet Union and Collective Security in Europe, 1933–39* (London, 1984) pp. 6–7; A. Ulam, *Expansion and Co-existence: Soviet Foreign Policy 1917–1973* (London, 2nd edn, 1974) pp. 183ff, pp. 209ff.
3. On the early Soviet reaction to the appearance of the Hitler cabinet see *ADAP*, C/I/1, no. 6, Dirksen to Bülow, 31 January 1933; ibid., no. 73, Dirksen to AA, 11 March 1933.
4. A review of the scathing Soviet press reaction to this speech, delivered in the immediate aftermath of the Reichstag fire, can be found in BK, ZSg. 133/52, 'Die Rede Hitlers im Sportpalast', 8 March 1933.
5. In this connection see *ADAP*, C/II/1, no. 161, unsigned memorandum [probably by Twardowski], 1 January 1934.
6. PAB, R83394, Dirksen to AA, 22 March 1933.
7. Weinberg, *Foreign Policy*, I, p. 27.
8. *ADAP*, C/I/1, no. 16, memorandum by Vogels of a Conference of Ministers, 8 February 1933.
9. Domarus, I/1, 23 March 1933, speech to the Reichstag, p. 236.
10. For the guidelines see PAB, R83394, unsigned memorandum, 18 March 1933.
11. Domarus, I/1, 23 March 1933, speech to the Reichstag, pp. 231, 236. On the Soviet reaction to the Four Power Pact see *ADAP*, C/I/1, no. 136, Dirksen to AA, 4 April 1933.
12. *ADAP*, C/I/1, no. 137, Dirksen to Bülow, 4 April 1933; ibid., no. 212, Dirksen to AA, 5 May 1933.
13. PAB, R83395, Dirksen to AA, 28 March 1933.

14. *ADAP*, C/I/1, no. 137, Dirksen to Bülow, 4 April 1933 (emphasis in the original).

15. Ibid., no. 142, memoranda by Thomsen, 7 April 1933, and Willuhn, 12 April 1933.

16. Ibid., no. 140, Neurath to the German embassy in Moscow, 5 April 1933, note 5.

17. Ibid., no. 312, unsigned memorandum, 14 June 1933. For the Soviet reaction see ibid., no. 325, Dirksen to Bülow, 19 June 1933; ibid., no. 331, memorandum by Bülow, 22 June 1933.

18. H. von Dirksen, *Moscow Tokyo London: Twenty Years of German Foreign Policy* (Oklahoma, 1952) p. 115. For Litvinov's views on the involvement of the German leadership see *Soviet Documents on Foreign Policy*. Selected and edited by J. Degras, 3 vols (London, 1951–3) [hereafter SDFP] 3, speech by Litvinov to the Central Executive Committee, 29 December 1933, pp. 48–61, here p. 56.

19. On Rosenberg's association with Ukrainian separatists immediately after the Nazi assumption of power see BK, ZSg. 133/52, Aktenvermerk Leibbrandt, 7 December 1933. Moscow fully realized that Rosenberg was hoping to incite these groups to action against the USSR, to which end he sought to encourage them with promises of a forthcoming anti-Bolshevik crusade that a coalition of powers comprising Germany, Britain, France, Italy and possibly Poland would carry out.

20. *ADAP*, C/I/2, no. 438, Twardowski to AA, 19 September 1933. Some three years later Hitler effectively confirmed these suspicions by telling the Estonian foreign minister that 'we were separated from Bolshevik Russia by so great a gulf that for ideological reasons we desired no closer connections or treaty arrangements of any kind with that country'. Ibid., C/V/2, no. 378, memorandum by Meissner, 17 June 1936.

21. In this connection see the recent study by E. E. Ericson III, *Feeding the German Eagle: Soviet Economic Aid to Nazi Germany, 1933–1941* (Westport, 1999).

22. See *ADAP*, C/I/2, no. 456, memorandum by Thomsen, 26 September 1933; ibid., no. 457, memorandum by Bülow, 26 September 1933.

23. Ibid., no. 487, Twardowski to AA, 10 October 1933.

24. Ibid., C/II/1, no. 163, Nadolny to AA, 5 January 1934.

25. G. Schramm, 'Basic Features of German Ostpolitik 1918–1939', in B. Wegner (ed.) *From Peace to War: Germany, Soviet Russia and the World, 1939–1941* (Oxford, 1997) pp. 11–25, here p. 23. On this, see also A. Kuhn, 'Das nationalsozialistische Deutschland und die Sowjetunion', in Funke, *Hitler, Deutschland und die Mächte*, pp. 639–53, here p. 646.

26. *ADAP*, C/I/1, no. 194, memorandum by Neurath, 28 April 1933.

27. BK, ZSg. 133/52, 'Einige Bemerkungen über die deutsch-sowjetischen Beziehungen im Jahre 1933', undated, but internal evidence suggests that the paper was drawn up in the autumn of 1933.
28. Hildebrand, *German Foreign Policy from Bismarck to Adenauer*, p. 137. The relevant passage from the Nuremberg speech reads: 'If a single people were to fall prey to Bolshevism in Western or Central Europe, this poison would continue its corrosive work and devastate today's oldest and most beautiful cultural possessions on earth. In taking this fight upon itself, Germany is but fulfilling, as so often in its history, a truly European mission.' In February 1934 Hitler declared to a gathering of German students that the triumph of Bolshevism in Europe would mean the complete annihilation of that 'Aryan spirit' upon which all culture was based. See Domarus, I/1, 3 September 1933, speech to the Party Congress, p. 299; ibid., 7 February 1934, speech to students in Berlin, p. 363.
29. G. Roberts, *The Soviet Union and the Origins of the Second World War: Russo–German Relations and the Road to War, 1933–1941* (London, 1995) p. 30, citing Suritz to Litvinov, 28 November 1935.
30. Ibid., pp. 31–2, citing Litvinov to Stalin, 3 December 1935.
31. For the views of the commander-in-chief of the German army during the 1920s, General von Seeckt, which were not untypical of German opinion at that time see J. Lipski, *Diplomat in Berlin, 1933–1939: Papers and Memoirs of Józef Lipski, Ambassador of Poland*, ed. W. Jedrzejewicz (New York, 1968) p. 37.
32. W. Michalka, *Ribbentrop und die deutsche Weltpolitik 1933–1940: Aussenpolitische Konzeptionen und Entscheidungsprozesse im Dritten Reich* (Munich, 1980) p. 270.
33. Z. Shore, 'Hitler's Opening Gambit: Intelligence, Encirclement, and the Decision to Ally with Poland', *Intelligence and National Security*, 14 (1999) pp. 103–22, here p. 110.
34. Dirksen, *Moscow Tokyo London*, p. 110.
35. Wagener, *Hitler: Memoirs of a Confidant*, pp. 49–50.
36. Ibid., pp. 51–2.
37. *DBFP*, 2/VI, no. 83, memorandum on the German–Polish Declaration of 16 November 1933, 27 November 1933.
38. *Official Documents Concerning Polish–German and Polish–Soviet Relations, 1933–1939*. Published by the authority of the Polish government (London, 1940) no. 6, Lipski to Beck, 12 November 1933.
39. Lipski, *Diplomat in Berlin*, pp. 124–5.
40. G. Krebs, *Japans Deutschlandpolitik 1935–1941: Eine Studie zur Vorgeschichte des Pazifischen Krieges*, 2 vols (Hamburg, 1984) I, p. 34.
41. On Soviet fears of Polish–German collaboration see PAB, R83396, Nadolny to AA, 11 December 1933. Commenting on the visit to Italy of

Litvinov, the Soviet foreign minister, the German ambassador in Rome drew special attention to the fears Litvinov had expressed of a German–Polish–Japanese combination against Russia. Ibid., Hassell to AA, 22 December 1933.

42. Brotherton Library, University of Leeds. Confidential US State Department central files. Germany: foreign affairs, 1930–1939, Dodd to State Department, 13 December 1933.

43. In August 1934 a Wilhelmstrasse circular summarizing the attitudes of the major powers towards the Franco–Soviet proposals revealed that the Polish objections were virtually identical with the German. BK, N1310/47, memorandum by Meyer, 16 August 1934. For the Polish position see also ADAP, C/III/2, no. 429, memorandum by Bülow, 14 January 1935; ibid., C/IV/1 no. 190, record of a conversation between Hitler and Beck, 3 July 1933. On the general incompatibility of the proposals with Hitler's plans and intentions see Weinberg, Foreign Policy, I, pp. 171, 183–4.

44. ADAP, C/III/2, no. 555, record of a conversation between Hitler and Sir John Simon, 25 March 1935.

45. ADAP, C/IV/1, no. 190, record of a conversation between Hitler and Beck, 3 July 1935.

46. IMT, vol. IX, Göring testimony, 14 March 1946, p. 308; Weinberg, Foreign Policy, I, pp. 193–4. For a useful review of Göring's activities in Polish–German relations see A. Kube, Pour le mérite und Hakenkreuz: Hermann Göring im Dritten Reich (Munich, 1986) pp. 103–18.

47. TBJG, Sämtliche Fragmente, I/2, 19 August 1935.

48. Hoover, Truman Smith Papers, Smith to the War Department, 25 November 1935. In his annual report for 1935 the British ambassador in Berlin also noted this possibility writing that Hitler's attitude towards Poland was 'no doubt influenced by the Russian peril and … Germany's mission to defend Western civilisation against Bolshevism. To Germany, Poland as a spear-head, a "brilliant second" in the move against Bolshevik Russia, might be an ally well worth the corridor. For with friendship between Germany and Poland, with a German fleet in command of the Baltic and a German air force assuring connection with East Prussia, the objections to the corridor would appear smaller. Alternatively, the crusade against the Bolsheviks might provide the means for compensating Poland elsewhere.' PRO, FO 371/19938/C143, Phipps to the Foreign Office, 6 January 1936.

Chapter 4

1. Wagener, Hitler: Memoirs of a Confidant, pp. 158–9.
2. Laqueur, Russia and Germany, p. 20.

3. *Daily Express*, 12 April 1919.

4. *ADAP*, B/XVI, no. 16, Bernstorff to AA, 21 October 1930.

5. M. Gilbert, *Winston Churchill: Documents*, vol. 5, pt. 2, *The Wilderness Years, 1929–1935* (London, 1981) memorandum by Prince Bismarck, 20 October 1930, p. 197.

6. On this aspect see G. T. Waddington, '"An idyllic and unruffled atmosphere of complete Anglo–German misunderstanding": Aspects of the Operations of the Dienststelle Ribbentrop in Great Britain, 1934–1938', *History*, 265 (1997) pp. 44–72, especially pp. 57ff.

7. R. Griffiths, *Fellow Travellers of the Right: British Enthusiasts for Nazi Germany 1933–1939* (Oxford, 1983) p. 139, citing *The Aeroplane*, 19 April 1933.

8. *Daily Mail*, 28 November 1933.

9. The Marquess of Londonderry, *Ourselves and Germany* (London, 1938) p. 21.

10. Ibid., p. 129.

11. N. Nicolson (ed.) *Harold Nicolson: Diaries and Letters 1930–1939* (London, 1966) 20 September 1936, p. 273. See also in this connection *DBFP*, 2/XVIII, no. 466, minute by Vansittart, 20 May 1937.

12. *DBFP*, 2/V, no. 139, Rumbold to Simon, 11 May 1933.

13. Ibid., no. 118, Simon to Rumbold, 8 May 1933. See also ibid., no. 126, Simon to Rumbold, 10 May 1933.

14. *ADAP*, C/I/1, no. 237, Hoesch to AA, 15 May 1933.

15. BK, ZSg. 133/44, memorandum by Rosenberg, 'Zweite Londoner Reise vom 4. bis 15 Mai 1933', 15 May 1933.

16. Griffiths, *Fellow Travellers of the Right*, p. 114.

17. PRO, FO371/16751/C10679, Kell to Vansittart, 4 December 1933.

18. House of Lords, Davidson Papers, memoranda by Davidson, 20 November 1933, 24 November 1933 [Waddington collection].

19. F. W. Winterbotham, *The Ultra Secret* (London, 1974) pp. 4–5; Winterbotham, *The Nazi Connection*, pp. 53–4.

20. BBL, R901/60976, memorandum, unsigned and undated, enclosed in Ribbentrop to Neurath, 4 February 1935.

21. Londonderry, *Ourselves and Germany*, pp. 84ff. See also I. Kershaw, *Making Friends with Hitler: Lord Londonderry and Britain's Road to War* (London, 2004) p. 138.

22. *DBFP*, 2/V, no. 36, Rumbold to Simon, 26 April 1933.

23. PRO, FO371/17369/W12257, Phipps to Simon, 24 October 1933.

24. *DBFP*, 2/VI, no. 305, Phipps to Simon, 22 February 1934.

25. Ibid., 2/XII, no. 651, notes of Anglo–German conversations held at the chancellor's palace, Berlin, on 25 and 26 March 1935.

26. *ADAP*, C/III/1, no. 84, Hoesch to AA, 12 July 1934.

27. PRO, FO408/64, Part LXVII, no. 78, Phipps to Simon, 19 July 1934.

28. *DBFP*, 2/XII, no. 651, notes of Anglo–German conversations held at the chancellor's palace, Berlin, on 25 and 26 March 1935.
29. *ADAP*, C/III/2, no. 555, record of a conversation between Hitler and Sir John Simon, 25 March 1935.
30. Ibid.
31. On Hitler's reaction to the naval agreement with Britain see Hildebrand, *Das Vergangene Reich*, pp. 474–6. For a succinct and revealing comparison of British and German aims during the negotiations see Kuhn, *Hitlers aussenpolitisches Programm*, pp. 172ff.
32. *ADAP*, C/IV/1, no. 131, unsigned memorandum, 4 June 1935. The day before the naval agreement was concluded Ribbentrop lunched with A. L. Kennedy of *The Times* and revealed his wish to introduce Baldwin to Hitler as he 'wants Baldwin to hear H[itler]'s ideas about Western solidarity against Bolshevism'. See G. Martel (ed.) *The Times and Appeasement*, 17 June 1935, p. 180.
33. *DBFP*, 2/XV, no. 383, Phipps to Hoare, 16 December 1935.
34. Ibid.
35. A. J. Toynbee, *Acquaintances* (London, 1967) p. 279.

Chapter 5

1. See Hitler, *Mein Kampf*, pp. 173, 318–9, 723–4. Hitler's first foreign press chief, Ernst 'Putzi' Hanfstaengl, cites him as early as 1924 as espousing the view that it was 'only in alliance with that hard-working, martially aware and racially unspoiled people, the Japanese, which is "without space" just like the German people and consequently our natural partner in the struggle against Bolshevik Muscovitism' that he could 'lead Germany into a new future'. See E. Hanfstaengl, *Zwischen Weissem und Braunem Haus: Memoiren eines politischen Aussenseiters* (Munich, 1970) pp. 167–8. Hitler's view of Japan in the 1920s is generally thought to have been influenced by the Munich-based geo-politician, Professor Karl Haushofer. See, for example, H. H. Herwig, 'Geopolitik: Haushofer, Hitler and Lebensraum', *Journal of Strategic Studies*, 22 (1999) pp. 218–41. For Haushofer's theories of geopolitics and the question of a German–Japanese alignment see E. L. Presseisen, *Germany and Japan: A Study in Totalitarian Diplomacy, 1933–1941* (The Hague, 1958) pp. 13–14.
2. Certain Japanese groups had made Hitler aware of their support and readiness for cooperation against Russia before the NSDAP came to power. See the reflections on a 1932 meeting between Hitler and Dr Okanouye in BBL, R43II/440, unsigned memorandum, 25 January 1935. On the general background to German and Nazi contacts with Japanese circles in Berlin in the later 1920s and early 1930s see J. W. M.

Chapman, 'A Dance on Eggs: Intelligence and the "Anti-Comintern"', *Journal of Contemporary History*, 22 (1987) pp. 333–72. Curiously, in view of his supposed concerns, even the Japanese ambassador is alleged to have raised with Nazi officials the issue of future collaboration against the USSR should the NSDAP ever come to power. See BK, ZSg. 133/42, Schickedanz to Rosenberg, 21 February 1931.

3. O. Tokushiro, 'The Anti-Comintern Pact 1935–1939', in J. W. Morley (ed.) *Deterrent Diplomacy: Japan, Germany and the USSR, 1935–1940* (New York, 1976) p. 23. See also, Krebs, *Japans Deutschlandpolitik*, I, p. 25.

4. E. Kordt, *Nicht aus den Akten* (Stuttgart, 1950) pp. 122–3. Speaking to a representative of the Japanese press in January 1932, Hitler gave no hint of his growing enchantment with Japan's martial spirit, but simply proclaimed that his movement necessarily opposed Bolshevism, expressed understanding for Japan's need to defend its national interests, and stated that the Nazi attitude towards Japan would be determined by nothing other than the amount of support it felt able to give to German attempts to overturn the Treaty of Versailles. *RSA*, IV/3, no. 2, Interview with Tokio Asahi Shimbun, 3 January 1932.

5. BBL, R43II/1454, Denkschrift Nr. 2 von Victor Spielmans, 'Die Lage im Fernen Osten und ihre Bedeutung', 6 January 1934.

6. PRO, FO371/16751/C10679, Kell to Vansittart, 4 December 1933.

7. *ADAP*, C/II/2, no. 237, Dirksen to Bülow, 4 February 1934; ibid., no. 267, Dirksen to AA, 17 February 1934. See also Hitler's remarks to Eugen Ott recorded in J. P. Fox, *Germany and the Far Eastern Crisis 1931–1938: A Study in Diplomacy and Ideology* (Oxford, 1985) p. 101. Dirksen represented something of an exception in the Wilhelmstrasse as an exponent of a close association with Japan. Although he was not a member of the NSDAP, he had socialized before 1933 with Goebbels from whom he may conceivably have acquired information about Hitler's views on Soviet and Far Eastern affairs. See *TBJG*, Sämtliche Fragmente, I/2, 4 and 21 January 1931. On Dirksen's views on policy towards Japan at the time of the negotiation of the Anti-Comintern Pact see, *ADAP*, C/IV/2, no. 479, Dirksen to Erdmannsdorf, 1 January 1936.

8. *ADAP*, C/II/1, no. 148, memorandum by Twardowski, 26 December 1933.

9. *IMT*, X, Ribbentrop testimony, 29 March 1946, p. 239. In an affidavit written the day before his execution Ribbentrop still maintained that the Anti-Comintern Pact was 'primarily an ideological pact' with a 'political weight against Soviet Russia'. Hoover, G. Henderson Papers, Csuz 79053-A, Joachim von Ribbentrop Affidavit, 15 October 1946.

10. The counsellor of the American embassy in Berlin noted that the inflammatory declarations made at the congress had 'afforded a welcome opportunity to the German press to enlarge on the duplicity of

Soviet policy, which on the one hand fraternizes with the bourgeoisie on the Council of the League and elsewhere, and on the other through the Comintern continues to preach world revolution'. NARA, State Department Decimal File 761.62/359, White to Hull, 5 August 1935.

11. Apart from the references made to the Bolshevik threat in discussions with official British representatives, most recently evident in Hitler's conversation with Simon in March 1935, and Ribbentrop's statements during the naval negotiations, the attraction of Germany's very public stand against Bolshevism was advertised in conversations conducted through private channels, and correspondence with prominent British personalities, As examples see PRO, FO800/295, Rennell to Hoare, 26 September 1935; PRO, FO800/290, Rothermere to Simon, 7 May 1935. For a summary of the various reactions to the declarations of the seventh Comintern congress see BK, ZSg. 121/334, unsigned memorandum, September 1935. The Japanese generally complained about the 'malicious' anti-Japanese nature of the speeches. The predictable Soviet response to British complaints was that 'the Comintern was not a Government institution or under Government control'. See *Daily Mail*, 4 September 1935.

12. For representative summaries see PAB, R85852, 'Russisches Lektorat. Die deutsch–japanische Geheimdiplomatie', 2 January 1936; ibid., unsigned and undated memorandum. Internal evidence suggests shortly after 8 January 1936.

13. Library of Congress, Washington D.C., [hereafter LoC], Dodd papers, Box 46, Dodd to Davis, 11 December 1935.

14. Presseisen, *Germany and Japan*, pp. 89–90; Weinberg, *Foreign Policy*, I, p. 244; *ADAP*, C/IV/2, no. 479, Dirksen to Erdmannsdorf, 1 January 1936. See also ibid., no. 416, memorandum by Erdmannsdorf, 18 November 1935.

15. Sommer, *Deutschland und Japan*, pp. 28ff.; Boyd, *The Extraordinary Envoy*, pp. 33ff.

16. On these developments see Sommer, *Deutschland und Japan*, pp. 29ff. In addition, the Japanese had their own reasons for wishing to proceed with the negotiations, including renewed difficulties with Russia on the Russo–Manchurian border. See, for example, PAB, R85851, DNB report, 4 May 1936.

17. *ADAP*, C/V/2, no. 362, memorandum by Meissner, 9 June 1936.

18. *Raumer mss*, fol. 18.

19. For example, in the *Zweites Buch* the only reference to Spain's value as an ally was in the context of its potential usefulness against France. Hitler, *Zweites Buch*, p. 217.

20. PRO, GFM34/3092, memorandum by Bülow-Schwante, 4 May 1936. For details of the German–Italian police agreement see J. Petersen,

Hitler-Mussolini: Die Entstehung der Achse Berlin-Rom 1933–1936 (Tübingen, 1973) pp. 438ff, p. 480. In 1937 the Germans organized a secret international police convention in Berlin, in which representatives from 15 nations took part, in order to discuss ways and means of suppressing Bolshevism. See BBL, NS19/256, memorandum by Bülow-Schwante, 24 August 1937.

21. Wiskemann, *The Rome–Berlin Axis*, p. 57.
22. *TBJG*, I/3/ii, 17 July 1936.
23. For further details on the economic exploitation of Spain during the Spanish Civil War see C. Leitz, *Economic Relations between Nazi Germany and Franco's Spain, 1936–1945* (Oxford, 1996); *GSWW*, I, pp. 316ff.
24. This view is supported by both the major works in Spanish and German on Hitler's policy towards the Spanish Civil War. See H-H. Abendroth, *Hitler in der spanischen Arena: Die deutsch-spanischen Beziehungen im Spannungsfeld der europäischen Interessenpolitik vom Ausbruch des Bürgerkrieges bis zum Ausbruch des Weltkrieges 1936–1939* (Nürnberg, 1970); A. Viñas, *La Alemania Nazi y el 18 de Julio* (Madrid, 1974). For the German leader's own retrospective confirmation of his motives see *Adolf Hitler: Monologe im Führerhauptquartier 1941–1944*. Aufgezeichnet von H. Heim. Herausgegeben und kommentiert von W. Jochmann (Munich, 2000) [hereafter Jochmann, *Monologe*] 19–20 February 1941, p. 284. For an interesting overview of the motives for and results to date of German intervention in Spain, written from the perspective of a career diplomat and stressing both the anti-communist political aspect and the economic benefits, see BBL, R901/61165, memorandum by Stohrer, February 1938.
25. H.-H. Abendroth, *Mittelsmann zwischen Franco und Hitler: Johannes Bernhardt erinnert 1936* (Scraptoft, 1978) p. 32.
26. Ibid., pp. 33–34; Abendroth, *Hitler in der spanischen Arena*, pp. 87 ff. See also Leitz, *Economic Relations between Nazi Germany and Franco's Spain*, p. 12.
27. J. von Ribbentrop, *The Ribbentrop Memoirs* (London, 1954) pp. 59–60.
28. See, for example, *ADAP*, C/V/2, no. 516, memorandum by Neurath of a conversation between Hitler and Horthy, 24 August 1936; *DBFP*, 2/XVII, appendix I, memorandum by Vansittart, 10 September 1936.
29. *DBFP*, 2/XVII, no. 84, minute by Sargent, 12 August 1936.
30. See PRO, FO371/408/66, Newton to Eden, 3 September 1936; PRO, FO371/19949/C6684, Newton to Eden, 25 September 1936.
31. On Ribbentrop's hopes in this direction see Michalka, *Ribbentrop und die deutsche Weltpolitik*, pp. 50ff; *IMT*, X, Ribbentrop testimony, 29 March 1946, pp. 230–2. For an assessment of Hitler's views on policy towards France between 1933 and 1936 see Hildebrand, *German Foreign Policy from Bismarck to Adenauer*, pp. 121ff.

32. See R. W. Mühle, *Frankreich und Hitler: Die französischen Deutschland-und Aussenpolitik 1933–1935* (Paderborn, 1995) pp. 97ff; pp. 247ff.

33. G. Warner, *Pierre Laval and the Eclipse of France* (London, 1968) pp. 93–4.

34. Domarus, I/2, 7 March 1936, speech to the Reichstag, pp. 590–1.

35. M. Muggeridge (ed.) *Ciano's Diplomatic Papers*, trans. S. Hood (London, 1948) [hereafter *CDP*] conversation with the Führer, 24 October 1936, p. 60.

36. W. Ritter von Schramm, *Sprich vom Frieden, wenn du den Krieg willst: Die psychologischen Offensiven Hitlers gegen die Franzosen 1933 bis 1939. Ein Bericht* (Mainz, 1973) p. 103.

37. T. Jones, *A Diary with Letters 1931–1950* (London, 1954) 4 September 1936, p. 245.

38. Ibid., 16 October 1936, p. 274.

39. *CDP*, conversation with the Führer, 24 October 1936, p. 58.

40. This measure, announced in late August 1936, was explained to the German public in terms of the growing military power of the USSR and its intervention in Spain. See Jacobsen, *Nationalsozialistische Aussenpolitik*, p. 457.

41. For the text of the memorandum see *ADAP*, C/V/2, no. 490, unsigned memorandum, August 1936. For a commentary on its provenance and significance, see W. Treue, 'Hitlers Denkschrift zum Vierjahresplan 1936', *VfZ*, 3 (1955) pp. 184ff. See further, especially for the role of Göring, whom Hitler made Reich plenipotentiary for the execution of the plan, Kube, *Pour le mérite und Hakenkreuz*, pp. 140ff; S. Martens, *Hermann Göring: 'erster Paladin des Führers' und 'zweiter Mann im Reich'* (Paderborn, 1985) pp. 66ff; R. J. Overy, *Goering: The 'Iron Man'* (London, 1984) pp. 46ff.

42. As Hitler said in October 1941, 'I write drafts of letters only concerning matters of quite fundamental importance, such as at the time of the Four Year Plan or last year concerning the Eastern action.' Jochmann, *Monologe*, 14 October 1941, p. 81.

43. *ADAP*, C/V/2, no. 490, unsigned memorandum, August 1936 (emphasis in the original).

44. Ibid., (emphasis in the original).

45. Ibid.

46. Hitler, *Mein Kampf*, p. 712.

47. Hitler, *Zweites Buch*, p. 223.

48. E. D. Susmel (ed.) *Opera Omnia di Benito Mussolini* (Florence, 1953) vol. 12, speech of 23 March 1919, p. 325.

49. *VB*, 29 July 1922.

50. Hitler, *Mein Kampf*, p. 721.

51. *RSA*, IV/1, no. 110, Interview with Il Popolo, [April] 1931. See also

ibid., IV/2, no. 84, Interview with *Sunday Graphic* and *Sunday News*, 5 December 1931.

52. See, for example, *DBFP*, 2/V, no. 358, Hadow to Vansittart, 24 August 1933; *ADAP*, C/I/1, no. 98, Hassell to AA, 18 March 1933; ibid., C/I/2, no. 485, Hassell to AA, 6 October 1933.

53. On this aspect see J. Calvitt Clarke III, *Russia and Italy against Hitler: The Bolshevik-Fascist Rapprochement of the 1930s* (New York, 1991).

54. PAB, R83396, Hassell to AA, 22 December 1933.

55. D. Mack Smith, *Mussolini* (London, 1993) p. 182.

56. Starhemberg, *Between Hitler and Mussolini*, p. 93.

57. *VB*, 9 September 1935.

58. *ADAP*, C/IV/1, no. 120, Hassell to AA, 30 May 1935. For analyses of Germany's exploitation of the crisis see M. Funke, *Sanktionen und Kanonen: Hitler, Mussolini und der internationale Abessinienkonflikt 1934–36* (Düsseldorf, 1970); and Petersen, *Hitler-Mussolini*, pp. 435ff.

59. *Documents Diplomatiques Français 1932–1939*, série 1, vol. IV (Paris, 1972) no. 113, Chambrun to Paul-Boncour, 15 August 1933.

60. BBL, NS8/116, memorandum by Strunk, 5 February 1936.

61. *ADAP*, C/V/1, no. 90, Papen to AA, 13 March 1936. Mussolini also argued that countries that 'opposed a rising nation' played into the hands of Bolshevism and would bring about the 'downfall of the West'.

62. Ibid., D/III, no. 40, Chargé d'Affaires in Italy to AA, 14 August 1936. The newly appointed and pro-German Italian Foreign Minister, Count Galeazzo Ciano, believed that events in Spain were 'driving Europe directly to a split between Communists and anti-Communists'. See ibid, no. 30, Hassell to AA, 6 August 1936.

63. *CDP*, conversation with the Führer, 24 October 1936, p. 57.

64. Ibid., conversation between Mussolini and Frank, 23 September 1936, pp. 43–8.

65. Ibid., conversation with the Führer, 24 October 1936, pp. 56–8.

66. M. Funke, 'Die deutsch-italienischen Beziehungen: Antibolschewismus und außenpolitische Interessenkonkurrenz als Strukturprinzip der "Achse"', in Funke, *Hitler, Deutschland und die Mächte*, pp. 823–46.

67. *Raumer mss*, fol. 36.

68. PRO, FO371/20743/C357, Phipps to Eden, 4 January 1937.

69. Ibid.

70. See *ADAP*, C/V/2, no. 624, German–Italian Protocols, 23 October 1936; *Daily Mail*, 2 November 1936.

71. *ADAP*, C/VI/1, no. 57, German–Japanese Agreement against the Communist International, 25 November 1936.

72. BK, ZSg. 121/14, 'Erklärung von Ribbentrop's [sic]', pp. 7–8.

73. *IMT*, XXXVI, doc. 416-EC, Niederschrift des Ministerrates am 4 September 1936, pp. 489–91. Göring is alleged to have repeated this

remark in an unpublished interview with a British journalist in December 1936. See S. Pons, *Stalin and the Inevitable War 1936–1941* (London, 2002) p. 66.

74. *TBJG*, I/3/ii, 2 December 1936.

Chapter 6

1. On Goebbels and national Bolshevism see especially his essay 'National-sozialismus oder Bolschewismus?' in *Nationalsozialistische Briefe*, 15 October 1925. For a brief introduction to the outlook of the Strasser faction see Stoakes, *Hitler and the Quest for World Dominion*, pp. 174ff.

2. *TBJG*, Sämtliche Fragmente, I/1, 15 February 1926 and 13 April 1926.

3. BBL, R55/450, memorandum by Taubert, undated, but written after 31 December 1944: 'Querschnitt durch die Tätigkeit des Arbeitsgebietes Dr Taubert (Antibolschewismus) des RMVP bis zum 31 Dezember 1944' [hereafter *Taubert mss*].

4. Ibid.

5. PRO, GFM34/1265, Goebbels circular, 8 December 1936.

6. BBL, NS43/17, Rosenberg to Schwarz, 16 January 1935.

7. See A. Ehrt, *Ein deutscher Todesweg* (Berlin, 1930); A Ehrt and J. Schweickert, *Entfesselung der Unterwelt: Ein Querschnitt durch die Bolschewisierung Deutschlands* (Berlin, 1932); A. Ehrt, *Totale Krise – Totale Revolution? Die 'Schwarze Front' des völkischen Nationalismus* (Berlin, 1933); *Terror: Die Blutchronik des Marxismus in Deutschland: Auf Grund amtlichen Materials bearbeitet von Adolf Ehrt und Hans Rosen* (Berlin, 1934); A Ehrt, *La Terreur Rouge: La Révolte Armée: Révélations sur l'organisation bolcheviste en Russie, en Allemagne et en France.* Introduction and conclusion by Nicolas Delile (Paris, 1934).

8. A. Ehrt, *Bewaffneter Aufstand! Enthüllungen über den kommunistischen Umsturzversuch am Vorabend der nationalen Revolution* (Berlin, 1933) p. 185.

9. The statistic is based on the *Personalakten* of individual Antikomintern members held at BBL.

10. Jacobsen, *Nationalsozialistische Aussenpolitik*, p. 453.

11. BBL, NS43/17, unsigned memorandum, 2 October 1934.

12. Ibid.

13. Ibid., unsigned memorandum, 10 October 1934.

14. BBL, NS43/18, memorandum by Reischauer, 'Tätigkeitsbericht Referat II', 28 February 1935; PRO, GFM34/458, German embassy Warsaw to AA, 16 June 1936.

15. NARA, T85/406, memorandum by Maass, 'Bericht über Reise nach Polen vom 2 bis 5 September 1934'.

16. PAB, R31832, Renthe-Fink to AA, 25 March 1936.

17. On the first tentative steps towards the Axis see Weinberg, *Foreign Policy*, I, pp. 234ff.

18. BBL, NS43/18, Gielen to Leibbrandt, 5 November 1935.

19. BBL, R43I/509, Aubert to Avenol, 13 June 1934. The following year Aubert founded the International Anti-Marxist Institute, also based in Geneva, the inauguration of which was attended in a private capacity by Alfred Gielen, a senior functionary of the Antikomintern. It was noted at the time by the German Consulate in Geneva that Aubert, who had originally concentrated his attacks on the Bolshevik system of government in the USSR, had more recently shifted his attention to 'the more general theme of the fight against international Marxism'. PAB, R31831, Truetzschler to AA, 13 June 1935.

20. *Taubert mss*, fol. 17.

21. PAB, R31832, memorandum by Roediger, 22 January 1936, and Heeren to AA, 17 April 1936.

22. Hoover, GDAV, box 177, Belgium, report by Gielen of a visit to Brussels, 31 October 1936. For Degrelle's conversation with Goebbels on 9 October 1936 see *TBJG*, I/3/ii, 10 October 1936.

23. BBL, NS43/18, report by Kommoss, 'Tätigkeitsbericht der Presseabteilung der Antikomintern, März 1936'.

24. See, for example, the issue of 25 September 1936 which carried articles about the lack of educational and healthcare resources in the USSR, a report about Popular Front agitation in Britain, and a catalogue of blood-curdling atrocities attributed to Republican forces and supporters entitled 'Red Murder in Spain'. Hoover, GDAV, box 192, AKND, 25 September 1936.

25. Ibid., 19 February 1938.

26. Ibid., 24 June 1938.

27. *Der Weltbolschewismus: Ein internationales Gemeinschaftswerk über die bolschewistische Wühlarbeit und die Umsturzversuche der Komintern in allen Ländern: Herausgegeben von der Antikomintern. In Verbindung mit den Sachkennern der ganzen Welt. Mit 400 Bilddokumenten, Karten und Anschauungstafeln* (Berlin-Leipzig, 1936). Internal Antikomintern correspondence reveals that work on this project was started in late 1933, and that drafts of most of the essays had been submitted by early 1935. *Der Weltbolschewismus* was not made available to the German public, probably because the diversity of the views on offer might conflict with given lines of German domestic propaganda. See BBL, NS43/17, memorandum by Ehrt, 22 January 1935; PAB, R31832, Ehrt to Hencke, 31 March 1936.

28. PAB, R31832, Bergen to AA, 30 April 1936.

29. A record of the conference proceedings can be located at PRO, GFM34/1265.

30. Nils von Bahr, a Swedish journalist living in Germany, had contributed a piece on Sweden's fight against Bolshevism to *Der Weltbolschewismus*, and had assisted Ehrt with the running of the Feldafing conference. During the initial stages of the Second World War he ran a German propaganda news agency in Stockholm called 'Skandiapress'. Immediately after the German defeat at Stalingrad he resurrected an unlikely scheme, first mooted in 1942, for a rapid postwar reconciliation between Germany and the West in order that together they might yet confront Russia. See Hoover, Deutsche Kongress Zentrale [hereafter DKZ] 16/AK, 'Wer ist Kapitän Nils von Bahr?' PRO, FO188/402, Tennant to Rabagliati, 7 January 1943.

31. Laqueur, *Germany and Russia*, p. 176.

32. Ibid.

33. Jacobsen, *Nationalsozialistische Aussenpolitik*, p. 454. There is a further brief survey of the Antikomintern's work in J. Sywottek, *Mobilmachung für den totalen Krieg: Die propagandistische Vorbereitung der deutschen Bevölkerung auf den Zweiten Weltkrieg* (Hamburg, 1976) pp. 104–6.

34. On the Antikomintern's involvement with these issues see PAB, R31832, Petmecky to Leibbrandt, 31 January 1936, and PRO, GFM34/458, Truetzschler to AA, 5 and 9 September 1936.

35. *DBFP*, 2/XVII, no. 233, Newton to FO, 23 September 1936.

36. J. Goebbels, *Bolshevism in Theory and Practice* (Berlin, 1936).

37. Ibid., p. 6. Goebbels' statements on conditions in Spain were largely based on material supplied by the Antikomintern which rapidly geared itself for a major propaganda offensive following the outbreak of the civil war. See Hoover, GDAV, box 187, unsigned memorandum, 5 February 1937.

38. Goebbels, *Bolshevism in Theory and Practice*, pp. 26–7.

39. Domarus, I/2, editor's comment, p. 645.

40. *Reden des Führers am Parteitag der Ehre 1936*, 'Die Proklamation des Führers auf dem Kongreß', 9 September 1936, pp. 23–4.

41. Ibid., 14 September 1936, 'Die Schlussrede des Führers auf dem Kongreß', pp. 70ff.

42. Domarus, I/2, editor's comment, p. 646.

43. NARA, State Department Decimal File, 761.62/395, Dodd to Hull,11 September 1936.

44. *TBJG*, I/3/ii, 9 September 1936. Note also in this context Hitler's rigid position on economic relations with the USSR, determined by his political convictions, despite the preference of Göring and others for closer ties. See Ericson III, *Feeding the German Eagle*, pp. 23ff; Pons, *Stalin and the Inevitable War 1936–1941*, p. 66.

45. NARA, State Department Decimal File, 761.62/413, Dodd to Hull, 23 October 1936.

46. NARA., 762.00/138, Smith to State Department, 1 October 1936.
47. PRO, FO371/19949/C6684, St Clair Gainer to Newton, 16 September 1936.
48. PRO, minute by Sargent, 2 October 1936.
49. BK, ZSg. 101/14, Presseanweisung, 28 November 193108

Chapter 7

1. On this aspect see Griffiths, *Fellow Travellers of the Right*, pp. 232–3.
2. *New York Times*, 26 November 1936. The German agreement with Austria referred to here is that signed in July 1936. For details see *ADAP*, C/V/2, editor's note, pp. 708ff.
3. *Manchester Guardian*, 26 November 1936.
4. *The Times*, 26 November 1936.
5. PRO, GFM34/561, memorandum by Schliep, 22 November 1936.
6. PRO, FO371/20285/F7274, Chilston to FO, 21 November 1936; PAB, Botschaft Moskau, 301. Schulenburg to AA, 21 November 1936.
7. *SDFP*, 3, Litvinov's speech to the Eighth (Extraordinary) Soviet Congress, 28 November 1936, pp. 220–6, here p. 223.
8. PRO, FO371/20286/F7927, Eden to Chilston, 21 December 1936.
9. PRO, FO371/20285/F7278, Clerk to FO, 26 November 1936.
10. *The Times*, 26 November 1936.
11. On Belgian views see PRO, FO371/20286/F7444, Ovey to FO, 30 November 1936; for Limburg-Stirium's attitude see PRO, GFM34/316, memorandum by Erdmannsdorff, 27 November 1936.
12. PRO, FO371/20286/F7443, Greenway to FO, 27 November 1936. See also *ADAP*, C/VI/1, no. 127, Prinz zu Wied to AA, 5 January 1937; ibid., C/VI/2, no. 284, Prinz zu Wied to AA, 18 March 1937.
13. PRO, FO371/20331/N6123, Watson to FO, 28 November 1936.
14. *ADAP*, D/I, no. 181, undated memorandum by Meissner, enclosed in Meissner to Neurath, 20 November 1936.
15. *Manchester Guardian*, 26 November 1936.
16. J. Gehl, *Austria, Germany and the Anschluss, 1931–1938* (London, 1963) p. 127. Speaking to the Heimwehr the same month Starhemberg had announced that as the Western powers were not strong enough to resist Bolshevism, it was necessary to 'set the idea of Fascism against Bolshevism' and for that purpose to 'bring the Fascist states into one front'. See *ADAP*, D/I, no. 186, Stein to AA, 27 November 1936. The Austro–German protocol signed during Schmidt's visit to Berlin, although recognizing that communism was the 'greatest danger menacing the peace and security of Europe', significantly spoke of a parallel rather than a common effort to contain it. Ibid., no. 177, AA to the German Legation in Vienna, 12 November 1936.

17. In this connection see *Raumer mss*, pp. 44–5.
18. See *ADAP*, C/V/2, no. 516, memorandum by Neurath, 24 August 1936; Ibid., C/VI/1, no. 55, Hassell to AA, 25 November 1936.
19. *CDP*, conversation with de Kánya, November 1936, p. 67.
20. Ibid.
21. *ADAP*, D/I, no. 181, undated memorandum by Meissner, enclosed in Meissner to Neurath, 20 November 1936.
22. Ibid., C/VI/1, no. 98, undated memorandum by Meissner, enclosed in Lammers to Stieve, 17 December 1936. Note also Rosenberg's remarks of 21 November 1936 to Franz Misak of the Hungarian newspaper *Uj Magyarsag* emphasizing the Bolshevik threat to the states of central Europe, and his urging, with the notable exception of Czechoslovakia, that they should work together against it. BK, ZSg. 133/53, unsigned memorandum, 21 November 1936.
23. *ADAP*, C/VI/1, no. 38, undated memorandum by Meissner, enclosed in Meissner to Neurath, 16 November 1936.
24. Ibid., no. 55, Hassell to AA, 25 November 1936.
25. On Romania's policy of 'balance' between Berlin and Moscow during and after 1936 see D. B. Lungu, *Romania and the Great Powers, 1933–1940* (Durham, 1989) pp. 99ff.
26. *ADAP*, C/VI/1, no. 43, Moltke to AA, 18 November 1938.
27. Ibid, no. 59, Moltke to AA, 26 November 1936.
28. PRO, GFM34/458, Moltke to AA, 28 November 1936.
29. See G. T. Waddington, '*Hassgegner*: German Views of Great Britain in the later 1930s', *History*, 81 (1996) pp. 22–39, here pp. 28–9.
30. *Reden des Führers am Parteitag der Ehre 1936*, 14 September 1936, 'Die Schlußrede des Führers auf dem Kongreß', p. 74.
31. PRO, FO371/408/66, Newton to Eden, 3 September 1936. Writing in 1946 Ribbentrop effectively confirmed this point, noting that Soviet–German enmity was so strong in 1936 that 'even our attitude to Britain had to be governed by the anti-Comintern policy. ... As loose a form as possible was chosen for the Anti-Comintern Pact, and prominence was given to ideology so as to remain diplomatically free should an alliance with Britain be possible'. Ribbentrop, *Memoirs*, p. 76.
32. Wolfgang Michalka stresses Ribbentrop's sceptical attitude at the outset of his ambassadorship in London, whereas contemporaries such as Ernest Tennant and Reinhard Spitzy insist that he was still quietly hopeful and favourable towards the idea of an agreement with Britain. See Michalka, *Ribbentrop*, pp. 112–13; PRO, PREM 1/335, 'Mr. E. W. D. Tennant's Relations with Herr von Ribbentrop'; R. Spitzy, *So haben wir das Reich Verspielt: Bekenntnisse eines Illegalen* (Munich, 1994) p. 98.
33. For negative press reactions see *Daily Mail*, 26 November 1936; *News Chronicle*, 26 November 1936. For details of Ribbentrop's efforts to

interest British statesmen in the notion of a crusade against communism, and the negative response these elicited, see *DBFP*, 2/XVII, no.
337, Eden to Phipps, 27 October 1936; and nos 485–6, Eden to Phipps,
18 December 1936.

34. PRO, FO/371/20285/F7237, Phipps to FO, 25 November 1936.
35. PRO, GFM34/258, Bielefeld to AA, 30 November 1936.
36. Sommer, *Deutschland und Japan zwischen den Mächten*, pp. 82–4.
37. On this aspect see *ADAP*, D/III, no. 27, Wegener to AA, 3 August 1936.
    Franco, according to Wegener, 'would like to be looked upon not only
    as the saviour of Spain but also as the saviour of Europe from the
    spread of Communism'.
38. Ibid., no. 137, Hassell to AA, 1 December 1936. For German surprise at
    the agreement see ibid., no 142, Neurath to Hassell, 5 December 1936.
39. PRO, FO371/19916/C9152, minute by Sargent, 29 December 1936.

Chapter 8

1. NARA, State Department Decimal File 761.62/421, Dodd to Hull, 6
   January 1937.
2. *TBJG*, I/3/ii, 2 January 1937.
3. NARA, State Department Decimal File 761.62/421, Dodd to State
   Department, 6 January 1937.
4. Fox, *Germany and the Far Eastern Crisis*, p. 210.
5. PRO, FO371/20732/C412, Beaumont-Nesbitt to Clerk, 14 January
   1937, enclosed in Clerk to FO, 15 January 1937; and minute by
   Rumbold, 20 January 1937.
6. PRO, FO371/20732/C497, Hotblack to Phipps, 18 January 1937,
   enclosed in Phipps to FO, 19 January 1937.
7. *TBJG*, I/3/ii, 28 January 1937.
8. Ibid.
9. Domarus, I/2, 30 January 1937, speech to the Reichstag, p. 671.
10. Kershaw, *Hitler: Nemesis*, p. 38.
11. *ADAP*, C/VI/2, no. 429, memorandum by Schmieden, 15 June 1937.
12. Ibid., no. 442, Meissner to Neurath, 29 June 1937.
13. PRO, FO371/20735/C3621, memorandum by Lothian, 4 May 1937,
    enclosed in Henderson to Vansittart, 10 May 1937.
14. For Hitler's reaction to this incident, and his heated remarks about the
    British attitude, see Domarus, I/2, 27 June 1937, speech at the Gau Party
    Congress, p. 703; Henke, *England in Hitlers politischem Kalkül*, p. 58.
15. ADAP, C/VI/2, no. 484, Henderson to Eden, 20 July 1937. This
    despatch appears to have been intercepted by Göring's *Forschungsamt*.
16. *Documents on International Affairs*, eds S. Heald and J. W. Wheeler-
    Bennett (London, 1936–1939) 1937, pp. 175–6.

17. Ibid., p. 177.
18. BK, ZSg. 121/14, 'Propaganda Anweisung, vom 31 März 1937. Richtlinien für die antibolschewistische Propaganda'.
19. Michels, *Ideologie und Propaganda*, p. 268.
20. On the composition and activities of the Sonderstab Köhn see ibid., pp. 266ff.
21. Hoover, GDAV, box 190, 'Die Tätigkeit der Anti-Komintern in Spanien während des Bürgerkriegs', undated. Internal evidence suggests after March 1939.
22. Ibid., 'Antibolschewistische Propagandatätigkeit des Ref. Pro/2 und der Anti-Komintern während des spanischen Bürgerkriegs', undated. internal evidence suggests after March 1939.
23. Ibid.
24. Ibid. 'Die Tätigkeit der Anti-Komintern in Spanien während des Bürgerkriegs', undated. Internal evidence suggests after March 1939.
25. Ibid.
26. See generally the reports referred to in notes 21 and 22. Other surviving Antikomintern documentation relating to the Spanish Civil War reveals that an Antikomintern liaison officer was attached to the staff of General Faupel, formerly chargé d'affaires at the German embassy in Madrid, and from February 1937 Hitler's special appointee as German ambassador to the Spanish nationalist government. The tasks of this individual, a certain Dr Schmitt, included cooperation with the Spanish nationalist authorities in overseeing the distribution of propaganda material and working towards the establishment of a general anti-Bolshevik organization comprising various groups including the Falange and the Catholic Church, which, once functioning, would be subordinated to governmental propaganda agencies. In June 1937 the Antikomintern also considered undertaking a humanitarian initiative in Spain, emulating a successful British effort, by arranging for a visit to Germany of 150 Spanish children comprising sons and daughters of serving nationalist soldiers as well as those of republicans who had fallen in battle. Such an undertaking, it was argued, would have an excellent propaganda effect both in Germany and abroad, not least for its potential 'tear-jerking' effects [*Tränendrüsen*]. It is not known whether this suggestion was acted upon. See respectively, Hoover, GDAV, box 187, unsigned memorandum, 5 February 1937, and ibid., memorandum by Gielen, 17 June 1937.
27. *Das Rotbuch über Spanien: Bilder, Dokumente: Zeugenaussagen: Gesammelt und herausgegeben von der Antikomintern* (Berlin, 1937).
28. See Hoover, DKZ/16/AK, draft circular letter prepared by the Antikomintern, 18 June 1937. BBL, R43II/1492a, Mahlo to Obersten Reichsbehörden/Reichsleiter/Leiter der Gliederungen und ange-

schlossene Verbände der NSDAP/Gauleiter/Referatsleiter, 21 June 1937; ibid., Taubert to Meerwald, 1 July 1937.

29. BBL, R43II/1492a, DNB Nacht-Ausgabe, 21 June 1937.
30. Hoover, GDAV, box 190, 'Die Tätigkeit der Antikomintern in Spanien während des Bürgerkrieges', undated. Internal evidence suggests after March 1939. On the *Rotbuch* see also H. R. Southworth, *Conspiracy and the Spanish Civil War: The Brainwashing of Francisco Franco* (London, 2002) p. 11.
31. See above p. 134.
32. *Taubert mss*, fol. 11.
33. H. Graham, *The Spanish Republic at War* (Cambridge, 2002) p. 60.
34. Ibid., p. 204.
35. On these issues see Pons, *Stalin and the Inevitable War 1936–1941*, pp. 42ff.
36. B. Lazitch, 'Stalin's Massacre of the Foreign Communist Leaders', in M. M. Drachkovitch and B. Lazitch (eds) *The Comintern: Historical Highlights. Essays, Recollections, Documents* (New York, 1966) p. 172.
37. On the fate of the Comintern during the purges see W. J. Chase, *Enemies Within the Gates? The Comintern and Stalinist Repression, 1934–1939* (New Haven, 2001); K. McDermott and J. Agnew, *The Comintern: A History of International Communism from Lenin to Stalin* (London, 1996) pp. 142ff; K. McDermott, 'Stalinist Terror in the Comintern', *JCH*, 30 (1995) pp. 111–30. In early February 1937 Stalin declared chillingly to Dimitrov: 'All of you there in the Comintern are playing right into the enemy's hands.' See I. Banac (ed.) *The Diary of Georgi Dimitrov, 1933–1949* (New Haven, 2003), 11 February 1937, p. 52. In the wake of the worst of the purges the German embassy in Moscow was quick to point out both the scale of the decimation wrought within the senior ranks of the Comintern, and, in consequence, the impact on the organization's effectiveness, which was no more apparent than in its lacklustre performance during the celebrations to mark the twenty-first anniversary of the Bolshevik revolution in October–November 1938. See NARA, T84/404, Schulenburg to AA, 19 November 1938, and Hoover, GDAV, box 197, von Dippelskirch [sic] to AA, 28 January 1939.
38. Hoover, GDAV, box 178, 'Kommunistischer Umsturzplan für Südamerika', AKND, 1 December 1937. The other articles can be found in the AKND issues for June and August.
39. Hoover, GDAV, box 196, memorandum by Gielen, 8 May 1936. The first opportunity for the Antikomintern to involve itself in South American affairs appears to have been provided by a dispute between Uruguay and the USSR, which subsequently became the subject of a confrontation in the League Assembly, arising from Uruguayan allegations of Soviet complicity in the communist uprisings that had taken

place in Brazil in November 1935. When this issue was discussed at Geneva between 20 and 23 January 1936, the Uruguayan delegate made some general references to Soviet interference in the internal affairs of other countries and to the connections between the USSR and the Comintern. The material upon which he based these allegations had been supplied by the Antikomintern through Dr Lodygensky of the Geneva-based *Entente Internationale contre la Troisième Internationale*. Ibid., memorandum by Gielen, 30 March 1936.

40. Ibid., memorandum by Gielen, 8 May 1936.
41. On these developments see ibid., memorandum by Dohms, 3 June 1937; ibid., unsigned note, 'Bücherversand an Ortega Martinez', 18 February 1938 (figures of shipments over a protracted period are unavailable, but between 25 January and 17 February 1938 more than 25 items were dispatched to Caracas); ibid., two memoranda [signature illegible, but probably that of Dohms], 14 November 1938 and 5 May 1939.
42. Hoover, GDAV, box 178, unsigned memorandum, 21 June 1937.
43. Ibid, memorandum by Dohms, 3 November 1937. Perhaps encouraged by this development Dohms subsequently suggested that the Antikomintern should produce a Portuguese language version of the *Informaciones Antibolcheviques*, a fortnightly Antikomintern newsletter that was distributed in Spain and South America. Ibid., memorandum by Dohms, 8 November 1937.
44. Ibid., unsigned memorandum, 14 September 1937. The Antikomintern subsequently drew up suggestions for 11 lectures with detailed preparatory reading materials for each.
45. NARA, T84/405, undated report by Stuckenberg. Following preliminary discussions in October 1936 between Nils von Bahr and leading figures of the Anti-Socialist and Anti-Communist Union, the Antikomintern mounted an exhibition in London that later visited Manchester, Leeds and Glasgow. According to Stuckenberg, over 150 people attended its opening ceremony on 2 February 1937, mostly MPs and leading figures from the world of economics. For a survey of the Antikomintern's efforts to monitor and promote anti-Bolshevism in Scandinavia during 1937 and early 1938 see Hoover, GDAV, box 195, 'Bericht über die antikommunistische Aufklärungsarbeit (Schweden, Norwegen, Dänemark, Finnland) in letzter Zeit', November 1937, and ibid., Renthe-Fink to the Antikomintern, 22 April 1938.
46. Hoover, GDAV, box 178, AKND, 1 June 1937. Five months later the AKND ran an article warning the British of Moscow's subversive role in the Palestine conflict. Ibid., AKND, 20 November 1937.
47. *Taubert mss*, fol. 12.
48. A copy of the 'interview' can be found in NARA, State Department Decimal File 761.62/435, Dodd to State Department, 1 April 1937. Note

Dodd's comment that the article was 'evidently intended to create the impression that the interview originated in New York, thus concealing Germany's major part in the project'.

49. In July 1937 the German government received an invitation to this event, which was evidently organized by a Mexican group and due to take place in Cuba in September. A response was not found among the papers of the Reich Chancellery. See BBL, R43II/1460, Chairman of the Mexican Middle Class Union to Hitler, 14 July 1937. The Antikomintern inspired gathering was scheduled to take place in Madrid following the end of the Spanish Civil War, but soon found itself overtaken by events, not least the embryonic Soviet–German rapprochement.

50. PAB, R100722, note by Hinrichs, 15 March 1937.

51. Hoover, DKZ/16/AK. *Contra-Komintern*, April 1937. The title of this publication was actually a throwback to the 1920s when an anti-communist newssheet of the same name, edited by one Melitta Wiedemann, had been in circulation. Following the Nazi seizure of power Ms Wiedemann appears to have sunk without trace. Whether the Antikomintern simply absorbed her activities and publication during the merger of the anti-communist associations in 1933 is unknown, but appears likely in view of the revival of the publication under exactly the same name, namely *Contra-Komintern: Kampforgan der Antibolschewistischen Weltbewegung*. For details see Sommer, *Deutschland und Japan*, p. 27, note 15.

52. Lacquer, *Germany and Russia*, p. 186. The author refers to a circular dispatch by Neurath of 17 April 1937, which, in view of the obscure reference he provides, I have been unable to locate.

53. Hitler was clearly uneasy at this time at the prospect of rank and file party members compromising the regime. 'The quality of the members of the Party was poor', he is said to have told a dinner guest in February. 'They were all very well for fighting Bolshevism in the street, but they were of little use for running the country, and [he] did not trust them to associate with foreigners without losing their heads.' PRO, FO371/20709/C1444, Phipps to Eden, 16 February 1937.

54. BBL, NS43/51, unsigned memorandum, 3 November 1936. For Rosenberg's objection to attempts by the ProMi to forbid collaboration between the APA and the Antikomintern see ibid., Rosenberg to Funk, 30 October 1936.

55. PRO, GFM34/900, minute by Neurath, 23 April 1937. For Hitler's October 1936 suggestion to Rosenberg about the proposed role in the fight against world Bolshevism see Cecil, *The Myth of the Master Race*, p. 124. Interestingly this suggestion was itself made as a possible compromise solution to an ongoing quarrel between Rosenberg and Ley.

56. *ADAP*, C/VI/2, no. 547, Humann-Hainhofen to Knauer, 5 September 1937.

57. For details on these developments see Sommer, *Deutschland und Japan*, pp. 82ff; G. Ciano, *Ciano's Diary 1937–38*, trans. A. Mayor, intro. M. Muggeridge (London, 1952) entries for 20–25 October inclusive, pp. 22ff; *ADAP*, D/I, no. 10, Hassell to Neurath, 20 October 1937.

58. NARA, State Department Decimal File 761.62/456, Grew to State Department, 13 November 1937.

59. PRO, FO371/20751/C8017, Henderson to Eden, 18 November 1937.

60. Henke, *England in Hitlers politischem Kalkül*, pp. 49ff., 77ff., 304.

61. NARA, State Department Decimal File 761.62/454, Dodd to State Department, 15 October 1937.

62. Waddington, 'Hassgegner', pp. 36–7.

Chapter 9

1. Hillgruber, *Hitlers Strategie*, p. 145.

2. For the record of the meeting see *ADAP*, D/I, no. 19, memorandum by Hossbach, 10 November 1937.

3. On the historiographical controversy generated by the Hossbach conference see D. Kluge, *Das Hoßbach-'Protokol': Die Zerstörung einer Legende*, (Leoni am Starnberger See, 1980). For an assessment of the significance of Hitler's remarks within the general context of Germany's foreign policy options in late 1937 see J. Wright and P. Stafford, 'Hitler, Britain and the Hossbach Memorandum', *Militärgeschichtliche Mitteilungen*, 42 (1987) pp. 77–123; similarly Weinberg, *Foreign Policy*, II, pp. 35ff.

4. BK, ZSg. 101/31, Kausch to Dertinger, 9 September 1937.

5. This and previous quotations taken from *Der Parteitag der Arbeit vom 6 bis 13 September 1937. Offizieller Bericht über den Verlauf des Reichsparteitages mit sämtlichen Kongreßreden* (Munich, 1938) 'Die große Schlußrede des Führers auf dem Kongreß', pp. 356ff.

6. Domarus, I/2, 1 January 1938, New Year proclamation to the NSDAP, p. 773. During the *Kampfzeit* Hitler had repeatedly quoted – quite out of context – the observation of the German historian Theodor Mommsen that the Jews were 'the ferment of decomposition of all peoples and states'. See, for example, HSA, no. 293, 'Ein Riesenbetrug'. Stichworte zu einer Rede, undated. Internal evidence suggests after 21 September 1921; ibid., no. 377, 'Die "Hetzer" der Wahrheit'. Rede auf einer NSDAP-Versammlung, 12 April 1922.

7. *TBJG*, I/5, 22 December 1937. This was not Hitler's first reference to the purges of the Soviet armed forces that had decimated the leadership corps during 1937. As was the case with many of his contemporaries, Hitler was baffled by these developments. 'Stalin is surely mad', noted Goebbels, paraphrasing the chancellor on 10 July 1937. 'There can be

no other explanation for his rule of blood [*Blutregiment*]. Then again, Russia knows nothing apart from Bolshevism. That is the danger that one day we will have to shatter.' Ibid., I/4, 10 July 1937.

8. On the significance of the Blomberg–Fritsch crisis see Kershaw, *Hitler: Nemesis*, pp. 51ff.; Weinberg, *Foreign Policy*, II, pp. 43ff. On the course of the *Anschluss* see Gehl, *Austria, Germany and the Anschluss*, pp. 166ff.

9. BBL, R901/60971, memorandum by Neurath, 14 January 1938; *ADAP*, D/V, no. 163, memorandum by Heeren, 17 January 1938.

10. On the origins of this further British approach for a general settlement with Germany see A. Crozier, *Appeasement and Germany's Last Bid for Colonies* (London, 1988). For a detailed analysis of Hitler's attitude to the colonial question in the 1930s see K. Hildebrand, *Vom Reich zum Weltreich: Hitler, NSDAP und koloniale Frage, 1919–1945* (Munich, 1969).

11. *ADAP*, D/I, no. 138, memorandum by Schmidt, 3 March 1938, enclosed in Neurath to Henderson, 4 March 1938.

12. On Hitler's attachment to the evolutionary path towards the *Anschluss* and the events of February–March 1938 in general see Gehl, *Austria, Germany and the Anschluss*.

13. See *ADAP*, D/I, no. 308, memorandum by Ribbentrop, 17 February 1938.

14. Ibid., D/II, no. 107, unsigned report with enclosures, [28?] March 1938.

15. Hamann, *Hitlers Wien*, pp. 462–3.

16. Hitler, *Zweites Buch*, p. 148.

17. Wagener, *Hitler: Memoirs of a Confidant*, p. 161.

18. *ADAP*, C/II/1, no. 68, memorandum by Köpke, 15 November 1933.

19. Ibid., C/IV/1, no. 128, Koch to AA, 3 June 1935.

20. Ibid., no. 105, AA Circular, 25 May 1935.

21. Ibid.

22. Ibid., C/IV/2, no. 580, Eisenlohr to AA, 23 February 1936.

23. BBL, NS8/44, The Final Fight Between Europe and Bolshevism. Address delivered by Mr Alfred Rosenberg at the Party Rally, Nuremberg 1936 (Munich, 1936) p. 21. In his speech the previous day Goebbels had spoken on similar lines, referring to the supposed Soviet air bases in Czechoslovakia as 'the starting points from which the Red bombers will attack Europe'. Goebbels, *Bolshevism in Theory and Practice*, p. 22.

24. VB, Sondernummer, 31 January 1937. Five days later, speaking in Hamburg, Goebbels too characterized the Czech–Soviet alliance as a 'great danger to European peace'. As such, it constituted an ideal instrument to help foment that chaos on the continent that the Soviets required in order to realize their 'nefarious schemes'. PRO, FO371/20709/C1092. Phipps to FO, 8 February 1937.

25. BBL, R43II/1496, 'Sudetendeutscher Dienst. Sonderausgabe. Die Parteien in der Tschoslowakei und ihre Stellung zum Bolschewismus', 19 March 1936.

26. PRO, GFM34/1265, Eisenlohr to AA, 7 June 1937.

27. On the abortive Czech–German contacts after the Rhineland reoccupation see Weinberg, *Foreign Policy*, I, pp. 312ff; for the assurances made by Prague to Berlin in late 1937–early 1938 see *ADAP*, D/II, no. 17, memorandum by Mackensen, 9 November 1937; ibid., no. 47, Eisenlohr to AA, 12 January 1938; ibid., no. 56, Eisenlohr to AA, 16 February 1938; BBL, R43II/1496a, memorandum by Ribbentrop, 31 March 1938.

28. BBL, R43II/1496a. Papen to Hitler, 1 December 1937.

29. Christie Papers, CHRS 180/1/5, record of a conversation with Göring, 3 February 1937 [Waddington collection].

30. Weinberg, *Foreign Policy*, II, p. 337.

31. On the Munich crisis in general see K. Robbins, *Munich 1938* (London, 1968); T. Taylor, *Munich: The Price of Peace* (London, 1979). Apart from the detailed treatment of German policy in Weinberg, *Foreign Policy*, II, p. 313ff, see R. Overy, 'Germany and the Munich Crisis: A Mutilated Victory?', in I. Lukes and E. Goldstein (eds) *The Munich Crisis, 1938: Prelude to World War II* (London, 1999) pp. 191–215.

32. For details of the May crisis and its repercussions see Weinberg, *Foreign Policy*, II, pp. 367ff; *ADAP*, D/VII, appendix H (iii), memorandum by Wiedemann, undated. Internal evidence suggests early September 1939.

33. *ADAP*, D/II, no. 144, Welczeck to AA, 1 May 1938; ibid., no. 189, minute by Weizsäcker, 22 May 1938.

34. Ibid., no. 379, Ribbentrop to Halifax, 21 August 1938.

35. Ibid., no. 510, unsigned memorandum, presumably by Ribbentrop, 17 September 1938.

36. *Documents Diplomatiques Français 1932–1939*, série 2, vol. XI (Paris, 1977) no. 291, François-Poncet to Bonnet, 22 September 1938.

37. PRO, FO371/21639/C14632, Ogilvie-Forbes to FO, 25 November 1938.

38. Domarus, II/1, 28 April 1939, speech to the Reichstag, p. 1151.

39. Jochmann, *Monologe*, 21 September 1941, p. 64.

40. In the wake of the 'May crisis' the Antikomintern's *Nachrichtendienst* reported that a 'Bolshevik rabble' had defaced the Masaryk monument in Mährisch-Schoenberg with the aim of inflaming public passions against the Sudeten Germans. See Hoover, GDAV, box 180, AKND, 24 June 1938.

41. H. Krebs, *Prag und Moskau* (Munich, 1938) p. 3. Other publications included a selection of previously published material from the pen of Leibbrandt, which appeared under his name as *Moskaus Aufmarsch gegen Europa* (Munich, 1938). There was also a collection of 12 lectures

by Rosenberg, Leibbrandt and a number of academics in a volume entitled *Europas Schicksal im Osten* (Breslau, 1938) edited by Hans Hagemeyer. The contributions dealt generally with aspects of German activity in eastern Europe apart from one essay, conspicuous by its inclusion, by Dr Karl Viererbl of the University of Berlin entitled 'Cultural Bolshevism and the Hatred of Germanism in Czechoslovakia.'

42. Krebs, *Prag und Moskau*, p. 23.
43. K. Vietz, *Verrat an Europa: Ein Rotbuch über die Bolschewisierung der Tschecho-Slowakei* (Berlin, 1938). Note the separation of the two compounds in the title, presumably to highlight the artificial nature of the Czechoslovak state. The Czech press deemed the book an exercise in 'war propaganda'. PRO, FO371/21763/8395. Newton to FO, 15 August 1938.
44. W. Treue, 'Die Rede Hitlers vor der deutschen Presse 10 November 1938', *VfZ*, 6 (1958) pp. 175–91, here p. 186.
45. See *ADAP*, D/IV, no. 81, directive by the Führer for the Wehrmacht, 21 October 1938; E. Kordt, *Wahn und Wirklichkeit: Die Außenpolitik des Dritten Reiches. Versuch einer Darstellung* (Stuttgart, 1947) p. 135. On Hitler's general reaction to Munich see Henke, *England in Hitlers politischem Kalkül*, pp. 187ff; Kuhn, *Hitlers aussenpolitisches Programm*, pp. 233ff; Weinberg, *Foreign Policy*, II, pp. 465ff.
46. Henke, *England in Hitlers politischem Kalkül*, pp. 204ff.
47. Weinberg, *Foreign Policy*, II, p. 484.
48. Earlier initiatives in this direction have been described above. See also BK, NS10/91, Raumer to Ribbentrop, 17 August 1937; *ADAP*, D/V, no. 34, memorandum by Ribbentrop, 31 March 1938.
49. Domarus, I/2, 20 February 1938, speech to the Reichstag, p. 802.
50. For the most important German–Polish exchanges see *ADAP*, D/V, no. 81, record of a conversation between Ribbentrop and Lipski, 24 October 1938; no. 101, memorandum by Ribbentrop, 19 November 1938; no. 119, record of a conversation between Hitler and Beck, 5 January 1939; no. 120, memorandum by Ribbentrop, 9 January 1939. See also ibid., D/VI, no. 101, memorandum by Ribbentrop, 26 March 1939.
51. *ADAP*, D/VI, no. 149, directive by Keitel, 3 April 1939; ibid., no. 185, directive by Hitler, 11 April 1939.
52. Ibid., no. 433, minutes of a conference, 23 May 1939.
53. See Roberts, *The Soviet Union and the Origins of the Second World War*, pp. 62ff. For a different view see Pons, *Stalin and the Inevitable War*, pp. 160ff.
54. *ADAP*, D/VI, no. 729, memorandum by Schnurre, 27 July 1939.

Chapter 10

1. On Ribbentrop's view of the German–Soviet rapprochement see G. T.

Waddington, 'Ribbentrop and the Soviet Union, 1937–1941', in D. N. Dilks and J. Erickson (eds) *Barbarossa: The Axis and the Allies* (Edinburgh, 1994) pp. 7ff.

2. C. J. Burckhardt, *Meine Danziger Mission 1937–1939* (Munich, 1962) p. 272.

3. *Documents Concerning German–Polish Relations and the Outbreak of Hostilities between Great Britain and Germany on September 3 1939.* Cmd. 6106 (London, 1939) no. 58, Henderson to Halifax, 24 August 1939.

4. Rosenberg considered the treaty with the USSR a 'moral loss of respect in the light of our by now twenty-year long struggle'. On the morning of 24 August 'the garden of the Brown House was reportedly littered with badges discarded by disillusioned party members'. Kershaw, *Hitler: Nemesis*, pp. 205–6.

5. *TBJG*, I/7, 24 August 1939.

6. U. von Hassell, *The von Hassell Diaries: The Story of the Forces Against Hitler Inside Germany, 1938–1944* (Boulder, 1994) pp. 66–7. Heinrich Hoffmann recalled a similar statement by Hitler: 'My Party members know and trust me; they know I'll never depart from my basic principles, and they will realise that the ultimate aim of this latest gambit is to remove the eastern danger.' H. Hoffmann, *Hitler was my Friend*, trans. R. H. Stevens (London, 1955) p. 256.

7. PRO, FO371/22986/C19451, Walters to Randall, 23 November 1939.

8. *ADAP*, D/VIII, no. 384, memorandum of a conference of the Führer with the principal military commanders, 23 November 1939.

9. Ibid., D/VIII, no. 654, record of a conversation between Hitler and Sven Hedin, 4 March 1940.

10. On reactions to German policy towards the Soviet–Finnish war see *TBJG*, I/7, 5 January 1940; 6 January 1940; *ADAP*, D/VIII, no. 511, memorandum by Scheidt, 5 January 1940.

11. Ribbentrop, *Memoirs*, p. 147.

12. Jochmann, *Monologe*, 5–6 January 1942, p. 180.

13. *ADAP*, D/VIII, no. 504, Mussolini to Hitler, 3 January 1940.

14. Ibid., D/IX, no. 1, record of a conversation between Hitler and Mussolini, 17 [sic] March 1940.

15. *TBJG*, I/7, 29 December 1939.

16. Ibid., 13 January 1940. Otto Dietrich saw Hitler's attitude to Stalin as broadly contingent on circumstances at any given time: 'With Stalin Hitler felt a certain solidarity, although he appraised the Russian's personality differently depending on his own political direction of the moment. As the high priest of Marxism and the enemy of his own ideology, Stalin was someone to be hated. After the non-aggression pact, Hitler was full of praise for his ally. When Stalin became his deadly foe again, he did not stop respecting him, but he refused to say a good

word for him.' O. Dietrich, *The Hitler I Knew*, trans. R. and C. Winston (London, 1957) p. 248. Although simplistic, there may be something to Dietrich's characterization of Hitler's attitude towards the Soviet leader.

17. *TBJG*, I/7, 1 October 1939 and 12 December 1939.
18. Ibid., 12 December 1939. It was perhaps in part because of the sustained activity of the Comintern that Hitler was at that time considering charging Rosenberg with the ideological protection (*Sicherung*) of the Party, state and Wehrmacht. Ibid., 9 December 1939.
19. On this point see especially the records of Hitler's numerous conversations with Admiral Raeder in *Führer Conferences on Naval Affairs* (London, 1946) volumes covering 1940 and 1941.
20. See *ADAP*, D/VIII, no. 636, memorandum by Schnurre, 26 February 1940.
21. On these developments see ibid., no, 677, memorandum by Ritter, 15 March 1940; ibid., D/IX, no. 238, Ritter to German embassy in Moscow, 12 May 1940; ibid., no. 300, memorandum by Ritter, 22 May 1940. On the change in the Soviet attitude see ibid., no 70. Schulenburg to AA, 9 April 1940; ibid., D/X, no 206, memorandum by Schnurre, 22 July 1940; *TBJG*, I/7, 27 July 1940.
22. *ADAP*, D/IX, no. 94, and note 5 thereto, Schulenburg to Weizsäcker, 11 April 1940.
23. Domarus, II/1, 1 January 1940, New Year proclamation to the NSDAP, p. 1441.
24. Ibid., 24 February 1940, speech at the Hofbräuhaus-Festsaal, p. 1465.
25. See, for example, J. Förster, 'Hitler turns East: German War Policy in 1940 and 1941', in Wegner (ed.) *From Peace to War*, pp. 115–33; Hillgruber, *Hitlers Strategie*, pp. 65ff, pp. 144ff.
26. A. Speer, *Inside the Third Reich: Memoirs by Albert Speer*, trans. R. and C. Winston (London, 1970) p. 173.
27. Hillgruber, *Hitlers Strategie*, p. 145.
28. H. Böhme, *Der deutsch-französische Waffenstillstand im Zweiten Weltkrieg* (Bonn, 1966) p. 59.
29. See, for example, *TBJG*, I/8, 12 April 1940, 20 May 1940 and 1 June 1940.
30. *ADAP*, D/IX, no. 1, record of a conversation between Hitler and Mussolini, 17 [sic] March 1940.
31. *TBJG*, I/8, 9 August 1940.
32. Hitler's determination ultimately to proceed against Russia aside, even supposed moderates such as Weizsäcker believed that Britain would require a further demonstration of German power before 'she leaves us a free hand in the East'. See F. Halder, *Generaloberst Halder: Kriegstagebuch*, ed. H.-A. Jacobsen, 3 vols (Stuttgart, 1962–64) [hereafter *Halder-KTB*] I, 30 June 1940.
33. BK, ZSg. 101/36, memorandum by Kausch, 15 July 1940.

34. Stalin had alarmed the Germans by demanding from Finland the nickel concession at Petsamo and by occupying areas in Lithuania which were nominally under German jurisdiction.
35. *Halder-KTB*, II, 31 July 1940 (emphasis in the original).
36. W. Warlimont, *Inside Hitler's Headquarters 1939–45*, trans. R. H. Barry, (Novato, 1964) pp. 111–12. Halder and Brauchitsch too felt strongly that Germany should continue to collaborate with the USSR to ensure the defeat of Britain. See *Halder-KTB*, II, 30 July 1940.
37. Jodl's memorandum can be found in *IMT*, XXVII, doc. 1776-PS, memorandum by Jodl on 'The Continuation of the War against England', pp. 301–3. For an analysis of the possibilities and problems connected with the 'peripheral strategy' see Hillgruber, *Hitlers Strategie*, pp. 178ff.
38. On the navy's attitude during 1940 see *GSWW*, IV, pp. 38–9.
39. See Michalka, *Ribbentrop*, pp. 247ff., 278ff.
40. Hilger, *Incompatible Allies*, p. 320.
41. Warlimont, *Inside Hitler's Headquarters*, p. 114.
42. J. von Herwarth, *Against Two Evils: Memoirs of a Diplomat-Soldier during the Third Reich* (London, 1981) p. 182.
43. On this aspect see especially A. Hillgruber, 'Die "Endlösung" und das deutsche Ostimperium als Kernstück des rassenideologischen Programms des Nationalsozialismus', *VfZ*, 20 (1972) pp. 133–53; and J. Förster, 'The Relation between Operation Barbarossa as an Ideological War of Extermination and the Final Solution', in D. Cesarani (ed.) *The Final Solution: Origins and Implementation* (London, 1996) pp. 85–102. See also, in the same volume, C. Streit, 'Wehrmacht, Einsatzgruppen, Soviet POWs and Anti-Bolshevism in the Emergence of the Final Solution', pp. 103–18, and O. Bartov, 'Operation Barbarossa and the Origins of the Final Solution', pp. 119–36.
44. Hillgruber, *Hitlers Strategie*, pp. 519–20.
45. As representative examples see R. Cecil, *Hitler's Decision to Invade Russia, 1941* (London, 1975) pp. 23ff, 167ff; J. Förster, 'Hitler turns East – German War Policy in 1940 and 1941', in Wegner (ed.) *From Peace to War*, pp. 115–33; Hildebrand, *Foreign Policy*, pp. 105ff; G. L. Weinberg, 'Der Überfall auf die Sowjetunion im Zusammenhang mit Hitlers diplomatischen und militärischen Gesamtplanungen', in R. G. Foerster (ed.) *Unternehmen Barbarossa: Zum historischen Ort der deutsch-sowjetischen Beziehungen von 1933 bis Herbst 1941* (Munich, 1993) pp. 177–85. Others who have acknowledged the importance of the ideological determinant behind Barbarossa include Ian Kershaw and Richard Overy. See Kershaw, *Hitler: Nemesis*, p. 461; and R. Overy, *Why the Allies Won* (London, 1995) p. 302, and more recently his *The Dictators: Hitler's Germany and Stalin's Russia* (London, 2004) p. 483.

46. This is the fundamental argument presented in H. W. Koch, 'Hitler's "Programme" and the Genesis of Operation "Barbarossa"', in H. W. Koch, *Aspects of the Third Reich* (London, 1988) pp. 285–322.

47. On this aspect see essentially G. Gorodetsky, *Grand Delusion: Stalin and the German Invasion of Russia* (New Haven, 1999).

48. C. Gerlach, *Kalkulierte Morde: Die Deutsche Wirtschafts und Vernichtungspolitik in Weißrußland 1941 bis 1944* (Hamburg, 1999) pp. 44–6, 59ff. Quotations from p. 45. Gerlach's conclusions about the economic impetus underpinning Barbarossa, and the methodology employed in reaching them, have been severely criticized in a recent Cambridge Ph.D. thesis on the interaction of war policy and planning for a final solution of the Jewish question in 1941. See T. Jersak, 'Hitler and the Interaction of War and Holocaust, 1941', Ph.D. thesis, Cambridge, 2000, pp. 49–50, 92–4 and footnotes thereto, 265.

49. R-D. Müller, 'Das Unternehmen Barbarossa als wirtschaftlicher Raubkrieg', in G. R. Ueberschär and W. Wette (eds) *'Unternehmen Barbarossa'. Der deutsche Überfall auf die Sowjetunion 1941: Berichte, Analysen, Dokumente* (Frankfurt am Main, 1991) pp. 125–57. See also more generally his contributions to *GSWW*, IV, 'From Economic Alliance to a War of Colonial Exploitation', pp. 118–224, and 'The Failure of the Economic "Blitzkrieg Strategy" ', pp. 1081–188.

50. G. R. Ueberschär, 'Hitlers Entschluss zum "Lebensraum"-Krieg im Osten: Programmatisches Ziel oder Militärgeschichtliches Kalkül?' in Ueberschär and Wette (ed.) *'Unternehmen Barbarossa'*, pp. 83–110, here p. 85. For a useful review of the historiography on Barbarossa down to 1997 see R-D. Müller and G. R. Ueberschär, *Hitler's War in the East, 1941–1945: A Critical Assessment* (Oxford, 1997) pp. 3–41.

51. *ADAP*, D/XI/1, no. 41, record of a conversation between Hitler and Sztójay, 10 September 1940.

52. *Kriegstagebuch des Oberkommandos der Wehrmacht (Wehrmachtführungsstab) 1940–1945*, 4 vols. Geführt von H Greiner und P. E. Schramm. Im Auftrag des Arbeitskreises für Wehrforschung, edited by P. E. von Schramm et al. (Frankfurt am Main, 1961–65) [hereafter *KTB OKW*] I, conference of 9 January 1941, pp. 253–9. On this occasion Hitler concentrated on the arguments that British hopes were placed in the USSR and that since Russia 'has to be beaten in any case, it is better to do it now, when Russian armed forces have no leaders and are poorly equipped and the Russians have to overcome great difficulties in their armament industry.'

53. See the postwar interrogations of Ribbentrop of 27 July 1945 and 25 August 1945 in PRO, WO208/3156 and WO208/3800.

54. *ADAP*, D/XI/2, no. 381, record of a conversation between Hitler and Antonescu, 23 November 1940.

55. Ibid., no. 606, record of a conversation between Hitler and Filov, 7 January 1941. For further denunciations of Soviet actions in the Baltic states see *TBJG*, I/8, 28 and 29 August 1940. 'One day we will have to settle accounts with Russia,' reiterated Goebbels on 24 August. 'When that day will come, I do not know, but I do know that it will come.'

56. According to Hitler, 'innumerable lives were saved by the fact that no newspaper or magazine article ever contained a word that could have let anyone guess what we were preparing.' Jochmann, *Monologe*, 17 and 18 September 1941, p. 61.

57. *ADAP*, D/XII/1, no. 222, record of a conversation between Hitler and Matsuoka, 1 April 1941.

58. Ibid., D/XI/2, no. 679, record of a conversation between Hitler and Mussolini, 21 January 1941.

59. The directive issued in December 1940 that finally confirmed the launching of Barbarossa.

60. *KTB OKW*, I, 3 March 1941, p. 341.

61. *Halder-KTB*, II, p. 346. Halder's record is substantiated in its essentials by notes made by another participant at this conference, Colonel-General Hermann Hoth. See J. Förster and E. Mawdsley, 'Hitler and Stalin in Perspective: Secret Speeches on the Eve of Barbarossa', *War in History*, 11 (2004) pp. 61–103. On the ideological dimension of the coming campaign Hoth noted: 'Battle of ideologies against Bolshevism. ... Russia a constant hotbed of social misfits. ... [Necessary] to eliminate Russian-Asiatic danger', p. 75.

62. See Y. Arad, Y Gutman and A. Margaliot (eds) *Documents on the Holocaust: Selected Sources on the Destruction of the Jews of Germany and Austria, Poland and the Soviet Union* (Jerusalem, 1981) no. 170, Commissar Order for 'Operation Barbarossa', pp. 376–7. More generally see J. Förster, 'Verbrecherische Befehle', in W. Wette and G. R. Ueberschär (eds) *Kriegsverbrechen im 20 Jahrhundert* (Darmstadt, 2001) pp. 137–51.

63. See especially *GSWW*, IV, pp. 491ff.

64. See J. Matthäus, 'Operation Barbarossa and the Onset of the Holocaust', in C. Browning, *The Origins of the Final Solution: The Evolution of Nazi Jewish Policy, September 1939–March 1942*. With contributions by Jürgen Matthäus (London, 2004) pp. 244–308, here pp. 248ff. See also H.-H. Wilhelm, 'Motivation und 'Kriegsbild' deutscher Generäle und Offiziere im Krieg gegen die Sowjetunion', in P. Jahn and R. Rürup (eds) *Erobern und Vernichten: Der Krieg gegen die Sowjetunion 1941–1945* (Berlin, 1991) pp. 153–82, and *GSWW*, IV, pp. 36ff, 518ff.

65. United States. Office of Chief of Counsel for the Prosecution of Axis Criminality, *Nazi Conspiracy and Aggression*, 11 vols (Washington, 1946–47) VIII, pp. 585–7.

66. H. B. Gisevius, *Adolf Hitler: Versuch einer Deutung* (Munich, [1963]), p. 471. See also Jochmann, *Monologe*, 17 and 18 September 1941, p. 61.
67. See Hildebrand, *Foreign Policy*, pp. 108–9, 113.
68. *ADAP*, D/XI/2, no. 660, Hitler to Mussolini, 21 June 1941.

Chapter 11

1. *TBJG*, II/1, 9 July 1941.
2. See, for example, Jochmann, *Monologe*, 8–10 August 1941, p. 55; ibid., 26–27 October 1941, p. 110.
3. C. Schroeder, *Er war mein Chef: Aus dem Nachlaß der Sekretärin von Adolf Hitler*, ed. A. Joachimsthaler (Munich, 1985) p. 113.
4. Jochmann, *Monologe*, 11–12 July 1941, p. 41.
5. *ADAP*, D/XIII/1, no. 134, Hitler to Mussolini, 20 July 1941.
6. *Staatsmänner und Diplomaten bei Hitler: Zweiter Teil. Vertrauliche Aufzeichnungen über Unterredungen mit Vertretern des Auslandes.* Herausgegeben und erläutert von Andreas Hillgruber (Frankfurt am Main, 1970) Anhang, record of a conversation between Hitler and Ōshima, 14 July 1941, pp. 541ff.
7. Brotherton Library, University of Leeds, microfilm 2249. Hitler's War. Papers from the Sammlung Irving, Institut für Zeitgeschichte, Munich, including the 1941 diary of Walther Hewel. Hewel Diary, entry for 11 July 1941. On Hitler's expectations of an armed clash between Britain and the USA, and his belief in the prospect of an Anglo–German alliance directed against America see Jochmann, *Monologe*, 25 July 1941, p. 47; ibid., 8–10 August, p. 56; ibid., 26–7 October 1941, p. 110. On the possibility of an outbreak of anti-Semitism in Britain following further reversals in the war see also ibid., 5 November 1941, p. 130.
8. In this respect see especially D. M. McKale, *Hitler's Shadow War: The Holocaust and World War Two* (New York, 2002) pp. 80ff.
9. *ADAP*, C/V/2, no. 490, unsigned memorandum, August 1936. Fears about potential Jewish machinations in times of crisis almost certainly played a part in the series of revisions and additions made to the Reich Citizenship Law, and other anti-Jewish measures enacted during 1937–38. For details see *The Holocaust: Selected Documents in Eighteen Volumes*, ed. John Mendelsohn. Vol. 1. *Legalising the Holocaust: The Early Phase 1933–1939* (New York, 1982) passim. For a brief description of these developments and their significance see W. Benz, *The Holocaust: A German Historian Examines the Genocide*, trans. J. Sydenham-Kwiet (London, 2000) pp. 24ff.; L. Dawidowicz, *The War against the Jews* (London, 1987) pp. 131ff; Longerich, *The Unwritten Order*, pp. 60ff.
10. The dispute with Poland can be traced in *ADAP*, D/V.

11. See especially 'Weltecho des jüdischen Meuchelmordes: Mitgefühl mit dem Opfer über die Bluttat', *VB*, 11 November 1938, and 'Juda träumt von der Weltherrschaft', *VB*, 29 November 1938. Following the Reichskristallnacht Hitler intervened directly in questions of German propaganda by cancelling a proposed series of radio broadcasts on Bolshevism scheduled for transmission by the *Reichssender Breslau* and ordering the station to concentrate 'exclusively' on the Jewish question. See BBL, NS43/37, memorandum by Hüttenrauch, 1 February 1939.

12. *ADAP*, D/IV, no. 158, record of a conversation between Hitler and Chvalkovsky, 21 January 1939.

13. *IMT*, vol. XXVIII, doc. 1816-PS, Stenographische Niederschrift von einem Teil der Besprechung über die Judenfrage unter Vorsitz von Feldmarschall Göring im RLM am 12 November 1938, pp. 499–542, here p. 538.

14. *Le Livre Jaune Français: Documents Diplomatiques 1938–1939. Pièces Relatives aux Événements et aux Négociations qui ont précédé l'Ouverture des Hostilities entre l'Allemagne d'une part, la Pologne, la Grande-Bretagne et la France d'autre part* (Ministère des Affaires Étrangères, Paris, 1939) no. 45, Lacroix to Bonnet, 7 February 1939.

15. Domarus, II/1, 30 January 1939, speech to the Reichstag, p. 1058.

16. See A. B. Rossino, *Hitler Strikes Poland: Blitzkrieg, Ideology and Atrocity* (Kansas, 2003) especially pp. 88ff, pp. 172ff, pp. 186ff.

17. *ADAP*, D/X, no. 101, memorandum by Rademacher, 3 July 1940. Only three weeks before Rademacher submitted his paper President Roosevelt had declared at Charlottesville, Virginia, that the USA would 'extend to the opponents of force the material resources of this nation'. See *The Times*, 11 June 1940. On the development of American policy after the fall of France see especially R. Dallek, *Franklin D. Roosevelt and American Foreign Policy, 1932–1945* (New York, 1995) pp. 233ff. On the Madagascar plan see, H. Jansen, *Der Madagaskar-Plan: Die beabsichtigte Deportation der europäischen Juden nach Madagaskar* (Munich, 1997); and most recently Browning, *The Origins of the Final Solution*, pp. 81ff.

18. See, for example, the terminology employed by Hitler in Domarus, II/1, 1 January 1940, New Year proclamation to the NSDAP, pp. 1441ff.

19. On this aspect of German propaganda in 1941 see especially J. Herf, *The Jewish Enemy: Nazi Propaganda during World War II and the Holocaust* (London, 2006) pp. 92ff.

20. Hoover, GDAV, box 32, ProMi-Informationsdienst, 'Der Bolschewismus als Waffe der Plutokratie', 24 June 1941.

21. Ibid., 'Juden sorgten die britische Weltkriegseinkreisung: Interessante Vergleiche zur Gegenwart', undated. Internal evidence is inconclusive. Senior figures from the Commonwealth were similarly tarnished by

accusations of complicity with Jewry. See the transcript of the radio broadcast of 21 June 1941 entitled 'Smuts, der Söldling der Plutokratie und des Judentums' in P. Aldag, *Worüber berichten wir heute: Unsere Gegner und ihr Krieg. Berichte aus dem 'Zeitgeschehen' des Großdeutschen Rundfunks in Zusammenarbeit mit der Anti-Komintern* (Berlin, 1941) pp. 55ff.

22. BK, R55/1398, ProMi-Informationsdienst, 'Judentum und Bolschewismus in England', 3 December 1941; ibid., 'Londons Ehe mit Moskau', undated. Internal evidence suggests late 1941. Hitler and Goebbels frequently spoke of Churchill's alleged susceptibility to Jewish influence, about which the latter article was about. See, as representative examples, Förster and Mawdsley, 'Hitler and Stalin in Perspective: Secret Speeches on the Eve of Barbarossa', p. 71, note 28, p. 72; Goebbels's *VB* leader of 6 July 1941, 'Der Schleier' reproduced in J. Goebbels, *Die Zeit ohne Beispiel* (2. Edn, Munich, 1942) pp. 237–40; Jochmann, *Monologe*, 18 October 1941, p. 93.

23. NARA, T84/404, *UdSSR-Dienst*, 'Die Komintern an die Arbeit: Die Plutokratien als Wegbereiter des bolschewistischen Terrors', 8 October 1941.

24. NARA, T84/407, *UdSSR-Dienst*, 'Europa gegen den Bolschewismus', 2 December 1941.

25. NARA, T84/405, *UdSSR-Dienst*, 'Warum die jüdischen Plutokraten Amerikas den Bolschewismus unterstützen', 4 July 1941. German radio had already made a broadcast along these lines three weeks before the launching of Barbarossa. See 'Das Massenelend in den Plutokratien, Nährboden für den Bolschewismus' in Aldag, *Worüber berichten wir heute*, pp. 35ff.

26. NARA, T84/405, 'Das Judentum als Bindeglied zwischen Bolschewismus und USA', 11 July 1941. The article relied for much of its information about the composition of Roosevelt's entourage on the report made in 1940 by the Dies Committee, set up to investigate 'un-American activities', which, by the end of its deliberations, claimed to have exposed over 200 communists in senior positions in the Roosevelt administration.

27. Ibid., 'Juden aller Länder vereinigt euch!' 26 August 1941 (my italics). In similar vein see Goebbels's lead article 'Die Juden sind schuld' in *Das Reich*, issue of 16 November 1941. Following the German declaration of war on the USA the SS produced a 50-page booklet explaining how and why 'Europe as a unified whole' was fighting for its existence against the 'Jewish British–American–Soviet front'. See Der Reichsführer SS (ed.) *Dieser Krieg ist ein weltanschaulicher Krieg* (Berlin, o. D.) Internal evidence suggests the turn of 1941–42. Quotations from pp. 25–6.

28. Jersak, 'The Interaction of War and Holocaust, 1941', pp. 284ff, 305ff.

Jersak has summarized the main ideas presented in his thesis in two articles: T. Jersak, 'Die Interaktion von Kriegsverlauf und Judenvernichtung: Ein Blick auf Hitlers Strategie im Spätsommer 1941', *Historische Zeitschrift*, 268 (1999) pp. 311–74; and T. Jersak, 'A Matter of Foreign Policy: "Final Solution" and "Final Victory" in Nazi Germany', *German History*, 21 (2003) pp. 369–91. In contrast to his criticisms of Christian Gerlach's argument that Operation Barbarossa was primarily determined by the 'bitter necessity of the war economy', Jersak finds rather less to object to in the same author's argument that Hitler announced the decision to proceed towards the annihilation of European Jewry at a meeting of senior Nazi functionaries the day after Germany declared war on the United States. Martin Moll, on the other hand, has detected serious defects in Gerlach's analysis of this issue. See respectively Gerlach, *Kalkulierte Mord*, p. 45; C. Gerlach, 'Die Wannsee-Konferenz, das Schicksal der deutschen Juden und Hitlers Grundsatzentscheidung, alle Juden Europas zu ermorden' in his *Krieg, Ernährung, Völkermord: Deutsche Vernichtungspolitik im Zweiten Weltkreig* (Zurich, 2001) pp. 79–152; Jersak, 'Die Interaktion von Kriegsverlauf und Judenvernichtung', p. 344, and note 138; M. Moll, 'Steuerungsinstrument im "Ämterchaos"? Die Tagungen der Reichs- und Gauleiter der NSDAP', *VfZ*, 49 (2001) pp. 215–73, especially pp. 219, 238ff. Of course, Jersak's seeming acceptance that Hitler made this *announcement* to the Gauleiter on 12 December 1941 does not contradict his point that the actual *decision* to proceed to the extermination of the European Jews had been taken several months earlier.
29. *TBJG*, II/3, 20 March 1942.
30. Domarus, II/2, speech at the Berlin Zeughaus, 15 March 1942, pp. 1849–50.
31. On this aspect see Kershaw, *Hitler: Nemesis*, pp. 523ff; *GSWW*, VI, pp. 510ff.
32. Virtually all the surviving records of Hitler's conversations with foreign dignitaries during 1942 reveal a striking concentration on military matters. See *Staatsmänner und Diplomaten bei Hitler: Zweiter Teil*, passim.
33. See primarily Kershaw, *Hitler: Nemesis*, pp. 3ff, 127ff, 339ff; Fest, *Hitler*, p. 647; Hildebrand, *Foreign Policy*, p. 106.
34. Jersak, 'The Interaction of War and Holocaust, 1941', p. 17.
35. In this respect see *TBJG*, II/1, 19 August 1941. During his meeting with Hitler on 18 August, Goebbels found the chancellor generally in good form, perturbed by, if anything, his underestimation of Soviet strength and the damage inflicted by British air raids, and healthily contemptuous of the results of the Churchill–Roosevelt summit, in which he saw an attempt by the British prime minister to improve his faltering

domestic position and a vain effort to persuade the USA to join the war. Moreover, whatever one makes of its validity, Jersak's argument that Hitler's supposed decision to exterminate the Jews was essentially a reaction to events can quite easily be turned on its head and transformed into a proactive initiative of the Führer's to radicalize Jewish policy using the Placentia Bay meeting, the Churchill–Roosevelt message to Stalin, and the 24 August Moscow broadcast as justification for such a measure. Moreover, for all his criticisms of Christian Gerlach's marginalization of the ideological determinants of Operation Barbarossa, Jersak pays relatively little attention to the work of other scholars of the Holocaust who have a rather different focus and perspective, notably Götz Aly and Susanne Heim who examine the radicalization of anti-Jewish policy from below. See G. Aly, '*Endlösung*': *Völkerverschiebung und der Mord an den europäischen Juden* (Frankfurt am Main, 1995); G. Aly and S. Heim, *Vordenker der Vernichtung: Auschwitz und die deutschen Pläne für eine neue europäische Ordnung* (Hamburg, 1991). Of related interest is Y. Lozowick, *Hitlers Bürokraten: Eichmann, seine willigen Vollstrecker und die Banalität des Bösen* (Zurich, 2000).

36. Jersak, 'Die Interaktion von Kriegsverlauf und Judenvernichtung', p. 319.
37. See Domarus, II/2, 30 January 1941, speech to the Reichstag, p. 1663.
38. See *TBJG*, II/1, 19 August 1941; Jochmann, *Monologe*, 25 October 1941, p. 106; *TBJG*, II/2, 13 December 1941; Moll, 'Steuerungsinstrument im "Ämterchaos"?' p. 239.
39. Kershaw, *Hitler: Nemesis*, p. 540.
40. *TBJG*, II/3, 15 February 1942.
41. Ibid., II/8, 8 May 1943.
42. BBL, NS18/225, unsigned memorandum, 10 May 1943.
43. G. L. Weinberg, *A World at Arms: A Global History of World War II* (Cambridge, 1994) p. 604.
44. Domarus, II/2, 21 March 1943, speech at the Berlin Zeughaus, pp. 2000–1.

Chapter 12

1. BK, ZSg. 101/20, 'Mitschriften der Anweisungen bzw Bestellungen aus der Pressekonferenz der Reichsregierung', 22 June 1941.
2. *VB*, 23 June 1941.
3. Ibid., 6 July 1941.
4. BBL, NS18/38, 'Sonderlieferung des Aufklärungs- und Redner-Information materials der Reichspropagandaleitung der NSDAP. Deutschland zum Endkampf mit dem jüdischen-bolschewistischen Mordsytem angetreten. Nur für Redner', undated, but clearly prepared before 22 June 1941.

5. On this aspect see also *Review of the Foreign Press 1939–1945.* Series A. Vol. V. *Enemy Countries: Axis Controlled Europe*, nos 93–117, 7 July 1941–22 December 1941 (ed.) Royal Institute of International Affairs (Munich, 1980) [hereafter *RFP*], no. 94, 14 July 1941; and BBL, R55/729, 'Political Review of Press and Radio', broadcast by Hans Fritzsche, undated. Internal evidence suggests July–August 1941.

6. PRO, FO371/29488/N4063. Foreign Research Press Service, German Section, 23 July 1941.

7. See respectively: PRO, FO371/26821/C7728. Campbell to FO, 9 July 1941; *RFP*, A/V, no. 95, 21 July 1941. In Norway German propaganda made reference to Quisling's 1930 publication 'Russia and Us' which had argued that Bolshevism was a conspiracy against European civilization and the 'Nordic ideals that have inspired it'. The issue of a struggle between the 'Nordic way of life' and 'Asiatic barbarism' was developed in detail in the Norwegian press.

8. *RFP*, A/V, no. 94, 14 July 1941.

9. *TBJG*, II/3, 24 February 1942.

10. *The Secret Conferences of Dr Goebbels October 1939–March 1943*, ed. W. A. Boelcke, trans. E. Osers (London, 1970) 17 April 1942.

11. See BBL, R55/1388. Presse-Rundschreiben, nos. II/1/42 and II/18/42 of 6 January 1942 and 22 April 1942.

12. Boelcke, *Secret Conferences*, 1–2 January 1942.

13. Ibid., 7–9 July 1942.

14. Ibid., 19 July 1942.

15. BBL, R55/1289. Taubert to Goebbels, 8 June 1942 and Taubert memorandum 25 June 1942. The army's *Propaganda-Kompanien* contained volunteer groups from the Baltic states, the Ukraine, and included Tartars and Cossack bands to help spread the word to the Russian people that Germany came as their liberator from Bolshevism. See OKW Weisung Nr 19, 8 July 1942, ibid.

16. PRO, FO371/31151/C5779. Campbell to FO, 5 June 1942.

17. *Taubert mss*, fol. 23.

18. Ibid., fols 25–6.

19. Information on the Antikomintern's activities in these respects can be found in BBL, R55/1288, Engelhardt to Goebbels, 12 September 1942; see also in the same file the two letters from Edelstein to Goebbels, 27 August and 11 September 1943. The Antikomintern's major European contacts can be traced in BBL, R55/1289, 'Kurze Übersicht der Länder mit denen die Auslansabteilung der Antikomintern in Verbindung steht und wo die Arbeit angelaufen ist', 15 May 1942.

20. See *Das Sowjet-Paradies: Ausstellung der Reichspropagandaleitung der NSDAP. Ein Bericht in Wort und Bild* (Berlin, 1942). Quotation from p. 35. Between October 1942 and March 1943 the ProMi and

Antikomintern planned to stage the 'Soviet Paradise' exhibition in Rome and Milan, together with further anti-Bolshevik exhibitions in Agram and Bordeaux. See BBL, R55/1297. Schmid-Burgk to Rau, 9 October 1942. The drawing of the distinction between the Bolshevik regime and the Russian people was, of course, nothing new. In April 1937 Germans had been reminded that their quarrel was not with the 'Slavic peoples' who were 'ruled and repressed by Bolshevism', but with the 'world revolution as promoted by the Comintern'. See BBL, NS6/226, Anordnung Nr 51/37, [signed by Hess], 19 April 1937.

21. Herf, *The Jewish Enemy*, p. 96.
22. *Warum Krieg mit Stalin? Das Rotbuch der Antikomintern* (Berlin, 1941).
23. Ibid., p. 57.
24. Herf, *The Jewish Enemy*, p. 92.
25. PRO, FO371/34476/1410. Minute by Roberts, undated, but after 9 January 1943.
26. The speech dealt largely with the impact of Stalingrad and the need for special measures to counter the 'assault by the steppes against our ancient and honourable continent, now that two thousand years' constructive work by western humanity is in danger'. See H. Heiber, *Goebbels*, trans. J. K. Dickinson (London, 1972) p. 289.
27. Boelcke, *Secret Conferences*, 12 February 1943.
28. The text of the speech can be found in PRO, FO371/34454/1288. Rosenberg also wrote an article on the struggle for Europe. While naturally avoiding any direct reference to the military reversals, he warned how all those Europeans who had allowed themselves to be 'put to sleep' by talk that the war in the east was a distant affair had recently had a rude awakening. *VB*, 30 January 1943.
29. PRO, FO371/36991/N149, MOI [communicated], 22 February 1943.
30. PRO, FO371/34566/C3277, *Polish Fortnightly Review*, 15 March 1943. It is interesting to note that in contrast to the USSR, which was held to have the aim of overrunning Europe, 'British and American "war aims" are not admitted to include anything practical or detailed' and that therefore 'it is deduced that they offer no security against Bolshevis-ation'. PRO, FO371/37741/C2921, PWE summary of 'German Propaganda and the German', 7 March 1943.
31. *TBJG*, II/8, 14 April 1943.
32. Ibid, 17 April 1943.
33. BBL, NS42/36, 'Tagesparole des Reichspressechefs', 14 April 1943. By the summer of 1943 the Katyn massacre had been exhausted in propaganda terms. On 6 June Goebbels reminded the Gauleiter that 'At the forefront of our propaganda stands the struggle against Jewry and Bolshevism. It must be applied across the broadest basis.' BBL, NS18/225, Goebbels to all Gauleiter, 6 June 1943.

34. BBL, R55/900, Taubert to Goebbels, 26 April 1943. In February 1943 Goebbels sanctioned a subsidy of 3,000,000 francs to help finance anti-Bolshevik exhibitions in Lyons and Marseilles that took place over the following summer. See BBL, Taubert to Goebbels, 24 June 1943.
35. BBL, R55/1359, Taubert to Goebbels, 5 June 1943.
36. *TBJG*, II/10, 16 November 1943.
37. Hoover, GDAV, box 206, 'Europäische antibolschewistische Propaganda-Aktion Propagandaplan', 22 November 1943.

Chapter 13

1. See, for example, *TBJG*, II/1, 9 July 1941.
2. On the positive attitude of the Turkish military to the possible destruction of Bolshevism by Germany see *ADAP*, D/XII/2, no. 621, memorandum by Kramarz, 12 June 1941. As part of the new order Hitler evidently intended to offer a further treaty of friendship to Turkey, presumably supplementing or replacing that of 18 June 1941. Turkey's role would then be to safeguard the Dardanelles, for 'No foreign power has any business in that part of the world.' Jochmann, *Monologe*, 8–10 August 1941, p. 56.
3. Domarus, II/2, proclamation to German people, 22 June 1941, p. 1731.
4. See Jochmann, *Monologe*, 8–10 August 1941, p. 55; ibid., 13 October 1941, p. 79. For Hitler's intentions towards Greece, *TBJG*, II/1, 9 July 1941.
5. *ADAP*, D/XIII/2, no. 424, record of a conversation between Hitler and Ciano, 26 October 1941.
6. Ibid. The previous month he had expressed the view that once 'the Asiatics had been driven out, Europe would no longer be dependent on any outside power; America, too, could "get lost" as far as we were concerned'. Ibid., no. 327, unsigned memorandum regarding the statements made by Hitler to Abetz, 6 September 1941.
7. Ibid., no. 372, memorandum by Lammers, 1 October 1941 (emphasis in the original).
8. Ibid., no. 76, RAM to Abetz, 5 July 1941. See also ibid., no. 527, AA circular, 1 December 1941.
9. *ADAP*, D/XIII/1, no. 114, unsigned memorandum regarding a conference held at the Führer's headquarters, 16 July 1941 (emphasis in the original).
10. Hoover, Phelps Papers, box 3, folder 16, 'Errors of the German policy in the Ukraine (1941–44)', 12 June 1947. In this respect see also the scathing criticisms of German occupation policy in the Ukraine and generally made by Hans von Herwarth while in American custody after

the war. Hoover, Murphy papers, box 77, interrogations of 'C' [von Herwarth], October 1945.

11. PRO, FO371/26721/C12176, minutes by Willard and Dew, 6 and 9 November respectively. The paper deals with German treatment of Ukrainians in Poland.

12. Hoover, Lerner Papers, box 5, PID 100-125. Krausskopf to Engel, 8 December 1942.

13. *TBJG*, II/8, 29 April 1943.

14. Ibid., 14 April 1943.

15. *Taubert mss*, fols 31–2.

16. *ADAP*, E/II, no. 46, Rosenberg to Koch, 17 March 1942.

17. S. Mayer, *Signal*, vol. 1 (London, 1979) p. 88.

18. On Finland's alignment with Germany after March 1940 and its role in the German–Soviet war see O. Vehvilainen, *Finland in the Second World War: Between Germany and Russia* (Basingstoke, 2002) pp. 74ff; *GSWW*, IV, pp. 429ff, 983ff.

19. *ADAP*, D/XII/2, no. 671, Stohrer to AA, 22 June 1941.

20. Ibid., D/XIII/1, no. 12, Stohrer to AA, 25 June 1941.

21. PRO, FO371/26940/ [document number missing]. Hoare to Eden, 3 July 1941. Upon making enquiries at the army ministry the British military attaché in Madrid reported that the Blue Division was little more than a symbolic gesture organized by the Falange, in whose ranks there was in any case not much enthusiasm for it, and, in the words of a senior Spanish officer, the main reason for its creation was probably the desire 'to take part in a victory parade in Moscow'. See Lubbock to MI3, 2 July 1941, ibid.

22. *KTB OKW*, I, memorandum by Lossberg, 21 December 1940, p. 996.

23. Ibid, conference of 9 January 1941, pp. 253ff.

24. *TBJG*, II/1, 19 August 1941.

25. *ADAP*, D/XIII/2, no. 510, record of a conversation between Hitler and Scavenius, 27 November 1941.

26. See, for example, the fulsome accounts of the proceedings in the *VB* of 26 November 1941.

27. See *ADAP*, E/I, no. 137, Weber to AA, 17 January 1942; ibid., E/II, no. 59, Ribbentrop to Killinger, 21 March 1942.

28. Ibid., E/I, no. 204, Schmieden to the German embassy in Turkey, 5 February 1942.

29. BBL, R43II/1428b, unsigned report on the situation in Bulgaria, 28 March 1942.

30. BBL, R901/61164. Moltke to Ribbentrop, 13 February 1943.

31. Ibid., Moltke to AA, 17 April 1943.

32. PRO, FO371/30927/C10191. Memorandum by Harrison, 19 October 1942.

33. *TBJG*, II/8, 8 May 1943.
34. Cited by M. Burleigh, *The Third Reich: A New History* (London, 2000) p. 796.

Overview and Epilogue

1. Overy, *Why the Allies Won*, pp. 76, 97–8.
2. Ribbentrop, *Memoirs*, pp. 170–1.
3. See N. Stone, *Hitler* (London, 1982) p. 219.
4. Kershaw, *Hitler: Nemesis*, p. 773.
5. BK, N1128/23, Das politische Testament Adolf Hitlers, 29 April 1945.
6. PRO, FO371/39086/C4916. Hoare to FO, 13 April 1944.
7. PRO, HW1/2843. Ōshima to Foreign Ministry, 20 May 1944.
8. For a review of German propaganda in these years see A. Smith Serrano, *German Propaganda in Military Decline, 1943–1945* (Durham, 1999).
9. *TBJG*, II/15, 10 February 1945.
10. *VB*, 30 December 1944.
11. R. Pois (ed.) *Alfred Rosenberg: Selected Writings* (London, 1970) pp. 145–6.
12. F. Genoud (ed.) *The Testament of Adolf Hitler: The Hitler–Bormann Documents February–April 1945*, trans. R. H. Stevens, intro. H. R. Trevor-Roper (London, 1959) pp. 103–4.
13. Ibid., p. 107.
14. Hoover, Lochner Papers, box 1, *Le Monde* [extract] 16 October 1945.
15. R. J. Overy, *Interrogations: The Nazi Elite in Allied Hands, 1945* (London, 2001) p. 319.

Bibliography

Unpublished Sources

A. Germany

1. Bundesarchiv: Berlin–Lichterfelde

NS 6 – Partei Kanzlei der NSDAP
NS 8 – Kanzlei Rosenberg
NS 18 – Reichspropagandaleiter der NSDAP
NS 19 – Persönlicher Stab Reichsführer–SS
NS 26 – Hauptarchiv der NSDAP
NS 42 – Reichspressechef der NSDAP
NS 43 – Außenpolitisches Amt der NSDAP
R 43 – Reichskanzlei
R 55 – Reichsministerium für Volksaufklärung und Propaganda
R 55 – Reichsministerium für Volksaufklärung und Propaganda [Formerly R 5001]
R 901 – Auswärtiges Amt Politische Abteilung (1920–1945)
62 Di 1 Dienststellen Rosenberg

Personal documents: Karl Baumböck, Paula Berth, Wilhelm Bockhoff, Lisbeth Bukowski, Adolf Ehrt, Ottokar Gaartz, Edith Genskow, Alfred Gielen, H. Griefe, Ernst Hartwig, Kaspar Häuser, Klaus von Keyserlingk, Adalbert Kungel, Johannes Maass, Dorothea Müller, Adele Petmecky, Dagmar von Raven, Hermann von Raumer, Herbert Reischauer, Joachim von Ribbentrop, Karl Stuckenberg, Eberhard Taubert

2. Bundesarchiv: Koblenz

Kle 616 – Antikomintern
N 1128 – Nachlass Adolf Hitler
N 1310 – Nachlass Neurath
R 6 – Reichsministerium für die besetzten Ostgebiete
ZSg 117– Presseausschnitt Sammlung Hauptarchiv der NSDAP
ZSg 121 – Presseausschnitt Sammlung Antikomintern
ZSg 133 – Sammlung zur nationalsozialistischen Außenpolitik

3. Politisches Archiv des Auswärtigen Amtes, Bonn

Botschaft London III
Botschaft Paris
Botschaft Moscow
Politische Beziehungen zu Deutschland
Miscellaneous

B. Great Britain

1. Public Record Office, London

Foreign Office General Correspondence : FO 371
Miscellaneous FO Papers
German Foreign Ministry Archives: GFM 33
German War Documents Project: GFM 34, GFM 35, GFM 36
Government Code and Cypher School: HW 1, HW 12, HW 13
War Office – Directorate of Military Intelligence (1917–1956): WO 208

Miscellaneous
CAB 21/942; HS 2/36; HW 15/21; KV 4/57; PREM 1/335; PRO 30/69 1815;
WO 32/5728; WO 106/5300; WO 219/5181

3. Brotherton Library, Leeds University

Records and Documents relating to the Third Reich. Group 8, reels 27–29:
   US State Department interrogation of senior German officials, 1945.
   (Microfilm)
Confidential US State Department Files. Germany: Foreign Affairs. 1930–
   1939. Decimal numbers 762 and 711.62. (Microfilm)
Hitler's War. Papers from the Sammlung Irving, Institut für Zeitgeschichte,
   München, including the 1941 diary of Walther Hewel. (Microfilm)

C. United States

1. Library of Congress, Washington

Papers of William E. Dodd
Papers of Loy Wesley Henderson

2. National Archives, Maryland

EAP 116 : Abteilung Sowjet–Union Archiv
State Department Decimal File: 761.00, 762.00

3. Hoover Institution, Stanford University, California

Gesamtverband Deutscher Antikommunistischer Vereinigungen

Miscellaneous Collections
World War II Subject Collection

D. Private Collections

Professor J. Erickson: Antikomintern-Pakte (1937–1939) [microfilms]
Professor B. Martin: Hermann von Raumer's *Lebenserrinerungen: Band V
1935–1938* [private manuscript, *Raumer Mss*, 1955]
Dr G. Stoakes: Völkischer Beobachter (1921–1928) [microfilms]
Dr G. T. Waddington: Selected documents from: Christie Papers, Churchill
College Archive, Cambridge; Davidson Papers, House of Lords Record
Office

Published Primary Sources

1. Collection of Documents

Akten zur deutschen Auswärtigen Politik 1918–1945, Serie A (1918–1925) vols
I–XIV, eds W. Bußmann and R. Thimme et al. (Göttingen, 1982–1995)
Akten zur deutschen Auswärtigen Politik 1918–1945, Serie B (1925–1933) vols
I–XXI, eds H. Rothfels and W. Bußmann et al. (Göttingen, 1966–1983)
Akten zur deutschen Auswärtigen Politik 1918–1945, Serie C (1933–1937) Das
Dritte Reich: Die ersten Jahre, vols I–VI, ed. H. Rothfels and R. Thimme et
al. (Göttingen, 1971–1981)
Akten zur deutschen Auswärtigen Politik 1918–1945, Serie D (1937–1941) vols
I–XIII, ed. J. S. Beddie et al (Baden-Baden, 1950–1970)
Akten zur deutschen Auswärtigen Politik 1918–1945, Serie E (1941–1945) vols
I–VIII, ed. I. Krüger-Bulcke and H. G. Lehmann (Göttingen, 1969–1978)
*Documents Concerning German–Polish Relations and the Outbreak of Hostilities
between Great Britain and Germany on September 3 1939*. Cmd. 6106
(London, 1939)
Documents Diplomatiques Français 1932–1939, série 1 (1932–1935) selected
vols (Paris, 1964–1984)
Documents Diplomatiques Français 1932–1939, série 2 (1936–1939) selected
vols (Paris, 1963–1986)
Documents on British Foreign Policy, Second Series, selected vols, eds E. L.
Woodward and R. Butler et al. (London, 1947–1984)
Documents on British Foreign Policy, Third Series, vols I–IX, eds E. L.
Woodward and R. Butler et al. (London, 1949–1955)
Documents on German Foreign Policy, series C (1933–1936) vols I–VI, eds P.
R. Sweet et al. (Washington, 1957–1983)
Documents on German Foreign Policy, series D (1937–1941) eds R. J. Sontag
(et al) vols I–XIII (Washington, 1949–1964)

Documents on International Affairs, selected vols, eds S. Heald and J. W. Wheeler-Bennett (London, 1936–1939)

Foreign Relations of the United States: Diplomatic Papers, selected vols (Washington, 1952–1959)

Foreign Relations of the United States: Japan 1931–1941, vol. II (Washington, 1943)

Führer Conferences on Naval Affairs 1939–1945 (London, 1946)

Hitler and his Generals: Military Conferences 1942–1945. The First Complete Stenographic Record of the Military Situation Conferences, from Stalingrad to Berlin, ed. H. Heiber, trans. R. Winter et al (London, 2002)

Der Hitler–Prozess 1924: Wortlaut der Hauptverhandlung vor dem Volksgericht München, vols 1–4, eds L. Gruchmann and R. Weber under Mitarbeit von O. Gritschneder (Munich, 1997–1999)

Hitler's War Directives 1939–1945, ed. H. R. Trevor-Roper (London, 1964)

Hitlers Weisungen für die Kriegsführung 1939–45: Dokumente des Oberkommandos der Wehrmacht, ed. W. Hubatsch (Frankfurt, 1962)

Kriegstagebuch des Oberkommandos der Wehrmacht (Wehrmachtführungsstab) 1940–1945, 4 vols. Geführt von H Greiner and P. E. Schramm. In Auftrag des Arbeitskreises für Wehrforschung. eds P. E. von Schramm et al. (Frankfurt am Main, 1961–65)

Le Livre Jaune Français: Documents Diplomatiques 1938–1939. Pièces Relatives aux Événements et aux Négociations qui ont précédé l'Ouverture des Hostilities entre l'Allemagne d'une part, la Pologne, la Grande-Bretagne et la France d'autre part (Ministère des Affaires Étrangères, Paris, 1939)

Nazi Ideology Before 1933: A Documentation, intro. and trans. B. M. Lane and L. J. Rupp (Manchester, 1978)

Nazi–Soviet Relations: Documents from the Archives of the German Foreign Office 1939–1941, eds R. J. Sontag and J. S. Beddie (Washington, 1948)

Official Documents Concerning Polish–German and Polish–Soviet Relations, 1933–1939. Published by the authority of the Polish Government (London, 1940)

Review of the Foreign Press 1939–1945, series A, vol. V (London, 1980)

Soviet Documents on Foreign Policy, ed. J. Degras, vol. III (New York, 1978)

Staatsmänner und Diplomaten bei Hitler: Zweiter Teil. Vertrauliche Aufzeichnungen über Unterredungen mit Vertretern des Auslandes, ed. A. Hillgruber (Frankfurt am Main, 1967–1970).

The Secret Conferences of Dr Goebbels October 1939–March 1943, ed. W. A. Boelcke, trans. E. Osers (London, 1970)

The Tokyo War Crimes Trial, eds R. Pritchard and S. M. Zaide, vols 1–22 (New York, 1981)

The Trial of the Major War Criminals before the International Military Tribunal, Proceedings, vols I–XXIII, Nuremberg 1947–1949; Documents in Evidence, vols XXIV–XLII (Nuremberg 1947–1949)

2. Papers, Letters and Speeches

Baynes, N. H. (ed.) *The Speeches of Adolf Hitler April 1922–August 1939*, vols I–II (Oxford, 1942)

Bouhler, P. (ed.) *Grossdeutsche Freiheitskampf: Reden Adolf Hitlers* (Munich, 1943)

Domarus, M. (ed.) *Hitler: Reden und Proklamationen 1932–45. Kommentiert von einem deutschen Zeitgenossen*, 2 Bde (Munich, 1965).

Genoud, F. (ed.) *The Testament of Adolf Hitler: The Hitler–Bormann Documents February–April 1945*, trans. R. H. Stevens, intro. H. R. Trevor-Roper (London, 1959)

Hill, L. E. (ed.) *Die Weizsäcker-Papiere, 1933–1950* (Frankfurt, 1974)

Jäckel, E. and Kuhn, A. (ed.) *Hitler: Sämtliche Aufzeichnungen 1905–1924* (Stuttgart, 1980).

Jochmann, W. (ed.) *Adolf Hitler: Monologe im Führerhauptquartier 1941–1944* (Munich, 2000)

Kotze von, H. and Krausnick, H. (eds) *'Es spricht der Führer': 7 exemplarische Hitler-Reden* (Gütersloh, 1966)

Muggeridge, M. (ed.) *Ciano's Diplomatic Papers*, trans. S. Hood (London, 1948)

Pois, R. (ed.) *Alfred Rosenberg: Selected Writings* (London, 1970)

Prange, G. W. (ed.) *Hitler's Words* (Washington, 1944)

Rosenberg, A., *Schriften aus den Jahren 1917–1921*, intro. A. Baeumler (Munich, 1943)

Race and Race History, ed. R. Pois (New York, 1974)

Roussy de Sales, R. (ed.) *My New Order: Hitler's Speeches* (New York, 1941)

Susmel, E. D. (ed) *Opera Omnia die Benito Mussolini*, vol. 12 (Florence, 1953)

United States. Office of Chief of Counsel for the Prosecution of Axis Criminality, *Nazi Conspiracy and Aggression*, 11 vols (Washington, 1946–1947)

Vollnhals, C. et al. (eds) *Hitler: Reden, Schriften, Anordnungen*, February 1925 and January 1933, 6 Bde (Munich, 1992–2003)

Hitler's Table-Talk 1941–1944, intro. H. R. Trevor-Roper (London, 1953)

Hitlers Tischgespräche im Führerhauptquartier, ed. H. Picker (Stuttgart, 1983)

3. Contemporary Works

Aldag, P., *Worüber berichten wir Heute: Unsere Gegner und ihr Krieg* (Berlin, 1941)

Antikomintern (ed.) *The Seventh World Congress of the Communist International* (Berlin, [1935])

Das Rotbuch über Spanien: Bilder, Dokumente, Zeugenaussagen (Berlin, 1937)

Enthüllungen über Moskau (Berlin, 1938)

Denkschrift über die Einmischung des Bolschewimus und der Demokratien in Spanien (Berlin, 1939)

Sie dienten dem Bolschewismus (undated)
Eckart, D., An alle Werktätigen (Munich, 1919) [Microfilm, Wiener Library, London]
Der Bolschewismus von Moses bis Lenin (Munich, 1924)
Ehrt, A., Ein deutscher Todesweg (Berlin, 1930)
Bewaffneter Aufstand! Enthüllungen über den kommunistischen Umsturzversuch am Vorabend der nationalen Revolution (Berlin, 1933)
Communism in Germany: The Truth about the Communist Conspiracy on the Eve of the National Revolution (Berlin, [1933])
La Terreur Rouge (la Révolte Armée): Révélations sur l'Organisation Bolcheviste en Russie, en Allemagne et en France (Paris, [1934])
Ehrt, A. and Schweickert, J., Entfesselung der Unterwelt: Ein Querschnitt durch die Bolschewisierung Deutschlands (Berlin, 1932)
Feder, G., Das Manifest zur Brechung der Zinsknechtschaft des Geldes (Munich, 1920) [Microfilm – Wiener Library, London]
Das Programm der NSDAP und seine weltanschaulichen Grundgedanken (Munich, 1930)
Goebbels, J., Bolshevism in Theory and Practice Speech delivered in Nürnberg on September 10 1936 at the Eighth National Socialist Party Congress (Berlin, 1936)
Der Angriff: Aufsätze aus der Kampfzeit (Munich, 1941)
Die Zeit ohne Beispiel (2nd edn, München, 1942)
Hagemeyer, H. (ed.) Europas Schicksal im Osten (Breslau, 1938)
Hitler. A., Der Weg zum Wiederaufstieg (Munich, 1927)
Die Reden Hitlers für Gleichberechtigung und Frieden (Munich, 1934)
Reden des Führers am Parteitag der Ehre 1936 (Munich, 1936)
Mein Kampf (Munich, 1939)
Reden des Führers am Parteitag Großdeutschland 1938 (Munich, 1939).
Der großdeutsche Freiheitskampf: Reden Adolf Hitlers. Vol. 1. September 1939 bis 10 März 1940 (Munich, 1940)
Hitler's Secret Book, intro. T. Taylor, trans. S. Attanasio (New York, 1961)
Hitlers Zweites Buch: Ein Dokument aus dem Jahre 1928. With a preface and commentary by Gerhard L. Weinberg, and foreword by Hans Rothfels (Stuttgart, 1961)
Mein Kampf, trans. R. Manheim (London, 1993)
Krebs, H., Prag und Moskau (Munich, 1938)
Leibbrandt, G., Moskaus Aufmarsch gegen Europa (Munich, 1938)
Bolschewismus und Abendland: Idee und Geschichte eines Kampfes gegen Europa (Berlin, 1939)
Londonderry, Marquess of, Ourselves and Germany (London, 1938)
Nilus, S., Protocols of the Meetings of the Learned Elders of Zion, trans. V. E. Marsden (London, [1948])
Reichsführer SS, Der (ed.) Dieser Krieg ist ein weltanschaulicher Krieg (Berlin, o.D., internal evidence suggests the turn of 1941–42)

Rosenberg, A., *Der Zukunftsweg der deutschen Außenpolitik* (Munich, 1927)
Der Bolschewismus als Aktion einer fremden Rasse (Munich, 1935)
Gestaltung der Idee: Reden und Aufsätze, 1933–1935 (Munich, 1936)
Pest in Russland: Der Bolschewismus, seine Häupter, Handlager und Opfer, ed.
    G. Leibbrandt (Munich, 1937)
Der Staatsfeindliche Zionismus (Munich, 1938)
Europa und sein Todfeind (Munich, 1938)
Tradition und Gegenwart: Reden und Aufsätze, 1936–1941 (Munich, 1941)
*Blut und Ehre: Ein Kampf für deutsche Wiedergeburt. Reden und Aufsätze von
    1919–1933*, ed. T. von Trotha (Munich, 1942)
Stadtler, E., *Der Bolschewismus und seine Überwindung* (Berlin, 1919).
Der kommende Krieg: Bolschewistische Weltrevolutionspläne (Berlin 1919).
Weltkrieg, Welttragödie und Weltbolschewismus (Berlin, 1919).
Bolschewismus als Weltgefahr (Düsseldorf, 1936).
Vietz, K., *Verrat an Europa: Ein Rotbuch über die Bolschewisierung der
    Tschecho-Slowakei* (Berlin, 1938).
*Das Sowjet-Paradies: Ausstellung der Reichspropagandaleitung der NSDAP. Ein
    Bericht in Wort und Bild* (Berlin, 1942)
*Der Parteitag der Arbeit vom 6 bis 13 September 1937: Offizieller Bericht über
    den Verlauf des Reichsparteitages mit sämtlichen Kongreßreden* (Munich,
    1938)
*Der Weltbolschewismus: Ein internationales Gemeinschaftswerk über die
    bolschewistische Wühlarbeit und die Umsturzversuche der Komintern in allen
    Ländern. Herausgegeben von der Antikomintern. In Verbindung mit den
    Sachkennern der ganzen Welt. Mit 400 Bilddokumenten, Karten und
    Anschauungstafeln* (Berlin-Leipzig, 1936).
Propaganda (Parteileitung der NSDAP – Propaganda Abteilung, München,
    1927)
*Terror: Die Blutchronik des Marxismus in Deutschland. Auf Grund amtlichen
    Materials bearbeitet von Adolf Ehrt und Hans Rosen* (Berlin, 1934)
*Totale Krise – Totale Revolution? Die 'Schwarze Front' des völkischen
    Nationalismus* (Berlin, 1933)

4. Memoirs and Diaries

Abendroth, H.-H., *Mittelsmann zwischen Franco und Hitler: Johannes
    Bernhardt erinnert 1936* (Scraptoft, 1978)
Banac, I. (ed.) *The Diary of Georgi Dimitrov, 1933–1949* (New Haven, 2003)
Burckhardt, C. J., *Meine Danziger Mission 1937–1939* (Munich, 1962)
Ciano, G., *Ciano's Diary, 1937–38*, trans. A. Mayor, intro. M. Muggeridge
    (London, 1952)
Ciano's Diary, 1939–43, ed. and intro. M. Muggeridge (London, 1947)
Dietrich, O., *The Hitler I Knew*, trans. R. and C. Winston (London, 1957)

Dirksen, H. von, *Moscow, Tokyo, London: Twenty Years of German Foreign Policy* (Oklahoma, 1952)

Goebbels, J., *Die Tagebücher von Joseph Goebbels: Sämtliche Fragmente. Herausgegeben von Elke Fröhlich im Auftrag des Instituts für Zeitgeschichte und in Verbindung mit dem Bundesarchiv*. Part I, 1924–1941. 4 Bde (Munich, 1987)

Die Tagebücher von Joseph Goebbels: Im Auftrag des Instituts für Zeitgeschichte und mit Unterstützung des Staatlichen Archivdienstes Russlands, Part I, 1923–1941. 9 vols, eds E. Fröhlich et al. (Munich, 1998–2003)

Die Tagebücher von Joseph Goebbels, Part II, Diktate (1941–1945) 15 Bde, eds E. Fröhlich et al. (Munich, 1993–96)

Halder, F., *Generaloberst Halder: Kriegstagebuch*, ed. H.-A. Jacobsen, 3 vols (Stuttgart, 1962–1964)

Hanfstaengl, E., *Zwischen Weissem und Braunem Haus: Memoiren eines politischen Aussenseiters* (Munich, 1970)

The Missing Years, intro. J. Toland (London, 1957)

Hassell, U. von, *The von Hassell Diaries: The Story of the Forces Against Hitler Inside Germany, 1938–1944* (Boulder, 1994)

Herwarth, J. von, *Against Two Evils: Memoirs of a Diplomat-Soldier during the Third Reich* (London, 1981)

Hilger, G. and Meyer, A. G., *The Incompatible Allies: A Memoir-History of German–Soviet Relations 1918–1941* (New York, 1971)

Hoffmann, H., *Hitler was my Friend*, trans. R. H. Stevens (London, 1955)

Jones, T., *A Diary with Letters 1931–1950* (London, 1954)

Kordt, E., *Wahn und Wirklichkeit: Die Außenpolitik des Dritten Reiches Versuch einer Darstellung* (Stuttgart, 1947)

Nicht aus den Akten (Stuttgart, 1950)

Lipski, J., *Diplomat in Berlin, 1933–39: Papers and Memoirs of Józef Lipski, Ambassador of Poland*, ed. W. Jedrzejewicz (New York, 1968)

Lüdecke, K. G. W., *I Knew Hitler: The Story of a Nazi Who Escaped the Blood Purge* (London, 1938)

Nicolson, H., *Harold Nicolson: Diaries and Letters 1930–1939*, ed. N. Nicolson (London, 1966)

Ribbentrop, J. von, *The Ribbentrop Memoirs* (London, 1954)

Schmidt, P., *Hitler's Interpreter*, ed. R. H. C. Steed (New York, 1950)

Schroeder, C., *Er war mein Chef: Aus dem Nachlaß der Sekretärin von Adolf Hitler*, ed. A. Joachimsthaler (Munich, 1985)

Speer, A. *Inside the Third Reich: Memoirs by Albert Speer*, trans. R. and C. Winston (London, 1970)

Spitzy, R., *So haben wir das Reich Verspielt: Bekenntnisse eines Illegalen* (Munich, 1994)

Starhemberg, Prince, *Between Hitler and Mussolini: Memoirs of Ernst Rüdiger Prince Starhemberg* (London, 1942)

Stresemann, G., *Gustav Stresemann: His Diaries, Letters and Papers*, ed. and trans. E. Sutton, vol. II (London, 1937)

Toynbee, A. J., *Acquaintances* (London, 1967)

Wagener, O., *Hitler: Memoirs of a Confidant*, ed. H. A. Turner (Jr) trans. R. Hein (New Haven, 1985)

Warlimont, W., *Inside Hitler's Headquarters 1939–45*, trans. R. H. Barry (Novato, 1964)

Winterbotham, F. W., *The Nazi Connection* (London, 1978)

5. Newspapers/Periodicals

Auf gut deutsch, Manchester Guardian, News Chronicle, News Service, New York Times, Nationalsozialistische Briefe, Das Reich, Der Stürmer, The Times, Völkischer Beobachter

Secondary Sources

Books

Abendroth, H-H., *Hitler in der spanischen Arena: Die deutsch-spanischen Beziehungen im Spannungsfeld der europäischen Interessenpolitik vom Ausbruch des Bürgerkrieges bis zum Ausbruch des Weltkrieges 1936-1939* (Nuremberg, 1970)

Mittelsmann zwischen Franco und Hitler: Johannes Bernhardt erinnert 1936 (Leicester, 1978)

Adamthwaite, A., *The Lost Peace: International Relations in Europe, 1918–1939* (London, 1980)

Aly, G., *'Endlösung': Völkerverschiebung und der Mord an den europäischen Juden* (Frankfurt am Maim, 1995)

Aly, G. and Heim, S., *Architects of Annihilation: Auschwitz and the Logic of Destruction*, trans. A. G. Blunden (London, 2003)

Baird, J. W., *The Mythical World of Nazi War Propaganda, 1939–1945* (Minneapolis, 1974)

Barclay, D. E. and Weitz, E. D. (eds) *Between Reform and Revolution: German Socialism and Communism from 1840 to 1990* (New York, 1998)

Baur, J., *Die russische Kolonie in München 1900–1945* (Wiesbaden, 1998)

Benz, W., *The Holocaust: A German Historian Examines the Genocide*, trans. J. Sydenham-Kwiet (London, 2000)

Bloch, M., *Ribbentrop* (London, 1992)

Böhme, H., *Der deutsch-französische Waffenstillstand im Zweiten Weltkrieg* (Bonn, 1966)

Bosworth, R. J. B., *Mussolini* (London, 2002)

Boyd, C., *The Extraordinary Envoy: General Hiroshi Oshima and Diplomacy in the Third Reich, 1934–1939* (Washington, 1980)

Bramsted, E. K., *Goebbels and National Socialist Propaganda 1925–1945* (Michigan, 1965)

Browning, C. R., *The Origins of the Final Solution: The Evolution of Nazi Jewish Policy, September 1939–March 1942*, with a contribution by J. Mathias (London, 2004)

Bullock, A., *Hitler: A Study in Tyranny* (London, 1962)

Burleigh, M., *The Third Reich: A New History* (London, 2000)

Burrin, P., *Hitler and the Jews: The Genesis of the Holocaust*, trans. P. Southgate (London, 1994)

Bytwerk, R. L., *Julius Streicher: Nazi Editor of the notorious anti-Semitic Newspaper Der Stürmer* (2nd edn, New York, 2001)

Calvitt Clarke III, J., *Russia and Italy against Hitler: The Bolshevik-Fascist Rapprochement of the 1930s* (New York, 1991)

Carr, W., *Arms, Autarky and Aggression: A Study in German Foreign Policy, 1933–1939* (London, 1972)

Cecil, R., *The Myth of the Master Race: Alfred Rosenberg and Nazi Ideology* (London, 1972)

Cecil, R., *Hitler's Decision to Invade Russia, 1941* (London, 1975)

Cesarani, D., (ed.) *The Final Solution: Origins and Implementation* (London, 1996)

Chase, W. J., *Enemies Within the Gates? The Comintern and the Stalinist Repression, 1934–1939* (New Haven, 2001)

Chickering, R., *We Men Who Feel Most German: A Cultural Study of the Pan-German League, 1886–1914* (London, 1984)

Crozier, A., *Appeasement and Germany's Last Bid for Colonies* (London, 1988)

Dallek, R., *Franklin D. Roosevelt and American Foreign Policy, 1932–1945* (New York, 1995)

Dawidowicz, L. S., *The War Against the Jews 1933–45* (Harmondsworth, 1987)

Drachkovitch, M. M. and Lazitch, B. (eds) *The Comintern: Historical Highlights. Essays, Recollections, Documents* (New York, 1966)

Erickson, J. and Dilks, D. (eds) *Barbarossa: The Axis and the Allies* (Edinburgh, 1994)

Ericson III, E. E., *Feeding the German Eagle: Soviet Economic Aid to Nazi Germany, 1933–1941* (Westport, 1999)

Fest, J., *Hitler*, trans. R. and C. Winston (New York, 1974)

Foerster, R. G. (ed.) *Unternehmen Barbarossa: Zum historischen Ort der deutsch-sowjetischen Beziehungen von 1933 bis Herbst 1941* (Munich, 1993).

Fox, J. P., *Germany and the Far Eastern Crisis 1931–1938: A Study in Diplomacy and Ideology* (Oxford, 1985)

Friedländer, S., *Nazi Germany and the Jews*, vol. 1, *The Years of Persecution 1933–39* (London, 1998)

Funke, M., *Sanktionen und Kanonen: Hitler, Mussolini und der internationale Abessinienkonflikt 1934–36* (Düsseldorf, 1970) (ed.) *Hitler, Deutschland und die Mächte: Materialien zur Außenpolitik des Dritten Reiches* (Düsseldorf, 1978)

Gasman, D., *The Scientific Origins of National Socialism: Social Darwinism in Ernst Haeckel and the German Monist League* (London, 1971)

Gehl, J., *Austria, Germany and the Anschluss, 1931–1938* (London, 1963)

Gerlach, C., *Kalkulierte Morde: Die deutsche Wirtschafts- und Vernichtungspolitik in Weißrußland 1941 bis 1944* (Hamburg, 1999)

Krieg, Ernährung, Völkermord: Deutsche Vernichtungspolitik im Zweiten Weltkrieg (Zurich, 2001)

Gilbert, M., *Winston S. Churchill*, vol. 5, *The Wilderness Years 1929–1935* (London, 1981)

Gollwitzer, H., *Die gelbe Gefahr, Geschichte eines Schlagworts: Studien zum imperialistischen Denken* (Göttingen, 1962)

Gorodetsky, G., *Grand Delusion: Stalin and the German Invasion of Russia* (New Haven, 1999)

Graham, H., *The Spanish Republic at War* (Cambridge, 2002)

Griffiths, R., *Fellow Travellers of the Right: British Enthusiasts for Nazi Germany 1933–39* (Oxford, 1983)

Haffner, S., *The Meaning of Hitler*, trans. E. Osers (London, 1988)

Hamann, B., *Hitlers Wein: Lehrjahre eines Diktators* (Munich, 1996)

Haslam, J., *The Soviet Union and Collective Security in Europe, 1933–39* (London, 1984)

Heiber, H., *Goebbels*, trans. J. K. Dickinson (London, 1972)

Heineman, J. L., *Hitler's First Foreign Minister: Constantin Freiherr von Neurath, Diplomat and Statesman* (Berkeley, 1979)

Henke, J., *England in Hitlers politischem Kalkül 1935–1939* (Boppard am Rhein, 1973)

Herf, J., *The Jewish Enemy: Nazi Propaganda during World War II and the Holocaust* (London, 2006)

Herzstein, R. E., *The War that Hitler Won: The Most Infamous Propaganda Campaign in History* (London, 1980)

Hildebrand. K., *Vom Reich zum Weltreich: Hitler, NSDAP und koloniale Frage* (Munich, 1969)

The Foreign Policy of the Third Reich, trans. A. Fothergill (London, 1973)

German Foreign Policy from Bismarck to Adenauer: The Limits of Statecraft, trans. L. Willmot (London, 1989)

Hildebrand, K. and Pommerin, R. (eds) *Deutsche Frage und europäisches Gleichgewicht: Festschrift für Andreas Hillgruber zum 60. Geburtstag* (Cologne, 1985)

Hillgruber, A., *Hitlers Strategie: Politik und Kriegführung 1940–1941* (Bonn, 1993)

Jäckel, E., *Hitlers Weltanschauung: Entwurf einer Herrschaft. Erweiterte und überarbeitete Neuausgabe* (Stuttgart, 1981)

Jacobsen, H.-A., *Nationalsozialistische Aussenpolitik, 1933–1938* (Frankfurt am Main, 1968)

Jahn, P. and Rürup, R., *Erobern und Vernichten: Der Krieg gegen die Sowjetunion* (Berlin, 1991)

Jansen, H., *Der Madagaskar-Plan: Die beabsichtigte Deportation der europäischen Juden nach Madagaskar* (Munich, 1997)

Kellogg, M., *The Russian Roots of Nazism: White Émigrés and the Making of National Socialism, 1917–1945* (Cambridge, 2005)

Kershaw, I., *Hitler 1889–1936: Hubris* (London, 1998)

Hitler 1936–1945: Nemesis (London, 2000)

Making Friends with Hitler: Lord Londonderry and Britain's Road to War (London, 2004)

Kluge, D., *Das Hoßbach-'Protokol': Die Zerstörung einer Legende* (Leoni am Starnberger See, 1980)

Kluge, U., *Soldatenräte und Revolution: Studien zur Militärpolitik in Deutschland 1918–19* (Göttingen, 1975)

Die deutsche Revolution: Staat, Politik und Gesellschaft zwischen Weltkrieg und Kapp-Putsch (Frankfurt am Main, 1985)

Koch, H. W. (ed.) *Aspects of the Third Reich* (London, 1988)

Krebs, G., *Japans Deutschlandpolitik 1935–1941: Eine Studie zur Vorgeschichte des Pazifischen Krieges*, 2 vols (Hamburg, 1984)

Kroll, F.-L., *Utopie als Ideologie: Geschichtsdenken und politisches Handeln im Dritten Reich* (Paderborn, 1998)

Kruck, A., *Geschichte des Alldeutschen Verbandes* (Wiesbaden, 1954)

Kube, A., *Pour le mérite und Hakenkreuz: Hermann Göring im Dritten Reich* (Munich, 1986)

Kuhn, A., *Hitlers Aussenpolitisches Programm: Entstehung und Entwicklung 1919–1939* (Stuttgart, 1970)

Laqueur, W., *Russia and Germany: A Century of Conflict* (London, 1965)

Lee, M. and Michalka, W., *German Foreign Policy 1917–1933: Continuity or Break?* (Leamington Spa, 1987)

Leitz, C., *Economic Relations between Nazi Germany and Franco's Spain, 1936–1945* (Oxford, 1996)

Longerich, P., *The Unwritten Order: Hitler's Role in the Final Solution* (Stroud, 2003)

Lozowick, Y., *Hitlers Bürokraten: Eichmann, seine willigen Vollstrecker und die Banalität des Bösen* (Zurich, 2000)

Lukes, I. and Goldstein. E. (eds) *The Munich Crisis, 1938: Prelude to World War II* (London, 1999)

Lungu, D. B., *Romania and the Great Powers 1933–1940* (Durham, 1989)

McDermott K. and Agnew J., *The Comintern: A History of International Communism from Lenin to Stalin* (London, 1996)

McKale, D. M., *Hitler's Shadow War: The Holocaust and World War II* (New York, 2002)

McKenzie, K. E., *Comintern and World Revolution 1928–1943: The Shaping of Doctrine* (London, 1963)

Mack Smith, D., *Mussolini* (London, 1993)

Martens, S., *Hermann Göring: 'erster Paladin des Führers' und 'zweiter Mann im Reich'* (Paderborn, 1985)

Matthias, E., and Morsey, R. (eds) *Das Ende der Parteien 1933* (Düsseldorf, 1960)

Mayer, A. J., *Politics and Diplomacy of Peacemaking: Containment and Counter-revolution at Versailles, 1918–1919* (London, 1968)

Mayer, S. L. (ed.) *Signal, Hitler's Wartime Picture Magazine*, 3 vols (Middlesex, 1976–9)

Mehnert, U., *Deutschland, Amerika und die 'gelbe Gefahr': Zur Karriere eines Schlagworts in der Grossen Politik, 1905–1917* (Stuttgart, 1995)

Merson, A., *Communist Resistance in Nazi Germany* (London, 1985)

Merz, K-U., *Das Schreckbild: Deutschland und der Bolschewismus 1917 bis 1921* (Frankfurt am Main, 1995)

Meyer zu Uptrup, W., *Kampf gegen die 'jüdische Weltverschwörung': Propaganda und Antisemitismus der Nationalsozialisten 1919–1945* (Berlin, 2003)

Michalka, W., *Ribbentrop und die deutsche Weltpolitik 1933–1940: Aussenpolitische Konzeptionen und Entscheidungsprozesse im Dritten Reich* (Munich, 1980)

Michels, H., *Ideologie und Propaganda: Die Rolle von Joseph Goebbels in der nationalsozialistischen Außenpolitik bis 1939* (Frankfurt am Main, 1992)

Militärgeschichtliches Forschungsamt (ed.) *Germany and the Second World War*, vols I–VI (Oxford, 1991–2001)

Morley, J. W. (ed.) *Deterrent Diplomacy: Japan, Germany and the USSR, 1935–1940* (New York, 1976)

Mühle, R. W., *Frankreich und Hitler: Die französische Deutschland- und Außenpolitik 1933–1935* (Paderborn, 1995)

Müller, R-D. and Ueberschär, G. R., *Hitler's War in the East, 1941–1945: A Critical Assessment*, trans. B. D. Little (Oxford, 1997)

Nekrich, A. M., *Pariahs, Partners, Predators: German-Soviet Relations, 1922–1941*, ed. and trans. G. L. Freeze (New York, 1997)

Nova, F., *Alfred Rosenberg: Nazi Theorist of the Holocaust* (New York, 1986)

Overy, R. J., *Goering: The Iron Man* (London, 1984)

Why the Allies Won (London, 1995)

Interrogations: The Nazi Elite in Allied Hands 1945 (London, 2001)

The Dictators: Hitler's Germany and Stalin's Russia (London, 2004)

Padfield, P., *Himmler: Reichsführer-SS* (London, 1990)

Plewnia, M., *Auf dem Weg zu Hitler: Der 'völkische' Publizist Dietrich Eckart* (Bremen, 1970)

Pons, S., *Stalin and the Inevitable War 1936–1941* (London, 2002)

Presseisen, E. L., *Germany and Japan: A Study in Totalitarian Diplomacy, 1933–1941* (The Hague, 1958)

Ritter von Schramm, W., *Sprich vom Frieden, wenn du den Krieg willst: Die psychologischen Offensiven Hitlers gegen die Franzosen 1933 bis 1939. Ein Bericht* (Mainz, 1973)

Robbins, K., *Munich 1938* (London, 1968)

Roberts, G., *The Soviet Union and the Origins of the Second World War: Russo-German Relations and the Road to War, 1933–1941* (London, 1995)

Rossino, A. B., *Hitler Strikes Poland: Blitzkrieg, Ideology, and Atrocity* (Kansas, 2003)

Seligmann, M., *Aufstand der Räte: Die erste bayerische Räterepublik vom 7 April 1919* (Grafenau, 1989)

Sharpe, A., *The Versailles Settlement: Peacemaking in Paris, 1919* (London, 1991)

Smith Serrano, A., *German Propaganda in Military Decline, 1943–1945* (Durham, 1999)

Sommer, T., *Deutschland und Japan zwischen den Mächten 1935–1940: Vom Antikominternpakt zum Dreimächtepakt - Eine Studie zur diplomatischen Vorgeschichte des Zweiten Weltkriegs* (Tübingen, 1962)

Southworth, H. R., *Conspiracy and the Spanish Civil War: The Brainwashing of Francisco Franco* (London, 2002)

Stoakes, G., *Hitler and the Quest for World Dominion: Nazi Ideology and Foreign Policy in the 1920s* (Leamington Spa, 1986)

Stone, N., *Hitler* (London, 1982)

Sywottek, J., *Mobilmachung für den totalen Krieg: Die propagandistische Vorbereitung der deutschen Bevölkerung auf den Zweiten Weltkrieg* (Hamburg, 1976)

Taylor, T., *Munich: The Price of Peace* (London, 1979)

Thies, J., *Architekt der Weltherrschaft: Die 'Endziele' Hitlers* (2nd edn, Düsseldorf, 1980)

Ueberschär, G. R. and Wette, W. (ed.) *Unternehmen Barbarossa: der deutsche Überfall auf die Sowjetunion 1941* (Paderborn, 1984)

Ulam, A., *Expansion and Co-existence: Soviet Foreign Policy 1917–1973* (London, 2nd edn, 1974)

Vehvilainen, O., *Finland in the Second World War: Between Germany and Russia* (Basingstoke, 2002)

Vieler, E. H., *The Ideological Roots of German National Socialism* (New York, 1999)

Viñas, A., *La Alemania nazi y el 18 de Julio* (Madrid, 1974)

Warner, G., *Pierre Laval and the Eclipse of France* (London, 1968)

Wegner, B., (ed.) *From Peace to War: Germany, Soviet Russia and the World 1939–1941* (Oxford, 1997)

Weikart, R., *From Darwin to Hitler: Evolutionary Ethics, Eugenics and Racism in Germany* (New York, 2004)

Weinberg, G. L., *The Foreign Policy of Hitler's Germany*, vol. 1, *Diplomatic Revolution in Europe, 1933–36* (London, 1970)

The Foreign Policy of Hitler's Germany, vol. 2, *Starting World War II, 1937–39* (New Jersey, 1994)

A World at Arms: A Global History of World War II (Cambridge, 1994)

Weitz, E. D., *Creating German Communism, 1990–1990: From Popular Protests to Socialist State* (Princeton, 1997)

Wette, W. and Ueberschär, G. R. (ed.) *Kriegsverbrechen im 20 Jahrhundert* (Darmstadt, 2001)

Whealey, R. H., *Hitler and Spain: The Nazi Role in the Spanish Civil War 1936–1939* (Kentucky, 1989)

Winterbotham, F. W., *The Ultra Secret* (London, 1974)

The Nazi Connection (London, 1978)

Wiskemann, E., *The Rome–Berlin Axis: A History of the Relations between Hitler and Mussolini* (London, 1949)

Zitelmann, R., *Hitler, Selbstverständnis eines Revolutionärs* (Hamburg, 1987)

Articles

Cassels, A., 'Was there a Fascist Foreign policy? Tradition and Novelty', *International History Review*, 2 (1983) 255–68

Chapman, J. W. M., 'A Dance on Eggs: Intelligence and the "Anti-Comintern"', *Journal of Contemporary History*, 22 (1987) 333–72

Eichholtz, D., 'Grossgermanisches Reich und Generalplan Ost', *Zeitschrift für Geschichtswissenschaft*, 28 (1980) 834–41

Förster, J. and Mawdsley. E., 'Hitler and Stalin in Perspective: Secret Speeches on the Eve of Barbarossa', *War in History*, 11 (2004) 61–103

Hauser, O., 'The Year 1937: The Decisive Turning-Point in British–German Relations', *Historical Studies*, X (1978) 132–46

Heilbronner, O., 'From Antisemitic Peripheries to Antisemitic Centres: The Place of Antisemitism in Modern German History', *Journal of Contemporary History*, 35 (2000) 559–76

Herwig, H. H., 'Geopolitik: Haushofer, Hitler and Lebensraum', *Journal of Strategic Studies*, 22 (1999) 218–41

Hillgruber, A. 'Die "Endlösung" und das deutsche Ostimperium als Kernstück des rassenideologischen Programms des Nationalsozialismus', *Vierteljahrshefte für Zeitgeschichte*, 20 (1972) 133–53

Jersak, T., 'Die Interaktion von Kriegsverlauf und Judenvernichtung: Ein Blick auf Hitlers Strategie im Spätsommer 1941', *Historische Zeitschrift*, 268 (1999) 311–74

'A Matter of Foreign Policy: "Final Solution" and "Final Victory" in Nazi Germany', *German History*, 21 (2003) 369–91

McDermott, K., 'Stalinist Terror in the Comintern: New Perspectives', *Journal of Contemporary History*, 30 (1995) 111–30

Moll, M., 'Steuerungsinstrument im "Ämterchaos"? Die Tagungen der Reichs- und Gauleiter der NSDAP', *Vierteljahrshefte für Zeitgeschichte*, 49 (2001) 215–73

Moore, G., 'From Buddhism to Bolshevism: Some Orientalist Themes in German Thought', *German Life and Letters*, 56 (2003) 20–42

Phelps, R. (ed.) 'Hitler als Parteiredner im Jahre 1920', *Vierteljahrshefte für Zeitgeschichte*, XI (1963) 274–330

(ed.) 'Hitlers 'Grundlegende' rede über den Antisemitismus', *Vierteljahrshefte für Zeitgeschichte*, 16 (1968) 390–420

Robertson, E. M., 'Zur Wiederbesetzung des Rheinlandes 1936', *Vierteljahrshefte für Zeitgeschichte*, 10 (1962) 178–204

Shore, Z., 'Hitler's Opening Gambit: Intelligence, Encirclement, and the Decision to Ally with Poland', *Intelligence and National Security*, 14 (1999) 103–22

Treue, W., 'Hitlers Denkschrift zum Vierjahresplan 1936', *Vierteljahrshefte für Zeitgeschichte*, 3 (1955) 184–210

'Die Rede Hitlers vor der deutschen Presse 10 November 1938', *Vierteljahrshefte für Zeitgeschichte*, 6 (1958) 175–91

Waddington, G. T., 'Hassgegner: German Views of Great Britain in the Later 1930s', *History*, 81 (1996) 22–39

'"An Idyllic Atmosphere of Complete and Unruffled Anglo–German Misunderstanding": Aspects of the Operations of the Dienststelle Ribbentrop in Great Britain, 1934–38', *History*, 265 (1997) 44–72

Wright, J. and Stafford, P., 'Hitler, Britain and the Hossbach Memorandum', *Militärgeschichtliche Mitteilungen*, 42 (1987) 77–123

Unpublished Works

Jersak, T., 'Hitler and the Interaction of War and Holocaust, 1941', Ph.D., Cambridge, 2000

Index